Michael Seymour is Assistant Curator in the Department of Ancient Near Eastern Art at The Metropolitan Museum of Art, New York. Prior to joining the Metropolitan Museum he worked for the Department of the Middle East at the British Museum, where he was co-curator of the special exhibition *Babylon: Myth and Reality*. He has also been a consultant to the World Monuments Fund on the site of Babylon, and an editor of the journal *Iraq*. He is co-author (with I. L. Finkel) of *Babylon: Myth and Reality* (2008).

'The city of Babylon and the idea of Babylon have co-existed as intertwined threads of intellectual and historical engagement for centuries. In the recent past Babylon was an emblem for Saddam Hussein's control over Iraq's past (ancient Babylon), present (reconstructed Babylon), and future (eternal Babylon). Since at least the sixth century BC, and up to modern times, Babylon has been entangled in discourses that transgress the boundaries between history, myth, fantasy and bias, while over the past century scientific archaeology has contributed to the mix. Michael Seymour teases apart the golden threads of Babylon's discourses, tracing each one in meticulous detail before reweaving them into a new and brilliant tapestry, presenting us in this adroit and learned book with a Babylon fit for the scrutiny of our age.'
 – Roger Matthews, Professor of Near Eastern Archaeology, University of Reading

'In this ambitious and all encompassing account of how the ancient city of Babylon has been studied, interpreted and received throughout history, Michael Seymour offers an exemplary study in the reception of the ancient world. Multiple manifestations of the notion of Babylon are explored, revealing the extent to which ancient civilisations have been appropriated according to different cultural contexts and priorities. The book presents an intoxicating mix of mythology, interpretation and fact from a wide variety of sources: both textual and visual. Through each of the chapters we see the exciting and complex journey that antiquities undertake once retrieved from the earth in which they were buried. One of the most important findings of the work is the extent to which ancient Mesopotamian culture is shown to have "lived on" in a range of conflicting and successive contexts. In this thoughtful and probing analysis, Seymour unravels the very idea of Babylon, revealing it to be a complex bundle of meanings and significances. He does a great service to archaeology, ancient history and cultural studies in telling this story of entanglement.'
 – Stephanie Moser, Professor of Archaeology, University of Southampton

'This is a brilliant first book by a rising star in Ancient Near Eastern studies. It comes at a critical moment when the ancient city of Babylon is under the spotlight as never before. After the coalition invasion of 2003 Babylon was turned into a military camp to universal international condemnation. Now the World Monuments Fund is helping with the conservation of the site and application has been made for Babylon to become a World Heritage Site. There have also been three major exhibitions about Babylon in the last few years, in Paris, Berlin and London, all with sumptuous catalogues, and the famous Cyrus Cylinder, found at Babylon in 1879 is currently the subject of a touring exhibition. Yet until now there existed no book that traced the exploration and excavation of Babylon against the wider backdrop of developments in European intellectual thinking and understanding. Michael Seymour does this with great skill and clarity, and has produced a book that not only examines the importance and significance of Babylon in the western and eastern traditions, but also provides a readable account of the history and excavation of the city. This will be an indispensable book both for scholars in a number of different fields and for laymen interested in the Ancient Near East.'
 – John Curtis, OBE, Keeper of Special Middle Eastern Projects, The British Museum

LEGEND,
HISTORY AND
THE ANCIENT CITY

BABYLON

MICHAEL SEYMOUR

I.B. TAURIS

LONDON · NEW YORK

Arts & Humanities Research Council

This publication is supported by the AHRC.

Each year the AHRC provides funding from the Government to support research and postgraduate study in the arts and humanities. Only applications of the highest quality are funded and the range of research supported by this investment of public funds not only provides social and cultural benefits but also contributes to the economic success of the UK. For further information on the AHRC, please go to: www.ahrc.ac.uk

Paperback edition published in 2016 by
I.B.Tauris & Co. Ltd
London • New York
www.ibtauris.com

Hardback edition first published in 2014 by
I.B.Tauris & Co. Ltd

ISBN: 978 1 78453 691 6
eISBN: 978 0 85773 607 9
ePDF: 978 0 85772 630 8

A full CIP record for this book is available from the British Library
A full CIP record is available from the Library of Congress

Library of Congress catalog card number: available

Typeset in Garamond Three by OKS Prepress Services, Chennai, India
Printed and bound by CPI Group (UK) Ltd, Croydon, CR0 4YY

MIX
Paper from
responsible sources
FSC FSC® C013604

Already was he bending over to
    Embrace my master's feet. 'Brother', said he,
    'Don't, for you're a shade, and shade you view'.
Standing, he said, 'You know now the degree
    Of love that warms me to you when it brings
Me to forget our insubstantiality:
    I treat our shadows still as solid things'.

                    Statius, author of the *Thebaid*, meets Virgil in
                    Purgatory (Dante, *Purgatorio* 21.130–6)

CONTENTS

LIST OF ILLUSTRATIONS

Fig. 1 Hammurabi of Babylon (1790–1752 BC) stands before the sun-god Shamash, from the Code of Hammurabi. Musée du Louvre. Photograph courtesy of Ariane Thomas.

Fig. 2 Stela of Marduk-apla-iddina II (721–710 BC, 703–702 BC). Vorderasiatisches Museum, Staatliche Museen zu Berlin. Photograph © bpk/Vorderasiatisches Museum, SMB/Olaf M.Teßmer.

Fig. 3 Reconstructed view of sixth-century BC Babylon from the north. Photograph © bpk/Vorderasiatisches Museum, SMB/Gudrun Stenzel.

Fig. 4 The Tower of Babel in the *Bedford Hours*. British Library. Photograph: public domain.

Fig. 5 The destruction of Babylon in the *Apocalypse of Angers*, 1377–82. Château d'Angers. Photograph: Kimon Berlin/Wikimedia Commons.

Fig. 6 The story of the doomed lovers Pyramus and Thisbe depicted on a medieval ivory casket. French, early fourteenth century. The Metropolitan Museum of Art, gift of J. Pierpont Morgan, 1917 (17.190.173a, b); The Cloisters Collection, 1988 (1988.16). Image © The Metropolitan Museum of Art.

Fig. 19 Preparations for Ishtar Gate reconstructions: sorting glazed-brick fragments in Berlin, 1927. Photograph © bpk/Vorderasiatisches Museum, SMB.

Fig. 20 The completed Ishtar Gate reconstructions at the Vorderasiatisches Museum today. Photograph courtesy of Alison Clark.

Fig. 21 Glazed-brick lion relief from the Processional Way. The Metropolitan Museum of Art, Fletcher Fund, 1931 (31.13.1). Image © The Metropolitan Museum of Art.

Fig. 22 The colossal Babylon set in D. W. Griffith's *Intolerance*, 1916. Photograph © Republic Pictures/Courtesy of Getty Images.

Fig. 23 Gertrude Bell at Babylon, 1909. Gertrude Bell Archive, Newcastle University, K 218. Photograph courtesy of the Gertrude Bell Archive, Newcastle University.

Fig. 24 Excavated ruins of the Northern Palace (left) and 1980s reconstructions at the Southern Palace (right) at Babylon. Photograph: author.

Fig. 25 Modern brickwork at the Southern Palace reconstructions, with Arabic inscription of Saddam Hussein. Photograph: author.

Fig. 26 Ceiling mural depicting Iraqi history, from Saddam Hussein's palace at Babylon. Photograph: author.

Fig. 27 Hanaa Malallah, *The God Marduk*, 2008. © Hanaa Malallah and the Trustees of the British Museum.

ACKNOWLEDGEMENTS

This book grew from my doctoral research, and I wish to thank Roger Matthews, Tim Schadla-Hall and Beverley Butler for their supervision of that project and support since. I owe a great debt to Stephanie Moser, who first introduced me to the study of representation in archaeology, supported me in pursuing this project and kindly read an early draft of this manuscript. I am also very grateful to my doctoral examiners, Stephanie Dalley and John Curtis, whose constructive criticism and advice formed a starting point for the further research that has resulted in the present book. I am doubly grateful to Dr Curtis, who subsequently recruited me to work for the British Museum and to contribute to the 2008–9 exhibition *Babylon: Myth and Reality* and its catalogue. The experience of researching and producing the exhibition was a hugely valuable one, for which I owe thanks to colleagues at the British Museum as well as at the département des antiquités orientales, Musée du Louvre, and at the Vorderasiatisches Museum, Pergamonmuseum, Berlin. I am grateful above all to Irving Finkel, lead curator of the British Museum exhibition, without whose good advice, support and encouragement I could not have produced this book. In New York, I am grateful for the support of Joan Aruz and my colleagues in the Department of Ancient Near Eastern Art at The Metropolitan Museum of Art. Particular thanks are owed to Sarah Graff, who kindly read a draft of the manuscript and provided valuable suggestions, to

Anne-Elizabeth Dunn-Vaturi for advice and assistance with images, and to Zainab Bahrani at Columbia University for discussing the project with me at a late stage.

I am greatly indebted to the UK Arts and Humanities Research Council, who both supported my original doctoral research and provided a further research grant enabling me to work on the expansion and conversion of the thesis for publication following the British Museum exhibition. I am also grateful to Alex Wright, my editor at I.B.Tauris, for showing great patience in allowing me time to revise and rework the manuscript, to Amy Himsworth and Sara Magness for their careful work as production editors, to Nadine el-Hadi for assistance in sourcing and licensing the images, and to the British Institute for the Study of Iraq for providing a small grant to assist with production costs.

Recently I have been involved with the World Monuments Fund's work at Babylon, as a result of which I have been able to visit the site itself and to work with Iraq State Board of Antiquities and Heritage staff there. I wish to thank both organizations for this opportunity, which has made it possible for me to visit Babylon at a time when this remains difficult for foreigners.

Finally, I am deeply grateful for the enormous degree of support I have received from family and friends, without which I could never have brought the book to publication. My special thanks are owed to Alex May, Andrew Swan, Anna Clement, Gabriel Moshenska, James Doeser, Sarah Readings, Rachel Dutta Choudhury and, always, Sirui Yan. To her, and to my parents, this book is dedicated.

Map 1 Location of Babylon and other ancient sites in modern Iraq.

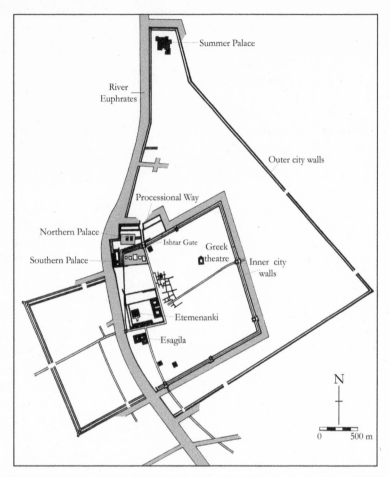

Map 2 The city of Babylon in the Neo-Babylonian period (sixth century BC).

CHAPTER 1

A CITY AND ITS GHOSTS

Working on behalf of the recently formed Deutsche Orient Gesellschaft (German Oriental Society), Robert Koldewey began excavations at Babylon in March 1899. By the standards of his British and French contemporaries in Mesopotamia, the excavation techniques he applied were slow and conscientious; nevertheless, they quickly revealed monumental buildings and vivid glazed-brick reliefs. Before the first year was out, it was clear that Koldewey had succeeded: after 2,000 years Babylon was emerging from the dust.

In their methods, German excavations between 1899 and 1917 resembled modern excavations far more closely than those of any predecessor. Crucially, they succeeded in identifying, tracing and recording the mud-brick architecture of the city. (The failure of nineteenth-century excavators in this respect is still visible in the enormous pits dug into some of Iraq's most important urban sites.[1]) Beyond the technical success, however, lay a more emotive achievement. This first year of excavations at Babylon could be seen as the end of a search that had begun in classical antiquity. Two millennia of fantastic and diverse visions of the famous city were in one sense ended by the excavations. Koldewey had uncovered Babylon itself. When the cultural significance of this action is appreciated, it is easy to understand the excavator's famous devotion to his excavation. He spent the vast bulk of the project's eighteen years at the site and would readily have spent more, as his first words in *The Excavations at Babylon* attest:

> It is most desirable, if not absolutely necessary, that the excavation of Babylon should be completed. Up to the present time only about half the work has been accomplished, although since it began we have worked daily, both summer and winter, with from 200 to 250 workmen.[2]

Despite the difficulties presented by the site, the results were spectacular. Brightly glazed brick reliefs showing dragons, lions and bulls quickly appeared as Koldewey's team excavated the monumental Ishtar Gate complex and the great Processional Way that ran through this, Babylon's grand northern entrance. The excavations also revealed the remains of temples, vast palaces and even the location of Babylon's ziggurat, the original Tower of Babel, but it was the blue-glazed bricks of the Ishtar Gate that would remain the strongest image to emerge from the ancient city. The discoveries culminated in Walter Andrae's painstaking reconstructions of the Processional Way and Ishtar Gate, displayed in Berlin's Vorderasiatisches Museum from 1930.[3] The original excavation of these vividly coloured reliefs, the actual decoration of ancient Babylon in its prime, was a powerful and exciting experience for the archaeologists, as their eventual display in Berlin was and is for the public.

The German excavations transformed modern knowledge of Babylon, and could be held to represent the moment at which legend was superseded by physical reality and the city entered the empirical, scientific domain of archaeological research. The moment, however, is incomplete. Though of huge archaeological importance, Koldewey's discoveries patently did not consign existing ideas about Babylon to the scrap heap. They might more accurately be said to have joined the existing cacophony of interpretation with a certain authority of voice, yet even the basis and extent of that authority are hardly simple matters. This book aims to explore what such moments mean in practice. If not immediate and total transformation, what is the effect of archaeology on the identity of a place people already know through other channels? Is there any way in which the archaeological moment of discovery is absolutely different from others – the traveller's visit and account or the artist's representation, for example? How do multiple, sometimes conflicting forms of knowledge co-exist and interact in the understanding of a single place? To ask these questions it is necessary to adopt a broader cultural and historical perspective on archaeological work itself: to view the development of archaeological approaches in their cultural context, and to consider the roles played by other, non-archaeological ways of engaging with the ancient past.

Human interest in antiquity and origins is a phenomenon far older and more varied than the academic disciplines of history or archaeology. We might even consider it universal, an aspect simply of being human, since ideas about the past are to be found everywhere and amongst everyone. The forms that our interest takes vary greatly, however, and such diversity produces its own challenges for the researcher. There are inherent difficulties to address in investigating a topic so broad, ranging widely over time and space and taking in a riot of disparate sources that includes fine art, poetry, theatre and music as well as history and archaeology. One approach to the problem is to follow the biography of a specific subject, idea, person or place, as is the case here; another is to focus on a broader topic (a field of scholarship or culture) at a particular time. In either case it is necessary to work across multiple subject areas, and to seek out connections that disciplinary boundaries in the present might tend to obscure.

Babylon is a city buried under its own mythology, transported through biblical and classical accounts into new worlds, and an afterlife that is sometimes so strange as to obscure an origin in any real place at all. The city has travelled, spread and transformed, which is precisely what makes it so interesting. The subject of this book then is not primarily the gradual rediscovery of Babylon archaeologically, though this certainly forms an important part. Rather, it is the history of that broader interest that continued to sustain Babylon in culture many centuries after the city itself had faded into obscurity. Much of the appeal is rooted in myth, but the aim of this book is not to establish simply that much of what has been written about Babylon over the centuries bears little relation to the realities of life in the ancient city itself. Instead its purpose is to explore the ways in which the stories created around Babylon in later times, with their varied and sometimes obscure connections to historical reality, can shed light on our own complex relationship with the ancient past. From an anthropological perspective legend and myth are useful, functional and necessary. One of the needs that they fulfil is that for frameworks into which present events can be fitted, and through which they might be understood. In this sense, historical narrative itself frequently plays a mythic role, selecting and drawing meaning from the mass of events with an eye to their understanding in the present.

A wider perspective may also help to address a recurring problem in studying the history of archaeology. It is common practice, particularly when writing of areas outside Europe, to treat the history of archaeology principally in terms of a succession of travellers and explorers, and if we are interested in Babylon we must certainly look at the people who visited and described the site. At the same time, however, it is important to recognize that the history of archaeology is one of intellectual development as well as physical exploration. We seek to understand why descriptions of Babylon by European travellers were written in the first place; why these changed over time; why, at a certain point, observation began to be supplemented by more formal survey and even excavation. The answers to these questions are often to be found not in the accounts of travellers themselves, but in the broader currents of European intellectual and cultural history. From this perspective, archaeology is a late arrival on a crowded stage, emerging only in the nineteenth century to vie with long-established traditions on the ancient past whose roots lay in theology, classical history, art, literature and more. Two millennia of accumulated thought, tradition, speculation, fantasy, philosophy and above all fascination preceded the first archaeological excavations at Babylon, and have since continued to flourish alongside archae-ological approaches.

To explore a topic so rich imposes its own constraints: I have had to be selective in the material discussed, and even then to treat too briefly a great many interesting individuals and stories. Some compensation, I hope, will be found not only in the breadth of the subject matter but also in the strange and revealing experience of following a city all the way from antiquity to the present day. Most of the journey takes place among ghosts and echoes: the fragments of the living city that in various ways survived its end. This, however, is no funereal procession. Babylon's ghosts are colourful and oddly creative – they take on lives of their own. Frequently they find new forms unimagined in the ancient Iraq where their journey begins. One wonders what the inhabitants of ancient Babylon would have made of the warlike Queen Semiramis of later tradition, or of the 'marriage market' of prospective wives described by Herodotus. They would certainly have been confused by talk of 'hanging' gardens, and much more so to discover that their city had gained a permanent association with the end of the world! Even the city's cataclysmic fall is a myth: the great destruction of popular imagination was for the Babylonians nothing more dramatic than a change of government. Yet all of these ideas have survived and developed in culture over the centuries, and even the most fantastic can contain echoes of a world with which the ancient Babylonians would have been much more familiar. As distant from the original as they might sometimes appear, they are still very much Babylon's ghosts.

Most ancient Mesopotamians, as far as we are able to tell, held rather pessimistic views on the next life. Myths describe a grey netherworld with no pleasures, whose inhabitants live in darkness and for whom the only food is dust. It is comforting to think that in one case at least they were mistaken: for the great city of Babylon itself, the afterlife has proven astonishingly rich.

CHAPTER 2

ANCIENT BABYLON

Very little is known of Babylon's earliest history. The city first appears in texts in the later third millennium BC,[1] one among many then thriving in southern Iraq. References of any kind to Babylon before the final century of the third millennium are very rare, but records of large offerings made to the temple of Enlil in Nippur during this century (while Babylon was part of an empire ruled from the southern city of Ur) suggest a city already of some size and wealth.[2] In the middle of the eighteenth century BC Babylon would emerge from relative obscurity to become the political centre of southern Mesopotamia, a position it was to maintain almost continuously for the next 1,400 years.

The site of Babylon lies on the Euphrates, approximately 85 km south of Baghdad. It is located towards the northern end of the great alluvial plain of southern Iraq, a landscape made of silts deposited by the Tigris and Euphrates rivers into a vast trough created by tectonic movement as the Arabian plate slips slowly east and north below the neighbouring Eurasian plate. The same collision is responsible for the creation of the Taurus and Zagros mountain ranges that define the northern and eastern borders of an area including all of Iraq as well as parts of modern Syria and Turkey. This area, known as Mesopotamia, thus incorporates several environmental zones, but it is in the flat alluvial plain of southern Iraq itself that Babylon is located. Home to the world's earliest cities,[3] the plain is subject to several important environmental constraints that have, since long before the foundation of Babylon, shaped its human occupation. The area is subject to very high temperatures and lies well beyond the reach of rain-fed agriculture. Even the small amount of precipitation this part of Iraq does receive is unevenly and unpredictably distributed: the bulk of a season's rain can fall in a single downpour, itself as harmful to crops as severe drought.[4] Human habitation is therefore entirely dependent on the two great rivers, and permanent settlement requires a system of irrigation. Once established, however, such a system could reap the benefit of rich alluvial soils and support extremely productive agriculture on the levees of canals. Most explanations of the region's early urban and associated economic development assume that the ability to produce large agricultural surpluses played an important role, though in quite what way is hotly disputed.[5] Herodotus was certainly impressed. In his fifth-century BC description he writes that:

> As a grain-bearing country Assyria {meaning Mesopotamia} is the richest in the world. No attempt is made there to grow figs, grapes, or olives, or any other fruit trees, but so great is the fertility of the grain fields that they normally produce crops of two-hundredfold, and in an exceptional year as much as three-hundredfold. The blades of wheat and barley are at least three inches wide. As for millet and sesame, I will not say to what an astonishing size they grow, though I know well enough; but I also know that people who have not been to Babylonia have refused to believe even what I have already said about its fertility. The only oil these people use is made from sesame; date-palms grow everywhere, mostly of the fruit-bearing kind, and the fruit supplies them with food, wine and honey.[6]

The infrastructure underpinning such abundance required constant maintenance, both of the system of irrigation canals and of a parallel system of drainage, since water can also bring salts to the surface by capillary action, rendering land too saline for agriculture. Although the requirements for organization of labour this need creates do not

seem to have been the primary driving force behind the earliest
urbanization during the fourth millennium BC, where the canal
systems employed are relatively modest, it is clear that by the middle
of the third millennium BC a great deal of labour must have been
organized to maintain major canals.[7] This very flat landscape is also
subject to changes in river courses, natural or artificially induced. As
is the case today, when dam projects and the competing water
demands of Iraq and its upstream neighbours Turkey and Syria are of
great political importance, in the ancient world control of water was a
significant source of power and conflict. Again there is some echo of
this in ancient Greek stories about Babylon, where massive
engineering projects to change water courses figure as an important
aspect of military strategy.[8]

Although there have been excavations at the site before and since, our
archaeological picture of Babylon derives primarily from work
conducted by the Deutsche Orient-Gesellschaft in the years 1899–
1917. These excavations of necessity concentrated on the later phases of
occupation, and particularly on the centre of the city as it was rebuilt by
Nebuchadnezzar II (604–562 BC) in the sixth century BC. The high
water table at Babylon has largely prevented direct exploration of its
earlier history. Some older monuments, including the famous
eighteenth-century BC Code of Hammurabi, were actually excavated
at the Iranian city of Susa; they had been looted from Babylon and
carried there in antiquity by the army of the Elamite king Shutruk-
Nahhunte (c.1185–1155 BC) in the twelfth century BC. More outrageous
items of booty from the same invasion were the cult statues of Marduk,
chief god of the city, and his consort Zarpanitu. Nebuchadnezzar II, the
most famous king of Babylon, took his name from the illustrious
predecessor who at the end of the twelfth century BC was able to recover
the statues and with them Babylon's honour and prosperity.[9]

The Old Babylonian period

Over the course of the third millennium BC, Mesopotamia changed
politically from a world of city states into one of larger polities, even
empires. First Akkad (a city whose exact location archaeologists have

so far been unable to establish), then Ur, then the rival powers of Isin and Larsa held sway over multiple cities in southern Iraq in the later centuries of the third millennium. Babylon's rise to a position of central political importance dates to the reign of Hammurabi (more accurately Hammurapi, 1790–1752 BC), the most famous of a dynasty of kings, sometimes called Amorite in reference to their likely tribal origin, who ruled from the early nineteenth century BC. Following a period of competition for territorial control that had been dominated by the cities of Isin and Larsa, Babylon managed to gain the upper hand, first at the head of a coalition, and later as sole power. By the end of Hammurabi's reign in the mid-eighteenth century BC, Babylon had achieved hegemony over not only southern Iraq but also a considerable area to the north. By this time the urban, literate world of Mesopotamia was already well over a millennium old, as in some form were the civic institutions that underpinned urban life. Certainly the latter include some legal framework, and so Hammurabi's modern epithet of 'lawgiver' is not quite deserved; it is rather his political and military successes that make him the most important figure of the period. His conquest of Larsa allowed him to claim the title of King of Sumer and Akkad (i.e. all of southern Iraq), and was followed by the acquisition of Mari to the north and eventually the Assyrian cities of Ashur and Nineveh.[10]

Once achieved, the pre-eminence established for Babylon among the cities of southern Iraq by Hammurabi was successfully defended, despite a significant challenge in the south of the region from the so-called Sealand dynasty.[11] The First Dynasty of Babylon, rulers of the city since the early nineteenth century BC, retained power and at least some of the territory won by Hammurabi until 1595 BC. An even more enduring legacy was that Babylon remained the principal political centre of southern Mesopotamia (which from this point forward we can justly refer to as Babylonia) until the reign of Seleucus I Nicator and the foundation of Seleucia on the Tigris at the end of the fourth century BC.

Quite appropriately even this, Babylon's real emergence as a powerful city, has become the subject of legend. Among the most important and iconic objects in the Mesopotamian collections of the

Musée du Louvre is the Code of Hammurabi, popularly known as the world's first code of laws (Figure 1). The text of the monument actually consists of a series of laws or precedents that might best be seen as examples of justice on the part of Hammurabi.[12] Significantly older lists of laws do exist,[13] though the quantity of laws and their presentation in this striking public format give the Code of Hammurabi a unique importance.[14] Its laws are still the first cuneiform texts to be studied by most students of Assyriology (the study of ancient Mesopotamian languages and literature).

Kassite Babylon

The fortunes of Hammurabi's successors waned over time, until eventually the gradual weakening of Babylonian power made it possible for the Anatolian Hittite Empire to launch a brief but highly successful military raid on Mesopotamia and even Babylon itself in 1595 BC. This incursion marks the end of the Old Babylonian period and the beginning of a more politically fragmented era that, from the Babylonian point of view at least, was to be dominated by a dynasty of Kassite kings. The Kassites first appear in Mesopotamian texts at the end of the eighteenth century BC, but it is only in the sixteenth that they come to play a major visible role in Babylon's story. With a non-Semitic language (that is to say, one unrelated to Babylonian) and coming probably from the Zagros mountains in Iran, Kassite families seem to have settled in Mesopotamia in increasing numbers throughout the seventeenth century BC, while at the same time a Kassite kingdom bordering that of Babylon existed and may have posed a military threat. Nonetheless, it was the Hittites under Murshili I (c. 1620–1595 BC) who brought a dramatic end to the First Dynasty of Babylon. Perhaps the Hittite presence would have been more lasting had it not been for court intrigue in the Hittite capital of Hattusha and the assassination of Murshili shortly after the 1595 BC raid. As it was, a much-weakened Babylon was fought over by its other neighbours. Although evidence for the sixteenth century BC is extremely sparse, it is thought that the 'Sealand' kings of the south briefly held Babylon itself before rule of the city and of the northern part of the southern Mesopotamian plain passed to the Kassites. The point at which Kassite control was established is also far from clear. The best available indicator is a later document recording that in c.1570 BC the Kassite king Agum II recovered the statues of Marduk and his consort Zarpanitu from the Hittite capital Hattusha (where they had been taken following the invasion of Murshili I) and returned them to the great temple Esagila at Babylon, a symbolically important act that seems to mark the legitimization, if not the exact beginning, of four centuries of Kassite rule.[15] By the mid-fifteenth century the Kassites had also won control of the southern territory formerly held by the Sealand dynasty, and thus the whole of Babylonia.

The Kassite period saw a partial return to a more rural pattern of settlement: archaeological survey data suggest that smaller settlements became more common in southern Mesopotamia as a whole, while numbers of larger settlements declined during the period.[16] On the other hand, there is evidence for substantial monumental building projects at Babylon and other cities under Kurigalzu I (?–1375 BC).[17] The Kassite state was large and to judge by its longevity successful, but never politically or militarily dominant internationally. Other powers of equal or greater significance during the latter half of the second millennium BC include the Hittite Empire in Turkey and Mitanni, a kingdom composed of small Hurrian states unified at around 1500 BC and at its greatest extent encompassing much of Syria and northern Iraq. The period has been characterized as an 'international age',[18] not least due to the remarkable archive known today as the Amarna letters. Found at the Amarna capital of Akhetaten, these documents reveal a correspondence between the pharaohs Amenophis III and Akhenaten and Kassite kings at Babylon, conducted in Babylonian cuneiform.[19] Tablets from Iraq, Syria, the Levant and Anatolia now confirm that similar correspondence – accompanied by gift exchange and intermarriage – occurred between kings across the Eastern Mediterranean and Middle East during the fifteenth and fourteenth centuries BC.

Kassite material and visual culture is distinct from that of the preceding Old Babylonian period, but also shows obvious continuity with the earlier Mesopotamian world. Perhaps the most distinctively 'Kassite' Babylonian artefacts are large stone land grants, called *kudurrus*, on which are carved texts, divine symbols and sometimes human beings. Even these monuments, however, are clearly Babylonian in their iconography and employ Babylonian cuneiform for their inscriptions. This is perhaps an early manifestation of a repeating pattern of assimilation in Babylon's history, whereby the city's conquerors would tend to emulate or adapt Babylonian cultural forms rather than attempting to impose their own. The reasons for this may well have varied over time, but certainly the tendency hints at the degree of cultural, religious and political cachet the city of Babylon held.

Elamites and others

During the reign of the Kassite king Kashtiliashu IV (1232–1225 BC) Babylon was sacked by the Assyrian army of Tukulti-Ninurta I (1243–1207 BC). The destruction, at least according to Assyrian texts, was substantial:

> [Tukult]i-Ninurta (I) returned to Babylon and brought [...]...
> [...] near. He destroyed the wall of Babylon (and) [pu]t the Babylonians to the sword. He took out the property of Esagil and Babylon amid the booty. He removed the great lord Marduk [from] his [dais] and sent (him) to Assyria. He put his governors in Karduniash (Babylon). For seven years Tukulti-Ninurta (I) controlled Karduniash.[20]

Babylon now came under Assyrian rule for the first time. It has been suggested that in describing this event in his royal inscriptions, Tukulti-Ninurta echoes the language of the much earlier kings of Akkad, Sargon and Naram-Sin, some of ancient Mesopotamia's first empire builders, investing himself with titles such as King of Sumer and Akkad and King of the Upper and Lower Seas (i.e. from the Mediterranean to the Persian Gulf).[21] 'In the midst of battle', the king declares,

I captured Kaštiliašu, king of the Kassites, (and) trod with my feet upon his lordly neck as though it were a footstool. Bound I brought him as a captive into the presence of Aššur, my lord. (Thus) I became lord of Sumer and Akkad in its entirety (and) fixed the boundary of my land as the Lower Sea in the east.[22]

Tukulti-Ninurta's reign was followed by a period of instability and upheaval across the Mediterranean and Middle Eastern world, affecting Assyria more directly than Babylonia and thus weakening Assyrian power over the latter. Kassite power was reasserted in Babylon (although Elamite interference may also have played some role in the weakening of Assyrian control) under Adad-shuma-usur (1216–1187 BC), Meli-Shipak (1186–1172 BC) and Marduk-apla-iddina I (1171–1159 BC). Eventually, however, a combination of Assyrian and Elamite military pressure proved enough to bring an end to the Kassite state. The Elamite king Shutruk-Nahhunte attacked the city c. 1159 BC; his son was installed as king of Babylon and it was at this time that a number of monuments from Babylon were carried off to the Elamite capital at Susa. Today the most famous of these is the Code of Hammurabi, but much more deeply felt at the time was the loss of the divine statue of Marduk.[23] The tradition of taking a city's god was an ancient one in Mesopotamia, and an act with significance of several kinds. The cult statue was naturally an object of great material value, but this was only the beginning. Cult statues in ancient Iraq were far more than images: in some sense, today imperfectly understood, they embodied the gods themselves. That it should be possible for a foreign army to loot a city and take the gods' statues suggested that the city had been forsaken by these deities. The loss of cult statues was thus a humiliating and traumatic experience and their recovery, even centuries later, an important matter of civic honour.

The short period of Elamite rule that followed was dogged by violent Kassite resistance, although the dynasty never returned to power. For the next several centuries Babylon was ruled by a succession of more-or-less local dynasties. Through a successful military campaign Nebuchadnezzar I (1125–1104 BC) of the Second Dynasty of Isin succeeded in recovering the statue of Marduk from

Susa, an event with tangible consequences for Babylonian cultural and religious identity. Marduk had already risen to prominence from his obscure third-millennium origins, but it is thought that his reinstallation in Babylon by Nebuchadnezzar marks his rise to the head of the regional pantheon. It was probably also during this period that the Babylonian Epic of Creation *Enuma Elish* first appeared, justifying Marduk's – and thereby Babylon's – pre-eminence through his heroic role in conquering the forces of chaos at the beginning of the world.[24]

Assyrian dominance

The achievements of Nebuchadnezzar I were considerable, but did not buy Babylonia long-term independence. Nebuchadnezzar himself appears to have been the most successful of the Second Dynasty of Isin kings, and throughout the reigns of his successors raiding by Aramean tribal groups revealed the limits of Babylonian state power. Meanwhile Assyrian fortunes had revived under Tiglath-pileser I (1114–1076 BC), and by the early first millennium BC Babylon was once again on the back foot politically and militarily. Successive kings of Assyria transformed their small state in northern Iraq into the dominant military power in the region, with a great empire covering most of the Middle East. Babylon was able to maintain its independence until the eighth century BC. From his accession in 745 BC, however, the Assyrian king Tiglath-pileser III campaigned increasingly in the south, initially against Chaldean and Aramean tribal enemies. By the end of his reign in 727 BC the whole of Babylonia was under direct Assyrian control. The brief reign of Shalmaneser V (726–722 BC) and the rise to power of the usurper Sargon II (721–705 BC) allowed Babylonia to reassert its independence under Marduk-apla-iddina II (the biblical Merodach-baladan), a ruler of the Chaldean Bit Yakin tribe who installed himself as king of Babylon in 721 BC, maintaining an independent kingship of Babylonia until finally ousted by Sargon in 710 BC (Figure 2). The eighth and seventh centuries BC saw regular rebellions against Assyrian rule from Babylonia, often led by the powerful Chaldean tribes of Bit-Dakkuri, Bit-Amukkani and Bit-Yakin, whose territory collectively stretched from the area of Borsippa, near Babylon, south along the Euphrates to the Persian Gulf.[25] Although largely sedentary, living in villages and even walled towns, the tribes apparently retained enough mobility to cause problems for Assyrian armies, possibly by making better use of the landscape and natural environment than their more powerful opponents.[26] They had less to lose from Assyrian campaigns than their neighbours in the cities of northern Babylonia.

Sennacherib in particular was to suffer constant setbacks in attempting to maintain Assyrian control over Babylonia. In 703 BC Marduk-apla-iddina capitalized on a revolt and briefly seized the throne of Babylon for a second time.[27] Sennacherib defeated the rebellion and installed Bel-Ibni, a Babylonian raised in the Assyrian court, as king of Babylon. Resistance persisted, however, and Sennacherib found it necessary to campaign against Marduk-apla-iddina again in 700 BC, at which time Bel-Ibni was also removed from the throne, and Sennacherib's son Ashur-nadin-shumi was installed as the new king of Babylon. Another serious Babylonian revolt against Assyria began in 694 BC, triggered by an Elamite invasion of Babylonia itself. Ashur-nadin-shumi was captured (apparently betrayed by Babylonian conspirators)[28] and a Babylonian, Nergal-ushezib, took up the kingship of the city. Nergal-ushezib's reign was brief: he was captured by the Assyrians in 693 BC and presumably executed. The rebellion continued under his successor Mushezib-Marduk, but Babylonia was no match for Assyria militarily. The city of Babylon itself was well defended and withstood a protracted siege, though not without great suffering. A contemporary legal text gives some sense of the deprivation:

> In the time of Mušēzib-Marduk, King of Babylonia, the land was gripped by siege, famine, hunger, want and hard times. Everything was changed and reduced to nothing. Two *qa* of barley sold for one shekel of silver. The city gates were barred, and a person could not go out in any of the four directions. The

corpses of men, with no one to bury them, filled the squares of Babylon.[29]

In 689 BC Babylon was finally sacked, although whether the city was taken by force or forced to surrender due to starvation is unclear. The destruction that followed was the culmination of years of violence in which it might be argued that Sennacherib's actions, along with the abolition of Babylon's independent kingship, were measures of last resort, essential to the conclusion of an exhausting five-year war.[30] Babylon had always held a special status in Mesopotamian culture, and surely such violence towards the city was not undertaken lightly. Nonetheless Sennacherib's own texts emphasize the totality of the destruction. The Bavian Inscription, carved on cliffs near the mouth of Sennacherib's irrigation canal for his capital at Nineveh, is explicit:

> I destroyed the city and its houses, from foundation to parapet; I devastated and burned them. I razed the brick and earthenwork of the outer and inner wall (of the city), of the temples, and of the ziggurat; and I dumped these into the Araḫtu canal. I dug canals through the midst of that city, I overwhelmed it with water, I made its very foundations disappear, and I destroyed it more completely than a devastating flood. So that it might be impossible in future days to recognize the site of that city and (its) temples, I utterly dissolved it with water (and made it) like inundated land.[31]

The destruction was especially shocking given Babylon's cultural and religious importance, and both Babylonian and Assyrian historical texts later seem to avoid the topic, at times attributing the devastation to a flood brought about by the wrath of Marduk.[32]

His attempts to install a loyal vassal as king of Babylon having failed, Sennacherib now took direct control of Babylonia.[33] Once again the statue of Marduk was removed, probably to Ashur.[34] The *Akitu Chronicle* records that during the statue's 20-year absence from Babylon the New Year festival did not take place.[35] All this occurred within the context of a broader depopulation of Babylonia in the late eighth and early seventh centuries BC. The deportations of subject populations to the Assyrian heartland served both to reduce the danger of dissent and rebellion and to provide labour for ambitious building programmes at Nineveh and for agricultural work in other parts of the empire.[36]

Sennacherib's son and successor Esarhaddon (681–669 BC) faced further rebellions, but also rebuilt Babylon after 11 years during which the city had apparently been abandoned following Sennacherib's destruction.[37] His inscriptions suggest that the rebuilding was accompanied by a reassertion of the piety and reverence towards Babylon that had traditionally been expressed by Assyrian kings and only briefly interrupted during the reign of Sennacherib. Brinkman summarizes their content as follows:

> In Esarhaddon's Babylon inscriptions, attention is focused on the divine framework within which the destruction and resurrection of Babylon occurred: malportent omina, the iniquitous conduct of the Babylonians (including misappropriation of temple funds), the destruction of the city by a severe flood, Marduk's decision to shorten the years of desolation (from 70 to 11), auspicious omina, and restoration. The Assyrians assembled a large group of workmen drawn – according to various versions – from all of Babylonia, from Assyria, and/or from conquered lands; and Esarhaddon claimed to have taken part in the work personally.[38]

Esarhaddon did not, however, install a new king on the throne of Babylon. Instead he aimed to resolve the problem through the Assyrian succession: two of his sons, Ashurbanipal and Shamash-shuma-ukin, were to inherit the kingdoms of Assyria and Babylonia respectively. This arrangement was intended not to divide the empire, but to place the two brothers in a close but unequal arrangement whereby ultimately Ashurbanipal held authority over both kingdoms. The succession occurred as planned and this dual monarchy held for some 16 years, during which time Ashurbanipal, as king of Assyria, continued his father's contribution to the rebuilding of Babylon and campaigned vigorously, extending and strengthening the Assyrian Empire. The return of kingship (in the form of Shamash-shuma-ukin) and the statue of Marduk (whether the original or a new statue produced in Assyria) were cause for great celebration in Babylonia but also Assyria, as recorded in texts of Ashurbanipal.

For much of Ashurbanipal's reign, the great military threats were posed by Egypt to the west and Elam to the east; Assyrian campaigns against both powers were successful and the empire's reach extended. In 652 BC, however, the system of dual kingship came to an abrupt end as Shamash-shuma-ukin turned against his brother, beginning the most serious of all the Babylonian revolts against Assyria. Whether the cause was overuse by Ashurbanipal of his prerogative as his brother's overlord or Shamash-shuma-ukin's perception that he was militarily able – with Elamite and tribal support – to stand against Assyria, the result was a devastating war, ultimately ruinous for both kingdoms. By the time the city of Babylon fell in 648 BC it had been under siege for two years. Again war was accompanied by famine and disease, and other cities in Babylonia also suffered grievously as the rebellion failed. Even after the reconquest of Babylon, the Assyrian army was occupied for several more years in campaigns of retribution against Elam, the tribes of southern Mesopotamia and those of the western desert. At the end of seven years of fighting, Assyria had successfully overcome all of its enemies, yet the campaign seems to have exhausted even this most formidable of military machines. After the rebellion there are no records of further Assyrian campaigns.[39] Ashurbanipal had triumphed, but the struggle had drained the Assyrian Empire's resources and perhaps even sown the seeds of its collapse. Shamash-shuma-ukin burned to death, though whether through suicide, murder or accident in the destruction of Babylon is unclear.[40] A prism of Ashurbanipal recording the events claims that the god Ashur himself threw Shamash-shuma-ukin into the flames.[41] The story of the two brothers survived into later, non-cuneiform tradition: a fourth-century BC papyrus fragment from Egypt carries an Aramaic version of the story.[42] It may even be the inspiration behind the Greek story of

Sardanapalus.[43] Whatever the details of his fate, Shamash-shuma-ukin is absent from the Assyrian relief showing Ashurbanipal taking Babylon's surrender and tribute.[44]

Following the war, Babylon was ruled by a king known as Kandalanu, for whom very little textual information survives.[45] Over the next two decades Babylonia recovered economically, but around the time of the deaths of Ashurbanipal and Kandalanu in 627 BC[46] it fell into political chaos. A new Babylonian leader, Nabopolassar, defeated an Assyrian army sent to Babylon and took the throne as an independent king of Babylonia. Assyria was never able to regain the upper hand, and in 612 BC Nineveh fell to a coalition of Babylonians and Medes. With support from its former rival Egypt, Assyria continued to hold north-western Mesopotamia, but the Assyrian and Egyptian forces were finally defeated decisively at the battle of Carchemish in 605 BC.[47] The overthrow of the Assyrian Empire altered the political landscape of the Middle East permanently, restoring Babylon to a central role.

Babylon triumphant: The Neo-Babylonian period

Under Nabopolassar (625–605 BC) and Nebuchadnezzar II (604–562 BC) a new dynasty established Babylon as capital of most of the area formerly ruled by the Assyrians from Nineveh, an empire extending from the Zagros mountains in the east to the Mediterranean Sea in the west. There is some reason to believe that this dynasty, today called Neo-Babylonian, itself had some links with the Assyrian court.[48] The Old Testament ascribes the dynasty the name Chaldean,[49] and modern scholarship has held that Nabopolassar was a member of the tribe of Bit Yakin, although evidence for this is actually very limited.[50] Whatever the dynasty's origins, the territory and administration Nabopolassar inherited were very much those of the Assyrian Empire.

The Babylonian kings also inherited the Assyrians' rivalry with Egypt for control of territory in the Levant. As crown prince, Nebuchadnezzar had already campaigned successfully against Egypt in the west. As king, he was required to maintain territory and to prevent subject states from shifting their allegiances or withholding tribute from the Babylonian crown. One such problem state was Judah. Twice, in 597 and 587–586 BC, Nebuchadnezzar was compelled to besiege Jerusalem in order to re-establish his authority. On the first occasion the Judaean king Jehoiachin, his family and other deportees were taken into exile in Babylon. On the second the city of Jerusalem was sacked, the temple looted and many more people deported from Judah to Babylon. The Book of Jeremiah suggests that further deportations occurred in 582–581 BC.[51] The next chapter will discuss this event and its significance in more detail; here it suffices to say that as a result of its centrality to the Old Testament this aspect of Nebuchadnezzar's reign has defined both the king and his city far more completely than could have been guessed at the time, since in fact no aspect of the procedure was particularly new or unusual, and there was already a long tradition of deportations of this kind. Assyrian military strength led to control over a huge geographical area during the early first millennium BC, but administration to deal with this expansion developed slowly and piece-meal. Tax and tribute from the provinces, vassals and puppet states made a major contribution to the wealth of the Assyrian heartland, but came with the increased complexity of ruling a large and disparate empire. Preventing uprisings on the fringes of the empire was a major concern for Assyrian kings and a number of policies developed to meet this need, among them mass deportations. When new territory was conquered or a rebellious vassal crushed, an increased imperial presence in the trouble spot was often complemented by the removal of large numbers of the indigenous population to the imperial core, effectively breaking up the rebellious population and reducing the potential for future resistance.[52] The practice was effective, and continued throughout the Neo-Assyrian and Neo-Babylonian periods until the Persian conquest of Babylon in 539 BC. The majority of the immigrant population were not slaves,[53] and some did rise to high status positions at the core of the empire (a possibility reflected in the career of the biblical Daniel, who receives a full Babylonian scribal education and ultimately achieves the status of trusted royal confidant). This last aspect of the deportations, also common if not as formalized in later empires, could be seen as a harmonizing, inclusive approach to creating and maintaining a viable imperial identity, and to effectively ruling a religiously and ethnically diverse empire. Non-Babylonian sources understandably take a dimmer view of the policy. Of these foreign sources one group – the biblical sources covering the Judaean Exile – have had an impact far greater than other ancient texts, including those of the imperial elites themselves, in forming a modern identity for ancient Babylonia. The capture and destruction of Jerusalem and subsequent deportation of Jews to Babylon is not only a major event from the perspective of the biblical authors, but one of enormous and continuing symbolic importance in Judaism and Christianity.

That the Judaean Exile should come to dominate Nebuchadnezzar's image and legacy would undoubtedly have come as a surprise to the king himself. In Babylonian terms his most significant acts were to secure the young empire established under his father Nabopolassar and to rebuild the city of Babylon itself as an imperial capital (Figure 3). The city as excavated by archaeologists in the early twentieth century is largely that constructed by Nebuchadnezzar in the early sixth century BC – precisely the period that is of most interest in terms of the Judaean Exile, but also that of Babylon's greatest world political significance. Nebuchadnezzar's achievements were listed in his building inscriptions and one text, known as *Nebuchadnezzar, King of Justice*, presents him as a model of the just king, maintaining law and order and punishing the wicked.[54] These qualities emulate those of Hammurabi, Nebuchadnezzar's most illustrious predecessor, and more concrete signs exist to show the king's reference to antiquity in his own inscriptions. Most strikingly, Nebuchadnezzar's monumental inscriptions appear in an archaizing script which imitates that of the Old Babylonian period, and thus the proclamations of a king who had reigned well over 1,000 years earlier.[55]

Nebuchadnezzar died in 562 BC and was succeeded by his son Amel-Marduk. It seems that the latter had once been out of favour and imprisoned, the victim of court intrigue.[56] That court life in

Babylon could be precarious is demonstrated by the speed of the succession that followed. Nebuchadnezzar had ruled for over four decades, but, although he may have acted as regent in the final years of his father's reign, Amel-Marduk lasted only two as king in his own right. He was murdered by his brother-in-law Neriglissar in 560 BC, the latter taking the throne. Neriglissar himself died not long after, in 556 BC, while his successor, his young son Labashi-Marduk, died, almost certainly murdered, after only three months on the throne. The crown now passed to Nabonidus (556–539 BC), a king who was to have more longevity, though not necessarily better fortune.

Did Nabonidus murder Labashi-Marduk? A stela of Nabonidus claims that 'Labashi-Marduk, a minor (who) had not (yet) learned how to behave, sat down on the royal throne against the intentions of the gods', going on to stress that 'I (Nabonidus) am the real executor of the wills of Nebuchadnezzar and Neriglissar, my royal predecessors!'[57] Dougherty makes the case for the defence, cautioning that there is no actual mention of the killing of Labashi-Marduk, nor of usurpation of the throne, and that since Nabonidus is keen to stress his links with Nebuchadnezzar and Neriglissar rather than to found a new dynasty, 'There is sufficient ground for the view that the last reign of the Neo-Babylonian empire was an integral part of the Neo-Babylonian dynasty'.[58] Nonetheless there are obvious political explanations for not mentioning murder or usurpation, and for supporting a claim to the throne with reference to earlier kings. It should be noted that the story is also known through the later Babylonian historian Berossus, whose account both preserves Nabonidus' indictment of Labashi-Marduk and states that the young king was murdered in a coup, with Nabonidus elevated to the throne by his co-conspirators.[59] The assumption should remain that Labashi-Marduk was murdered, and that Nabonidus was the beneficiary, if not the leader, of a violent coup.

Nabonidus was not himself part of the royal family. He describes himself as one who had not expected the role, and had no thought of kingship, even as 'the son of a nobody',[60] but his background was certainly not a humble one. He had spent his life close to power, claims in his inscriptions to have served kings from Nebuchadnezzar onward faithfully, and he may even be the 'Labynetus of Babylon' who appears in Herodotus brokering peace between Lydia and Media.[61] Nonetheless, Nabonidus' own account suggests that his accession was sufficiently unexpected as to require a more than usual degree of divine sanction:

> (This is) the great miracle of Sin that none of the (other) gods and goddesses knew (how to achieve), that has not happened to the country from the days of old.

> That (you), Sin, the lord of all the gods and goddesses residing in heaven, have come down from heaven to (me) Nabonidus, king of Babylon! For me, Nabonidus, the lonely one who has nobody, in whose (text: my) heart was no thought of kingship, the gods and goddesses prayed (to Sin) and Sin called me to kingship.[62]

Inscriptions of his mother Adda-Guppi, the high priestess of the moon god Sin at Harran, also claim that the moon god called Nabonidus to kingship,[63] and his own inscriptions suggest that throughout his reign Nabonidus focused to an unusual degree on the cult of Sin. The moon god was always a major figure in the Babylonian pantheon; normally, however, a king's devotion would be directed primarily towards Babylon's patron deity Marduk and his son Nabu. From the surviving textual sources it appears that Nabonidus' particular devotion to the moon god stemmed from his upbringing, and especially from his remarkable mother. Adda-Guppi strikes an imposing figure even at a distance of two-and-a-half millennia. The fact that her name survives at all puts her in a tiny minority among ancient Mesopotamian royal women; that long texts should survive describing her life is almost unique. A text on two stelae found at Harran is known today as the 'autobiography' of Adda-Guppi. As well as suggesting power, these texts attest to what – particularly in the ancient world – seems to have been an incredibly long and healthy life. If the 'autobiography' is to be believed, Adda-Guppi lived happily to the age of 104. 'My eyesight was good (to the end of my life)', she tells us, 'my hearing excellent, my hands and feet were sound, my words well chosen, food and drink agreed with me, my health was fine and my mind happy. I saw my great-grandchildren, up to the fourth generation, in good health and (thus) had my fill of old age'.[64]

Just how far Nabonidus' devotions and cultic behaviour actually diverged from the expectations of his court is difficult to judge, in part because several of the key surviving sources are unambiguously anti-Nabonidus propaganda. A prime example is the gathering of gods' cult statues from other cities in Babylon prior to the Persian invasion. The gods' entry into the city was conceived as a matter of their own choosing, and indeed not all local gods did enter Babylon on this occasion. Following the conquest, however, it was easy to level the charge that the statues had been brought into the city against their will (hence their subsequent failure to protect the city or its king).[65]

The most puzzling aspect of Nabonidus' reign is his long absence from Babylon itself. In around 553 BC Nabonidus travelled to Teima in north-western Arabia, where he stayed for the next ten years, leaving his son Bel-sharra-usur – the biblical Belshazzar – as regent in Babylon. This arrangement, certainly highly irregular, was also far from satisfactory, since there were cultic duties which only the king could perform and which therefore went neglected for a decade. The reasons for Nabonidus' decision to stay away are unclear. From his own account of events it would seem that there had been a rebellion against the king by priests and citizens of Babylon, Borsippa, Nippur, Ur, Uruk and Larsa, all of whom refused to contribute to the rebuilding of the Ekhulkhul temple of Sin at Harran. Whatever the connection, it seems that Babylon was also suffering seriously from disease and famine at the time of Nabonidus' departure.[66]

A tradition preserved in the Dead Sea Scrolls, known as the *Prayer of Nabonidus*,[67] claims that it was the king himself who suffered from a disease:

{I, Nabonidus}, was (there) smitten with [the evil bushāna-disease] for seven years, and when, from [that] time, I became as [a dying man(?), I prayed to the Most High] and he forgave my sin. (Thereupon) a holy man who was a Judean fr[om the Exiles, came to me saying], 'Proclaim (your forgiveness) and write it down so as to give honour and glo[ry] to the name of [the Most High]'.[68]

Other possible causes are political and economic: there is every reason to believe that Nabonidus set out to conquer and control Arabian trade routes, since the value of trade in aromatics and spices was enormous and rising during the sixth century BC. This explanation, however, accounts only for the Babylonian presence in general. It does not explain why the king of Babylon himself might want or need to be present, neglecting his political and religious duties in Babylon all the while. One anti-Nabonidus text, the *Verse Account of Nabonidus*,[69] asserts that during the years of his absence the Babylonian New Year festival known as *akitu*, apparently the most important in the calendar,[70] could not be performed. The king acted as a mediator between human and divine worlds, a role that seemingly could not be played by Belshazzar as regent. The *Verse Account* is a propagandistic text, but the hiatus in the *akitu* festival is real enough: it is confirmed by Nabonidus' own royal chronicles:

> The king did not come to Babylon for the [New Year] ceremony of the month of Nisannu; the god Nabû did not come to Babylon, the image of the god Bêl did not go out of Esagila in procession, the festival of the New Year was omitted.[71]

Nabonidus returned to Babylon in 543 BC. By this time, however, the balance of power in the Middle East was shifting. Cyrus II of Persia in southern Iran had come to the throne in 559 BC and led a successful rebellion against the western Iranian empire of Media, overthrowing its king Astyages. From here had followed the conquest of Turkey, including the Lydian Empire of King Croesus, leading ultimately to a position whereby Cyrus was strong enough to mount a challenge for the Babylonian throne. His armies defeated those of Nabonidus and Belshazzar at the battle of Opis in 539 BC, allowing Cyrus to enter Babylon peacefully as a conqueror (a fact stressed in the Cyrus

Cylinder, the Persian king's own account of his conquest, of which more below). Probably the lack of resistance had also to do with elements friendly to Cyrus inside the city. The most popular theory has been that priests of Marduk at Esagila, disaffected due to Nabonidus' favouring the moon god Sin, were responsible both for the ease of Cyrus' entry into Babylon and the composition of propagandistic documents such as the *Verse Account* and Cyrus Cylinder.

The fates of Nabonidus and Belshazzar are uncertain. According to the third-century BC historian Berossus, Nabonidus was captured but not executed, and was given land in Carmania (Kerman, in southeastern Iran), a remote outpost of the vast new empire created by Cyrus.[72]

Babylon in the Persian Empire

The conquest of Babylon by Cyrus in 539 BC has been understood in later tradition as the fulfilment of Old Testament prophecy. The language of that prophecy was fiery and pointed to a total destruction, but in fact the conquest marked a relatively quiet transition between the end of the Neo-Babylonian dynasty and the beginning of Persian rule. Babylon lived on, now as part of the vast Achaemenid Empire. Far larger than any political unit that had preceded it, the empire built by Cyrus and his successors stretched from the Eastern Mediterranean in the west far into Central Asia in the east. Not that Babylon was now a small fish in a big pond: the city remained a royal capital, albeit one of four,[73] a major administrative centre and surely the world's largest commercial centre. Cyrus himself was anxious to support an image of continuity, as can be seen in the text of the famous Cyrus Cylinder. A foundation inscription excavated at Babylon by Hormuzd Rassam in the late nineteenth century,[74] the Cylinder describes Cyrus restoring religious and cultural life in Babylon to its proper order following the strange reign of Nabonidus. The document is Babylonian in format, language and in its dedication to Marduk, chief god of the city. It is a document of the city's conquest, unquestionably an important historical event in itself, but its modern fame really rests on a particular aspect of this conquest – the end of the Judaean Exile – and on a close connection with the Bible.

Babylon during the two centuries of Persian rule (539–330 BC) continued to play an important political, cultural and economic role, now as part of a much larger empire.[75] The famous return to Jerusalem and commencement of the Second Temple period belies the fact that the whole region remained subject to the rule of a foreign empire, administered in part from Babylon. Following Cambyses' successful campaign of 525–522 BC, that empire also incorporated Egypt, removing the only remaining major power in the region and effectively guaranteeing that the small kingdoms of the Levant could exist only as subjects of Persia. Nonetheless, the support the Cyrus Cylinder gives to the biblical account of the return to Jerusalem[76] has encouraged many to see it as an ancient charter of human rights.[77] This it certainly is not; instead it is a document expressing benevolent kingship. The idea that people could have 'rights' independent of the will of the king and the gods is a very modern one, and was simply alien to the world in which the text was produced. Nor was Persian rule always accepted: Persian kings faced further Babylonian rebellions, one of which may have caused Xerxes to close Esagila, the great temple of Marduk, and perhaps even to destroy the cult-statue of the god himself.[78]

Alexander

Like Cyrus, Alexander entered the most heavily fortified city in the world through open doors, having defeated the incumbent king in battle elsewhere.[79] In the Macedonian case a series of victories over Persian forces culminated in the battle of Gaugamela (331 BC), at which the Persian army was decisively defeated and following which the Persian king Darius III fled. His attempts to organize further resistance to Alexander failed, and having outlived his usefulness he was ultimately murdered by his erstwhile allies. Our principal sources on these events are Greek. A Babylonian astronomical diary gives the dates of Alexander's defeat of Darius at Gaugamela and entry into Babylon with precision, but sadly does not include any additional information on the event.[80]

It has been argued that Alexander's rule should be seen as a continuation of Achaemenid government, with the real break coming only in the fragmentation of the empire following his death in 323 BC.[81] This conception certainly fits with the specific fate of Babylon. Alexander had intended it for his capital, and had begun work on restoring the city's temples, including Esagila and the ziggurat Etemenanki, in the grand tradition of his predecessors.[82] Famously his Macedonian generals are reported to have become increasingly dismayed at Alexander's willingness to adopt Persian court customs and manners, notably in accepting divine honours.[83] Particularly unacceptable was the idea that Macedonians, proud of what they saw as their more egalitarian traditions, might have to perform *proskynesis* (prostrating oneself, kneeling or bowing in obeisance) before Alexander.[84]

One of Alexander's greatest projects at Babylon[85] was an ephemeral one: the funeral pyre of his companion Hephaestion, who had died at Ecbatana (modern Hamadan in western Iran) in 324 BC. Diodorus describes the destruction of an enormous stretch of city wall to create a pyre measuring around 200 metres on each edge.[86] This was then lavishly decorated. Diodorus writes that:

> Upon the foundation course were golden prows of quinqueremes in close order, two hundred and forty in all. Upon the catheads each carried two kneeling archers four cubits in height, and (on the deck) armed male figures five cubits high, while the intervening spaces were occupied by red banners fashioned out of felt. Above these, on the second level, stood torches fifteen cubits high with golden wreaths about their handles. At their flaming ends perched eagles with outspread wings looking downward, while about their bases were serpents looking up at the eagles. On the third level were carved a multitude of wild animals being pursued by hunters. The fourth level carried a centauromachy rendered in gold, while

the fifth showed lions and bulls alternating, also in gold. The next higher level was covered with Macedonian and Persian arms, testifying to the prowess of the one people and to the defeats of the other. On top of all stood Sirens, hollowed out and able to conceal within them persons who sang a lament in mourning for the dead.[87]

We need not credit the particular details, but again according to Diodorus, whose source is the Alexander historian Cleitarchus, Alexander 'showed such zeal about the funeral that it not only surpassed all those previously celebrated on earth but also left no possibility for anything greater in later ages'.[88] This would certainly be fitting behaviour for Alexander, a self-styled Achilles who in Hephaistion had lost his Patroclus. The tragic sequel, in June 323 BC, was the death of Alexander himself, following two weeks of fever.[89] The circumstances of his death in Babylon, surrounded in the classical accounts by dark portents and warnings from Chaldean sages, remain disputed. Malaria, typhoid and poisoning have all been suggested, though the latter seems unlikely.[90]

Few of Alexander's own building projects at Babylon had time to reach fruition. The ziggurat was not restored (Strabo records that simply clearing the rubble of the ziggurat required the work of 2,000 men for two months, and that the work was not continued by any of Alexander's successors[91]). Meanwhile, what had seemed under Alexander the nascent process of orientalizing a Hellenistic empire was to reveal itself in the subsequent centuries as the opening of conduits for Hellenistic art and culture to spread into large parts of Western and Central Asia.[92] A process that had begun under the Achaemenid kings was accelerated, and with it the flow of art and ideas east and west. From this time onward, Hellenistic influence can be strongly felt in the material culture of Mesopotamia, and indeed much farther east.

Babylon fades from view

For all the power and longevity of the image of a cataclysmic fall of Babylon, the truth is that the city's end came very gradually, and through political and economic changes rather than military force. At the end of the fourth century BC Seleucus Nicator, having secured for himself the provinces of Western Asia in the battle for succession fought among Alexander's former generals, founded a new capital at Seleucia on the Tigris, greatly expanding a pre-existing settlement on the site.[93] The new city became a major centre for trade, and from this point onward Babylon's decline proved unstoppable, though it remained a bastion of cultic and scholarly activity. By the first century AD the temples of Babylon seem to have been among the last places in which the cuneiform script was in regular use and the old documents could be read.

We do not possess a clear picture of the rate of Babylon's decline in economic importance or its depopulation over the centuries. It is thought that the city never recovered from the Parthian sack of 127 BC, and after this date it is probably more accurate to imagine a city of ruins than anything resembling its former imperial pomp. Nonetheless, the journey from world capital to complete abandonment was extremely long, probably in the order of 1,500 years. Ibn Hauqal, writing in the tenth century AD, records a small village at Babel.[94] By the time of Rabbi Benjamin of Tudela's visit in the twelfth century even this seems at last to have vanished. Several villages continue to surround the site even today, but from the twelfth century onwards the major local settlement was the present town of al-Hillah. In a sense this fading from view is an end even more complete than a violent destruction. Babylon's last days proved as unspectacular and went just as unnoticed by posterity as its beginning.

Babylonian ghosts

The summary above is intended simply to give some historical context to what follows, to outline Babylon's place in the history of the ancient Middle East, and to present an approximate historical and archaeological view from which to proceed in looking at other visions of the ancient city. The principal subject of this book is not the ancient city itself but its reception and representation, its afterlife. Before moving on to later tradition, therefore, it is perhaps worth pausing to consider the substantial body of myth, legend and lore that developed around the city of Babylon within ancient Mesopotamian culture itself.

To begin at the Beginning, Babylon was not only the centre of the universe but also the site of the world's creation. If this is to overstate the Mesopotamian view of the second and first millennia BC it is to do so only slightly. *Enuma Elish*, the epic poem describing the world's creation in a form probably adjusted to fit the political reality of Babylon's resurgence under Nebuchadnezzar I in the late twelfth century BC, makes Marduk the hero god who is able to create order from chaos. Defeating the monstrous army of Tiamat, the primordial sea, Marduk is able to create the world and of course its centre, Babylon.[95] The rise of Marduk in the pantheon, supplanting earlier supreme gods such as Enlil, is thought to coincide in particular with Nebuchadnezzar I's recovery of the god's statue from Susa, whence it had been taken as war booty following the fall of the Kassite dynasty. This event itself took on the quality of legend, and Nebuchadnezzar himself acquired a heroic reputation in Babylonian culture.

Babylon was a city of sufficient import to play a role in the mythology of others. One highly mythologized area of Mesopotamian historiography concerns the rise and fall of the kings of Akkad at the end of the third millennium BC. Sargon of Akkad created a polity that covered all of Mesopotamia, claiming to have campaigned from the 'Upper Sea' (the Mediterranean) to the 'Lower Sea' (the Persian Gulf).[96] Small wonder then that as the real founder of what was arguably Mesopotamia's – even the world's – first empire, Sargon's name grew in stature until, long after his death, he acquired the status of a legendary hero-king, with attributes comparable to those of Gilgamesh, the legendary king of Uruk. As great as Sargon's fame, however, was the infamy that would attach to his grandson Naram-Sin. In life Naram-Sin seems to have been a highly successful king, a military leader in the mould of his illustrious predecessor (he is also, incidentally, the first ancient Mesopotamian king known to have had himself deified, appearing with the horned cap of a deity on a victory stela).[97] The decline of Akkadian power with which his name was to become associated seems in fact to have begun only after his reign. In legend, however, he became the king who both caused and presided over the city's catastrophic downfall. Texts describe in detail the city of Akkad's abandonment by the gods following Naram-Sin's impious rebuilding of the temple of Enlil at Nippur, which he is said to have carried out despite not receiving the necessary favourable omens.[98] A further legend of impiety, however, concerns Sargon and the very foundation of Akkad. The *Weidner Chronicle*[99] gives the impression that against the will of Marduk Sargon took soil from Babylon in order to found a new settlement, either Akkad itself or another city nearby, which in a further transgression he made so bold as to name Babylon.[100] From this point onward Marduk turned against the kings of Akkad, and when Naram-Sin committed further offences (the text says that he 'destroyed the people of Babylon'), Marduk's wrath came in the form of Gutian invaders from Iran, leading to chaos and collapse and finally giving sovereignty 'of the whole world' to King Shulgi of Ur.[101] The overall impression is that the building of Akkad is a hubristic attempt to found a new Babylon or to create a mirror image of the city, and thus the history of Akkad becomes a facet in a story of divine favour and destiny that is really Babylon's.

None of this accords very well with our history of the period: Babylon's rise to pre-eminence among the cities of southern Iraq did not occur until centuries after the fall of Akkad. For the time of Sargon we have only the very limited evidence mentioned at the beginning of this chapter that Babylon even existed. Nonetheless, the perception that Babylon was a city of extreme antiquity seems to have been widely held, the Epic of Creation being only one example of interest in the city's origins and ancient past. Ancient Mesopotamian kings with an eye to posterity recorded their achievements in a variety of ways, among the more important of which was the burial of foundation inscriptions in new constructions and restorations of temples, city walls and palaces. Burying foundation documents was a standard practice throughout Mesopotamian history, and the discovery of such documents by later kings during their own restoration works was considered auspicious. Later periods in Babylon see an acute awareness of royal predecessors and the city's antiquity, expressed most visibly in Nebuchadnezzar II's use of an archaic script in his building inscriptions. To render the script of Hammurabi's era accurately on the monuments of Nebuchadnezzar required epigraphic scholarship to bridge well over a millennium of change, and indeed evidence does exist of scribal study of earlier scripts. Tablets from Babylon and Borsippa show clearly that Neo-Babylonian scribes collected and studied ancient documents bearing earlier scripts, even to the point of reconstructing lost sound values with some accuracy.[102] As well as this technical aspect, the practice clearly shows a reverence for Hammurabi himself, a consciousness of Babylon's great history and the achievements of earlier rulers. The king himself took his name from another predecessor, the Nebuchadnezzar who had recovered the statue of Marduk for Babylon some 500 years earlier and whose glorious reign had also become a part of the city's legend.

When Cyrus of Persia in his turn conquered Babylon in 539 BC, his propaganda echoed that of Nebuchadnezzar II in format and language. Among the many remarkable qualities of the Cyrus Cylinder is the extent to which it is a conventional Babylonian document. In format, language, script, even its devotion to the Babylonian god Marduk,[103] the Cylinder emphasizes continuity with local tradition. It even refers to the auspicious discovery of an inscription of Ashurbanipal, to Cyrus an ancient king, during Persian building works. At the same time as linking himself with the long tradition of Babylonian kingship, of course, Cyrus also succeeded in demonizing his immediate predecessor, Nabonidus. This legendary Nabonidus, neglectful, irresponsible and possibly insane, has gone on to have a long and interesting life of his own in culture, as we shall see in later chapters. Cyrus' presentation of his own and Nabonidus' behaviour lived on through biblical tradition. Interestingly, Cyrus' account of his conquest also followed what seems from a later perspective to have been a consistent pattern of conquerors of Babylon emphasizing their peaceful entry into the city, their reverence for its gods, and their responsible kingship and civic works. Accounts of Alexander's behaviour, in particular, mirror those of the founder of the dynasty he conquered.[104]

All of these are mythologized representations of Babylon in their own right, legends that thrived even within the living city itself. They lie at the beginning of a long tradition. Babylon was destined to engender myths, fantasies and legends so powerful as eventually to occlude the ancient city itself. That transformation begins with the biblical and ancient Greek accounts of the city, and it is to these sources that we now turn.

CHAPTER 3

TYRANTS AND WONDERS:
THE BIBLICAL AND CLASSICAL
SOURCES

By the first century AD the cuneiform writing system was nearing
extinction. Babylon appears to have been one of the last centres in
which the script survived, preserved in venerable temple institutions
such as Esagila, but such isolated pockets of cuneiform scholarship
were doomed to wither away. The latest dated cuneiform texts known
today were written in the first century AD.[1]

The demise of cuneiform, and more particularly of the ability to
read cuneiform documents, is of enormous significance to the nature
of Babylon's survival. For 2,000 years Babylon would be known only
through foreign sources, and not until the mid-nineteenth century
would the chronicles, literature, mythology and scholarship of
ancient Mesopotamia become accessible once again. The content and
character of the non-cuneiform ancient sources on Babylon is
therefore of paramount importance to our story. The two principal
groups of sources available after the extinction of cuneiform are
biblical texts and the accounts of classical Greek authors. The two
groups possess characteristics of language, subject matter and focus
that distinguish them from one another in broad terms, but each
also contains considerable internal variety. Their content includes
mythology and folklore, ethnographic and geographical observations,

detailed historical accounts, moral commentaries and more besides. The biblical and classical sources are the building blocks from which the entirety of European tradition on ancient Babylon is ultimately derived.

At one remove from the ancient Mesopotamian sources themselves, in considering the biblical and classical sources we repeatedly encounter questions not only of factual accuracy but also of perspective. There is a need to address problems of accuracy and the limitations of the ancient sources' knowledge of the Babylonia they describe, but just as important are the perspectives which, if limited in terms of accurate description of the city, reveal much about Babylon's place in the wider world. When dealing with glimpses of an enigma such as the Hanging Gardens, it is natural to become impatient for more reliable information, yet amid the difficulty of distinguishing the real from the legendary in these accounts we have material as precious as any native source: contemporary chroniclers of Babylon as seen from without.

Biblical sources

With the exception of the Book of Revelation, all the biblical sources on Babylon are to be found in the Old Testament and Apocrypha. Including Revelation, they form a corpus composed at different times over the course of a millennium and in several languages – Hebrew, Aramaic and Greek – as well as a variety of political and cultural settings. It is therefore all the more remarkable that to a great extent the biblical narratives concerning Babylon are actually focused on a very short period in the city's history. Almost all references to Babylon in the Bible relate to the city of the sixth century BC under the rule of the Neo-Babylonian kings and their Persian successors. Many of these passages are individually the subject of voluminous scholarship, far beyond the scope of the present book. Here we simply give a summary account of the most influential themes in terms of Babylon's later reception.

Genesis

If this claim to historical focus seems at first rather far-fetched, it is perhaps because of the timeless, mythic character of the best-known of all biblical stories surrounding Babylon: the Tower of Babel.

Now the whole world had one language and a common speech. As men moved eastward, they found a plain in Shinar and settled there.

They said to each other, 'Come, let us make bricks and bake them thoroughly'. They used brick instead of stone, and tar for mortar. Then they said, 'Come, let us build ourselves a city, with a tower that reaches to the heavens, so that we may make a name for ourselves and not be scattered over the face of the whole earth.'

But the Lord came down to see the city and the tower that the men were building. The Lord said, 'If as one people speaking the same language they have begun to do this, then nothing they plan to do will be impossible for them. Come, let us go down and confuse their language so they will not understand each other.'

So the Lord scattered them from there over all the earth, and they stopped building the city. That is why it was called Babel – because there the Lord confused the language of the whole world. From there the Lord scattered them over the face of the whole earth.[2]

The story involves a play on words: Babel sounds like the Hebrew verb *balal*, to confuse.[3] The narrative is intended to explain the origin of multiple languages, but the tale of a city whose great size and pride have led to hubris, decay, fragmentation and confusion has struck a chord with writers and artists through the ages. The narrative is set in a mythical past and at first sight appears wholly unconnected with the historical realities of sixth-century BC Babylon. Where then does it originate?

A Mesopotamian origin of some kind for the Tower is relatively easy to demonstrate, since the Tower of the Genesis text contains several elements that reflect the qualities of a Mesopotamian ziggurat: the building materials of baked brick and bitumen are referred to specifically. Particular reference to the ziggurat Etemenanki at Babylon itself is a slightly different matter (of which more below), but the image of a Babylonian city dominated by a ziggurat comes through unambiguously.

Mesopotamian influence is clear not only in the building described. Following the Tower of Babel narrative is one of the biblical passages most clearly paralleled in Mesopotamian literature: genealogies following the Flood,[4] with lifespans considerably shorter than those that preceded it. These have parallels in the early part of the Sumerian King-List, in which a similar gradual reduction towards more plausibly mortal lifespans occurs. This correspondence is the more interesting because although the Tower of Babel story only makes sense as a foreign (Judaean) interpretation of the monuments,[5] one aspect is strangely reminiscent of an ancient Mesopotamian explanation for death. In the myth known as *Atra-hasis*, humanity has been created to serve the gods, but humans in large numbers are found to be noisy.[6] Angered, the great god Enlil sends cataclysmic floods, but soon enough population returns to an unacceptable level. Only by inventing death can numbers be regulated. The Tower seems to carry a similar implication that human affairs might be regulated based on the comfort of the gods rather than a system of moral punishment and reward, and for this and other reasons it has been suggested that the story might be a borrowing from Mesopotamia. No similar cuneiform text survives, however, the only possible reference being the case of a single omen stating that 'If a city rises to the interior of heaven like a mountain peak, that city will be turned to rubble.'[7] This correspondence is probably coincidental, however, and it should be noted that the Tower's physical destruction (as opposed simply to the cessation of construction due to the confusion of tongues) is not part of the Genesis account at all, appearing instead in the *Jewish Antiquities* of Josephus,[8] whose first-century AD elaboration and moral interpretation of the story has had an enormous impact on later representations. (He also makes Nimrod the Tower's architect, following the implication of Genesis 10,[9] and is responsible for introducing a prophecy from the Sibyl paralleling the Genesis account.[10]) Perhaps more significant are the Babylonian tradition of Babylon as the first city (as in the creation epic *Enuma Elish*) and the inscriptions of Neo-Babylonian kings that describe raising the top of Etemenanki to 'to vie with the heavens'.[11] It is another passage, however, that gives the clearest of all indicators of the influence of Babylonian literature on the Book of Genesis: the account of the Flood, whose Babylonian equivalent was discovered by George Smith to public astonishment in 1872.[12] Part of the Babylonian Epic of Gilgamesh, the narrative is so close to that of Genesis as to admit of no doubt that the two are directly related.

Nimrod is not mentioned in Genesis 11, but in Genesis 10 (originally a separate text) is described as the son of Cush, son of Ham, and as 'a mighty hunter before the Lord'.[13] Attempts have been made to link him to figures in Mesopotamian literature.[14] Whatever the name's origin, he is clearly presented as the founder of Mesopotamian civilization: Genesis 10 describes him founding cities first in Babylonia (including Babylon and Akkad), then in Assyria (including Nineveh).[15]

Exile

There are widely divergent views on the date of the Yahwist Source, and thus that of the Tower of Babel and much other material in Genesis. Traditionally, the material has been regarded as the oldest in the Bible, dating to the tenth–ninth century BC; more recently, it has been argued that some or even all of the Yahwist Source should be dated much later, to the sixth century BC.[16] This is a hugely complicated and multi-faceted question on which there is no scholarly consensus, but it is relevant here that from the narrower perspective of Near Eastern political history and Mesopotamian influence there is some reason for considering the sixth century BC as a natural candidate for the crucial period during which many legends drawn from or influenced by the Babylonian world entered Judaean religion and ultimately the Old Testament. In the sixth century BC,

Babylon and Judah underwent a period of extremely close interaction – events, indeed, around which a substantial part of the Bible is structured – known variously as the Jewish Exile, Judaean Exile and Babylonian Captivity. We have already seen something of the Babylonian view of these events in Chapter 2. To recap, Nebuchadnezzar II, after successfully securing the borders of his empire against the Babylonians' main western rival, Egypt, still had to deal with rebellions and dissent in the provinces. One rebellious vassal state was Judah, whose revolts in 597 and 587 BC required Nebuchadnezzar to besiege and recapture Jerusalem twice, on the second occasion sacking and looting the city and its temple. Large numbers of people, including the king and court, were deported from Jerusalem to Babylonia, where a majority of them stayed and became integrated into Babylonian society.

Though in agreement with the Babylonian sources on the basic facts of the case, the biblical perspective on these events is profoundly different. Above all else, the experience of exile is presented as a traumatic separation of a people from its beloved homeland. The best-known expression of this deep spiritual loss is Psalm 137, 'By the Rivers of Babylon we Sat Down and Wept':

By the rivers of Babylon we sat down and wept
As we remembered Zion.
On the willow trees there
We hung up our lyres,
For there those who had carried us captive
Asked us to sing them a song,
Our captors called on us to be joyful:
'Sing us one of the songs of Zion.'
How could we sing the Lord's song
In a foreign land?

If I forget you, Jerusalem,
May my right hand wither away;
Let my tongue cling to the roof of my mouth
If I do not remember you,

If I do not set Jerusalem
Above my chief joy.

Remember, Lord, against the Edomites
The day when Jerusalem fell,
How they shouted, 'Down with it, down with it,
Down to its very foundations!'
Babylon, Babylon the destroyer,
Happy is he who repays you
For what you did to us!
Happy is he who seizes your babes
And dashes them against a rock.[17]

No hint of this feeling is to be found in the matter-of-fact Babylonian sources, and indeed one might even question the universality of such strength of bitter feeling among the Judaeans themselves. The Assyriologist and historian of Mesopotamian archaeology' Mögens Trolle Larsen offers a provocative counterpoint to the biblical perspective:

> When the Jewish elite was sent from the provincial outpost of Jerusalem to Babylon, it was somewhat the same as sending the intellectuals of Poznań into exile in Paris – it is a wonder that any of them wanted to go back after sixty years, and of course relatively few did; but those who chose to return were full of the rage of injured pride, a feeling they poured into their dreams and prophecies.[18]

History has room for both these narratives, one current pushing toward the maintenance of a distinct identity, strengthened in exile, the other toward assimilation into Babylonian life.[19] If the story of the exile is structured by opposition to Babylon, much of the content of the Old Testament is nonetheless steeped in Babylonian culture.

The three major biblical versions of the Exilic story are to be found in 2 Kings,[20] 2 Chronicles[21] and (as prophecy) Jeremiah.[22] This, on a par with the Exodus (whose Old Testament form seems itself to have been heavily influenced by the Babylonian Captivity),[23] is a case of forced migration on which later Jewish and Christian traditions have focused as a touchstone for all righteous struggle against oppression. In both 2 Kings and 2 Chronicles the siege of Jerusalem and Captivity are the subject of final chapters, although the two accounts end at different points. 2 Kings finishes with the release of Jehoiachin:

> In the thirty-seventh year of the exile of King Jehoiachin of Judah, on the twenty-seventh day of the twelfth month, King Evil-merodach Amel-Marduk of Babylon in the year of his accession showed favour to king Jehoiachin. He released him from prison, treated him kindly, and gave him a seat at table above the kings with him in Babylon. Jehoiachin, discarding his prison clothes, lived as a pensioner of the king for the rest of his life. For his maintenance as long as he lived a regular daily allowance was given him by the king.[24]

2 Chronicles, though only treating the period of the Captivity very briefly, extends to the rule of Cyrus and the Judaeans' release. Specifically its final two passages, repeated at the beginning of Ezra (1 and 2 Chronicles, Ezra and Nehemiah, originally formed a single book),[25] offer one of the Bible's most famous links with archaeology, in that the text relates closely to that of the Cyrus Cylinder, one of the most important primary sources on the transition between the Babylonian and Achaemenid empires.[26] The passage runs:

> In the first year of King Cyrus of Persia: The Lord, to fulfil his word spoken through Jeremiah, inspired the king to issue throughout his kingdom the following proclamation, which he also put in writing:

> The decree of King Cyrus of Persia: The Lord the God of heaven has given me all the kingdoms of the earth, and he himself has charged me to build him a house at Jerusalem in Judah. Whoever among you belongs to his people, may the Lord his God be with him, and let him go up.[27]

The proclamation is completed in Ezra:

> Whoever among you belongs to his people, may his God be with him, and let him go up to Jerusalem in Judah, and build the house of the Lord the God of Israel, the God who is in Jerusalem. Let every Jew left among us, wherever he is settled throughout the country, be helped by his neighbours with silver and gold, goods and livestock, in addition to the voluntary offerings for the house of God in Jerusalem.[28]

A variant of the same text also appears in the Apocrypha, in 1 Esdras.[29] The 'house' is the Second Temple, another major Old Testament theme. The Cyrus Cylinder, one of many written versions of a proclamation made by Cyrus, includes specific provisions for the return of gods and people to their home cities, and it is widely agreed that the biblical passage refers to the same proclamation. That the examples given are Mesopotamian and Elamite and do not include Jerusalem simply reflects the Babylonian context of the cylinder in particular. Nonetheless, it is clear enough that the passage in Ezra does not give the exact words of Cyrus, who was not himself a convert to Judaism. His place in the story as liberator, however, has accorded him a sympathetic portrait in the biblical accounts and, by extension, later histories. Babylon and its earlier kings, by contrast, are subject to some of the most fiery condemnations of Jeremiah and Isaiah. In one passage in Isaiah, an explicit link is made between the king of Babylon and Lucifer (Lucifer is the Latin Vulgate translation of *Helel ben Shahar*, rendered in English as Son of Dawn, Son of the Morning, Day Star or Shining One).[30] The reference is contained in a song mocking the fallen king of Babylon:

> How you have fallen from heaven,
>   morning star, son of the dawn!
> You have been cast down to the earth,
>   you who once laid low the nations!
> You said in your heart,

'I will ascend the heavens;
I will raise my throne
above the stars of God;
I will sit enthroned on the mount of assembly,
on the utmost heights of the sacred mount.
I will ascend above the tops of the clouds;
I will make myself like the Most High.'
But you are brought down to the realm of the dead,
to the depths of the pit.
Those who see you stare at you,
they ponder your fate:
'Is this the man who shook the earth
and made kingdoms tremble,
the man who made the world a wilderness,
who overthrew its cities
and would not let his captives go home?'[31]

Daniel

In Isaiah, the 'morning star' is never named,[32] and the identity of the last king of Babylon is a significant problem in other biblical accounts. Not all of the names of the Neo-Babylonian kings survive into the Old Testament, and from the biblical sources alone the chronology is not always clear. The problem of royal names and chronology is even more apparent in Daniel, yet in many ways it is here that we find the definitive biblical version of Babylon; a detailed image of the Babylonian court that has inspired and informed most other representations of the city since. The world represented is Neo-Babylonian and Achaemenid, although the Aramaic text itself dates to several centuries after the time of Nebuchadnezzar. As with much apocalyptic literature, the accurate prediction of later events in the text, written as prophecy, gives us a relatively unproblematic guide to the earliest date of composition.[33] This approach, placing it in the reign of the Seleucid king Antiochus IV Epiphanes (175–164 BC), remains the best available guide to the dates of Chapters 7–12, although Chapters 1–6 are

more problematic.[34] In terms of composition, there is a break
between Chapters 6 and 7. The cycle of Babylonian rule –
Nebuchadnezzar II followed by Belshazzar followed by 'Darius the
Mede' (whose identification has proven difficult)[35] – in Chapters
1–6 is repeated in Chapters 7–9. The break coincides with two
other changes: the onset of visions in the narrative and a markedly
more negative attitude toward the Babylonian kings.

The narrative follows the career of the prophet Daniel, a Judaean
interpreter of dreams in the courts of successive kings of Babylon.
Such a career for a Judaean in Babylon is plausible,[36] but the figure of
Daniel in the Bible is likely to be a composite. Collins argues that the
tradition of a great prophet of this name is older than the Babylonian
Captivity:

> [T]he figure of Daniel may be more akin to Enoch than to Ezra
> or Baruch. The Bible contains no reference to a prophet by this
> name outside the actual book of Daniel. In the book of Ezekiel
> (an actual prophet of the exile) we do, however, have two
> references to Daniel. Ezek. 14:14 says that when a land sins
> against God 'even if these three men, Noah, Daniel and Job
> were in it, they would deliver only their own lives.' Ezekiel
> 28:3 taunts the king of Tyre: 'Are you wiser than Daniel?' It
> would appear from these references that Daniel was the name of
> a legendary wise and righteous man.[37]

Although it could be argued that Ezekiel refers to a revered
prophet of his own day, likening Daniel to those of legend, this seems
less probable than the explanation given above by Collins. If the
origins of a Daniel tradition lie further in the past, however, the
setting for the biblical text is clearly and specifically the Neo-
Babylonian and Persian court of the sixth century ·BC. The main
substance of the early part of the Book of Daniel is a series of dreams
and omens that Daniel interprets. The main king whom Daniel
serves is Nebuchadnezzar, but the narrative also features Belshazzar
and Darius the Mede. The absence of the other Neo-Babylonian
kings, and particularly Nabonidus as the last of the dynasty, reflects

the later date of the source. Belshazzar, the son of Nabonidus, was never king of Babylon, but acted as regent at Babylon during his father's absence in Arabia,[38] and both the length of that absence and the fact that Belshazzar is remembered as king in the Book of Daniel suggest that his role as regent was more than token. In Daniel the regency becomes a reign as full king and Nabonidus is forgotten, although in reality the latter had returned from Arabia well before the Persian conquest. Perhaps the fact that Nabonidus was forgotten in this way reflects the final success of Cyrus, who had taken care to ensure that his predecessor's name and memory were systematically erased.[39]

One Daniel story of particular importance in later tradition is that of the Fiery Furnace. Three Hebrews, Shadrach, Meschach and Abednego, refuse to worship a huge golden idol set up by Nebuchadnezzar, who has them thrown into the fire. Once in the furnace the three are unharmed. Worse, Nebuchadnezzar can see *four* men walking in the fire and, he observes, 'the fourth looks like a god'.[40] Nebuchadnezzar is struck both by the faith of the Jews and the power of their god and, if not going so far as to convert, issues a remarkable decree: 'Anyone, whatever his people, nation, or language, if he speaks blasphemy against the God of Shadrach, Meshach and Abed-nego, is to be hacked limb from limb and his house is to be reduced to rubble; for there is no other god who can save in such a manner'.[41] The story is a good example of the ambiguity of Nebuchadnezzar's role in Daniel. Not only an oppressor, he acts in many ways as a sponsor to Daniel and other Jews, and is prepared to take Daniel's advice and accept his interpretations of dreams.

Perhaps the most famous episode from Daniel is that of Nebuchadnezzar's seven years in the wilderness.[42] The story is thought to have arisen from cuneiform texts that actually concerned Nabonidus. The Cyrus Cylinder and *Verse Account of Nabonidus* in particular furnished details of Nabonidus' supposedly heretical behaviour prior to the fall of Babylon.[43] The king's perceived neglect of the capital and its cults, combined with his apparent attempt to elevate the role of the moon-god Sin (and with it his mother Adda-

Guppi's temple to the same god at Harran) at the expense of Babylon's Marduk priesthood provided great scope for Persian anti-Nabonidus propaganda. The Dead Sea Scroll text known as the *Prayer of Nabonidus*[44] added another layer to what was already becoming more of a legend than a biography: in this version Nabonidus 'lived apart from men' for seven years while suffering from what may have been a disfiguring disease.[45] In Daniel, the disease is transformed again, becoming seven years of madness and God's punishment not for Nabonidus' heresy but for Nebuchadnezzar's pride,[46] while the downfall of the city itself is associated with Belshazzar. Where the Babylon of Nabonidus now passed to the Persian Cyrus, that of Daniel's Belshazzar is ruled by an aged Darius the Mede.[47]

This attribution of stories originally associated with Nabonidus to Nebuchadnezzar is not an isolated conflation of historical identities. The name of Nebuchadnezzar in Hebrew, Aramaic and later Arabic writings came to be associated with other figures, including two much more recent invaders of Jerusalem, the Roman emperors Vespasian and Titus. Al-Biruni (973–1048 AD), observing the attribution of Nebuchadnezzar's identity to the Roman emperors, commented that 'It seems that the people of Jerusalem call everybody who destroyed their town Nebuchadnezzar'.[48] Although the Book of Daniel shows confusion in the identity of his successors, there is a reasonable argument for an intentional conflation of Nabonidus and Nebuchadnezzar in this case. If the authors drew directly on Babylonian sources, the conflation must have been conscious. If conflation occurred in a chain of intermediate written or oral sources it might still have been conscious and deliberate, because unless the story at some stage replaced the name Nabonidus with 'king of Babylon', someone in the chain must have read or heard Nabonidus but written or said Nebuchadnezzar. Clearly the substitution of one historical name for another is very different from the gradual corruption of a single name, e.g. our own Nebuchadnezzar (or the other Hebrew variant, Nebuchadrezzar) from the Babylonian Nabu-kudurri-usur. Most probably, stories involving any king of Babylon tended eventually to attach to the famous name of Nebuchadnezzar.

The problem of Nabonidus' absence from the biblical accounts is exacerbated by equal confusion over the identity and place of his son, the crown prince Belshazzar. In his study of Nabonidus and Belshazzar, Dougherty summarizes 13 ancient non-cuneiform accounts of the succession, with considerable variation in the sequence of rulers given.[49] By far the most famous role played by Belshazzar, however, is that given in the Book of Daniel, in which, as king of Babylon, he presides over a great feast, serving his nobles from gold and silver taken by Nebuchadnezzar from the Temple in Jerusalem. In this moment of supreme blasphemy God's punishment arrives, prefigured by the writing on the wall, a mysterious warning that only Daniel can read. He explains the portent to Belshazzar as follows:

'You praised the gods of silver and gold, of bronze, iron, wood and stone, which cannot see or hear or understand. But you did not honour the God who holds in his hand your life and all your ways. Therefore he sent the hand that wrote the inscription.
'This is the inscription that was written:
Mene, Mene, Tekel, Parsin
'This is what these words mean:
Mene: God has numbered the days of your reign and brought it to an end.
Tekel: You have been weighed on the scales and found wanting.
Peres: Your kingdom is divided and given to the Medes and Persians.'[50]

Belshazzar honours Daniel for relaying this warning, making him the third highest officer in the empire, but to no avail. Mere hours later Babylon falls to the invading Persians.

The latter part of Daniel consists of apocalyptic visions. It is certainly significant from the standpoint of later portrayals that the only apocalyptic text in the Old Testament is set in Babylon, but a description of the destruction of the city is not itself part of the Daniel apocalypse. The visions are too abstract to belong to any geographical place, although they are used to couch specific history and geography in the vaguer terms of prophecy. Daniel's vision of the 'time of the end'[51] begins with a war between the kingdoms of the north and the south. These are Hellenistic kingdoms. Daniel 11 alludes to the rise of Alexander and to the subsequent division of his empire among the generals:

> 'Now then, I tell you the truth: Three more kings will appear in Persia, and then a fourth, who will be far richer than all the others. When he has gained power by his wealth, he will stir up everyone against the kingdom of Greece. Then a mighty king will appear, who will rule with great power and do as he pleases. After he has appeared, his empire will be broken up and parcelled out toward the four winds of heaven. It will not go to his descendants, nor will it have the power he exercised, because his empire will be uprooted and given to others.'[52]

The Babylonian Captivity is a defining experience in the Old Testament: beyond the accounts of Nebuchadnezzar's siege of Jerusalem, the deportation to Babylon and the return to Jerusalem granted by Cyrus themselves, much of the Old Testament was written and/or set in Babylonia. Beyond even this there is a further association apparent in the Mesopotamian literary traditions on which Old Testament narratives frequently draw, famous examples being Nahum and the Song of Songs. To later readers, of course, this interweaving of literary traditions was less visible than the presentation of the history of the Captivity itself. In this history the fate of sinful Babylon, if not strictly apocalyptic, took on a far more dramatic character than that suggested by the Cyrus Cylinder. The most vivid description is found in Jeremiah:

> Therefore marmots and jackals will skulk in it, desert-owls will haunt it; never more will it be inhabited and age after age no one will dwell in it. It will be as when God overthrew Sodom and Gomorrah along with their neighbours, says the Lord; no one will live in it, no human being will make a home there.[53]

Revelation

The only New Testament apocalypse, and indeed the only New Testament source on Babylon,[54] Revelation is much later than any of the other biblical accounts mentioned here, dating to the late first century AD.[55] It is also very different in its composition and purpose from any of the Old Testament sources. Although it makes constant reference to the Old Testament, using references familiar to Christians to mask politically dangerous statements, the subject matter is contemporary, with Babylon a metaphor for the Roman world and for Rome itself. This symbolic role, of course, has not prevented Revelation from acting simulataneously as a source for ideas and imagery on the historical Babylon. The Whore of Babylon first appears here, embodying the corruption of Rome, Babylon and the pagan world:

> One of the seven angels who held the seven bowls came and spoke to me; 'Come,' he said, 'I will show you the verdict of the great whore, she who is enthroned over many waters. The kings of the earth have committed fornication with her, and people of the world have made themselves drunk on the wine of her fornication.' He carried me in spirit into the wilderness, and I saw a woman mounted on a scarlet beast which was covered with blasphemous names and had seven heads and ten horns. The woman was clothed in purple and scarlet, and decked out with gold and precious stones and pearls. In her hand she held a gold cup full of obscenities and the foulness of her fornication. Written on her forehead was a name with a secret meaning: 'Babylon the great, the mother of whores and of every obscenity on earth.' I saw the woman was drunk with the blood of God's people, and with the blood of those who had borne their testimony to Jesus.[56]

Both the woman and the beast have been understood to represent Babylon,[57] and the vivid apocalyptic imagery of Revelation has undoubtedly informed many later representations of the city. Alongside this imagery, the language and even the moral message of

Revelation were to become part of the standard tool-kit for describing and representing Babylon in later ages. Of course, this is not a message first conceived here, nor is all the symbolism original. The passage above, for example, recalls Jeremiah:

> Babylon has been a golden cup in the Lord's hand,
> To make all the earth drunk;
> The nations have drunk of her wine,
> And that has made them mad.[58]

Nonetheless, the anthropomorphic representation of Babylon in Revelation is a significant step even from the sinful King of Babylon of Isaiah. Once created, she is a figure whose identity infuses all the others. The historical fall of Babylon, the Persian conquest of 539 BC, now becomes permanently entwined with the violent, hallucinatory, apocalyptic visions of Revelation. Thus begins Babylon's transformation from a real, physical location in Mesopotamia to a spiritual one in the providential narrative of Christian history. Babylon here was not only Rome, but all of human worldliness and wickedness, the site of crisis at which the great battle of the Apocalypse would take place and from whose destruction the New Jerusalem would finally emerge.

Classical sources

The two most sustained and detailed surviving ancient Greek descriptions of Babylon come from Herodotus[59] and Ctesias of Cnidus, the latter via the later historian Diodorus Siculus.[60] These accounts, along with the almost entirely lost description of Berossus, have proven highly influential, informing sources on Babylon from antiquity to the present. Of the three, the earliest and today the best known is that of Herodotus, and it is with this account that any consideration of the influence of classical sources on Babylon must begin.

Herodotus

The first feature that differentiates Herodotus' description of Babylon from the biblical accounts is that a description is exactly what it is. It consists of an examination of the layout, architecture, population and customs of the city, and in this respect has no biblical counterpart. With the single grand exception of the Tower of Babel, almost no description is given of any of the city's physical features in the Old Testament; by contrast, Herodotus offers a topographical survey complete with detailed accounts of the more remarkable buildings. It was here that Greek audiences could first encounter the walls of Babylon, later to be numbered among the seven wonders of the world. In Herodotus' description, the city:

> Is surrounded by a broad deep moat full of water, and within the moat there is a wall fifty royal cubits wide and two hundred high (the royal cubit is three inches longer than the ordinary cubit). And now I must describe how the soil dug out to make the moat was used, and the method of building the wall. While the digging was going on, the earth that was shovelled out was formed into bricks, which were baked in ovens as soon as a sufficient number were made; then using hot bitumen for mortar the workmen began by revetting with brick each side of the moat, and then went on to erect the actual wall. In both cases they laid rush-mats between every thirty courses of brick. On the top of the wall they constructed, along each edge, a row of one-roomed buildings facing inwards with enough space between for a four-horse chariot to pass. There are a hundred gates in the circuit of the wall, all of bronze with bronze uprights and lintels.[61]

This short passage alone has been the focus of much speculation on Herodotus and the veracity of his account. There are plenty of details to work with, from the impossible height of the wall and the 100 gates,[62] to the accurate description of baked bricks, use of bitumen and layers of matting. Other details lie somewhere between: the thickest of Babylon's inner city walls were indeed enormous, validating Herodotus' claims, but whether chariots actually did run along them (or even in a protected roadway between the two main banks)[63] is another matter.

Many inaccuracies and inconsistencies in the ancient descriptions of Babylon are not readily explained as mistakes, nor do they necessarily stem from ignorance. In the case of Herodotus, particular historical circumstance and the establishment of a new genre should be considered. Herodotus balanced a claim to authority based on personal observation and research with a concern for entertainment and giving pleasure to the listener or reader.[64] The elements of narrative and entertainment were recognized in antiquity, and not always valued. Aristotle's description of Herodotus as a *mythologos*, a teller of myths,[65] was not intended as a complement. In an early but highly influential use of Assyriology to interrogate ancient Greek sources, the Assyriologist A. H. Sayce set out to question Herodotus' claims about Babylon one by one.[66] Working methodically through his account, Sayce's 1883 study effectively – at the time it must have seemed fatally – demolished the authority of Herodotus' description and undermined the belief that he had ever actually visited Babylon. Although he was despairing of Herodotus the historian, however, Sayce did have a clear view of what, if not accurate historical description, the value of Herodotus could be for the modern student:

> The net result of Oriental research in its bearing upon Herodotos is to show that the greater part of what he professes to tell us of the history of Egypt, Babylonia, and Persia, is really a collection of 'märchen,' or popular stories, current among the Greek loungers and half-caste dragomen on the skirts of the Persian empire. For the student of folklore they are invaluable, as they constitute almost the only record we have of the folklore of the Mediterranean in the fifth century before our era [...]. After all, it is these old stories that lend as great a charm to the pages of Herodotos as they do to those of Mediæval travellers like Mandeville or Marco Polo; and it may be questioned whether they are not of higher value for the history of the human mind than the most accurate descriptions of kings and generals, of war treaties and revolutions.[67]

Surviving fragments of ancient folklore and legend are indeed a
precious resource. If the entirety of Herodotus' account were proven
false there would still be great value in its reading. It would surely
still be included here, since stories and ideas can be significant from
the point of view of representation long after they have been
discredited as historical sources, or indeed without ever having
seriously pretended to that status in the first place. There may be no
clearer example of this than Babylon, but it is not a unique case.
Perhaps the closest parallel is Venice, whose great cultural impact on
the modern European imagination has little to do with historical
particulars, save perhaps the life of Casanova. Tanner's 1992 study of
the city's cultural identity is entitled *Venice Desired*:

> As the greatest and richest and most splendid republic in the
> history of the world, now declined and fallen, Venice became an
> important, I would say central, site (a topos, a topic) for the
> European imagination. And more than any other city it is
> inextricably associated with desire. Desire of Venice, desire for
> Venice, desire in Venice – this is a crucial force and feature in
> European literature from Byron to Sartre.[68]

This seductive Venice of the imagination has something in common
with many European images of Babylon. Such imagined cities have
something to tell us about our own culture, our modes of thought
and our organization and structuring of the world around us. For all
this, however, the historical accuracy of ancient sources does matter,
even when we focus on historiography and representation. We need to
be able to distinguish between observation, hearsay and imagination
in Herodotus if we are to understand just what it was about Babylon
that he wanted to communicate, and to differentiate the city he
describes from what we would be prepared to call the historical
reality, however limited and imperfect our own knowledge of the
latter. Assessing the veracity of Herodotus' statements is not the
primary work of this book, but disentangling the historiography that
leads to more recent representations is, and it is worth noting that
contemporary scholarship is currently undoing much of Sayce's

original argument. Herodotus' description of Babylon has regained some of its lost credibility.[69]

Herodotus made no mention of the Hanging Gardens of Babylon, a surprising omission with several possible explanations. Either Herodotus did not actually visit Babylon, or there were no such gardens there to describe, or he had no knowledge of or access to royal gardens – we would, after all, expect their use to be highly restricted. Following Sayce, but supported by separate references to the gardens in Berossus (via Josephus), Ctesias (via Diodorus Siculus) and Strabo, the consensus has been that Herodotus either did not visit Babylon himself, or more specifically did not visit the royal palace.[70] Stephanie Dalley has argued that Herodotus did not mention the gardens because there were none, and that the gardens described by other authors were in fact those of Sennacherib at Nineveh.[71] This is not the first analysis to locate the gardens elsewhere. E. A. Wallis Budge suggested the 'palace of Cyrus' at Ecbatana as another potential site based on the account given by Hyginus[72] and on Pliny's attribution of the gardens to Cyrus.[73] Further, he argued, 'It is possible that statements about the garden of Cyrus were transferred to the Hanging Garden, and, as a matter of fact, the accounts of it are so contradictory that they cannot all be referring to the same thing'.[74]

The debate on the gardens' location continues. Julian Reade has suggested that the western outwork, a massive structure between Babylon's Southern Palace and the Euphrates traditionally interpreted as a treasury or fort because of its unusually thick walls, might equally be the foundations for garden terraces, and that this location would tally with the descriptions of classical authors.[75] Reade also stresses that Nineveh is not positively identified as the site in any textual source, and that 'In fact the classical writers who describe the Hanging Gardens or are quoted by other writers as doing so, whatever the intricacies of textual transmission, are unanimous that what they are attempting to describe are gardens at Babylon'.[76]

The idea that Babylon and Nineveh could have been conflated in the relevant Greek sources has been taken up by Marc Van De Mieroop, who argues that a Mesopotamian literary construct existed that treated the fortunes and histories of the two cities as closely related and inversely proportional, and that the deliberate representation of parallels between them could have contributed to their conflation in foreign sources.[77] There is no doubt that such conflation exists to some degree: accounts in which the Tigris runs through Babylon and the Euphrates through Nineveh are not unusual, nor a tendency to refer to the whole of Mesopotamia as Assyria and to treat the Neo-Assyrian and Neo-Babylonian periods as a single, continuous empire (in which they may have had a point).[78] Later sources also suggest the possibility that Nineveh was sometimes referred to as 'Babylon' or 'Old Babylon'.[79] The argument does have some problems, however. While the engineering works of Sennacherib to water his own spectacular gardens at Nineveh do support these as a candidate, and indeed much more evidence survives for royal gardens at Nineveh than Babylon,[80] Herodotus may not have seen gardens for another reason. As Dalley notes, had there ever been Hanging Gardens at Babylon, they would have disappeared by the time of Herodotus, since the course of the Euphrates through the city changed early in the Persian period and made such a garden impossible. (Nor could he have seen first-hand the gardens of Nineveh, whose palaces and imperial architecture had long since been destroyed.)

The nature and extent of confusion between Babylon and Nineveh in the Greek sources in this case is still the subject of much debate. As well as drawing attention to this issue, however, Dalley's analysis of the sources in terms of the Assyrian royal gardens at Nineveh has also brought to light many problems with Sayce's original argument against Herodotus having visited Babylon.[81] These include: the existence of a probable route for the royal road from Sardis to Susa consistent with Herodotus' description; the conclusion that Xerxes did not completely destroy the temple and statue of Marduk in Babylon,[82] making it plausible that Herodotus or a contemporary informant could have seen both this and the New Year *akitu* festival;[83] late inscriptions contradicting Sayce's assertion that Nineveh was completely deserted in the time of Herodotus, and therefore his informants for that city could not have been local; and that Herodotus' claim that the Babylonian name for Aphrodite was Mylitta has some validity.[84]

Herodotus' description covered far more than physical monuments. A large part of his account could be termed ethnographic,
describing customs and beliefs the writer himself records as a
detached observer. The customs he describes are frequently
outlandish and certainly not literally true, but there are some links
suggesting origins either in fact or in Mesopotamian myth and
folklore. What is far less clear is Herodotus' purpose in recording
them. There is some ambiguity in his assessment of the traditions he
describes, making it difficult at times to be sure whether his approval
of them is genuine or satirical. Some critics argue for the latter,[85]
while others suggest that a negative approach is the essence of
Herodotus' 'ethnographic' writing: 'Herodotus notes points which
distinguish this people from others, and especially points which a
Greek finds odd, and therefore repellently interesting. Oddity is an
ethnocentric principle [. . .]. Woman bites louse is news. Herodotus
thus seems not so much the precursor of Malinowski and Boas, as of
Strange as it Seems and *Believe it or Not*.'[86]

Herodotus describes as the 'most ingenious' of the Babylonian
customs the marriage market, a system whereby bride-prices paid for
the prettiest wives are used as dowries for the plainest, thus ensuring
everyone can get married and at the same time redistributing wealth
(because a rich man will pay a high bride price while a poor man will
seek a high dowry). He comments that 'This admirable practice has
now fallen into disuse and they have of late years hit upon another
scheme, namely the prostitution of all girls of the lower classes to
provide some relief from the poverty which followed upon the
conquest with its attendant hardship and general ruin'.[87] Arieti sees
Herodotus' approval here as sarcastic:

> The arrangement seems to make for a contented community.
> Yet several elements of humour in the description – the over-
> poetical term 'grew ripe for marriage' [. . .] the unquestioned
> ranking by the auctioneer of the girls' relative beauty (can there
> be no debate about who is more beautiful?), and again
> Herodotus's breaking into direct quotation of the auctioneer's
> speech – 'Who will take the least money for this one?' –

suggest perhaps that Herodotus has his tongue in his cheek. Of course, he may be using a rhetorical device: if this is the *best* custom, how horrible must the other customs be![88]

In a detailed analysis of the origins of the story, Richard McNeal thinks Herodotus sincere in his approval, but does perform the important task of teasing out plausible Greek origins for the idea. All the Babylonian evidence (primarily in the form of marriage contracts and law codes) weighs against any suggestion that the story might be rooted in observation or folk memory in Babylonia itself. McNeal argues that the involvement of the state in arranging marriage, the financial exchange and the basis of the system in contest are all more suggestive of a Greek context than a Mesopotamian one,[89] reflecting specifically 'the competitive world of the small city state, suspicious of outsiders, protective of its womenfolk, intent upon the accomplishment of a public social policy at the expense of individuals, a functioning oral society in which, at the same time, coined money is the means of facilitating commercial transactions'.[90] The marriage market may also be a manifestation of a particularly Greek kind of philosophical experimentation with ideas of social justice, again following the assumption that the state can play an active role for the good of the community.

Another certainly inauthentic Babylonian custom described by Herodotus is that of bringing the sick out into the street, where they receive advice from passers-by. Herodotus asserts that there are no doctors in Babylonia, which would presumably have struck a Greek audience as quite backward. He is of course mistaken. Herodotus could not have known the extent of the debt, but in reality the Hippocratic corpus itself drew heavily on Babylonian medicine.[91]

The final Babylonian custom described by Herodotus is ritual prostitution in the temple of Aphrodite, something he claims every woman is obliged to perform once in her life.[92] Whether he approves of the other traditions he describes or not, Herodotus leaves no room for ambiguity here, describing it as the 'one custom amongst these people which is wholly shameful'.[93] The potential for later conflation with the biblical Whore of Babylon and image of the city of sin is obvious, but the two traditions developed independently and for different reasons. In the biblical case the root cause is Nebuchadnezzar's behaviour toward Jerusalem; for Herodotus and other Greek authors, the spur is only partly political grudge; another very large factor is a fascination with the exotic, and the use of the distant east both as a site for fantasies and as a negative 'other' against which the merits of Greek culture could be defined. This was hardly an ideal starting point for cultural understanding, of course, but such interest was not always parochial or mean-spirited. We must not forget that at the very start of his description Herodotus offers his own straightforward judgement on Babylon: that 'it surpasses in splendour any city in the known world'.[94]

Ctesias

The other lengthy Greek description of Babylon is that of Ctesias of Cnidus, a doctor in the Persian court. Although his *Persica* in 23 books has not survived, his work does appear in the epitomes of Diodorus Siculus and Photius.[95] The former includes his description of Babylon. Diodorus cites Ctesias throughout this description, and is known elsewhere to have borrowed whole passages from Megasthenes and Agatharchides.[96] His goal in writing the *Bibliotheke Historica* was a complete synthesis of available historical knowledge, not a personal or necessarily always original account. Although impossible to confirm, it seems that parts of Ctesias' description of Babylon have been copied verbatim or near-verbatim in Diodorus. Current scholarship on Diodorus is in agreement that his account of Babylon uses Ctesias as its main source, with some elements probably drawn from the late fourth-century BC historian Cleitarchus, although in his introduction to Book 2 of the *Bibliotheke Historica* Murphy is keen to emphasize that Diodorus does not deserve the charge of 'being an uncritical compiler and plagiariser of earlier works to which he himself added nothing of his own, no insights, no grand unifying themes'.[97] References to the description of Ctesias largely match with the Diodorus account, although one important possible addition is the Hanging Gardens: Budge argued that Diodorus did not quote this part of his description from Ctesias,[98] although it is unclear on what basis. References to Ctesias as the authority being used are dotted about the Diodorus text, apparently acting as occasional reminders that Ctesias is the source rather than specific citations.

Despite Ctesias' apparent tendency to doubt Herodotus (as one commentator observes, 'A marked feature of Ctesias' account is a tendency to disagree with Herodotus [...] whether or not he had better information (for example, in the case of Darius's fellow conspirators against Pseudo-Smerdis, Herodotus has five names right out of six, while Ctesias has only one)',[99] much of the content of the description as known from Diodorus is fantastic, and came to be recognized as such even in antiquity.[100] He claimed to have used Achaemenid royal archives to produce his *Persica*, though oral tradition and stories heard at the Persian court seem more probable sources for much of the account. Introducing their edition of his work, Llewellyn-Jones and Robson observe that 'Ctesias was writing something different from Herodotus; the *Persica* is a very original work based on a combination of personal observation and the plentiful information he learned from the rich oral tradition embedded within the Iranian court, and a healthy dose of Greek inquisitiveness about their eastern neighbours wrapped up, undoubtedly, in some semi-mythology too'.[101]

Diodorus/Ctesias' history begins with the life of Ninus, the first king of Asia and founder of the city of Ninus (Nineveh), who 'set about the task of subduing the nations of Asia, and within a period of seventeen years he became master of them all except the Indians and Bactrians'.[102] The account then lists Ninus' conquests, from Egypt to Iran and Central Asia.[103] Although much of the Ctesias account has the feel of a story of origin set in a distant and mythical past, this list suggests not a truly ancient kingdom but one of the great empires of the first millennium BC, and is more representative of the maximum extent of the vast Achaemenid Empire than of the work of an early conqueror, but even a greatly reduced form (such as that created by the Neo-Assyrian expansion) would describe an empire on a scale that had not been established before the ninth century BC. To take Ctesias' description of the founding of Nineveh, occupied since the seventh millennium BC, or of the first empire in Asia, which an archaeologist might associate with the kings of Akkad in the third millennium BC, as references to great antiquity is an error encouraged by the mythological components in the narrative. Ctesias could not have realized the city's true age, and could plausibly be referring to later imperial building works in any of the Assyrian capitals. He is probably attempting to describe the origins of the Assyrian Empire;[104] that its provinces resemble those of the contemporary Persian Empire reflects the understanding that the empires succeeding one another in Asia inherited one another's territory.

The city of Ninus (Nineveh), founded by the king Ninus, is described by Ctesias as being located on the Euphrates, and as the largest city not only of its own time, but of all time.[105] Both these attributes would better fit Babylon, since Nineveh was actually located on the Tigris and Babylon exceeded it in size. Still, the city described is not Babylon, at least in the author's mind, since the founding of the latter by Semiramis is subsequently related and later events set in Ninus show clearly that Nineveh is intended. It has been argued that the identification of Babylon in the account is also suspect, since some of the palace decoration described by Diodorus[106] sounds very much like hunting scenes from Assyrian palace reliefs.[107] However, although the scene described is reminiscent of an Assyrian relief, the rest of the description could only apply to Babylon, featuring glazed-brick reliefs unmistakeably of the kind used by Nebuchadnezzar, and with whose effect and technical mastery Ctesias was clearly impressed ('all kinds of wild animals had been depicted on the bricks before they were fired and which faithfully mimicked reality in the ingenuity of their colouring').[108] The description thus involves at least some direct reference to Babylon, and it is not impossible that even the description of subject matter is roughly accurate and that we are missing images of the king hunting that did once exist in the city. Koldewey himself felt that he had identified a match for the hunting scene description in the Persian Building during his excavations at Babylon.[109] Another possibility is that, just as Nineveh appears here on the Euphrates, the art of the two cities has been conflated; both, after all, were drawn on in the monumental imperial architecture of the Persia in which Ctesias lived.[110]

Ninus is important as a founder, but Ctesias (or at least Diodorus) devotes much more space to Semiramis. Her birth, life and marriage to Ninus, her succession to the throne upon the death of Ninus, the founding of Babylon, her achievements as sole sovereign, the decadence of her descendants and the fall of Nineveh, under Sardanapalus, to Arabaces the Mede are all covered at length. It is only in Ctesias' account that we find the mythical life of Semiramis, daughter of Derceto, founder of Babylon and warrior queen. She is accorded no such achievements in Herodotus, who only describes her as 'responsible for certain remarkable embankments in the plain outside the city [Babylon], built to control the river which until then used to flood the whole countryside'[111] – a description that fits well with Strabo's observation of a folk tradition identifying Semiramis as a great builder existing in many locations throughout Western Asia[112] – and instead concentrates on the building works of Nitocris, a figure possibly based on a queen of Sennacherib known by the Assyrian name Zakutu and the Aramaic name Naqia, who as the mother of Esarhaddon rose to enormous power during the latter's reign. This remarkable queen seems to have been directly involved with the religious and military affairs of the day, built palaces, and is even depicted on a relief behind the king. She has herself been suggested as a source for some aspects of Semiramis in later legends.[113]

After a birth and early childhood reminiscent of the Moses story, Ctesias' account has Semiramis waging war disguised as a male soldier and proving herself a great military strategist. After succeeding her husband Ninus, she goes on to campaign in lands as distant as Ethiopia and India; in the latter, like Alexander, she is faced with the challenge of fighting against an army with terrifying war elephants. Ctesias also describes her as bloodthirsty, selecting soldiers from her army to sleep with before having them executed the following morning, to avoid the risk of having to share or cede her power to a husband. Finally, she is transformed into a dove. That the Semiramis biography is originally the work of Ctesias is confirmed by Athenagoras:

For if detestable and god-hated men had the reputation of being gods, and the daughter of Derceto, Semiramis, a lascivious and blood-stained woman, was esteemed a Syrian goddess; and if, on account of Derceto, the Syrians worship doves and Semiramis (for, a thing impossible, a woman was changed into a dove: the story is in Ctesias), what wonder if some should be called gods by their people on the ground of their rule and sovereignty [. . .] and others for their strength, as Heracles and Perseus; and others for their art, as Asclepius?[114]

Semiramis' transformation into a dove was a myth that had survived well enough to require only a casual allusion to be understood in Ovid's *Metamorphoses*.[115] (Curiously, this seemingly ideal tale of transformation is not recounted; Ovid's main 'Babylonian' story is the tragic romance of Pyramus and Thisbe.)

If Semiramis' deeds do relate to historical events in Mesopotamia, that relationship is tangled and convoluted in the extreme. The name Semiramis has long been thought to derive from that of the Assyrian queen Sammuramat,[116] leaving us to reconcile a Neo-Assyrian queen with the builder of Babylon. Time and place are wildly out of line with the historical character of Sammuramat, but can be accounted for in part by phenomena already discussed, namely the conflation of Nineveh and Babylon and a lack of awareness of the distance in time between the foundation of either Nineveh or Babylon and the rise of the Neo-Assyrian Empire. Further, Sammuramat's career was exceptional: she was a queen of Shamshi-Adad V (823–811 BC) but seems to have acted as vice-regent or co-regent during the reign of her son Adad-nirari III (810–783 BC)[117] and even to have gone to war herself. Nonetheless, the etymological link between Sammuramat and Semiramis has been questioned and an alternative suggestion based on a Syrian deity has been suggested.[118] Ctesias himself refers to an existing Syrian tradition of deifying Semiramis by worshipping the dove.[119] The Semiramises of both Herodotus and Ctesias would thus become goddesses rendered as historical characters, rather than historical characters with divine or mythological embellishments.

Following the detailed biography of Semiramis, Diodorus presents
the reader with the key classical account of the decadence, sloth and
luxury of the kings of Assyria, exemplified in the characters of
Semiramis' son Ninyas and the last of her line, Sardanapalus
himself.[120] Other rulers are not recorded (save one Teutamos, said to
have sent reinforcements to the Trojans under the command of
Memnon). Diodorus/Ctesias comments, 'There is no urgency to
record all the names of the kings and the number of years each
reigned since there was nothing done by them worthy of mention'.[121]

The description of Ninyas is intended as a typical example of
Assyrian kingship:

> After Semiramis' death, her and Ninus' son, Ninyas, succeeded
> to the throne and ruled peacefully, not emulating in any way his
> mother's fondness for war and her adventurous spirit. For in the
> first place he spent all his time in the palace, seen by no one
> except his concubines and attendant eunuchs, and sought
> luxury and idleness and the total avoidance of suffering and
> anxiety, thinking that the goal of a happy reign was to enjoy
> every kind of pleasure without restraint.[122]

By Greek lights Semiramis appears heroic in comparison with her son;
even 'love of war' is intended as a virtue. The faults of Ninyas are also to
some extent those seen by Greek writers in Persian kings: decadence,
luxury, softness and a retreat from contact with the world outside
the palace, and especially from war. Clearly the palace culture of the
ancient Middle East as a whole contributed to this impression among
Greek writers, but it also served in its condemnation of oriental
corruption to highlight the 'Greek' values of austerity and the public
forum. Passages such as the description of Ninyas are criticisms not only
of the character of individuals but also of a form of government, in the
same vein as Aeschylus' *Persians*.[123] The environment, they suggest,
engenders and reinforces the faults of individuals unfit to rule.

The description of Sardanapalus shows the result of many generations
of such decadent hedonism. The following passage provided the
inspiration for the Sardanapalus familiar in modernity from Byron's

famous 1821 play of the same name,[124] and is a strong candidate for the original template for what was to become the modern literary and artistic trope of the oriental despot:

> Sardanapallus, who was the thirtieth in succession after Ninus who founded the Empire and the last Assyrian King, surpassed all the others who came before him in luxury and idleness. For apart from the fact that he was never seen by anyone outside the palace, he lived the life of a woman, and spent his time with his concubines, spinning purple cloth and working the softest fleeces, and he took to wearing female clothing and made up his face and his whole body with white lead, and other things courtesans customarily use, more delicately than any luxury-loving woman. He purposely adopted a woman's voice and during his drinking sessions not only did he continually enjoy such drinks and food as were capable of providing the most pleasure, but he also pursued the delights of sex with men as well as women; for he freely enjoyed intercourse with both, not worrying at all about the shame engendered by the deed.[125]

For quite different reasons, the fall of the Assyrians was given a moral dimension comparable to that of the Old Testament accounts of the punishment of Nineveh and Babylon. Sardanapalus' defeat was not presented as inevitable, however, although the tendency to decadence is at one point his undoing. Following the successful defence of Ninus (Nineveh) against several attacks Sardanapalus, unaware of the defection to Arabaces of a Bactrian army on its way to support him, lets his guard down too soon. He gives a feast, distributing good food and wine to his soldiers, upon which 'the whole army fell to carousing'.[126] Arabaces' army takes them by surprise in the night. Retreating into the city, Sardanapalus is powerless as the garrisons surrounding Nineveh, drawn from across the empire, defect one by one to the side of the rebels. Even now, however, the city walls and stores are sufficient to survive a siege for two years. 'But in the third year great storms of rain fell without cease, with the result that the Euphrates became swollen, inundated part of the city, and overturned the wall for twenty stades'.[127] At this point Sardanapalus, seeing all is lost, builds the famous pyre containing his wealth, his royal robes, his concubines and eunuchs, and consigns himself 'to the flames along with all of them and the palace itself'.[128]

Although this is the primary account from which all later descriptions of Sardanapalus are derived, it seems that Ctesias was not the first to write about this character in Greek. A surviving fragment of Hellanicus of Lesbos gives a tantalizing hint of oral tradition on Sardanapalus, mentioning the existence of stories portraying him sometimes as a hero, sometimes as decadent and weak, and rationalizing the two by invoking two Assyrian kings of the same name.[129] Was the same variety of stories available to Ctesias?

Who was Sardanapalus? The name itself seems to be a corruption of Ashurbanipal (Ashur-bani-apli). Nineteenth- and early twentieth-century Assyriology took this to be the case and saw the Greek and Assyrian names and characters as synonymous. More recently it has been suggested that the name is a conflation of more than one Assyrian king's name, combining elements of Ashurbanipal and Esarhaddon.[130] However, in the case of the fourth-century BC Aramaic papyrus preserving the story of the civil war between Ashurbanipal and Shamash-shuma-ukin (see Chapter 2) Ashurbanipal does indeed become Sardanapal.[131] The story of the conflict between the brothers as related in the papyrus is in many ways a reversal of the story of Sardanapalus as told by Ctesias. Here, as in life, it is Shamash-shuma-ukin who finds himself under siege. Like Sardanapalus, he barricades himself in his palace (at Babylon, not Nineveh) and subsequently perishes – though not in flames, but in an accident while attempting to march on Nineveh. Given that the very existence of the Aramaic account suggests wide dissemination of the story, and that the parallels between the two are so pronounced, it seems plausible that the Sardanapalus of Ctesias is indeed an echo of the war between Ashurbanipal and Shamash-shuma-ukin, preserving the name of one king but the fate of the other.[132] The story moves away from Babylon, and the last kings of Assyria after the great Ashurbanipal are forgotten, allowing the grisly end of Shamash-shuma-ukin at Babylon to be recycled as the fall of Nineveh.

What of language and translation? Ctesias could not have possessed the skills of a classically trained Babylonian scribe, i.e. mastery of Assyrian and Babylonian, the main Akkadian dialects, of Sumerian, and by implication of several enormous cuneiform sign-sets. He could not have read for himself the *Verse Account of Nabonidus* (a priestly account written in Babylonian emphasizing the king's neglect of his city and people), though indirect access to Babylonian literary traditions is more plausible. Van De Mieroop highlights Babylonian elements in Ctesias' account of the destruction of Nineveh, judging that 'it seems probable that Ktesias used a Babylonian source relating the destruction of Nineveh' and that, unbeknownst to Ctesias, this source in turn paralleled Assyrian accounts of Sennacherib's sack of Babylon in 689 BC and was styled to emphasize retribution for that destruction.[133] These links are convincing, but do not preclude transmission via intermediate oral sources. It seems that spoken Aramaic has been grossly under-estimated as a source for Ctesias, since the classic early analyses of his account pre-dated the discovery that Aramaic was the lingua franca of the Achaemenid Empire. This point brings a range of new possibilities into play, the implications of which are discussed by Dalley.[134] Dalley focuses on wisdom literature in Aramaic and the recitation traditions of the Persian court, arguing that the flexibility of historical setting in Aramaic tales of kings is a strong candidate for much of the geographical and historical confusion in Ctesias' account. Examples of similar, more securely documented processes of this kind of corruption are pertinent here, most importantly the story of Ahiqar the Sage.[135] The papyrus describing the war between Ashurbanipal and Shamash-shuma-ukin is another case in point. In terms of transmission, and particularly of explaining the survival of names and fragments of history from the cuneiform world occurring in otherwise very distant sources, Aramaic written and oral sources probably form the missing connection in many more cases than we are able to prove. Such sources would surely give us a far better understanding of the information on Mesopotamian history that was available to the Hellenistic world. These, however, are not the only sources whose loss we must lament. What a different picture might appear if one text above all had survived. For the non-Babylonian wishing to know something of the land and its people, the guide most perfectly placed was surely Berossus.

Berossus

Ctesias and Herodotus provide a wealth of information on Babylon, some of it accurate and all of it interesting. Both of these extended accounts were written by Greek visitors to Mesopotamia, however, while an equivalent account by a member of the society they purported to describe has not survived. A Babylonian priest, Berossus wrote a history of Babylonia in Greek, known either as *Babyloniaca* or *Chaldaica*, at a time when cuneiform texts were still known and understood, though Aramaic had long been the lingua franca in most of Western Asia. He was native to the society of which he wrote, and through cuneiform had direct access to far more information than any Greek writer could hope to. Josephus' description of the *Babyloniaca* suggests that Berossus' history went back even as far as the legendary world of *Atra-hasis*. Introducing his account of the Neo-Babylonian kings, he explains:

> My witness here is Berossus, a Chaldaean by birth, but familiar in learned circles through his publication for Greek readers of works on Chaldaean astronomy and philosophy. This author, following the most ancient records, has, like Moses, described the flood and the destruction of mankind thereby, and told of the ark in which Noah, the founder of our race, was saved when it landed on the heights of the mountains of Armenia. Then he enumerates Noah's descendents, appending dates, and so comes down to Nabopolassar, king of Babylon and Chaldaea.[136]

Sadly, almost nothing of the work has survived.[137] It has been suggested that Berossus' history was ultimately forgotten because it did not fit well with the existing dominant account of Mesopotamian history, that of Ctesias, omitting key figures such as Ninus and Semiramis.[138] The account is now known only through the citations and quotations of later writers, principally Flavius Josephus and Eusebius of Caesarea. Even these fragments, however, contain a great deal of useful information, and it is clear that Berossus had access to an accurate record of the Neo-Babylonian succession, including the lengths of each king's reign, that could only have come from Babylonian chronicles.

Where Berossus' account is remembered at all in classical literature, it is commonly altered and mythologized. In what is probably an already quite garbled version of an original with some Babylonian root, Berossus is quoted as reporting a festival called *Sakaia*, five days during which slaves rule their masters.[139] The idea resurfaces in Plutarch, whose Semiramis persuades Ninus to allow her to rule for five days before using her new power to imprison him.[140] Diodorus does not mention an origin in Berossus, attributing the story to 'Athenaeus and certain other historians'.[141] The story is further embroidered in the fifth century AD by Paulus Orosius, whose *History Against the Pagans* was one of the most widely read and influential historical texts in medieval Europe.[142] As well as elaborating the account of Semiramis' depravity,[143] Orosius makes the distinctively Christian addition of a mystical numerological link with Rome.[144] This corruption of the source raises questions about the original content of Berossus, particularly with regard to chronology. It is safe to agree that 'of all the lists of neo-Babylonian monarchs that have survived, the arrangement of Berossus most closely corresponds to that of the cuneiform documents,'[145] but we know his arrangement only through those of Josephus and Eusebius,[146] whose apparent quotations of the same passage in Berossus differ. Eusebius also preserves the list of Alexander Polyhistor, who also claimed to use Berossus as his source and again produced a different account.[147]

Claiming to quote Berossus directly, Josephus gives an account so strikingly accurate in those details that can be checked against the cuneiform sources as to make all the more tantalizing those that cannot. To the names and reigns of the Neo-Babylonian king, all quite accurately preserved, Berossus adds details of murder and conspiracy not mentioned in the terse Mesopotamian royal chronicles:

Nabuchodonosor [Nebuchadnezzar] fell sick and died, after a
reign of forty-three years, and the realm passed to his son
Evilmerodach [Amel-Marduk]. This prince, whose government
was arbitrary and licentious, fell a victim to a plot, being
assassinated by his sister's husband Neriglissar, after a reign of
two years. On his death Neriglissar, his murderer, succeeded
to the throne and reigned four years. His son, Labarosoardoch
[Labashi-Marduk], a mere boy, occupied it for nine months,
when, owing to the depraved disposition which he showed, a
conspiracy was formed against him, and he was beaten to death by
his friends. After his murder the conspirators held a meeting, and
by common consent conferred the kingdom upon Nabonnedus
[Nabonidus], a Babylonian and one of their gang.[148]

Table 1 shows the accuracy of Berossus' account.

To the known Babylonian historical texts Berossus adds human
detail in the form of the plots against Amel-Marduk and Labashi-
Marduk. That this information is absent from the cuneiform sources,
however, should prompt a note of caution. Were the details of the
murders handed down through oral tradition, through written
sources, now lost (but necessarily of a very different kind to the
official records from which the details of regnal years were obtained),
or are they simply creative additions to suit the Greek style of
historiography and a Greek audience (in which case the further
question arises whether they necessarily originate with Berossus at
all, or with a later redactor)? With the same caveat in mind, we
should still take seriously Berossus' account of Babylon's conquest
and the fate of Nabonidus, which again fleshes out the information
given by the cuneiform sources:

In the seventeenth year of [Nabonidus'] reign Cyrus advanced
from Persia with a large army and, after subjugating the rest of
the kingdom, marched upon Babylonia. Apprised of his
coming, Nabonnedus led his army to meet him, fought and was
defeated, whereupon he fled with a few followers and shut
himself up in the town of Borsippa. Cyrus took Babylon, and

Table 1. The accuracy of Berossus' account of the reigns of the Neo-Babylonian kings.

Ruler (as best known in English)	Babylonian name	Called in Josephus	Actual reign[149]	Reign in Josephus
Nabopolassar	Nabû-apla-uṣur	Ναβοπαλάσσαρον	626–605 BC	21 years
Nebuchadnezzar	Nabû-kudurri-uṣur	Ναβουχοδονόσορον	605–562 BC	43 years
Amel-Marduk	Amel-Marduk	Ευειλμαράδουχος	562–560 BC	2 years
Neriglissar	Nergal-šar-uṣur	Νηριγλισάρου	560–556 BC	4 years
Labashi-Marduk	Labaši-Marduk	Λαβοροσοάρδοχος	556 BC	9 months
Nabonidus	Nabû-na'id	Ναβοννήδω	556–539 BC	17 years

after giving orders to raze the outer walls of the city, because it presented a very redoubtable and formidable appearance, proceeded to Borsippa to besiege Nabonnedus. The latter surrendering, without waiting for investment, was humanely treated by Cyrus, who dismissed him from Babylonia, but gave him Carmania for his residence. There Nabonnedus spent the remainder of his life, and there he died.[150]

Berossus, Amyitis and the Hanging Gardens

Berossus is one of the key sources for the Hanging Gardens. He apparently attributes their construction to Nebuchadnezzar, and confusion in his account of Babylon and Nineveh is less likely than in those of Ctesias or Strabo.[151] Some doubt is raised by the fact that we know Berossus through Jewish and Christian writers, since in later tradition Nebuchadnezzar became almost a generic 'king of Babylon', but the correspondence to what is known of Nebuchadnezzar's life seems too good for such a coincidence. Berossus sets out to counter the Greek perception that Semiramis was, in general, responsible for Babylon's architectural wonders,[152] and it is in this context that he gives one of the clearest indications of his Babylonian source material: an account of Nebuchadnezzar's construction work at Babylon that not only finds confirmation in the cuneiform sources but can be convincingly matched with a particular text. Robartus van der Spek has highlighted strong parallels between the East India House inscription of Nebuchad-nezzar and Berossus' description of the city, showing that Berossus describes the same works, and in the same order, as the monumental stone inscription now held in the British Museum.[153] The correspondence between the two texts is remarkable, with one significant exception: the description of the Hanging Gardens. No cuneiform source mentions the gardens, yet Berossus' description of them appears in what is otherwise a list directly modelled on a known Babylonian inscription. This is more than a minor idiosyncrasy: given Berossus' accuracy on other points, his mention of the gardens should have special importance. How might their inclusion be explained? The passage on the gardens itself is very brief:

> within this palace [Nebuchadnezzar] erected lofty stone terraces, in which he closely reproduced mountain scenery, completing the resemblance by planting them with all manner of trees and constructing the so-called Hanging Garden; because his wife, having been brought up in Media, had a passion for mountain surroundings.[154]

By placing this description within a detailed account of Nebuchadnezzar's building works, Berossus ties the gardens' construction not only to a specific king, but even to a particular place: Nebuchadnezzar's Southern Palace. This and details in other classical sources have prompted attempts to locate the gardens at or near the palace, including Robert Koldewey's candidate, the so-called 'vaulted building', and the recent suggestion of the great western outwork between palace and river, previously interpreted as a fortified keep or treasury, as a possible location.[155] Nonetheless, it is worth considering the possibility that the addition of the gardens to the account was made by another writer, again rendering Berossus more acceptable to a Greek audience.

A key to the story's origin may be Nebuchadnezzar's mountain-loving bride. Berossus is the first author to identify the king who built the gardens of Babylon as Nebuchadnezzar, and to give a name, Amyitis, to his queen. Little notice has been taken, however, of the fact that he makes these identifications in two quite different parts of his narrative. His mention of Amyitis comes in reference to her marriage for political reasons. Nebuchadnezzar, at this time the Babylonian crown prince, is married to Amyitis, daughter of Astyages (and granddaughter of Cyaxares) to cement a Babylonian–Median alliance.[156] Berossus is thus the first to rationalize the Iranian origin of the queen in the story, but he does so in a separate and thoroughly unromantic description of the politics of the rising Neo-Babylonian dynasty. For this reason it seems highly unlikely that the marriage has been invented by Berossus (or a later editor) to dovetail with his description of the gardens, in which he neither names Amyitis nor refers to the other passage.[157] Dovetail it does, however, and perfectly. For Berossus the queen's point of origin is Media and thus its capital Ecbatana, high in the Zagros mountains. All versions of the story rely on the king's wife coming from a mountainous country – Persia in Diodorus, unnamed in Curtius[158] – to a very flat one. The greatest such contrast in the entire region was that between mountainous Media (the site of Ecbatana, modern Hamadan, is 1,850 m above sea level, surrounded by peaks of over 3,000 m) and Babylonia, one of the flattest landscapes on earth.

Several conclusions can be drawn. First, that the good fit between a romantic Hanging Gardens story that seems to depend on its queen coming from Media and Berossus' far more matter-of-fact description of Nebuchadnezzar's marriage is, at least, a remarkable coincidence, since the two appear in the text for different reasons and seem quite independent of one another. To introduce the two details, bearing in mind that neither appears in an earlier Greek source and that their use implies knowledge of both the landscape of Media and the political situation – hardly known to the Greeks – of the Babylonian-Median alliance against Assyria, would be quite a feat on the part of any later redactor. Second, that the identification is made by an author who elsewhere criticizes the tendency to confuse Nineveh with Babylon (as in the case of Semiramis) and who gives a highly credible political reason for the marriage. Certainly he does not confuse Nebuchadnezzar with an earlier Assyrian king. Third, that if a romantic story about Nebuchadnezzar and his Iranian bride underlies the tale, it follows that even the pre-Berossus version demonstrates some link to knowledge of Nebuchadnezzar.

Although Berossus is aware of the story, his treatment of it implies that it does not originate in the Babylonian official sources, as indeed we would not expect it to. Instead, the combination of a narrative that has the qualities of myth and storytelling with a demonstration of specific knowledge of political events in Babylon and a folkloric interest in the contrast between Iranian and Babylonian landscapes makes a Persian court origin for the story much more plausible than fourth-century Greek invention, and incidentally confirms that

Ctesias, who had prolonged access to just such court stories, is more likely than Cleitarchus to have provided the basis for the Hanging Gardens account given by Diodorus. Having reached this conclusion, it seems more than coincidence that the (sadly very limited) evidence for Old Persian literature suggests an extremely good fit. Those tales thought to have an Old Persian origin in the Greek sources and the *Shahnameh* are noted for the innovation of stories centred on romantic love; they also involve journeys to distant lands.[159] The physical descriptions of the gardens are a separate matter. The (spuriously) precise descriptions of their construction and engineering found in the classical sources are probably best explained as Greek embellishment, even allowing for the possibility that they preserve some echo of Sennacherib's gardens at Nineveh. They are conspicuous by their absence from Berossus' brief account.[160]

Taken together, the impression is of a Median or Persian oral tradition that originated at a time when Nebuchadnezzar's marriage to a Median princess[161] was still well known, survived in Persian court tradition – with the appropriate substitution of a Persian princess – and thus reached Ctesias, at which point the particular identities of king and queen might have been lost even if they had not been before, since Ctesias had no apparent knowledge of the Babylonian history that would have allowed him to place these individuals in context. Berossus knew both versions of the story.

Novels and romances

Apparently quite distinct from the histories described above, two fragmentary early novels feature Babylon. These are the *Ninus* romance and the *Babyloniaca* of Iamblichos.

The *Ninus* romance is an early first-century AD Greek novel, known today from four papyrus fragments. Its authorship is uncertain, two possibilities being Chariton, author of the novel known as *Callirhoe* and citizen of Aphrodisias, once known by the name of Ninoe (Ninus), and one Xenophon of Antioch, referred to in the *Souda* (a lexical/encyclopaedic volume dating to the tenth century AD) as the author of a *Babyloniaca*.[162] The novel's style and format do not draw on any Mesopotamian source,[163] nor does the novel appear to involve any attempt to represent the difference of another culture per se. Although the plot is uncharacteristic of its genre and might therefore owe something to an origin as Hellenized and mythologized Mesopotamian history,[164] McCall is right to describe the use of the names Ninus and Semiramis as 'merely historical ciphers in a romantic plot which involved a shipwreck, warfare and love scenes'.[165] The protagonists and their behaviour are not easily recognized as their namesakes in Greek histories, let alone as historical figures in ancient Iraq. *Ninus* does, however, provide us with an interesting case in the use of historical allegory. The two points of interest here are the apparent selection of some but not all available historical information on the topic and the role of barbarian 'historical ciphers' such as Ninus and Semiramis in this literary form.

Turning first to the question of available historical information, the probable source for *Ninus* is Ctesias' *Persica*. Although Herodotus' description of Babylon is older, and mentions the names Ninus and Semiramis,[166] it does not connect the two characters, does not mention Derceto, Semiramis' mother according to Ctesias/Diodorus and apparently in *Ninus*, and does not contain the description of Assyrian military campaigns, known through Diodorus to have been present in Ctesias and the likely inspiration of Ninus' campaign in Armenia in the *Ninus* romance. To accept that the writer had knowledge of Ctesias' narrative, however, is also to accept that they were prepared to disregard and contradict that history as readily as to borrow from it. Most interesting is the character of Ninus' beloved, unnamed in the surviving fragments.[167] As the bride-to-be of Ninus and daughter of Derceto,[168] it is highly unlikely that the female protagonist of *Ninus* was *not* named Semiramis. If this is correct, however, we must next explain the metamorphosis apparently undergone by Semiramis between her incarnation in the *Persica* and that in *Ninus*. In the former she is a fearsome warrior, ruling alone, sleeping with and then executing her soldiers, and leading an ambitious military expedition to India. In other accounts Semiramis does not simply survive Ninus, but tricks him out of his sovereignty.[169] If later legend is any guide, the author would not have needed Ctesias to tell him that Semiramis was a bold and warlike figure: this much was probably canonical and widely known. The character in the *Ninus* romance, by contrast, proves too shy to reveal her feelings for Ninus to his mother, while Ninus' parallel speech to Derkeia is a stylistic highlight of the work.[170] While the novel as we know it is fragmentary, and there is certainly the possibility of Semiramis performing more boldly in lost parts of the novel, this incident alone departs completely from the portrait available to the *Ninus* author from historical sources. We can conclude that the writer consciously decided to make this departure, considering the representation of an ideal character more important than historical veracity in this context.

The *Babyloniaca* of Iamblichos, surviving only through an epitome in the *Bibliotheke* of Photius, bears even less resemblance to any historical account. The plot is described in detail by Photius,[171] and as Stephens and Winkler write:

> If there was any suspicion that the patriarch was capable of pulling our leg, this would be the place to exercise it. According to him, the hero and heroine roam throughout the Near East pursued by two eunuchs whose noses and ears have been cut off. They encounter bees with poisoned honey, a lesbian princess of Egypt, a cannibalistic brigand, look-alike brothers named Tigris and Euphrates who happen to be exact doubles for the hero, and a rather dignified farmer's daughter whom the heroine forces to sleep with an executioner who is really a priest of Aphrodite who helps his son Euphrates break jail by dressing in the farmer's daughter's clothes.[172]

Iamblichos' identity itself seems to have been partially mythologized. The *Souda* claims he was born a slave,[173] while Photius writes that he had a Babylonian slave for a tutor, and it was from him that Iamblichos originally heard the story of the *Babyloniaca*.[174] Whatever the truth of the matter, the effort in both cases is to give some extra interest to the story through its exotic origin.

The most famous classical romance set in Babylon, though today its original setting is largely forgotten, is the tragedy of Pyramus and Thisbe. The story appears in Ovid's *Metamorphoses*:[175]

Pyramus, who was handsomest of men
and Thisbe, of a loveliness unrivalled
in all the East, lived next to one another
in Babylon, the city that Semiramis
surrounded with a wall made out of brick.[176]

Kept apart by their parents, the lovers are able to communicate
through a small crack in the wall separating their two homes.
Desperate but unable to kiss, they arrange to meet by a tall mulberry
tree near the tomb of Ninus.[177] Thisbe arrives first, but is scared away
by a passing lion; fortunately for her the lion has just eaten. Pyramus
arrives to sée his beloved's cloak – dropped during her escape – now
chewed by the lion and stained with the blood of its earlier kill, and
naturally despairs. Believing Thisbe dead, he impales himself upon
his own sword. Returning to discover his body and wracked with
grief, Thisbe uses Pyramus' still-warm blade to take her own life. Her
last words are a prayer that the two lovers be permitted to lie together
in death, and that the mulberry will remember their deaths in the
crimson colour of its berries, which until this day had been white.

Today, the story is best remembered as the play performed by
Shakespeare's rude mechanicals in *A Midsummer Night's Dream*. Its
drama and tragedy, however, are of a higher order, and are far better
preserved in another of Shakespeare's works: Ovid's Babylonian
Pyramus and Thisbe find more than an echo in *Romeo and Juliet*.

A dual inheritance

There are sharp contrasts between the biblical and ancient Greek
historical traditions with regard to Babylon, not only in specifics but
also in the nature of their interest and attitudes towards Mesopotamia.
The almost ethnographic passages on Babylonian culture found in
the Greek historians' works have no substantial biblical parallel,
while the Old Testament is richer in moral allegory, asserting a
providential meaning for the history of Babylon that has defined the
city's place in culture ever since. This is a difference not primarily of
the availability of information, but of purpose and of situation. The

biblical texts incorporate a familiar land and culture into a history centred on divine judgement; the Greek accounts aim to describe a land and culture unfamiliar to their audience.

Detail outweighs moral judgement in the Greek sources, leading to a rich quasi-ethnographic resource for later historians to draw on and adapt. The reverse is true of the biblical descriptions: moral judgement is the point, description incidental. Further, morality for Jews and Christians is in any case primarily the province of scripture, to be sought in the Bible rather than in pagan histories or ancient Greek legends. In the longer term a clear distinction would emerge in the way the two categories of source were put to use, whereby classical sources can be seen to have greater influence on academic reconstructions of Babylon and cultural detail in visual representations, and biblical accounts on the moral representation of Babylon and the selection of subject matter in art and literature. At the same time, the two traditions would not be treated in isolation from one another, and indeed at times strenuous efforts would be made to reconcile and integrate the two.

With all their complications and contradictions, by Late Antiquity the biblical and classical accounts comprised all the information available on Babylon, and indeed all that would be available for many centuries to come. Babylon itself had vanished, as had its vast cuneiform literature and the expertise required to read it. How would medieval scholars deal with the accounts that survived? And how would those adventurous Europeans who actually visited Mesopotamia interpret the mysterious ruins of its ancient past? The great city they would find would henceforth be Baghdad. At Babylon they would meet only the huge, almost featureless mounds beneath which the city of Nebuchadnezzar lay concealed, and upon which layers of folklore and legend would continue to accumulate.

CHAPTER 4

THE EARTHLY CITY: MEDIEVAL AND RENAISSANCE APPROACHES

By the time that Paulus Orosius compiled his influential universal history in the fifth century AD, the Babylon of Nebuchadnezzar was already a distant memory. The cuneiform script had become completely extinct by the early centuries AD, but the period at which Babylonian chronicles were effectively lost as direct sources is much earlier, since the third-century BC account of Berossus seems to have been the last significant point of direct transmission between the Babylonian and Greek historical sources.[1]

Orosius' *History Against the Pagans* divided history into four epochs: the ages of Babylon, Macedon, Carthage and Rome. The scheme, which was intended to allow comparisons between the epochs, was one of the most influential aspects of the work, and is repeated in other medieval universal histories. So too was the manner in which they were compared, for Orosius was interested above all in the moral significance of his subject matter. The medieval European historical treatment of Babylon – indeed of the entire ancient world – can be characterized in the broadest terms as a process of organization and rationalization of vast quantities of textual evidence. This rationalization was not limited to the resolution of apparent conflicts between sources, but had a religious and moral aspect that frequently required new structures and interpretations to be applied to historical narratives. Nor was the exercise an abstract one. Rather, with the idea of a timeless morality, analysis of past behaviour informed an understanding of political life in the present, and is well reflected in the adaptation of historical legend to contemporary political need.[2]

In an article focusing on this political aspect of medieval historiography, Gabrielle Spiegel argues that 'the medieval chronicler utilized a very fluid perspective with regard to past and present. The search for the past was guided by present necessities; but so, too, the historical understanding of the past for its part determined the rhetorical presentation of contemporary events'.[3] Thus the past was not entirely elastic, rather perceptions of past and present were intertwined, each understood as bearing upon the other. The practice of attempting a degree of cultural relativism and an understanding of past actions in their contemporary cultural context – a quality valued in modern historians and not unknown in antiquity; witness the writings of Herodotus – is extremely rare in medieval historiography. The nearest approach is to be found in attempts to address the problem for Christian authors of allotting a proper place to virtuous pagans such as Dante's Virgil, who in the *Divine Comedy* must ultimately dwell in Limbo, debarred from heaven though spared the pains of hell. More generally, the focus on understanding the past in a manner useful for contemporary morality led to judgements that were more absolute.

The problem of difference in medieval perceptions is a recurring one: models of medieval worldviews as essentially similar or essentially alien to our own both have some validity and have co-existed in a shifting balance in modern historical thought.[4] Most treatments of the antecedents of archaeological exploration have fallen into the former category, insofar as the most relevant sources have been assumed to be the accounts of the few European travellers who visited ancient sites in the Middle East. Understood as fieldwork, these reports have been treated in effect as precursors to archaeological studies – a view which, while not entirely misleading, does tend to overemphasize these works' separation from other medieval approaches to the distant past and to overstate their importance in terms of intellectual history. Most medieval journeys to the Middle East were made either for commercial reasons or as pilgrimages, not for any kind of scholarly research.[5] The tendency is to privilege the on-the-spot observations made by travellers and explorers, antiquaries, treasure-hunters and eventually – when is a matter of personal preference, for the division is conceived as a question more of degree than of type – archaeologists. What unites the group is direct observation of ancient sites, and in general it is this element that has normally been sought in looking for antecedents to archaeological work. Later spectacular discoveries and their success in penetrating into the public consciousness have served to reinforce this perspective. As Hudson remarks:

> What British archaeology achieved overseas, indeed, was largely responsible for narrowing the meaning of the word 'archaeology'. In Crete, in Egypt, in Mesopotamia and elsewhere in the Middle East and around the Mediterranean, the great discoveries which caught the attention of the public were made as the result of digging. Sir Leonard Woolley, Sir Arthur Evans, Sir Max Mallowan and others earned their knighthoods and made their reputations by their skill and good fortune in finding wonderful things underneath vast quantities of sand and earth. They were the excavator-knights, the finders of buried treasure, who fired the imagination of their fellow countrymen and brought archaeology to the attention of the popular press and therefore of the man in the street. Since the 1920s archaeology, for most people, has been practically a synonym for excavation.[6]

The visitors to Babylon do form some kind of continuum, and their personal experiences and different approaches have affected the development of new ways of understanding the past, but taken in isolation do little to explain the later development of archaeological approaches. They are self-evidently not the key drivers for the development of the humanist rational–empirical approach to the past that underpins the modern discipline of archaeology. Our approach must therefore involve two parts: the first a survey of the visitors to Babylon and their accounts; and the second a consideration of the broader spectrum of engagement with the ancient city in European intellectual and artistic tradition.

Travellers and their accounts

The shrinking and final disappearance of Babylon as a settlement is only hinted at in the available historical sources. Perhaps the last reference to a living settlement is that of Ibn Hauqal, who mentions a small village of Babel as late as the tenth century.[7] By the time of the earliest medieval European travellers' accounts, even this village had apparently disappeared, though as today others existed around the fringes of and even on the site. In any case, biblical accounts led medieval travellers to expect a deserted ruin.

Benjamin of Tudela

A key medieval source for European knowledge of Asia is the *Itinerary* of Rabbi Benjamin ben Jonah of Tudela, a Spanish merchant whose travels, begun around 1160, probably lasted until 1173.[8] The *Itinerary*, unpublished until 1543[9] and known to us only in abridged form, covers a vast area, including most major cities and holy places of the Middle East and extending as far east as China, its primary aim being to record the situation of Jews across the world. The *Itinerary* describes Babylon first, then al-Hillah and finally the Tower of Babel (in fact the site of Birs Nimrud, ancient Borsippa).[10] Benjamin's account of the Tower records that local people were afraid to venture near the site as it was infested with snakes and scorpions.[11] He also describes an ancient but functioning synagogue, and the site of the Fiery Furnace of Daniel:

> Near at hand, within a distance of a mile, there dwell 3,000 Israelites who pray in the Synagogue of the Pavilion of Daniel, which is ancient, and was erected by Daniel. It is built of hewn stones and bricks. Between the Synagogue and the Palace of Nebuchadnezzar is the furnace into which were thrown Hananiah, Mishael, and Azariah, and the site of it lies in a valley known unto all.[12]

There is some doubt as to whether Benjamin actually visited Babylon, or indeed ever travelled as far to the east as the scope of his account implies. The preface, written later and apparently by a different author, describes the *Itinerary* as the account of 'what he saw' and 'what he heard'. Introducing his translation of the *Itinerary*, Asher argued that these were to be understood as two distinct sections of the work.[13] The account includes the names of the principal Jewish leaders and elders in towns until the journey reaches Baghdad, after which these are almost entirely absent. According to Asher, this is where 'what he saw' ends and 'what he heard' begins. If this is strictly true, it would seem that he saw Mosul and Nineveh (Mosul's principals are listed, and it appears in the itinerary before Baghdad), but not Babylon, Hillah or the Tower of Babel. It is true that once in Iraq there were good reasons to stop at Baghdad:

> Bagdad, at his time the seat of the Prince of the captivity [a Jewish leader claiming descent from King David, whose description forms a large part of Rabbi Benjamin's section on Baghdad], must have attracted numerous Jewish pilgrims from all regions, and beyond doubt was the fittest place for gathering those notices of the Jews and of trade in different parts of the world, the collecting of which was the aim of R. Benjamin's labours.[14]

All this said, if we are less strict about the division of the book into two parts there is nothing to prevent the supposition that Benjamin might have made a trip to Babylon from Baghdad. The information given is plausible and certainly does not fit with the more fantastic accounts of his travels in the far east that, in any case, may have been introduced into the account by later compilers.[15]

In terms of Rabbi Benjamin's experiences in Iraq, it is worth noting Signer's comment on his written Hebrew:

> A reading of the Hebrew text of the *Itinerary* reveals more about Benjamin. He writes in a rather formal medieval Hebrew. His Hebrew is suffused with Arabic forms. This would certainly indicate that Benjamin knew Arabic. It was probably his

mother tongue. Arabic gave Benjamin the linguistic key to the
world he set out to explore in Asia and Africa. Benjamin's
knowledge of Arabic also opens up a path toward a deeper
understanding of his intellectual milieu.[16]

In this respect Benjamin was atypical of European travellers to the
Middle East. Despite the long history of European orientalism, the
field has never been large, and until at least the nineteenth century was
so dominated by the study of classical Arabic effectively as a dead
language that European *speakers* of Arabic were at all times extremely
rare.[17] Arabic would not have been the only available channel for
communication, but Benjamin's account does contain intriguing
fragments of folklore and local tradition relating to the places he
visited in Iraq, including Babylon. His inclusion of a site understood to
be the location of the Fiery Furnace is a prime example. On the other
hand, this biblical connection is representative of another
characteristic of Benjamin's account: that although based on first-
hand observation its description is inevitably informed by scripture
and religious interest. Thus his inclusion of the detail that the site of
the Tower is now filled with snakes is liable to be the product not only
of experience (whether direct or via an informant) but equally of
Benjamin's noting a striking confirmation of the prophecy of Jeremiah.

Marco Polo and Baghdad as Babylon

Some travellers identify Baghdad as modern Babyloh, or New Babylon.
Marco Polo gives the impression of assumed continuity between the
two cities, describing 'the great city of Baldach or Bagadet, anciently
called Babylon'.[18] His late thirteenth-century account is therefore of
Babylon's heir, which in a sense Baghdad was. The conflation of the two
cities is a mistake, but as the last in a succession of powerful cities
dominating the political landscape of the Middle East from central
Iraq Baghdad was indeed the political legatee of Babylon and, as
Marco Polo's description made clear, a worthy successor:

In Baghdad, which is a very large city, the Caliph of all the
Saracens in the world has his seat, just as the head of all the

Christians in the world has his seat at Rome. Through the midst of the city flows a very large river, by which travellers may go to the Indian Sea.

It is in Baghdad that most of the pearls are pierced that are imported from India to Christendom. Here too are woven many fabrics of cloth of gold and silk, known as *nasich* and *nakh* and and cramoisy, very richly decorated with beasts and birds. It is a great centre for the study of the law of Mahomet and of necromancy, natural science, astronomy, geomancy, and physiognomy. It is the largest and most splendid city in all these parts.[19]

Others realized that Baghdad was distinct from the site of Babylon, but still referred to the former as New Babylon (John Eldred) or simply Babylon (Anthony Sherley, Johann Schiltberger, Robert Coverte). Given the apparent tendency of Greco-Roman writers to refer to Nineveh as Babylon or Old Babylon, we can appreciate that the identification of Babylon with multiple sites involves more than the misidentification of ruins such as Birs Nimrud and 'Aqar Quf (of which more below) as the Tower of Babel.

St Odoric

Friar Odoric of Pordenone travelled from Venice to China's Pacific coast in the early fourteenth century. The journey was so remarkable that Odoric, who was eventually beatified, gained a reputation for having had divine protection, and stories of miracles associated with him began circulating during his own lifetime.[20] His account, probably dictated upon his return, includes many strange and fantastic peoples, but much of its geography is sound and he is generally agreed to have actually made the journey he describes. The account was in any case the by-product rather than the goal of his journey. He travelled as a missionary, and states explicity that he 'crossed the sea and visited the countries of the unbelievers in order to win some harvest of souls'.[21] His description of Iraq is minimal but does include the Tower of Babel, which he describes as four days' journey from Baghdad. He passed it, according to his own account, on the way northwest from Yazd, although his translators and editors have suggested that this may be a mistake on his part, the route appearing in effect as a massive detour westward in his itinerary; the alternative proposed by Chiesa is that he came into Iraq via Soltaniyeh in north-western Iran.[22] The distance given from Baghdad is credible for Babylon and thus makes the ruined ziggurat visible at Birs Nimrud a plausible candidate for the site Odoric believed to be the Tower of Babel. He makes no comment on the site to give us any clue. Although he discusses Baghdad Odoric never mentions the city by name, either as Baghdad or Babylon. He describes 'Chaldea', meaning either the vicinity of Baghdad or Iraq more generally, as 'a great kingdom', and notes that its people have 'a language of their own'. He also describes reversal of gender norms for dress:

> The men are comely, but the women in sooth of an ill favor. The men indeed go smartly dressed and decked as our women go here, and on their heads they wear a kind of fillet of gold and pearls; whilst the women have nothing on them but a miserable shift reaching to the knees, and with sleeves so long and wide that they sweep the ground. And they go barefoot with drawers hanging about their feet, and their hair neither plaited nor braided, but in complete dishevelment; and as here among us the men go first and the women follow, so there the women have to go before the men.[23]

This puzzling inclusion does not seem to accord with any known tradition. The best explanation, as with some customs described in the more fantastic Far Eastern parts of the narrative, is that Odoric simply uses a reversal of European norms in order to express the difference of this strange land.

Johann Schiltberger

In 1396, at only 15 years old, Johann Schiltberger of Bavaria was captured at the battle of Nicopolis. He spent the next five years as a prisoner of the sultan Bajazet, and in 1402 both slave and captor fell into the hands of Timur (Timur-e lang, Tamerlane). Schiltberger provides a mixture of first- and second-hand accounts of Timur's campaigns, but his personal experience was enormous: he travelled with Timur's army and court to Siberia, Central Asia, Egypt, Arabia (where he is claimed by his modern editors, P. Bruun and J. Buchan Telfer, to have been the first Christian visitor to Mecca and Medina),[24] and of course Mesopotamia. On his eventual escape and return to Bavaria, where he arrived in 1427, his narrative was recorded. As extraordinary as any aspect of his story is the testament this account offers to his powers of memory. Schiltberger was apparently illiterate, and 'The various incidents of his career in the East are recounted without method, and were evidently related just as the recollection of them occurred to him',[25] yet the content of his account, or at least that part of it based on first-hand experience, is remarkably ungarbled and factually accurate. Schiltberger's illiteracy seems almost an advantage in this respect, since he is not subject to the burden of reconciling his own experience with that of his predecessors or literary tradition. Babylon, however, is an exception to this general rule. Telfer believes that Schiltberger's relation of the dimensions of the walls of Babylon, clearly from Herodotus, is the one and only indication of a literary source in the entire account.[26] This may be going too far, since even within the description of Babylon itself there is the almost obligatory reference to Jeremiah and Isaiah: 'none can get there because of the dragons and serpents, and other hurtful reptiles, of which there are many in the said desert'.[27] This is far from clear-cut, however: an intimate knowledge of the Old Testament is itself no indicator of literacy in fifteenth-century Europe, and while it does seem strange that he chooses the same biblical reference as his literate forebears, it is conceivable that the fulfilment of Jeremiah's prophecy may have struck Schiltberger in such a way as to cause him to include the added detail in the same manner. We could even believe that this is straightforward observation, with no intentional reference to a source at all. In terms of the specific reference, however, the coincidence would be remarkable.

Schiltberger also refers to Baghdad as Babylon, and describes Timur's conquest of the city in 1401 (to which he was not a first-hand witness). Schiltberger's testimony often emphasizes the violence and cruelty of Timur, and here he describes the destruction of Baghdad:

> Tämerlin besieged it for a whole month, during which time he undermined the walls, took the city and burnt it. Then he had the earth ploughed and barley planted there, because he had sworn that he would destroy the city, so that nobody should know whether there had been houses or no.[28]

His account of the Tower of Babel includes a description of Baghdad (this time called 'New Babylon' to distinguish it from the 'great Babylon'),[29] and there is no reason to think that he did not visit the city. Schiltberger describes Baghdad as a grand city in which Persian as well as Arabic is spoken, with an enormous hunting ground or menagerie. He also tells us that Great and New Babylon are separated by a river called the Schatt (Tigris).[30] This is hard to interpret: the ruins of Babylon lay far downstream on the Euphrates. Perhaps, like some later travellers, he refers to what are actually the ruins of ancient canal systems between Falluja and Baghdad. The tower that Schiltberger found was Birs Nimrud, confirmed both by his description of distances, which Bruun demonstrated are correct for Birs Nimrud,[31] and in a name we encounter for the first time here: 'Marburtirudt', which Bruun reasonably suggests stands for 'Marbout Nimroud', or prison of Nimrod.[32] Schiltberger understood the whole name to refer to the king who built the tower, and was therefore nearer than he apparently knew to the biblical view that the builder was Nimrod.

John Mandeville

In these early travellers' accounts of Babylon we can see the strong effect of writers' expectations and religious convictions on personal observation. Biblical references framed as observation abound in most accounts: the claim that the ruins of Babylon are filled with snakes and other dangerous creatures is found in Benjamin of Tudela,[33] Friar

Odoric,[34] Johann Schiltberger,[35] Leonard Rauwolf[36] and Anthony Sherley,[37] and is apparently based on various translations of Jeremiah and Isaiah's prophetic descriptions of the city's fate. One measure of this influence is the mid-fourteenth-century account of 'Jehan de Mandeville', better known as Sir John Mandeville, in which both the author and the journey described are probably fictitious. Even if the narrative is authentic in the sense of referring to a real journey, it was nonetheless constructed almost entirely by compiling and embellishing existing literature. Despite this limitation Mandeville, whose real identity remains unknown, gives an account comparable in detail and content to that of Rabbi Benjamin (whose Hebrew description he could not have read), mainly by describing the fulfilment of Old Testament prophecy. Whether or not readers believed the more fantastic elements of the narrative (in the tradition of Pliny's monstrous races, see below), 'Mandeville's Travels was certainly the most famous travel text, and generally one of the most popular works of prose of late medieval Europe'.[38]

This is not to say that Mandeville did not make errors. His Babylon, for example, is conflated with another great Eastern city: Cairo. In the Middle Ages one of Cairo's several names was *Bab al-Yun*, retained by Coptic Christians and remembered today in the quarter of the old city known as Babylon. (There is also an Egyptian tradition that the name derives from Nebuchadnezzar's military adventures, which in reality never reached this far.) As a result, Mandeville's Babylon was the destination of the holy family on their flight into Egypt; and of Joseph, sold by his brothers; most importantly it was the seat of the present Egyptian sultan. At the same time it was the city of Nebuchadnezzar and the story of the Fiery Furnace. To further complicate matters, Mandeville was aware of another city, located further to the east:

Do understand that the Babylon which I speak of at the moment, where the Sultan lives, is not Babylon the Great, where happened the Confusion of Tongues, when the Tower of Babilon was being built. The walls of it were sixty-three furlongs high, and it is in the deserts of Arabia as you go

towards the kingdom of Chaldea. But it is a long time since
anyone dared approach that wretched place; for it is waste, and
so full of dragons and snakes and other venomous beasts that no
man dares come near it.[39]

Mandeville knew something of the location, combining biblical
and classical information – 'That same city of Babylon the Great
was set in a fair plain, which was called the field of Senaar, on the
River Euphrates, which ran through the city at that time'[40] – but
his geography drifts into talk of more distant and legendary
realms: Cathay (China) and the mystical, mythical kingdom of
Prester John:

> From that Babylon where the Sultan dwells [i.e. Cairo] to
> Babylon the Great is forty days' journey, travelling north-east
> through the desert. And Babylon the Great is not subject to the
> Sultan but to the King of Persia. He holds it of the Great Caan
> [Khan], who is a great emperor – indeed the greatest in the
> world, for he is lord of the great land of Cathay and many other
> countries, and a great part of India. His land marches with
> Prester John's land; and he has such great lordships that he
> knows no end of them. He is greater and beyond comparison
> mightier than the Sultan. Of his great state and majesty I
> intend to speak later, when I come to it.[41]

Leonard Rauwolf

The sixteenth century saw a substantial rise in the number of
accounts of Mesopotamia and its ancient sites, and a gradual increase
in detail. In an excellent review of these, Ooghe observes that 'printed
Mesopotamian travel narratives jumped from being virtually non-
existent prior to 1530 to numbering at least 19 in the second half of
the century alone'.[42] A good example of this flourishing interest is
the account of Leonard Rauwolf, a Bavarian physician who travelled
from 1573 to 1576, coming to Baghdad in October 1574. His
account of the journey was first published in 1583. He describes

Babylon, 'The oldest capital in Chaldaea' lying to the east of 'Elugo' (Falluja).[43] He found it,

> Completely destroyed, and uninhabited it lies still; close behind it stands the high Tower of Babylon, that the children of Noah (who first settled in this land after the great flood) tried to build up to Heaven.[44]

Rauwolf's city of Babylon must have been the remains of ancient canals he saw on his journey to Baghdad, and his Tower of Babel must be the ruined ziggurat at 'Aqar Quf.[45] This seems to be the first account in which 'Aqar Quf, ancient Dur Kurigalzu, is mistaken for the Tower of Babel. Although a long way north of the real site of Babylon and much nearer to Baghdad, there is a logic to the identification: if the ruins of canals en route to Baghdad were taken as the remains of the city of Babylon, the prominent ruined ziggurat at 'Aqar Quf would present itself as a much more obvious candidate for the Tower than a ruin far to the south that in any case fewer travellers would ever have seen. Moreover, the visible remains of reed matting inserted between courses of mud-brick in the ziggurat's construction match perfectly the description of Herodotus. These factors, combined with an understanding of Baghdad as Babylon's direct successor supporting the assumption that the two are located close together, are enough to explain the emergence of a tradition that the remains of the Tower of Babel were to be seen at 'Aqar Quf.

John Eldred

The Englishman John Eldred was in southern Iraq in 1583, and gives a short account of Babylon. The location he gives is at first a little puzzling:

> In this short desert, between the Euphrates and Tigris, formerly stood the great and mighty city of ancient Babylon, many of the old ruins of which are easily to be seen by day-light, as I, John Eldred, have often beheld at my good leisure, having made three several journeys between Aleppo and New Babylon.[46]

To travel from Aleppo to Baghdad ('New Babylon') meant going
south-east along the Euphrates, or more likely in parallel to it in the
desert at some distance to the west, coming close to the Tigris only as
one approached Baghdad, and not travelling far enough south to
come near to the site of Babylon at all.[47] Budge describes Eldred as
coming to 'Aqar Quf 'when he was coming down the Tigris from
Môsul'.[48] He may have had reason to assume that the route was a
desert crossing to Mosul followed by a journey down the Tigris, but
this is not what Eldred wrote and it is more probably the Euphrates
caravan route to which he refers. Hilprecht has it that Eldred, like
Rauwolf and the Venetian merchant-traveller Gasparo Balbi, saw
'Aqar Quf while travelling east from Falluja to Baghdad, and that
like them he mistook the ruins of ancient canals for the city of
Babylon.[49] This explanation seems to accord better with Eldred's
description, the 'short desert' presumably being the stretch between
Falluja and Baghdad. The description of the Tower is compatible
with 'Aqar Quf:

> Here also are yet standing the ruins of the old Tower of
> Babel, which, being upon a plain ground, seemeth afar very
> great; but the nearer you come to it, the lesser and lesser
> it appeareth. Sundry times I have gone thither to see it,
> and found the remnants yet standing, above a quarter of a
> mile in compass, and almost as high as the stone work of
> Paul's steeple in London; but it showeth much bigger. The
> bricks remaining of this most ancient monument be half a
> yard thick, and three quarters of a yard long; being dried
> in the sun only: and between every course of bricks, there
> lieth a course of mats, made of canes, which remain sound
> and not perished, as though they had been laid within
> one year.[50]

Eldred's immediate successors give similar accounts: Anthony
Sherley[51] and John Cartwright[52] both apparently interpreted the
ziggurat at 'Aqar Quf as the Tower of Babel. Jean Baptiste Tavernier,
visiting in 1652, also believed 'Aqar Quf to be the Tower, although

he also recorded a local tradition that the tower was built by an Arab prince to protect his subjects in time of war.[53] In common with other travellers he gives detail of the bricks and reed matting used, though there is no explicit statement of their excellent correspondence with the description of Herodotus.

There is one other potential 'Tower of Babel' deserving of mention here. It is often assumed that the enormous – and still standing – ninth-century Malwiya minaret of the Great Mosque at Samarra was another presumed Tower of Babel, or at least that its shape influenced depictions of the Tower in European art, to some of which it bears a quite striking resemblance. Nothing in the European travel accounts, however, suggests that this might be the case. The earliest known European description of Samarra is that of Anthony Sherley, who with his brother, Robert, made a celebrated trip as an emissary of Queen Elizabeth to the court of Shah 'Abbas of Persia at the close of the sixteenth century.[54] The site does not seem to have been much visited by European travellers, and none mistook the Malwiya minaret for the Tower of Babel. John Newberry, visiting in 1580, did refer to its area as *Eski* (old) Baghdad,[55] but this does not suggest the site of Babylon. Baghdad did, after all, succeed Samarra as a capital and the name reflects this. Most importantly, illustrations of the Malwiya minaret do not seem to have been in circulation in any form, making it unclear how the image could have passed into European art.[56]

Pietro Della Valle

Accounts of the sixteenth-century kind contain some basic information on routes and curious sights, but basically focus on contemporary concerns (naturally, far more detail was recorded of the living city of Baghdad than anything relating to the ancient past), and treat ancient sites such as Babylon only incidentally. A significant shift in emphasis comes with the visit of Pietro Della Valle, whose role as a methodological precursor to archaeological study of the area has been emphasized by Blunt and more recently Invernizzi.[57] An Italian nobleman abandoning Rome for travel to soothe romantic disappointment (successfully: he was to marry in

Iraq), he is best known for what, in hindsight, seems an important first:

> He is alleged to have been the first person to copy a cuneiform inscription, something he indeed did in Persepolis on October 13th–14th 1621. This claim, however, requires certain qualifications, for his copy is not entirely correct, and a cuneiform line was copied in Persepolis a short time earlier by Don Garcia de Silva y Figueroa, ambassador of Spain in Isfahan from 1617 to 1624, whom Della Valle himself met at the court of Shah Abbas. Nevertheless, it is a fact that, while the report published by the Spanish aristocrat had no particularly strong influence on seventeenth-century European culture, the wider diffusion and uninterrupted success of Pietro Della Valle's letters over the following centuries give special importance to the copy of the Persepolitan inscription he published.[58]

He also correctly deduced that the inscription was to be read from left to right.[59] This act of recording, however, is not so much an isolated step in itself as a reflection of the extent to and manner in which Pietro Della Valle's approach to the ancient sites he visited during his travels differed from those of his predecessors. Della Valle copies, sketches, explores, and even:

> Probing the remains with his pick at different points, endeavours to get a clear idea of the structure of the unknown monument standing in front of him. In the curiosity of knowledge, we are here confronted with what is apparently the earliest example of an excavation sounding in Mesopotamia, and certainly the earliest recorded such sounding.[60]

Invernizzi rightly stresses the distinctly empirical and, significantly from an archaeological point of view, physical character of Della Valle's attempt to find out about the site. Pietro Della Valle does not represent a break from so much as a culmination of the interest shown by his recent predecessors;[61] nonetheless the genuinely new

aspects of his approach require explanation. Within an existing
European tradition of travel writing it seems that leisure, education,
inclination and a moment in cultural and intellectual history – more
of Della Valle's native Rome than of the Middle East – combined to
facilitate an account that was not only more detailed than its
predecessors, but which derived in part from close physical
examination, demonstrating in the process that there was indeed
something to be learned from the study of the ruins themselves.

The most remarkable products of Pietro Della Valle's visit to
Babylon are visual. Among his retinue was a Flemish artist, who
produced sketches that were intended to form the basis for a future
painting.[62] Although the painting seems never to have been made
and the sketches themselves have not survived, they were the source
for three images in Athanasius Kircher's *Turris Babel*[63] (of which
more below), where their naturalism contrasts sharply with the
fantastic images making up the bulk of the illustration. They are
recognizable depictions of Tell Babil, the northern mound at Babylon
and site of Nebuchadnezzar's Summer Palace, to which the ancient
name of the city still attached. The images show ruined and formless
mounds totally unlike any previous European depiction of Babylon.
Kircher's work also contributed to Pietro Della Valle's influence in
another way, including a Latin translation of the account of Babylon
(the primary sources are in Italian, letters to Della Valle's friend
Mario Schipano)[64] thereby making the description accessible to a
larger European readership.

Another notable development of the late-sixteenth and
seventeenth centuries is the beginning of (known) collecting of
ancient material from Babylonia by European travellers. This was
nothing on the scale of later export of Mesopotamian antiquities, just
as Della Valle's investigations at Tell Babil bore no resemblance to
the huge excavations of the nineteenth century. Della Valle himself
brought back souvenirs: inscribed bricks from Babylon and Ur. (A
curious Babylonian stamp seal, to which has been added a
Hellenistic-era head in profile, is also known to have been in Italy
as early as the seventeenth century. Understandably, prior to the era of
modern excavations the later portrait was misinterpreted as that of

Nebuchadnezzar.[65]) Still, he was not the first: the Austrian Georg Christoph Fernberger, visiting in the late sixteenth century, collected a brick from the 'Tower of Babel', though this is long since lost.[66]

The changing role of observation

It would not be quite true to say that Pietro Della Valle worked from observation where others did not – the value of seeing something for oneself is implicit in any travel account – but we could perhaps say that his observation resulted in an account that was critical in a way that those of Rauwolf or Sherley were not. These travellers, to read their narratives today, give the impression of trusting the Bible far more than their own eyes, and indeed this may very well have been the case. There is still great value in the classic characterization of a medieval model of the universe given by C. S. Lewis in *The Discarded Image*:

> They [medieval writers and thinkers] are bookish. They find it very hard to believe that anything an old *auctour* has said is simply untrue. And they inherit a very heterogenous collection of books [...]. Obviously their *auctours* will contradict one another. They will seem to do so even more if you ignore the distinction of kinds and take your science impartially from the poets and the philosophers; and this the medievals very often did in fact though they would have been well able to point out, in theory, that poets feigned. If, under these conditions, one has also a great reluctance flatly to disbelieve anything in a book, then here there is obviously both an urgent need and a glorious opportunity for sorting out and tidying up.[67]

'At his most characteristic', argues Lewis, 'medieval man was not a dreamer nor a wanderer. He was an organiser, a codifier, a builder of systems.'[68] To this extent he denies his subject the creativity of other ages, and this claim we can treat with reasonable scepticism. The emphasis Lewis places on the perceived importance of classification and the resolution of all these *auctours* or canonical sources, on the other hand, is astute and still widely accepted. The judgement was not, it should be stressed, intended to disparage the medieval scholar (indeed Lewis himself greatly valued a very similar version of intellectual clarity and order).[69] *The Discarded Image* set out to help modern readers appreciate medieval and Renaissance perspectives, and in the case of our sources for these periods the view above does indeed help to do this. We are interested in a particular mode of acquiring and dealing with knowledge, and the crucial observation is that textual authorities play a role in medieval travel accounts quite different to that seen in their modern equivalents, where the value is often seen to lie in being able to supplement, revise or even refute an earlier authority. The modern instinct, perhaps through a combination of the historical experience of later New World navigators and the drive for empirical research which has grown ever stronger in the centuries following the Enlightenment, is to identify the work of travellers to distant lands as discovery of the new, to base their value upon this, and thus to be left if anything a little disappointed by the repeated confirmations of biblical or classical sources we find in earlier travel accounts. At worst, this can leave the reader revelling too much in the curios: for 'originality' in the account of Friar Odoric, for example, one might turn to his fantastic descriptions of monstrous races far to the east, dismissing the more practical and indeed accurate geographical content, or indeed the affirmation of scripture that is so important in the account of the more learned Benjamin of Tudela. What if, to adopt the perspective Lewis suggests, we instead identify the work of these accounts as clarification, and their value as the individual's contribution to a self-referentially complete and harmonized model of the universe? The first step in doing so would be to recognize the strong intellectual imperative for such a project. To turn to a contemporary of Lewis and fellow expert in medieval thought, Morton Bloomfield stated:

> [N]o proper understanding of medieval literature is possible without a good knowledge of the Christian categories of thought and beliefs. Yet medieval man was also the heir of late classical antiquity and of barbarian cultures, and their categories of thought, their literary genres, their points of

view, were also part of his heritage. He was well aware of a secular tradition which had not been completely transformed by Christianity.[70]

There were problems to be solved, conflicts and puzzles as well as the important business of collecting together and consolidating the sum of knowledge available from past authorities, and arching over the whole the question of incorporating this knowledge within a single religious framework. From this perspective another kind of contribution to knowledge is apparent, and one that perhaps shows the works of the medieval travellers in a better light. The reward for adopting this slightly alien perspective is that it now becomes easier to identify real intellectual common ground between medieval and Renaissance efforts and later studies of Babylon. The need to place what one learns within a model of the universe, for example, is not itself a goal whose pursuit disappears or even fades; it is the method of that pursuit that changes. What we are really studying is an aspect of the slow transition from a medieval drive to understand a web of great but finite complexity to a present-day pursuit of simplicity that is epitomized in the elegance of contemporary characterizations of physical law, reduced to a handful of forces from whose interaction the variety and complexity of our universe is now believed to derive. This cosmological example is not so far as it appears from changes in the way we know the human past. For scholars in the social sciences, and humanities too, the twentieth century was a time of model-building and the search for underlying principles, albeit that this search met with far less success than that in the physical sciences. Again, what differentiates this effort from the 'medieval' work of codification and classification is a shift in emphasis between the careful study of existing sources and the more-or-less empirical acquisition of new data with a view to establishing and refining consistent rules and principles.

To return briefly to the accounts of monstrous races, these too can be seen as part of the incorporation of knowledge into a grand framework. They actually originate in classical geographies, notably the *Natural History* of Pliny the Elder,[71] and we could most accurately say that it is not their existence but their increasingly awkward inclusion next to a more prosaic observed world that is distinctively 'medieval'.[72] A comparable problem – and solution – can be found in the medieval treatment of hagiography and the miracles of the saints. Kendall takes the example of the Venerable Bede's *Historia Ecclesiastica*, in which,

> We see a double image. There is the dispassionate, scientific observer, meticulously sifting the evidence of the past, and there is also the child of the Dark Ages, embracing the most superstitious elements of popular legend.[73]

Arguing that the crucial tool in Bede's resolution of such diverse material is expert rhetoric, Kendall draws a conclusion as to the nature of his achievement:

> [Readers] may be conscious of the juxtaposition of what we can loosely call historical and hagiographical narrative. But once the juxtaposition is seen as an accurate reflection of the discontinuity of the sixth age [i.e. 'the time of grace extending from the advent of Christ to the second coming and the last judgement'], conditioned by preexisting narrative conventions, the magnitude of Bede's achievement becomes apparent. The *History* is a finally unified version of the totality of man's experience from the mundane to the miraculous, in and beyond time.[74]

So the process is one of reconciling not merely discordant sources but substantially different types of source and modes of thought. Even putting aside the religious interpretation of this 'discontinuity', the historian can appreciate the need to preserve all sorts of sources against a background of great philosophical and theological flux and tension. Medieval travel accounts were subject to the same pressures, and so both a degree of conservatism and a desire to be inclusive rather than sceptical make good sense. As with Pliny's monstrous races, however, the very preservation of knowledge in new contexts is a form of change in itself.

Although by no means a radical departure, the account of Pietro Della Valle does indeed represent a significant contrast to its predecessors. Its author questioned and tested, and in order to do so he had to have faith in the usefulness of his own observations. The difference in his approach can hardly be seen as a consciously impious or heretical act, but the difference is there nonetheless, and in its very method Della Valle's account challenges a certain theocratic kind of knowledge. The truth of scripture and the canon, it implies, is not precisely literal and not, as a historical document, complete. The possibility of separating mythos and logos in conceptions of the truth of scripture originates in acts of just this kind. This can hardly have been his own view of the event, but when we see this conflict of authority manifest itself explicitly in the nineteenth and twentieth centuries, we will be reminded of the figure of Pietro Della Valle, tentatively exploring the ruins he believed to be the foundations of the Tower of Babel.

Medieval and Renaissance histories, art and literature

Babylon in Late Antique Christian theology
The great doctors of the Western Church have tangibly shaped all aspects of European religious and intellectual culture. The impact of St Augustine, St Ambrose, St Jerome and Gregory the Great on Christian doctrine and Western philosophy is difficult to overstate. Particularly important for our purposes are St Jerome and St Augustine, two of the most prolific, and later most famed, of all Christian writers in Latin, both of whom contributed substantially to Babylon's image and place in world history.

In one sense the significance of St Jerome (Eusebius Sophronius) has already been discussed, because his especial importance lies in the translation of works discussed in the previous chapter. His Latin version of Eusebius of Caesarea's *Chronicon* kept accessible to scholars a work that preserves chronological information on Mesopotamia from Berossus, Megasthenes and Abydenus.[75] As well as transmitting specific information on Mesopotamia, Jerome's translation of the *Chronicon* also preserved (and extended, from 327 up to 378 AD) Eusebius of Caesarea's synchronization of pagan and Christian chronologies for world history.[76] Further, the translation helped the work to achieve its status and influence as a key chronicle of history and much-used source on chronology in medieval Europe.[77] Jerome's commentaries on Daniel, Jeremiah and Isaiah are also relevant to the later study and interpretation of these key sources on Babylon. Important as they are, however, all of these achievements are utterly dwarfed by Jerome's masterpiece of biblical translation, the Latin Vulgate Bible.

The so-called Old Latin version of the Bible began to emerge in Africa and Western Europe during the second century AD.[78] Reference to it as a single version is purely for convenience; one could more accurately speak of a heterogenous corpus of Old Latin versions, including multiple versions of books and no single version of them all. Jerome's work, produced over 22 years *c*.383–405, was far more than simply a standardization. It was a return to primary sources, since Jerome was the first to translate the Old Testament into Latin from the Hebrew. Previously translators had worked only from the Greek Septuagint, which had its own school of justification as an inspired work and which Jerome's translation took centuries to supersede.[79] Supersede them it did, however, and with profound consequences. Contemporary biblical translations into English take their form not because they are based on those of Jerome, but because they have adopted his insistence on rendering the text as faithfully to the original language of composition as possible.

St Augustine is important to Babylon's story in two respects: his impact upon what became a dominant Christian conception of history in general, and his location of Babylon in particular within that history. Augustine played a key role in introducing the Judeo-Christian concept of linearity, destiny and finity into Latin historiography with *The City of God*.[80] The same work is significant for its use of Babylon. Developing the role of Babylon from Revelation's allegory of Rome, *The City of God* was, ironically, a response to Alaric's sack of Christian Rome in 410 AD. Composed from 413 to 426, the work addresses the threats to Christendom occasioned by the weakening and collapse of the Western Empire, and by the pagan reaction against Christianity as some Romans held the new religion responsible for the fall of the eternal city.[81] These concerns rendered the nature of history and of historical change particularly urgent to Augustine.

Against the prevailing sense of disaster in the Empire, shared by Jerome (the latter, in common with other theologians, identified Rome with the fourth beast seen by Daniel,[82] signifying the last kingdom before the Apocalypse),[83] Augustine's work focuses on the argument that the Christian God's kingdom is not earthly. He looks forward to the Last Judgement as heralding a bright future for Christians in a heavenly Jerusalem,[84] reached through the pilgrimage, including trials such as Rome's, that is the earthly City of God.[85] The glory of Rome was the Romans' earthly reward for 'the virtues by which they pursued the hard road that brought them at last to such glory', but 'It was not God's purpose to grant these men eternal life with the angels in his heavenly city'.[86] This could be achieved only through Christian piety and observance.

Augustine takes Revelation's original allegorical use of Babylon (the Old Testament accounts, whatever their broader implications, do refer to the city of Babylon itself) and develops it, explicitly removing its geographical ties and situating it instead in human hearts. In philosophical terms, Augustine is even able to move beyond the Christian context in his distinction between the two cities:

> [N]otwithstanding the many great nations that live throughout the world with different religious and moral practices and are distinguished by a rich variety of languages, arms and dress, nevertheless there have arisen no more than two classes, as it were, of human society. Following our Scriptures, we may well speak of them as two cities. For there is one city of men who choose to live carnally, and another who choose to live spiritually, each aiming at its own kind of peace, and when they

achieve their respective purposes, they live such lives, each in its own kind of peace.[87]

Augustine writes that 'the two cities were created by two kinds of love: the earthly city by a love of self carried even to the point of contempt for God, the heavenly city by a love of God carried even to the point of contempt for self'.[88] In his commentary on Psalm 65, Augustine explicitly names Babylon and Jerusalem in these terms.[89] This distinction, and its elevation from specific geography and history to a place in history as structuring principle, have survived: their modern expression in Zionism and Rastafari is discussed in Chapter 7. Augustine is also arguably the originator of the notion that something external to time in the world (God, the heavenly city) exists, thereby engendering a focus on destiny and redemption in the future over the search for meaning in the present.[90] This focus, which also survives into modernity, gives the role of Babylon as the materialist earthly city a further connotation of inward-looking folly.

Medieval Arabic sources

There is one explicit reference to Babylon in the Quran.[91] It is to be found in *Al-Baqarah* (*The Cow*), in a warning against rejecting the teachings of the Quran and listening to devils, who 'teach men witchcraft and that which was revealed to the angels Harut and Marut at Babylon'.[92] The reference is to a pre-Islamic narrative in which the angels laugh at humans for their weakness in succumbing to sin. God instructs them to choose two of the most virtuous of their number (Harut and Marut) to live on earth, with earthly desires. This they do, and as God predicts fall into sin, tempted by a Persian princess into wine and adultery. The angels' punishment was to be thrown into a well for all eternity (a site at Babylon known as the 'pit of Daniel' gained a reputation as the location of the well). The Quranic passage is interpreted quite differently, as angels are considered infallible in Islamic theology. The standard interpretation is that Harut and Marut were sent to Babylon to test humans by revealing forbidden knowledge in the form of magic and instructing mortals not to imitate them. Naturally many failed the test.

Although Babylon was not accorded the same prominence as in Christian literature,[93] other Arabic sources preserve Greek traditions on the city.[94] Greek chronologies for Mesopotamia were collected and compared by Abu-Raihan Muhammad Ibn 'Ahmad al-Biruni (973–1048 AD [362–440 AH]). His *Chronology of Ancient Nations* includes three Mesopotamian chronologies, one Assyrian and two Babylonian. The work was highly influential and has been important in the long-term preservation of now lost sources and other information. Sachau, its translator, wrote that:

> It is a standard work in Oriental literature, and has been recognised as such by the East itself, representing in its peculiar line the highest development of Oriental scholarship. Perhaps we shall one day find the literary sources from which Albîrûnî derived his information, and shall be enabled to dispense with his extracts from them. But there are other chapters [...] regarding which [...] the author had learned the subject from hearsay among a population which was then on the eve of dying out.[95]

Al-Biruni's Assyrian chronology runs for 1305 years, and among other points of interest offers relative dates for the sack of Troy and the reign of King David, while the Assyrian and Babylonian chronologies cover periods of 241 and 428 years, respectively. In the Assyrian chronology the first king is Belus,[96] followed by Ninus, founder of Nineveh. Al-Biruni states that Abraham was born in the 43rd year of Ninus' reign, although all the reigns given are plausible for mortal kings – the very long reigns attributed to early kings in Sumerian, Akkadian and Hebrew lists are absent. Al-Biruni's founder of Babylon is Nimrod:

> According to some chronicler, Nimrôd ben Kush ben Ham ben Noah, founded a kingdom in Babylonia twenty-three years after the confusion of languages. And that was the earliest kingdom established on earth.[97]

The phrase 'some chronicler' is typical of al-Biruni's vagueness regarding sources for these chronologies. He cites 'Western authors' as sources for the story of Sardanapalus[98] and his downfall at the hands of Arbaces.[99] The content of his version is sufficient to confirm Ctesias as the origin, but not necessarily as one of the actual works used by al-Biruni – likely intermediaries are Diodorus Siculus and Photius. Ctesias is not the source, however, for the Babylonian chronologies. The first of these concerns the beginning of Babylon's history: the city is founded by Nimrod, while in an interesting piece of etymological tidying up Semiramis is made the founder of Samarra.[100] She is succeeded not by Ninyas, as in Ctesias, but by a Zameis, whose name reappears in the seventeenth-century chronology of Athanasius Kircher (see below). Al-Biruni's second Babylonian chronology runs from a 'Nebukadnezar the First'[101] up to Alexander the Great, totalling 428 years. The last Neo-Babylonian king is 'Belteshassar' (reigned four years), followed by 'Darius the Median, the First' (17 years) and 'Cyrus, who rebuilt Jerusalem' (nine years). Of all the known chronologies for Babylon on which al-Biruni might have drawn, this one accords best with that of Daniel, where Cyrus is also preceded by a mysterious (and aged) Darius the Mede. Nebuchadnezzar II (the name Nebuchadnezzar is in fact remembered, here as in other Arabic sources, as 'Bukht-Nassar') is illustrated in two medieval copies of the text in the act of destroying Jerusalem.[102] Bukht-Nassar and the Judaean Exile are also remembered in the twelfth-century account of Yaqut al-Rumi al-Hamawi. Interestingly, Nebuchadnezzar also retains an association with large-scale canal engineering.[103]

Arab historians were limited to the same group of non-cuneiform sources as their European counterparts. Writing in the late fourteenth century, Ibn Khaldun used classical sources to give a brief account of Babylonia in volume two of his great universal history, but a fuller account had to wait until the late sixteenth century and the universal history of Müneccimbaşı (Ahmed ibn Lutfullah, d. 1702). Müneccimbaşı account drew on European as well as Islamic sources, and his information on Assyria and Babylonia came from the former. These kingdoms, along with the

Seleucid and Ptolemaic dynasties, were novelties 'previously barely known to Islamic historiography'.[104]

Nimrod receives frequent mention, and is ascribed several roles: settler as in Genesis 10, builder of the Tower, sinner against God, monstrous giant and magician. One story has Nimrod attempting to use eagles to ascend to heaven and make war on God.[105] The play on words of the confusion of tongues' Babel/*balal* also survives, as *ta-balal-a*, to get mixed up.[106] As in the Western tradition, Nimrod and Nebuchadnezzar were the names which survived most prominently, and both carried strongly negative associations. The city of Babylon itself became that of 'witchcraft and wine',[107] and 'Babylonian eyes' became those that enchanted.[108] According to al-Bakri, 'Ali refused to pray at Babil, considering it cursed and calling it a 'graveyard'.[109] The reference recognizes both the antiquity and the pagan nature of the site, and indeed Babylon retained a reputation as the oldest city in Iraq.[110] More prosaically, Babylon was regularly included in the medieval Arabic geographies. The descriptions, like those of medieval European travellers, are generally laconic, but the antiquity and great size of the site are recognized. To describe Iraq as 'Babylonia' is criticized as anachronistic – meaning that it still occurred – in the tenth-century *Geography* of al-Muqadassi.[111]

Late Antique and medieval Hebrew sources

A further interesting facet of Nimrod's identity bridges the medieval Islamic and Hebrew sources. A tradition in the Aggada makes him the antagonist of Abraham as he confronts his religious doubts, while Qur'anic references to these struggles of Abraham (which do not name Nimrod) are understood to belong to the same tradition.[112]

A key medieval source from the point of view of Jewish historiography is the *Sefer ha-Qabbalah* (*Book of Tradition*) of Abraham Ibn Daud, composed in Spain 1160–1 AD (4921 AM). The work was highly influential, achieving a status in Jewish culture similar to that held by Orosius or Isidore of Seville in medieval Christian historiography.[113] Ibn Daud was concerned with demonstrating the antiquity and continuity of rabbinical tradition, and this in itself is historiographically important, in that it marks a difference from the

Augustinian Christian model, stressing an unbroken tradition of experience and a repetition of patterns, with biblical events acting as precedents for episodes in later Jewish history.[114] As in Augustine, Babylon's significance is rendered timeless, but here for a different reason, one more akin to the Greek cyclical conception of history. Here the Babylonian Captivity becomes a hardship that will recur throughout Jewish history.

Although developed within rabbinical tradition, the *Sefer ha-Kaballah* relies more heavily on Ibn Daud's own study of biblical texts than on existing scholarship.[115] In the resulting chronology Nebuchadnezzar attacks Jerusalem in the first, 18th and 23rd years of his reign. In the first attack he carries off Jehoiachim, Daniel and the three companions of the Fiery Furnace. In the second he takes Jehoiachin and some 17,000 captives (Ibn Daud notes a contradiction with the figure of 3,023 given by Jeremiah, arguing that this is the figure for heads of families). It is not until his final attack that he destroys the Temple and captures Zedekiah.[116] Forty-seven years later, Ibn Daud's Belshazzar is betrayed by his own officers in fulfilment of Isaiah 21.5.[117] All of these events occur in the mid-fourth millennium dating from the creation of Adam, with the destruction of the Temple in 3362.[118]

Although influential in Jewish scholarship, Ibn Daud's work fell out of favour in Christian historiography. In the mid-sixteenth century Calvin attacked the commentary on Daniel of Don Isaac Abravanel, which was based on the chronology of the *Sefer ha-Qaballah*.[119] The attack did much to discredit rabbinic historical scholarship generally, and Ibn Daud's Babylonian chronology in particular, in the emergent Protestant Christianity of Northern Europe.

An altogether different kind of Mesopotamian legacy can be felt through the Babylonian Talmud, whose compilation in Late Antique Iraq resulted in the incorporation of much cuneiform-derived material. Particularly notable for the transmission of information on magic and medicine from cuneiform into Aramaic, the Babylonian Talmud also contains historical traditions, some rooted in cuneiform sources, others matters of legend and lore. The Babylonian Talmud represents the compilation and redaction of centuries of Jewish scholarly tradition in Mesopotamia. Despite its spiritual resonance, the end of the Babylonian Captivity had certainly not meant an end to Jewish life in Iraq; on the contrary it was only the beginning. As noted in Chapter 3, there is no reason to think that more than a minority of Judaeans took advantage of the right of return granted by Cyrus, and over the centuries Iraq's Jewish population increased. The scholars behind both content and compilation of the Babylonian Talmud were descendents of the Judaeans brought to Babylonia by Nebuchadnezzar, working at the great Talmudic academies of Sura and Pumbeditha, as well as smaller centres such as Nehardea and Mahuza.

Other traditions, Persian and Armenian

In Persian as in Arabic literature some influence came through Jewish tradition and the Babylonian Talmud, ensuring the survival of the names of Nimrod, Nebuchadnezzar and Daniel, as well as a memory of the Babylonians as great astronomers in Persian as well as Western culture. It is worth noting that in medieval Arabic tradition there were two possible founders of Babylon. One was Nimrod, originating with the Genesis account as interpreted by Josephus; the other came from Persian literature. In the Persian tradition Babylon was founded by a line of kings beginning with an evil and semi-monstrous Arab king named Zahhak,[120] whose successor Kavus seems to share characteristics with the Nimrod of Arabic tradition. He was reputed to have built the Tower of Babel[121] and to have built seven palaces at Babylon, each of a different stone or metal, corresponding to the seven planets. To this king is also attached the legend of an attempt to reach heaven using eagles, ascribed to Nimrod in the Arabic sources.[122]

Legends of Semiramis also spread to Persia, while a separate Armenian tradition also grew up around the legendary queen. The eighth-century AD account of Moses Khorenati describes Semiramis leading an invasion of the Lake Van area (and thus presumably the kingdom of Urartu, Assyria's neighbour and sometime rival power) and building a great city there – for which Urartian ruins are a probable inspiration.[123] The invasion is prompted by her desire for the youthful Ara the Fair, a semi-divine hero,[124] but despite her order that he be captured alive he is killed in the fighting. Semiramis attempts to resurrect Ara, until finally she resorts to dressing a substitute as the king and announcing to his people that he has returned to life.

Early European images

Early European artistic images of Babylon or Babylonians are concentrated around three subjects: episodes from the Book of Daniel, the Tower of Babel and the Book of Revelation.[125] A common image is that of Shadrach, Meshach and Abednego in the Fiery Furnace. The message of trust in God protecting the faithful is a powerful one with obvious resonance for early European Christians. The scene, featuring only Shadrach, Meshach and Abednego, is depicted in the Catacombs of Priscilla in Rome, in a fresco dating to the late third century AD. Their cruciform poses are repeated in many later illustrations, including some of the most lavish depictions of scenes from Daniel. These are the spectacular surviving manuscripts of Beatus of Liebana's eighth-century *Commentary on the Apocalypse* (in fact a compilation of existing commentary). Twelfth-century copies of the manuscript featuring a distinctive, North-African influenced graphic style contain some of the most vivid illustrations related to Daniel and Revelation in medieval art. The most celebrated version is the *Silos Apocalypse*, produced at the monastery of Santo Domingo de Silos, Cantabria.[126] The depiction of the Fiery Furnace in this instance features an angelic protector of the three men, as well as larger images of the enthroned Nebuchadnezzar and courtiers worshipping the idol. Another twelfth-century manuscript illustration comes from the Bible of Etienne Harding, representative of a tradition where Shadrach, Meschach and Abednego are represented as young children.[127] Here, the largest figure is again Nebuchadnezzar, plump and ornately dressed. A smaller figure appealing to him may be Daniel. As an illustration to a personal Bible the scene is an easy choice to understand: espousals of humility and piety reflected well on the wealthy and powerful patron of the work. A more lavish representation can be seen in a fifteenth-century German image of the scene.[128] In this image the Jews in the furnace are calm and in prayer, and the fire itself seems to emanate from them as a kind of radiance or corona. Around and above them are smooth grey arches; below is a chaotic scene dominated by Nebuchadnezzar's servants standing awkwardly as they try to shield themselves from the flames. The impression is of shielding mortal eyes from the sight of God.

The other common genre of Daniel images is the interpretation of Nebuchadnezzar's dreams. These scenes may be lavish[129] or extremely dark,[130] but only a few are markedly orientalizing.[131] Nebuchadnezzar's dreams have also been illustrated in manuscripts of Dante's *Divine Comedy*. One example shows Nebuchadnezzar's dream of a statue whose head is of gold, body and arms of silver, stomach and thighs of bronze, legs of iron and feet of iron and clay (Daniel explains that the golden head represents Nebuchadnezzar himself, the rest of the body those kingdoms that will follow his own, down to the division of Alexander's empire among his generals), in an image that also includes the figures of Moses, St John the Baptist, St John the Evangelist and the archangels Michael, Raphael and Gabriel.[132]

Images of the siege of Jerusalem focus on the city itself, with the Babylonians included as an encircling army in European costume. The best-known examples come from manuscript illustration. A detailed comparison of representations of Jerusalem and Babylon would be interesting in its own right; here we must focus on the latter, noting only that in Christian art the two are frequently juxtaposed, following the opposition between Babylon and the New Jerusalem set up in Revelation and reinforced by St Augustine. Nebuchadnezzar's attacks on Jerusalem are not forgotten in the representation of his character from Daniel. Indeed, one notable siege illustration is an illumination of the opening letter to the Book of Daniel itself.[133]

The Tower of Babel is perhaps the most common image of all. An exceptional late medieval illustration of the Tower is that found in the *Bedford Hours*, a lavish fifteenth-century book of hours illustrated in Paris (Figure 4).[134] As in many other medieval illustrations, the tower and its building techniques are contemporary. So too are the costumes of the builders, and of king Nimrod and his architects, who from this point on appear in most images of the tower. The *Bedford Hours* image, though exceptional in the quality of its production, is typical in all these features of medieval manuscript illustrations of the Tower of Babel. It is interesting to note that, despite the explicit moral role of the tower as a warning against ambition and pride, it could simultaneously act as a showcase for developments and achievements in the medieval mason's art.

Despite the challenges presented by its often bizarre imagery, illustrations of the Book of Revelation are not uncommon in medieval art. The Whore of Babylon,[135] holding the golden cup and seated upon the beast with seven heads, is one such image, while again the Beatus manuscripts such as the *Silos Apocalypse* furnish some of the most vivid images, including of the destruction of Babylon itself. The most impressive of all medieval representations of the apocalypse, however, is the incredible late fourteenth-century *Apocalypse of Angers*, in which the subject matter, conventions and vivid imaginative qualities of manuscript illustrations of Revelation are rendered in large-scale tapestries of astonishing elegance and beauty (Figure 5).[136] The work, still displayed at the Château d'Angers, is monumental: the apocalypse is depicted in six tapestry sections, each around 4.5 m in height and with a combined length of over 100 m.[137]

Medieval images of events in the ancient past employ contemporary architecture and costume and only rarely feature visible 'oriental' motifs. They do not attempt to reconstruct the fashions of past ages: no equivalent yet existed of the later Renaissance antiquarian and numismatic studies on which the first attempts at such authenticity would be based.[138] Instead they lend emphasis and colour to a knowledge of Near Eastern antiquity that was necessarily based purely on textual sources, and from which little information on appearances could be derived. They served to fire the imagination, and to breathe life into the accounts they illustrated. Much the same could be said of those references to ancient Mesopotamia that occurred in the decoration of churches,[139] and which were available to a broader public than manuscripts, which after all were barred to most on grounds of literacy and expense. Some tapestries would also have had a wider audience: it is thought that the *Apocalypse of Angers* itself was hung in Angers Cathedral on some feast days.

Secular contexts for the illustration of Babylon are fewer. One notable survival is the story of Pyramus and Thisbe, retold by Boccaccio in the *Decameron* and by Chaucer in his *Legend of Good Women*.[140] An ivory box in the collections of the Metropolitan Museum of Art shows something of the medieval cultural context for the story, including it alongside other episodes from courtly literature, including Aristotle teaching Alexander, Phyllis riding Aristotle, and the assault on the Castle of Love (Figure 6). Certainly there are differences between what would be considered 'canonical' Babylon stories in the medieval and Renaissance worlds and in later periods, partly as a consequence of the greater medieval reliance on Latin (as opposed to Greek) sources. The medieval image of Semiramis – very positive, as one of the Nine Worthy Women – was based on a story absent from the Greek accounts, but told by the Roman historian Valerius Maximus. On hearing of a revolt in Babylon whilst at her toilette, Semiramis pauses to lead an army to crush the rebellion before returning to finish combing her hair. She is identifiable in medieval images by her long, unbrushed hair – symbolism which may feature in the Venus of Botticelli's *Primavera*.[141] More explicitly, the theme survives beyond the Renaissance and into the Baroque paintings of Guercino, who produced three major versions of Semiramis receiving word of the revolt.[142]

Returning to scriptural sources, a different model of feminine virtue and physical courage was the image of Judith beheading Holofernes in his tent, thereby preventing the sack of Bethulia. In the Book of Judith, Holofernes is a general of Nebuchadnezzar, though this Nebuchadnezzar was 'king of the Assyrians, and reigned in Nineveh'.[143] The story has long been understood to relate to its own, second- to first-century BC political context, with competing theories on the identity of 'Nebuchadnezzar'. The subject of Judith beheading Holofernes appears regularly in medieval manuscripts, and has been treated by many artists, including Giorgione, Michelangelo, Lucas Cranach, Caravaggio and Artemisia Gentileschi; more recent notable examples include works by Francisco Goya and Gustav Klimt.

Babylon in medieval cosmology: the case of Dante

Although its references to Mesopotamia are all brief, Dante's *Divine Comedy* is important here for two reasons. First, the contemporary and later influence of Dante's work in general lends enormous weight to the mentions it does make of Babylon in terms of representation. Second, the *Divine Comedy* is essentially a moral categorization of human beings by type, based in large part on the personal values and prejudices that in many (though by no means all) cases Dante shared with other Christian thinkers of his age. The *Divine Comedy*'s careful classification of sin and virtue is exactly the kind of grand model C. S. Lewis had in mind when writing *The Discarded Image*.[144] The model successfully integrates biblical and classical traditions, as well as applying itself to Dante's contemporary world.[145] Its categories and hierarchies hold many surprises for the present-day reader. Alexander, for example, is to be found in the river of blood around the seventh circle of hell, with Attila and other 'tyrants, who took to sword and pillaging',[146] while Saladin is placed in Limbo, the first circle of hell and the best fate available to a non-Christian in this scheme.[147] Both placements at first seem anachronistic in an age of religious crusades, yet the treatment of Saladin must be reconciled with the awful fate Dante writes for the Prophet Mohammed. The author cannot be mistaken for displaying a great tolerance of Islam.[148]

The only mention of the city of Babylon is in the highest reaches of heaven, as a great trial that has been passed:

> Oh what great wealth, crammed down in there, among
>> These richest coffers which, below on earth,
>> Were goodly husbandmen, and true seed flung.
> Here they have life and joy in just that worth
>> Of treasure, earned in banishment and weeping
>> In Babylon, and scorning gold for dearth.[149]

The biblical reference is to Psalm 137, and the role of Babylon is that of purgatory-on-Earth. More use is made of the Babylon of Revelation, in the sense that Dante's visions in the earthly paradise[150] relate closely to those of Revelation. Unlike Augustine, Dante uses them for the condemnation of Rome, but the meaning is nonetheless quite different from that of Revelation itself. This time the attack is directed at Christian Rome, and the corruption of the Church.

Despite such scant reference to the city as a whole, several characters associated with Babylon are treated individually. Semiramis is found very early on, in the second circle of hell, reserved for sexual sinners and battered by an eternal storm. She is grouped with, among others, Cleopatra, Tristan and the lovers of the *Iliad*: Achilles, Paris, Helen. Virgil describes her to Dante:

'The first of those of whom you question, she's
    Empress of many tongues,' he then replied
    'And so undone with lechery that her decrees
Mingled her lust into her law and tried
    To shift away from her own acts the blame
    Which to her own loose conduct had applied.
Queen Semiramis was her earthly name;
    We read she was to Ninus wife and heir.
    She held the land which is the Sultan's claim.'[151]

This account is enough to confirm that Dante's Semiramis is a combination of those described by Ctesias and Athenaeus, via Diodorus Siculus and presumably a Latin translation or epitome. One possible source is Orosius who, as has already been noted, emphasized and elaborated Semiramis' sexual transgressions.[152] Certainly his *History Against the Pagans* was a particularly popular and much-reproduced work in the Middle Ages.[153] Further, although a name is not given it seems likely that Dante designates Orosius as a 'little light' in the fourth heaven, that of the sun,[154] supporting the suggestion that he used and respected Orosius' work.[155]

Other aspects of the account show contemporary influence. 'The land which is the Sultan's claim' suggests that Dante, like John Mandeville and others, understood Babylon to be an ancient name for Cairo, although the reference is perhaps too vague to be sure. More significantly, while Semiramis' behaviour is drawn from classical sources, the moral dimension of Virgil's comment on that behaviour is framed in an apparently original way. The Semiramis of Ctesias certainly does not try 'to shift away from her own acts the blame'. She is a semi-mythical barbarian queen and, like a Greek immortal, is presumed not to care. Whatever the case, a wide gulf separates Semiramis from Babylon's other representative in hell, Nimrod. Interestingly the latter is not identified with Ninus, Ctesias' founder of Babylon, and no attempt is made to resolve this apparent conflict of founders. There is some indication that for Dante the conflict did not occur. On the one hand, some later sources suggest the concept of a dispersal immediately after the confusion of tongues, followed by a re-founding of Babylon; on the other, Nimrod, when we finally reach him in the lowest reaches of hell, is clearly a creature of another age.[156] Nimrod is in the ninth circle for his treachery to God, and is conceived as one of the giants who made war on heaven. While the previous levels of hell have involved dire and violent punishments, the giants are simply chained and still appear very dangerous. Nimrod is given the longest description of any of them, and even has a speech, though it is nonsense. As Virgil explains to Dante:

> He told me: 'He condemns himself in speech.
>   This is the Nimrod, through whose evil spurred,
>   We cannot speak one language, each to each.
> Let's leave him standing there, nor waste a word
>   For every language is the same to him,
>   As his own to us, senseless, absurd.'[157]

The monstrous, chained, giant Nimrod is part of the climax of the *Inferno*, and is much more prominent than the later passage, in the *Purgatorio*, where we encounter a figure more familiar to us. Here Dante and Virgil walk along a path where the proud are depicted to be trodden underfoot, and see Nimrod witnessing the ruin of his tower. The two representations are not factually inconsistent, but that of the *Inferno* certainly does conflict with the Nimrod of our medieval illustrations of the Tower, of which that described in the *Purgatorio* seems more representative. Moral teaching lies at the heart of all these works, and in this respect the monstrous giant who wars against heaven and the man who is misguided merely by dint of ambition and pride are very different. The latter description is an example from which one is intended to learn humility, the former a shocking image from which one can learn only fear: of Nimrod, of God, and of hell.[158]

Nebuchadnezzar is not one of the characters Dante meets, and he receives only a brief reference:

> And Beatrice [Dante's love and guide through Heaven] took the role on Daniel thrust,
>> In saving Nebuchadnezzar from the ire
>> That rendered him so cruel and unjust.[159]

Considering Dante's theme of sin and redemption and Nebuchadnezzar's biblical fame, this cursory treatment is strange. One explanation may lie in the complications of the Book of Daniel itself. Dante's original source presents two morally quite different versions of the king, only one of whom finds any kind of redemption. Dante's model is intended to punish and reward tendencies more than specific actions, and specific actions are always taken to be indicative of the whole personality of those he meets in the *Divine Comedy*. The system works by rule, not degree, and although individuals in the *Purgatorio* may display a mixture of virtues and vices, they are consistent. Nebuchadnezzar's shifting pattern of cruelty, madness and submission to wise counsel is difficult to incorporate. Dante's apparent resolution of the problem, a simpler arc of sin and, through Daniel, redemption, involves a sleight of hand, but is also a very neat, very medieval solution.

Dürer and the image of the apocalypse

The religious politics of the Reformation profoundly influenced Babylon's place in European cultural life, as the 'violent conflict for souls' unfolding in northern Europe turned the image of the apocalypse into a tool for sectarian mud-slinging.[160] Babylon was caught up in this battle as reformers drew on the language of Revelation to attack the present-day city of sin they saw increasingly in the Roman Church.

Early signs of the blurring between the Babylon of Revelation and the contemporary, lived world can be seen in the famous *Apocalypse* woodcuts of Albrecht Dürer, published in 1498. Dürer's Whore of Babylon is a richly adorned courtesan in contemporary Venetian dress (Figure 7).[161] The 'peoples of the Earth' drawn to her also wear contemporary dress, and notably include a monk and a Turk in the foreground. All this, however, is set amid the fantastic visions of Revelation. The Whore of Babylon herself is the main focus of the image, holding aloft the golden cup filled with obscenities.[162] She rides upon a seven-headed beast, while above her the angels prophesying Babylon's destruction[163] and the armies of the Knight Called Faithful and True[164] descend upon the world. In the background the city of Babylon itself erupts in flame.

In depicting the complex, hallucinatory visions of Revelation Dürer faced a particular challenge, greater than that of his medieval predecessors. Following Luther's views (Dürer's admiration for Luther is well documented, although he remained a Catholic throughout his life), his images had to remain subordinate to – and thus strictly illustrative of – the text. As as result, 'Where the imaginings of the text are most implausible Dürer was obliged to be most literal'.[165] The result was as original as it was dazzling.

Produced at the close of the fifteenth century, Dürer's *Apocalyspe* was to influence practically all northern European printed illustrations of the subject in the sixteenth,[166] as the theme's role in the imagery of the Reformation developed. The association in reformist minds between vice-ridden, corrupt Babylon and the comtemporary Roman Church could be expressed through devices similar to those by which Dürer had mixed visionary and material, ancient and contemporary elements in his woodcuts. Of particular importance, given the impact and dissemination of Luther's own German translation of the New Testament, published in 1522 and better known as the *September Testament*, are the images produced for this publication by Lucas Cranach, whose apocalypse woodcuts were strongly influenced by those of Dürer but also carry clear attacks on Rome. Making the link explicit, Cranach's *Destruction of Babylon* used Rome as depicted in Hartmann Schedel's 1493 *Nuremberg Chronicle* as its model.[167] From the abstract symbol of worldliness Babylon had become through the influence of St Augustine, it was once again returning to a physical locus; and as in the day of St John the Divine that locus was Rome.

Pieter Bruegel and the Tower of Babel

By far the most famous images of the Tower of Babel today are the late sixteenth-century paintings of Pieter Bruegel the Elder (Figure 8). Bruegel produced three paintings of the Tower, of which two survive.[168] Filled with minute detail and showing a masterful understanding of architecture, the paintings are also famous for the strong political statement they made by placing the Tower of Babel, symbol of pride and decay, in a contemporary Flemish setting. They were much imitated, providing the basic model for a major genre in the late sixteenth and early seventeenth centuries.

Familiar settings can be misleading. The artist acquired the nickname 'peasant Bruegel' for his depictions of everyday peasant life, and for a long time his work was considered to be very straightforward and not at all intellectual. It was often asserted, following the biographical account of Carel van Mander, that Bruegel was by birth a peasant himself.[169] This was never a view easily reconciled with darker, stranger works such as *The Triumph of Death* or *Dulle Griet*, and twentieth-century scholarship on Bruegel made the traditional position increasingly untenable. Charles de Tolnay, the author most responsible for promoting a new perspective on the artist,[170] is now generally seen as having gone too far in his portrayal of Bruegel as a radical and member of the House of Love, but the considerable literary and scholarly content of his works is now widely acknowledged. As for his peasant scenes, many are now seen as far more pessimistic and satirical than was once thought. Very little biographical information survives about the artist himself, although there is some limited evidence suggesting that he associated with a humanist intellectual circle including the cartographer Abraham Ortelius.[171] He probably produced some risqué work that does not survive: on his deathbed he seems to have ordered his wife to burn some of his drawings.

Whether, as has often been suggested, this work was strongly political, however, is far from clear.[172]

Information on Bruegel's cultural and intellectual influences must therefore be drawn from the paintings themselves. There is sufficient iconographic evidence in Bruegel's oeuvre to suggest that the artist had a considerable familiarity with the ideas of Erasmus, who seems to be the source for many of the proverbs and puns illustrated in his paintings.[173] Perhaps more importantly, Bruegel's work seems to follow an Erasmian prescription for the visual representation of history. Erasmus thought it stupid and pointless to attempt to reconstruct the past by 'dressing Flemings in Greek costumes', and rather felt that the aim was to make the past live in the present.[174] This position on visual art (on which subject Erasmus wrote rarely) is a direct extension of his broader position that the writers of classical antiquity had tangible and practical lessons for life in the present. Bruegel takes the same approach, and does so with intelligence and great emotive force. His *Massacre of the Innocents*[175] is perhaps the most compelling of all demonstrations of the past 'living in the present'. By placing this awful scene in a mundane contemporary setting, Bruegel brings perhaps even more horror to the subject than the painfully graphic depiction of the same event by Rubens.[176] More prosaically, there is a good chance that Bruegel refers here to political events of his own day, and to persecution of Calvinists and others by the Inquisition.[177] This much also applies to the Tower of Babel paintings. The architecture of the tower itself is classical, but the town over which it looms is sixteenth-century Antwerp. In terms of a contemporary political meaning, it is quite likely that Nimrod in the Vienna painting actually represents Philip II of Spain.[178] Spanish rule in the Netherlands included an active role for the Inquisition, and if we accept that Bruegel had links to prominent humanists such as Ortelius this would certainly have affected his own circle. The suggestion that Nimrod and the Tower's builders might be Philip and his supporters is rather clearer in the Tower of Babel paintings produced by some followers of Bruegel than in his own work, however, and interestingly the Rotterdam panel does not feature Nimrod at all.[179] Figures in Lucas van Valckenborch's Tower of Babel paintings feature obviously Spanish costume, a more open criticism available to the Protestant Valckenborch, who had already fled the Inquisition to settle in Germany.

As with a great deal of Bruegel's work, there are multiple additional meanings and even ambiguity in the main theme.[180] Thus, while the towers certainly refer to doomed pride, they also seem to have a role in the utopian ideas of the day. The confusion of tongues was an important theme, not least because of wider issues regarding linguistic and especially religious diversity in the Low Countries. It has been pointed out that the vast number of Tower of Babel paintings produced by Dutch and Flemish artists in the later sixteenth and early seventeenth centuries appear at just the same time as the production and publication of the first Polyglot Bible. There can be no doubt that questions of language in this context were bound up with questions of religion and the politics of the Reformation. Bruegel himself is not known to have been a Protestant, but there are several instances in his work that suggest he was part of the very broad base of criticism of the Catholic hierarchy and its privileges. (A very small feature in the centre of the Rotterdam painting shows what looks like a cardinal's procession moving up the Tower, though it is ambiguous enough that the artist could easily have denied that any such impression was intended.[181]) The limitations of human division and failure to some extent imply the potential to succeed through unity, whether of language or religion, and the idea that despite its pessimistic primary message a second, more utopian strand exists in Bruegel's paintings is plausible, indeed almost characteristic: that celebration, sympathy and satire are so closely bound up in works such as *Wedding Feast* helps to explain why the satirical aspects of the work went so long unrecognized. Similarly, while the relevance of the Tower of Babel is moral, it is rather more than a simple didactic moral lesson on pride; in some ways it is a contemporary moral theological question left unresolved.

Bruegel's towers themselves are gigantic structures, classical in their architecture and quite unlike the contemporary towns and harbours at their feet. The model is the Colosseum, the greatest known building of antiquity and of course one associated with Rome.

The influence of Bruegel's choice has been enormous, but he was not the first to base his Tower on the Roman monument. A 1547 etching by Cornelis Anthonisz is probably the earliest example. In this image the tower is depicted as falling, almost exploding, as a terrified populace (some of whose poses are obviously modelled on famous classical sculptures) run for safety from falling masonry.[182] Nor would Bruegel actually have needed to travel to Italy in order to gain detailed architectural knowledge of the Colosseum: an excellent alternative source was available in the form of prints made by Hieronymus Cock, whom Bruegel knew personally. He did go, however, working in Rome for about five years. It is known that during this period he worked closely with the miniaturist Giulio Clovio, probably painting landscape backgrounds to Clovio's figure work.[183] Through Clovio Bruegel had access either to a Gerard Horenbout image in the *Grimani Breviary*, to Clovio's close copy of it for the *Farnese Hours*, or to both.[184] The extent to which this image forms the model for Bruegel's towers may not be immediately apparent in isolation, but if it is compared with more traditional manuscript illustrations the connection appears very strong indeed. The colossal scale of the tower in the *Grimani Breviary* is an innovation, as is the deep, naturalistic landscape in which it is set. It was for their landscape painting (although the genre did not yet exist independently) that northern artists were appreciated in Italy, and Bruegel himself went on to transform this important aspect of Netherlandish art. Building on the work of Joachim Patinir, Bruegel developed the concept of the 'world landscape', using a combination of techniques to incorporate views over vast composite landscapes into his compositions.[185] The Tower of Babel is one example: in one sense the setting is Antwerp; in another, as the viewer appreciates instinctively, it is the world at large. The towers do not fit perfectly into the world landscape model, in that one would normally expect more prominent mountainous alpine elements, although these do occur in paintings of the subject by other artists following Bruegel. Nonetheless it can be seen that Bruegel contrives to present a much larger area, and from a more elevated perspective, than his subject strictly requires, altering perspective in order to do so. Compare the view from a raised foreground with that of a more clear-cut example, such as Bruegel's own *Landscape with the Fall of Icarus*, and the nature of the genre becomes more apparent.

A great deal, perhaps too much, has been read into the architectural feasibility of Bruegel's depictions and the many paintings that followed. If the structure appears possible from an engineering perspective, is the implication that humanity can potentially succeed in its endeavours? On the other hand, are failings in the architecture incidental or meaningful in the paintings' message?[186] A further sense in which the architecture is meaningful is surely the connection with Rome. In Protestant prints of the same period, the Babylon of Revelation was equated not only with imperial Rome but with the papal Rome of the present.[187] Babylon was an important Reformation motif, used far more often against the Catholic Church than in its defence. The ruined triumph of imperial Roman architecture would make an excellent symbol through which to criticize hubris in the contemporary Roman power. There is no compelling reason to think that Bruegel was not an orthodox, practicing Catholic, let alone that he was a member of the House of Love, but this does not necessarily preclude veiled criticism of the earthly trappings of his faith.

The Tower of Babel pictures relate to present and past in several ways. They contain probable references to specific people and issues of the artist's day, more universal messages about pride, hubris and possibly even utopia; most importantly, they demonstrate a quite complex basis for the location of a historical subject in a present-day setting. All of these features fall under the general heading of relating to and understanding the past. When European travellers visited Babylon in the sixteenth century they noted that, as they had read, the city was destroyed and its ruins had become infested with wild beasts. The value of further empirical investigation on-site was not yet at all obvious. New knowledge of the past, for a scholar like Erasmus, lay in the study and interpretation of texts. The value of that knowledge, and in one sense even its culmination, lay in the application of these readings to the contemporary world, and clearly Bruegel made a greater contribution in this respect than the travellers who visited and described the site of Babylon in his day. Bruegel's paintings represent a sophisticated engagement with the distant past, and rather than a secondary use of the available information or a fancy, they also represent an active position on the relevance and meaning of that past in the present.

Bruegel's paintings sparked the development of an entire genre. Between the mid-sixteenth and early seventeenth centuries there appeared dozens of paintings and drawings of the Tower of Babel, some by students of Bruegel himself, treated in an often almost identical manner. Hendrick van Cleve, Lucas and Marten van Valckenborch, Pieter Brueghel the Younger, Abel Grimmer and many more produced images following the basic format of Bruegel's paintings.[188] The architectural details of the towers in these images tend to be modelled on classical ruins, particularly the Roman Colosseum, while the surrounding towns and harbours are recognizable as towns in the artists' contemporary environments. Bruegel had created a vision of the Tower that, though entirely of his own creation, has defined the monument's appearance in the European imagination ever since.

Athanasius Kircher

No Mesopotamian visual reference points were available for Bruegel's Tower of Babel paintings, or for any other European image of Babylon, prior to the late seventeenth century. Arguably the first are the drawings commissioned by Pietro Della Valle on his travels, showing a present-day tell (Tell Babil, which for Della Valle was the Tower of Babel), and with the inscribed bricks brought to Europe during the seventeenth and eighteenth centuries by Della Valle, Engelbert Kämpfer, who visited Iran in 1686,[189] and the Abbé Barthélemy.[190] These still constitute a meagre resource – the Della Valle images show only a tell, and reveal nothing of its contents. Nonetheless, such images and the descriptions they accompanied began to play a role. The scholar whose work most clearly bridges the gap between Renaissance and modern thought on Babylon, as on so many topics, is the seventeenth-century Jesuit priest, collector *extraordinaire* and polymath Athanasius Kircher.

Kircher's *Turris Babel* is a unique theological and historical work, incorporating the observations of Pietro Della Valle, the implications of Old Testament chronology, the Babylonian histories of Ctesias and Herodotus, the moral aspects of the story of the Tower of Babel and a treatise on linguistics.[191] Fascinated by languages and their origins (he is best known to Egyptologists for his serious but unsuccessful attempt to decipher hieroglyphs), Kircher had a strong interest in the Genesis confusion of tongues and hence the Tower of Babel. He was not alone in treating the question of the original, so-called Adamic, language spoken by Adam and Eve in the Garden of Eden; the most commonly held view was that the Hebrew of the Pentateuch must represent that language, and that all others were created by the confusion of tongues. From this starting point, Kircher took a philological approach, considering many languages and seeking to understand their relationships to one another. In effect the great work was almost a universal history of language: its goal was to explain how languages had multiplied and spread since Babel.[192]

Turris Babel confronts the present-day reader with the full extent of the epistemological gulf between seventeenth-century and contemporary academic thought, and gives the lie to the quite deceptive modern intelligibility of some travel accounts of its time. It also challenges the tendency to assume that, on the basis of knowledge building up in a linear and cumulative way, scholarly works such as Kircher's will tend to be more 'modern' in their assumptions and arguments than less scholarly works, such as travel accounts, that rely more heavily on hearsay, folklore and contemporary common knowledge. *Turris Babel* is a supremely scholarly work drawing on a multitude of sources, and the Babylon Kircher presents is in some ways the most complete version we will encounter in any source, yet when taken as a whole it is more obviously alien to a modern archaeological or historical account than the narratives of the ancient Greek historians. In trying to resolve all available knowledge about Babylon, Kircher created a work that required of its reader a great openness to the divine, the magical and the fantastic. The combination of completeness and implausibility is not a coincidence but the direct result of the challenge Kircher set himself. *Turris Babel* works to achieve a harmony, consistency and completeness that is simply impossible, and in so doing creates a vision of Babel that is rich and strange in equal measure. Nor did Kircher's scholarship inhibit his imagination: his attention to the sources is studious, yet with them he builds a description of Babylon far more detailed and complete than they could possibly allow.[193]

Kircher's dating for the foundation of Babylon takes as its basis the life of Noah. He offers three sequences of dates, counting forward from the beginning of the world; based on the age of Noah; and counting forward from the Flood, at which point the world had existed for 1657 years.[194] According to this system he places a co-regency of Nimrod and Belus (the Bel known from classical sources, the Babylonian god Marduk) at the end of the second millennium, with both their deaths in the 1996th year of the world (the 940th of Noah's life and the 340th since the Flood). They are immediately succeeded by Ninus, who nine years later also becomes king of Assyria. This must owe something to Diodorus, whose Ninus 'set about the task of subduing the nations of Asia, and within a period of seventeen years he became master of them all except the Indians and Bactrians'.[195] Accordingly Ninus is succeeded by Semiramis, but here Kircher diverges from Diodorus, and as in the chronology of al-Biruni she is succeeded not by Ninyas but by Zameis. Nimrod reigns for at least 250 years, against Ninus' and Semiramis' shorter but still lengthy reigns of 52 and 42 years, respectively.[196] These should not necessarily be taken to imply natural lifespans, since Semiramis was the contemporary of Ninus, but the pattern of a gradual reduction in life expectancy follows the model of the Old Testament. The many images in *Turris Babel* were mainly designed by Conraet Decker and were commissioned by Kircher for the purpose. They present a great variety of views of the Tower and the city, although conforming to a general pattern similar to that of the Flemish painters whereby Roman ruins and Egyptian obelisks were mixed with more contemporary architecture. Nimrod, Ninus and Semiramis are all shown in Roman military dress.[197]

One of the problems with producing a consistent representation of the Tower of Babel was the contradiction between its apparent destruction very early in human history and the accounts of its existence, and indeed destruction at human hands, in Greek histories. Kircher adopts Orosius' solution to this problem: a second Tower, built by Ninus and Semiramis. This interpretation apparently still held some currency for Rich and Keppel in the early nineteenth century. (Indeed a similar problem is still being resolved today, in that Herodotus describes a temple that was once thought, by the time of his visit to Mesopotamia, to have been completely destroyed by Xerxes.[198]) This position, however, hardly begins to account for the array of towers presented as images in the book, which range from a gigantic neo-classical wedding cake to the nondescript tells recorded by Pietro della Valle's artist. As well as the Tower(s) of Babel, illustrations include views of the entire city and of the Hanging Gardens. The former is laid out on a grid pattern, after Herodotus, with the river (only one, contradicting other maps in the book where the Tigris and Euphrates meet in Babylon) running through the centre, and monumental buildings in the centre of the city and on either side of the river. The whole city is surrounded by a moat, with bridges running into the walls at regular intervals through the 100 gates mentioned by Herodotus. Despite the tendency towards classical architecture, particularly in the Tower, an Asian setting is indicated: in the foreground figures in exotic dress, some mounted on elephants, move towards the city.

Perhaps the most remarkable elements of *Turris Babel* are Kircher's attempts to bring scientific and humanistic analysis to bear on those aspects of the Tower of Babel tradition hardest to interpret literally, namely the attempt to build the tower up to heaven and the subsequent confusion of tongues. This approach simply does not admit of allegory, and Kircher graphically demonstrates the impossibility of building a tower to reach heaven. That impossibility, furthermore, is argued not in philosophical or theological but in mechanical terms, on the basis of the astronomical insight that the nearest heavenly body, the moon, is simply *too far up*. Kircher calculates that to reach the moon the tower would require three million tonnes of material, stand 178,672 miles high, and would tip the Earth from its axis (Figure 9). The combination of biblical literalism and Enlightenment astronomy used to reach this conclusion seems absurd, particularly when rendered as a visual image, but the case is a perfect microcosm of the challenges Kircher faced in studying the Tower of Babel. The domains of theology, philosophy and empirical research had begun to chafe against one another in unexpected and sometimes alarming ways.

Rembrandt

Images based on the Book of Daniel continue in the sixteenth and seventeenth centuries, one common subject being Belshazzar's Feast. Typically such images showed the king's more or less orientalized banqueting hall, guests and sometimes the writing on the wall, but by far the most famous and important example is in almost every way atypical: Rembrandt's masterpiece *Belshazzar's Feast* (*c.*1636–8) has much more to do with the artist's unique religious vision and approach to the representation of history and the Bible than with the art of his contemporaries (Figure 10). Rembrandt's huge canvas focuses tightly on Belshazzar himself, revealing only a small group of bystanders and a single table from the great feast. Belshazzar, recoiling, stares in horror at the writing on the wall as it appears before him. He is dressed in an orientalizing costume that was almost certainly copied, along with the king's pose, from a Pieter Lastman painting of *Esther and Ahasuerus*.[199] Other figures in the painting also have models in earlier paintings,[200] though Belshazzar's is the only one to feature an oriental costume of any kind. Rembrandt took no part in the wave of interest in Persian costume then current among Dutch painters, nor in the vogue for Turkish costume that had preceded it.[201] His major source of 'oriental' costume was probably the Jewish population of Amsterdam,[202] alongside, as here, figures in other paintings. In truth, all treatment of historical accuracy in terms of material culture seems utterly irrelevant here. The elements that matter are Rembrandt's portrayal of the king, his personality, his emotions, and of the divine writing itself.

The painting's inscription has been the subject of much debate. Written in Hebrew characters, it contains the Aramaic inscription *mene mene tekel upharsin*. Its format, however, is highly peculiar, arranging the letters not in horizontal lines but vertical columns. Attempting to read the inscription normally, i.e. in horizontal lines right-to-left, produces nonsense. The device is a response to a scholarly problem arising from the Daniel account of the incident: why, in the court of the king of Babylon, could only one person (Daniel) not only interpret but even *read* an inscription given in the Near Eastern lingua franca of Aramaic? The solution of vertical columns can be traced to the Babylonian Talmud, where it is attributed to Rabbi Samuel,[203] and was probably given to Rembrandt by the famous Amsterdam Rabbi Menasseh ben Israel.[204]

In one sense, then, the painting is very scholarly, but its purpose is not to mystify and its central, emotional meaning is immediate and direct. In the figure of Belshazzar Rembrandt captures the mixture of alarm, fear and guilt that are the real subject of the painting. This is an encounter with the divine whose human dimension was of great importance to Rembrandt, as would also be the case in many of his later biblical works. Lit by the writing on the wall, the skin tones of the king break with artistic convention: where normally cold and warm tones are alternated, here Rembrandt uses exclusively warm tones, contributing to the work's theatrical quality. The king's pose, at once turning towards and pulling away from the writing, causes his figure to fill a large part of the canvas, physically dominating it and contributing to the movement as the surrounding figures also react to the apparition.[205] The king himself is middle-aged and his face lined. Rembrandt offers a Belshazzar who is careworn, strangely ordinary for all his pomp. This is a picture of a rich and powerful man discovering his own ruin, and of the power of God over mortals. Just as much as Bruegel, Rembrandt is an artist concerned with the meaning of his historical subject in the present.

CHAPTER 5

DISCOVERIES AND FANTASIES: ENLIGHTENMENT AND MODERN APPROACHES

Explorers, antiquaries and archaeologists

The seventeenth and eighteenth centuries saw huge changes in European intellectual culture. Enlightenment scholarship brought forth new ideas and new approaches to studying the world in a flood, from the models for understanding sensory experience proposed by Bacon and Descartes to the transformative contributions to physics and mathematics of Newton and Leibniz. The network of scholars was international, the scope of their researches cross-disciplinary, and sooner or later the implications of their work came to be felt in almost every area of scholarship. It should come as no surprise that over the course of the eighteenth century descriptions of ancient sites such as Babylon came to exhibit far more in the way of empirical inquiry than those of the past.

Early eighteenth-century attempts to establish the site of Babylon already have a somewhat different character from their predecessors. The existence of two distinct proposed sites for the Tower of Babel may have spurred some empirical research and comparison with ancient sources. The Dominican monk Pére Emmanuel de St Albert makes explicit mention of two possible sites for Babylon, both of which he visited in 1700, and of which neither is 'Aqar Quf.[1] Rather, he identifies a problem that would puzzle visitors until the time of Koldewey: the apparently competing sites of Birs Nimrud, which he describes as lying in Arabia, and the ruins on the eastern bank of the Euphrates, that is the actual ruins of Babylon. Jean Otter, visiting in May 1743, apparently had no confusion regarding the site, insofar as it was in the general area of Hillah, and was aware of a surviving local tradition of calling all or part of it Babel. Otter, an orientalist who would later become professor of Arabic at the Collège de France, cites not other recent travellers but rather the 'Géographe Turc' (meaning Ahmed Dede Müneccimbaşı, author of the seventeenth-century universal history *Camiu'd-Düvel*, 'The Chronology of Nations')[2] and the Qur'anic reference to Harut and Marut.[3]

Niebuhr and Beauchamp

The late eighteenth century is notable for two particularly influential visitors' accounts of Babylon: those of Carsten Niebuhr and the Abbé Joseph de Beauchamp. Writing his history of the field in 1904, Hilprecht saw their accounts as an important transitional point. In introducing the two he drew a firm distinction between their approaches and those of their predecessors,[4] describing the latter as 'Travellers, whose education was limited, and missionaries who viewed those ruins chiefly from a religious standpoint,' in contrast to the 'strictly scientific interest in the ruins of Babylon' shown by Niebuhr, Beauchamp and their successors.[5]

Carsten Niebuhr travelled in Asia between 1761 and 1768, visiting the area of Babylon in 1765. The account of Babylon forms part of his *Reisebeschreibung nach Arabien und andern umliegenden Ländern*.[6] As the only surviving member of the six-man scientific expedition sent by Frederick V of Denmark, Niebuhr was obliged to write as a polymath and did so with dazzling success. Not the least of his abilities, however, was a prosaic one: the careful attention to detail he brought to his recording. This proved of immense value both to the early excavators benefiting from his maps and plans, and perhaps even more to the decipherers of cuneiform scripts. The inscriptions Niebuhr copied at Persepolis were later used by Georg Grotefend to make the first steps in the decipherment of Old Persian, a success which in turn would contribute to the unlocking of the more complex syllabic cuneiform scripts.

Pierre Joseph de Beauchamp, then vicaire général in Baghdad, visited Babylon twice during the 1880s. As well as conducting modest investigations of his own at the ruins, Beauchamp questioned one of the diggers for bricks at the site. Nebuchadnezzar's baked bricks from the site made an excellent modern building material and had long been recycled for use in new buildings in the surrounding area – indeed the process would continue throughout the nineteenth century. Beauchamp was given a remarkable account:

> I was informed by the master mason employed to dig for bricks that the places from which he procured them were large thick walls and sometimes chambers. He has frequently found earthen vessels, engraved marbles, and about eight years ago a statue as large as life, which he threw amongst the rubbish. On one wall of a chamber he found the figure of a cow, and of the sun and moon, formed of glazed-bricks. Sometimes idols of clay are found representing human figures.[7]

This was the most accurate description of the contents of the Babylon mounds yet to occur in a European source. Beauchamp did not have the means to discover what a good informant he had found, but the glazed-brick bull reliefs and Babylonian terracottas discovered by much later excavators are clearly the objects to which the mason refers.

Beauchamp took care to confirm Niebuhr's measurements, including making his own calculations of Babylon's latitude.[8] This detail reflects a broader change: as the numbers of travellers increased, and as a greater and more permanent European imperial presence was being established in many parts of the world, European mapping of the world was becoming more accurate and more complete. The ability to give precise coordinates to something as exotic as Babylon has its own impact. The site is no longer a vague area on the edge of the known geography, but a manageable part of it that submits to its rules as easily as anything else. As such edges of known geography became less common, so they became increasingly interesting, even fetishized.[9] In the nineteenth century, the tension between discovery and the exhaustion of these boundaries is most clearly reflected in the fame and fascination of Henry Morton Stanley and David Livingstone's meeting on the shores of Lake Tanganyika. Stanley emphasizes the fact that the last certain location he had for Livingstone was 10° S on the Eastern coast of the continent, and that with Livingstone having been 58 months in the interior this knowledge would be of no help.[10] Africa, in other words, was still beyond such control. By enlarging the known, controlled world, geographical expertise equally shrank the unknown. The role of mystery and mythology in understandings of faraway places such as Babylon was being gradually eroded, although it could be argued that the value of what remained exotic and beyond reach correspondingly increased.

Claudius Rich

Claudius Rich was East India Company Resident in Baghdad 1808–21, and visited Babylon in 1811 (Figure 11). This visit, in the form of Rich's *Memoir on the Ruins of Babylon*, first published in the *Mines de l'Orient* in 1813 and subsequently reproduced as a separate book, was by far the most detailed report on the site yet produced.[11] Not only is Rich's observation thorough, but his knowledge of earlier sources, many of which were not available to him while he was writing in Baghdad, is impressively wide-ranging. These qualities lead to an account at once based on empirical observation and informed by older sources, whether biblical, classical or the reports of travellers, and thus acts as a review of these sources based on Rich's own experience. Thanks partly to the author's own ability in Arabic, Turkish, Persian and Hebrew, the *Memoir* is also an interesting, if not very complimentary, source on local knowledge and stories relating to various parts of the site.

Rich's account includes the journey from Baghdad to Hillah, detailing the route and distances. This journey includes a dried up canal known as the 'Naher Malcha, or *fluvius regius*, the work, it is said, of Nebuchadnezzar'.[12] In discussing Babylon itself, Rich works south to north across the mounds, describing each one in some detail. He also provides a series of views of the mounds on two of his three plates. (The third is a now quite famous plan of Babylon, by far the most accurate yet produced.) In the course of the description, he resolves a number of points arising from earlier travellers' accounts. This is not incidental, but at times feels like the structuring principle and purpose of his description; in this, it is distinguished from all other travel accounts referred to here with the possible exception of the far later (and in tone rather more quarrelsome) *By Nile and Tigris* of E. A. Wallis Budge.[13] Rich felt strongly that there was a need to improve on what he saw as the incomplete and misleading sources available. To demonstrate his point (and extremely helpfully from our perspective), the author introduces his account by describing his own first impressions of Babylon explicitly in relation to the preconceptions he was conscious of bringing with him to the site:

I have frequently had occasion to remark the inadequacy of general descriptions to convey an accurate idea of persons or places. I found this particularly exemplified in the present instance. From the accounts of modern travellers, I had expected to have found on the site of Babylon more, and less, than I actually did. Less, because I could have formed no conception of the prodigious extent of the whole ruins, or of the size, solidity, and perfect state, of some of the parts of them; and more, because I thought that I should have distinguished some traces, however imperfect, of many of the principal structures of Babylon. I imagined, I should have said: 'Here were the walls, and such must have been the extent of the area. There stood the palace, and this most assuredly was the tower of Belus.' – was completely deceived: instead of a few insulated mounds, I found the whole face of the country covered with vestiges of building, in some places consisting of brick walls surprisingly fresh, in others merely of a vast succession of mounds of rubbish of such indeterminate figures, variety and extent, as to involve the person who should have formed any theory in inextricable confusion.[14]

Rich therefore set out to describe the site in the greatest possible detail, an exercise that provided him with the tools to unpick the claims of earlier travellers to an impressive extent. For example, he seems to have been the first writer to have realized that many of the ruins described by even his immediate predecessors were in fact canals.[15] He deduced this partly from references to foliage, of which there is little on the site itself (he also suggests that this is probably due to the rubbish contained in the mounds being unsuitable soil for plants) save the Kasr tree (of which more below), which he describes as a badly damaged but still leaf-producing evergreen.[16]

While his stated aim is to confine himself almost entirely to on-the-spot description of the site, Rich does in fact devote considerable attention in his account to questions of correspondence with the claims of classical authors and with the confirmation of Old Testament prophecy. Throughout, he relies on and refers to the *Geographical System of Herodotus Examined and Explained* of Rennel,[17] and subsequent English visitors such as Robert Ker Porter, George Keppel and James Silk Buckingham tended to use Rennel's textual perspective and Rich's observations in conjunction.[18]

Rich is notable because he was prepared to challenge details of Herodotus based on his own observations, but he does not express any great doubt in the authority of classical authors in general, much less the claims of Isaiah and Jeremiah. Indeed, he had little reason to. At this stage, there was no very great conflict with these sources, even for an author placing a very high value on empirical observation. The confusion and desolation Rich saw fitted very well with Babylon's prophesied destruction, even to the point of the ruins being home to 'many dens of wild beasts'.[19] Confirmations of detail from classical accounts are also forthcoming: 'From the yielding nature of the soil I can readily conceive the ease with which Cyrus dug a trench round the city, sufficient to contain the river', he reports, referring to an event described in Xenophon's *Cyropedia*.[20]

A final merit of Rich's account, no doubt enhanced by the author's long residence in Iraq and linguistic ability, is its incidental coverage of local and non-European tradition relating to the site, a subject that is only now reappearing in archaeological discourse generally.[21] A memorable conversation occurs on top of the mound Rich calls Mujelibè:

> The summit is covered with heaps of rubbish, in digging into some of which, layers of broken burnt brick cemented with mortar are discovered, and whole bricks with inscriptions on them are here and there found: the whole is covered with innumerable fragments of pottery, brick, bitumen, pebbles, vitrified brick or scoria, and even shells, bits of glass, and mother of pearl. On asking a Turk how he imagined these latter substances were brought there, he replied, without the least hesitation, 'By the deluge'.[22]

Mujelibè in this case is Tell Babil, also called Maqlub, although other travellers refer to the Kasr area by the same names.[23] Koldewey too knew the Kasr by the name 'Mudshallibeh', 'the overturned'.[24]

Rich also gives a full account of the legend attaching to the single, ancient tree on the Kasr, which he tells us is locally known as *Athelè*. According to local tradition, this tree alone was spared in the destruction of Babylon, 'that it might afford Ali a convenient place to tie up his horse after the battle of Hellah [Hillah]!'.[25] Hereafter, this story appears several more times in the travel accounts.[26] Although *Memoir on the Ruins of Babylon* gives the impression that it was already well known, it seems to be the first published report of its existence, at least as a single tree.

Rich resists the obvious but etymologically unlikely conclusion that the word *birs*, as in Birs Nimrud, was a corruption of the Arabic *burj*, or tower. He also seems to have consulted Iraqi scholars on its meaning. In a footnote he writes:

> The etymology of the word *Birs* (برس) would furnish a curious subject for those who are fond of such discussion. It appears not to be Arabic, as it has no meaning which relates to this subject in that language, nor can the most learned

persons here [in Baghdad, where *Memoir on the Ruins of Babylon* was written] assign any reason for its being applied to this ruin.[27]

The account provoked considerable debate between the author and other scholars, most importantly the great geographer of India James Rennel, and prompted Rich to revisit the site and publish a *Second Memoir on the Ruins of Babylon* in 1818.[28] The posthumous *Narrative of a Journey to the Site of Babylon*[29] is a compilation of these accounts, the original journal of his expedition to Babylon from which the *Memoir* was written, a reprint of an article by Rennel on Rich's 1815 account of the topography of Babylon, and the account of an 1821 journey from Basra to Shiraz and Persepolis. The debate between Rich and Rennel is significant because it provides the first serious example of the authority of textual scholarship on Babylon being challenged on the basis of observations made at the site. Although an important cartographer and surveyor himself, where Rennel contests points made by Rich he is defending not only his own scholarship but to some extent that of Herodotus. Rich, in turn, is an early contributor to a process that over the course of the nineteenth and early twentieth centuries would progressively undermine the primacy of classical and biblical accounts of the ancient Near East, displacing them from the centre of scholarly debate as archaeology in the region developed.

Rich was an avid collector, most notably of oriental manuscripts, and collected archaeological material during his time in Iraq, including bricks from Babylon stamped with the name of Nebuchadnezzar and cuneiform tablets – though at this stage they could not be read, with some doubting whether the script was really written language at all. This collection, later sold to the British Museum by Rich's widow, has some claim to being the first of its kind in Europe:

There had indeed existed certain collections of Oriental gems and cylinders and, as early as the seventeenth century, 'that vain and curious traveller' Pietro della Valle had brought back to Italy inscribed bricks from the ruins of Babylon and Ur, and

later, at the end of the eighteenth century, the Abbé de
Beauchamp had also gathered bricks from Babylon. But Rich's
collection was the first that could be called representative, for it
included several classes of ancient Babylonian antiquities, as
well as Oriental manuscripts and coins.[30]

Despite this, both Rich's investigations and his collecting were on a
very small scale in comparison to what would follow. Away from
Babylonia, in northern Iraq, the age of large-scale British and French
Assyrian excavations was about to begin.

Botta, Layard and large-scale excavation:
The rediscovery and reception of Assyrian art

The background to the great age of Assyrian excavation was as much
political as scholarly. The politics of European imperial competition
within the Ottoman Empire would have forced both England and
France to engage more heavily in Mesopotamia by the 1840s,
regardless of precedent. By this period the processes that would
ultimately lead to the delineation of the present-day Middle East, from
the formation of new boundaries and borders to the construction of the
concept of the 'Middle East' itself,[31] were well underway. In terms of
the ancient Near East, the excavations would give the modern world its
first substantial contact with ancient Mesopotamian visual culture: the
iconic reliefs and winged bulls of the Assyrian palaces.

Today, large-scale European excavations in the nineteenth-century
Ottoman Empire are popularly assumed to have been simple matters
of imperial plunder, driven by a desire for conquest and power. The
extent to which this assumption bears close examination varies. In
the Mesopotamian case imperial military concerns, Anglo-French
competition and political positioning were definitely factors, though
not the only ones, and even within the realm of politics the Ottoman
Empire, which granted permission for excavations and export of
antiquities, was no powerless victim of European deception. The
picture, inevitably, is more complicated.[32]

The diplomat with antiquarian interests, Rich, was followed in
1842 by a diplomat appointed specifically because of them, Paul-Émile

Botta as French Consul in Mosul at the suggestion of Jules Mohl, the leading orientalist and secretary of the Société Asiatique in Paris. Botta was originally on the right path to excavate Nineveh, following Rich's correct attribution of the city to the Nebi Yunus and Kuyunjik mounds. Botta planned at first to work on Nebi Yunus, but was forced to bow to strong local opposition due to the shrine on top of that mound (Nebi Yunus means 'tomb of Jonah'). Botta dug at Kuyunjik from December 1842 to May 1843,[33] but did not find the palaces of Sennacherib and Ashurbanipal that lay beneath. Instead he was led away by discoveries of carved stone at the nearby site of Khorsabad. This mound quickly yielded spectacular architectural discoveries. Encountering a vast and ornately decorated palace, Botta revised his view, henceforth believing Khorsabad to be the site of Nineveh. Texts were later to reveal the site as ancient Dur-Sharrukin, an important but short-lived Assyrian capital, and the palace Botta found as that of Sargon II (722–705 BC), founder of that city.

In contrast to the French governmental decision to place Botta in Mosul, Austen Henry Layard's, and therefore Britain's, entry into competition for the spectacular discoveries and museum pieces of Assyria was a matter more of an accident than design. Despite the precedent set by Rich, whose finds from the area were purchased by the British Museum after his death and whose antiquarian work had attracted public attention, the Museum itself displayed its then customary attitude to non-classical antiquity, giving neither money nor further thought to Mesopotamia.[34] Layard himself was supposed to be on his way to Ceylon (Sri Lanka) for the purpose of practicing law when he met Botta at Mosul in 1842.[35] The encounter was fortuitous, however, since the young Layard possessed both the education and the ambition necessary to appreciate the value of Botta's discoveries and to dream of conducting similar excavations himself. On a personal level, Layard and Botta seem to have liked each other from the first.[36] Later, Layard would praise the generosity of his French counterpart:

M. Botta lost no time in communicating his remarkable discovery [i.e. the first discoveries at Khorsabad] to the principal scientific body in France. Knowing the interest I felt in his labours, he allowed me to see his letters and drawings as they passed through Constantinople; and I was amongst the first who were made acquainted with his success. And here I gladly avail myself of the opportunity of mentioning, with the acknowledgment and praise they deserve, his disinterestedness and liberality, so honourable to one engaged in the pursuit of knowledge. During the entire period of his excavations, M. Botta regularly sent me not only his descriptions, but copies of the inscriptions, without exacting any promise as to the use I might make of them. That there are few who would have acted thus liberally, those who have been engaged in a search after antiquities in the East will not be inclined to deny.[37]

At a political level Layard had a potent tool for getting his wish: the report of discoveries that would heap glory upon France and bring the monuments of legendary Nineveh to Paris itself. The appeal to British cultural pride and Anglo-French competition was necessarily indirect, however. The British and French governments behaved in different ways with regard to this kind of imperial cultural competition, and although it is not true that the British state provided no help in the acquisition and study of antiquities,[38] France was – as Layard and other British excavators were not slow to point out – far more generous in its direct support. Perhaps it would be fair to say that the British government, and the trustees of the British Museum, generally viewed the acquisition of antiquities as a meritorious service to be rendered to the state by private individuals, to be given practical help where possible, and whose efforts might subsequently be better compensated in terms of honour and recognition than financial renumeration. It was therefore initially through the private sponsorship of Stratford Canning, the British ambassador to the Sublime Porte in Constantinople, that Layard was able to return to the area and excavate at Nimrud in 1845.

Like Botta, Layard was initially unable to excavate at Nebi Yunus, nor even at Kuyunjik, the reason being that both tells were visible from Mosul, lying just across the Tigris. He initially attempted to hide his work from local authorities, though in light of its eventual scale this seems a little hard to fathom. The situation was certainly embarrassing for Canning, who later had to obtain a retroactive permission on Layard's behalf. As Russell observes:

> This was not India, and while Britain was a major imperial power, so was the Ottoman Empire. The Assyrian sculptures were obtained through diplomatic channels, by the British ambassador [Canning] approaching the Ottoman sultan, hat in hand, asking if Britain might have any pieces that the sultan did not need.[39]

Nonetheless, it was this attempt to employ large numbers of men in digging colossal sculptures out of a nearby tell and yet somehow maintain a low profile that led Layard to dig at Nimrud, ancient Kalhu (Nimrud, site of the former Assyrian capital Kalhu, is not to be confused with Birs Nimrud, ancient Borsippa, near Babylon). Here, excavating what turned out to be the palace of Ashurnasirpal II, Layard became convinced that this, rather than Khorsabad or the Kuyunjik and Nebi Yunus mounds, was the site of biblical Nineveh. Like Botta at Khorsabad, he had concluded that the city he had discovered was too grand *not* to be that of Nineveh. As a result, neither Layard's *Nineveh and its Remains* nor Botta's *Monuments de Ninive*[40] describe Nineveh, instead treating ancient Kalhu and Dur-Sharrukin respectively. Layard did return to Nineveh itself, however, and his work there was continued by Hormuzd Rassam, resulting in further collections of reliefs from palaces of Sennacherib and Ashurbanipal, now held in the British Museum alongside those of Ashurnasirpal II and Tiglath-Pileser III from Nimrud.

Following Layard's spectacular initial successes, Canning was able to recoup his expenses from the British government and to persuade the British Museum to take responsibility for further work in Assyria, but this handing over to government and even the entry of the Assyrian sculptures into the national collection were contentious.

Layard himself was exceptional in arguing that the sculptures had any great merit aesthetically, as art in their own right. 'It is impossible to examine the monuments of ancient Assyria,' he claimed, 'without being convinced, that the people who raised them had acquired a skill in sculpture and painting, and a knowledge of design and even composition, indicating an advanced state of civilization'.[41] Even so, he and others sympathetic to the cause of acquiring the sculptures thought that their chief merit lay in their position in art history, as distant precursors to the genius of classical Greece. Purists did not even concede this as a virtue, arguing instead that the purpose of the sculpture collections of the British Museum was to display what was finest and best in the ancient traditions in order to provide instruction to the artists of the present. No such instruction, it was held, was to be gained from studying the sculptures of Assyria. The most important proponent of this view was Richard Westmacott the Elder, who as a trustee of the museum and leading figure in art criticism wielded considerable power.[42] Ultimately the Assyrian sculptures were accepted into the collection, but certainly not on equal terms with those of classical antiquity. Like the statuary of ancient Egypt, they were treated as curiosities and crude steps in the early history of art, far from the perfection of the Parthenon marbles and the associated concept of ancient objects embodying achievements that the present might seek to emulate. Even Layard did not go so far as to suggest that the Assyrian sculptures could bear comparison with the best of ancient Greek art. Instead he made the argument for a historical connection, seeing the discoveries of Sir Charles Fellows at Xanthos in Lycia (also recent arrivals at the British Museum; also disliked by the purist Westmacott) as a kind of bridge:

> The Xanthian marbles [. . .] are remarkable illustrations of the threefold connection between Assyria and Persia, Persia and Asia Minor, and Asia Minor and Greece. Were those marbles properly arranged, and placed in chronological order, they would afford a most useful lesson; and would afford even a superficial observer to trace the gradual progress of art, from its primitive rudeness to the most classic conceptions of the Greek

sculptor. Not that he would find either style, the pure Assyrian or the Greek, in its greatest perfection; but he would be able to see how a closer imitation of nature, a gradual refinement of taste, and additional study, had converted the hard and rigid lines of the Assyrians, into the flowing draperies, and classic forms of the highest order of art.[43]

Something like this principle did eventually come to govern the arrangement of the museum's principal sculpture galleries, with the lasting consequence that the sculpture galleries are still arranged in the order Egypt, Assyria, Asia Minor, Greece (Parthenon).[44] Even among students of the field, Layard's more enthusiastic view was an exception. Henry Rawlinson argued that Layard's finds were of the highest value, but for their historical importance and the cuneiform inscriptions they carried rather than their imagery:

> I still think the design in general crude and stiff, the execution careless, the grouping confused and fantastic. I am sure, in fact, that modern art alone cannot desire instruction from the marbles of Nineveh, and that the mere connoisseur in statuary will be offended at the inelegant (sometimes even grotesque) forms. But far be it from me to declare the marbles valueless on this account [...]. The marbles of Nimrud will be, in my opinion, an honour to England, not in the exclusive department of art, but in that more worthy field, a general knowledge of the early world.[45]

Nor would Rawlinson countenance the idea that Greek art owed any debt to that of Assyria.[46] His views on the qualities of the Assyrian sculptures as art were so negative as to offend the sometimes touchy Layard, notwithstanding that the latter was every bit as invested as Rawlinson in the European traditions that placed the art of classical Greece at the pinnacle of human achievement, and had even expressed similar negative sentiments.[47]

Layard's encounter with Botta and his discoveries in 1842 had changed his life. He returned home a hero, 'Layard of Nineveh'.

Nineveh and its Remains, however, suggests a personality that, notwithstanding the author's genuine and long-term interest in the ancient past of the region, would have found plenty of other occupation on his journey even if excavating tells had played no part in it (indeed, he had taken a commission from the Royal Geographical Society before setting out). The book is more travel narrative than antiquarian study, and its author took as great an interest in his contemporary Ottoman setting as in ancient Mesopotamia. This interest is often very positively expressed, though this is not the case in his dealings with officials. Layard's own rather high-handed approach, and perhaps problems of communication, led at times to friction with the local and Ottoman authorities. His account is not sympathetic to these other interests: Reade describes the book as 'one of the most damning accounts of Ottoman imperial administration ever written'.[48] The criticism falls into a broad genre: negative depictions of Ottoman government by representatives of the other Great Powers would accumulate through the late nineteenth and early twentieth centuries, and would be employed as a justification for the eventual division of the empire and introduction of British and French Mandates in the Middle East. More positively, Layard's concern with the present also gives his work considerable value as a travel account. From the so-called 'devil-worshippers' (Yezidis) to the governors of regions through which Layard passed, his book is valuable as a mid-nineteenth-century European's experience of contemporary Iraq, as well as the country's ancient past.

Beyond their mistaken association with Nineveh, Botta and Layard's publications share very little and were decidedly different in nature. Frederick Bohrer has discussed the different aims and methods of dissemination employed in England and France in some detail,[49] but to summarize the most important differences we can look specifically at these two publications of 1849 by Layard and Botta themselves. Layard's was a popular book – exceptionally popular, in fact[50] – and its commercial success was furthered both by extensive coverage of the Assyrian discoveries as they reached London in the *Illustrated London News* and by the publication of an even cheaper abridgement of Layard's already relatively affordable work, *A Popular Account of the Discoveries at Nineveh*.[51] In France, meanwhile, *Monument de Ninive* represented the other extreme. Botta's work was published in five large volumes, lavishly illustrated and produced, and absolutely beyond the reach of all but the very richest. Next to the mass-production of *Nineveh and its Remains*, *Monument de Ninive* looks like a Renaissance masterpiece, produced under elite patronage and for the particular benefit of the patron. This, in fact, is not so far from the truth of the matter. *Monument de Ninive* was indeed produced in tiny numbers and mainly for patrons of the work. It could more fairly be compared to Layard's own *The Monuments of Nineveh*[52] and *Second Series of the Monuments of Nineveh*,[53] expensive large-format works again produced in small numbers and for a very exclusive audience, although *Monument de Ninive* was a grander production even than these. Unlike them, however, it was the principal means of disseminating information about the discoveries, there being no perceived popular appetite for or benefit in a publication equivalent to *Nineveh and its Remains*. Had such a book been written, it remains possible that this assumption would have been borne out, since Layard's sales were built on the foundation of regular coverage of Assyrian antiquities in the *Illustrated London News*, whose weekly circulation of approximately 100,000 (which in the mid-nineteenth century would imply a much higher actual readership) dwarfed the sales of even very successful books of the time.[54] The publication did have a Parisian opposite number in *l'Illustration*, but the latter did not parallel the remarkable enthusiasm for the Assyrian discoveries shown by the *Illustrated London News*.

Partly in consequence of this difference in publication formats, Layard presents himself in a manner far more consistent with other travellers and travel writers, particularly the other Englishmen who had visited Mesopotamia earlier in the nineteenth century. In style his work is reminiscent of Ker Porter or Buckingham. Botta seems more in tune with a savant tradition, for which the supremely lavish 23 volumes of the *Description de l'Égypte* provided the publication model.[55] Whether such a difference can be ascribed to national scholarly traditions as such is far from clear, however, since they can be explained at least as well through the different levels of state interest and support the two excavators received. Whatever the case, *Nineveh and its Remains* reads as a story of adventure and discovery, and finds its closest parallels in other travel accounts. This is the field in which the style of the book comes to make the most sense, far more so than in comparison with a lavish, visually stunning and above all expensive production such as *Monument de Ninive*, or a book as excavation report such as Koldewey was later to produce with *Wiedererstehendes Babylon*.[56] It is a captivating book because its author is a fine travel writer possessed of an elegant style. The details of the excavations themselves, which are really only sketched, are clearly secondary to the work of producing an engaging account and creating for the reader a vivid sense of place. Layard is extremely successful in both these respects, and it is perhaps for this reason as well as the inherent interest of the Nineveh story that he is popularly remembered as a rugged adventurer rather than the cultured aesthete who would go on to become a politician, diplomat and collector and connoisseur of fine art. By the same token, it is easy to criticize the manner in which the mid-nineteenth-century Assyrian excavations were conducted, and to paint Layard as a coarse treasure-hunter, unconcerned with the historical value or context of his discoveries. Such a view is grossly unfair to a man who, acting largely on his own initiative precisely because he did see the great historical value of the Assyrian mounds, was also a pioneer of excavation in Mesopotamia, and whose recording, in the form of fine and accurate drawings of the discoveries themselves,[57] was of an extremely high quality in its own light. Later excavators deserve credit for developing better approaches and realizing the value of stratigraphy and context, but the reverse is not true: the mid-nineteenth-century excavators do not deserve censure for their failure to account for data they did not know could be successfully recovered from an archaeological site, nor for their view that the most useful thing they could do was recover large numbers of stone reliefs and cuneiform tablets for study. The subsequent 150 years of Mesopotamian archaeology and Assyriology have proven them only partially wrong in this latter respect, so dependent on the nineteenth-century excavations are we for the cuneiform archives and art that today still form the bulk of available data on ancient Assyria and the focus for its study.

One interesting facet of the Assyrian discoveries is that they lent dramatic material and visual support to an idea of world history that was in any case pervasive in mid-nineteenth-century England. The rise and fall of empires was a subject normally studied through ancient authors, where the classical idea of a cyclical pattern leading ultimately to the pinnacle of Rome dominated ideas of historical development.[58] These models explained Britain's place at the pinnacle of world civilization, and its ability to wield power over the once mighty states of the Eastern Mediterranean and Middle East. They were seen to receive substantial physical proof in discoveries such as Layard's. They also prophesied decline and fall of even the mightiest, as Shelley famously observed in *Ozymandius*, but like their Roman predecessors most British imperialists solved this problem through the crude device of seeing their creation, for no better reason than self-interest, as the end and perfection of the process.[59]

The museums themselves took quite different attitudes to the Assyrian material. The French project was supported by the government throughout, whereas available records suggest the British Museum's position lay somewhere between grudging acceptance of and outright hostility to Layard's finds, which the trustees considered aesthetically inferior to the classical sculpture they saw as the Museum's main business. Egyptian material generally suffered the same fate, and the second-class status of both sets of antiquities is reflected in the sums the trustees were willing to spend on them, in sharp contrast with Greco-Roman antiquities.[60] Despite the trustees' reservations, however, a vast quantity of Assyrian sculptures did enter the British Museum, celebrated on their arrival by enthusiastic coverage in the *Illustrated London News*.

The excavation methods themselves were distant from those of modern archaeology. The main method for extracting the sculptures consisted of finding the edge of a relief-decorated wall and tunnelling alongside it, removing reliefs along the way. Sometimes this could be done in open trenches; at others it was necessary to tunnel deep into the mounds, shoring up the tunnels to prevent their caving in. Paintings by one of the artists who worked with Layard, F. C. Cooper, give some sense of the method and its dangers.[61] For shipping it was necessary to minimize weight, and therefore the thick panels were cut down to only a few inches in thickness. Nonetheless they remain extremely heavy, and require great care to move safely even with the best modern equipment and professional heavy artefact handlers. For workmen at the time of the excavations, the movement of the objects must have been very dangerous. On occasion large pieces, in particular the winged bulls and lions, were deliberately cut into pieces for transport – the repairs made on their reassembly are still visible.[62] Assyrian antiquities went first down the Tigris on rafts to Basra before being shipped on to London and Paris. In the British case they travelled via Mumbai, where at least one large shipment was temporarily unpacked for display at the docks. Losses and damage were inevitable under these circumstances; the most tragic case was that of the French expedition of Fulgence Fresnel, Felix Thomas and Jules Oppert, which lost an entire shipment of Mesopotamian finds in the Tigris in 1855 after being attacked.[63] Material left *in situ* fared no better. Exposed to wind-blown dust, huge temperature changes and moisture, surfaces of reliefs left exposed on site after excavation were quickly damaged, eroding the usually very shallow reliefs and inscriptions. Exposure to the elements remains a huge problem for sites and monuments in Iraq.[64]

Layard at Babylon

Based on large-scale excavation, Layard and Botta's work was invasive and physically destructive. Their successors caused perhaps greater damage, particularly in southern Iraq where the difficulty of tracing mud-brick architecture, often combined with a lack of interest in doing so as excavators searched for stone monuments or caches of cuneiform tablets, meant that excavations frequently dug through buildings. This different character of sites in the south was one reason why Layard did not replicate his Assyrian successes at Babylon. He did attempt to excavate at the site, but was discouraged by early results. There were no stone reliefs here of the kind found at Nimrud and Nineveh, nor did it seem possible to glean much information about the ancient city's layout beyond what had already been identified by Rich.[65] In this respect Layard shared the frustration of his predecessors. He was prepared to cast doubt on the idea of a great square agreeing with the vast dimensions for the city wall given by Herodotus and encompassing Birs Nimrud, as several nineteenth-century visitors had proposed,[66] although like them he did not realize that one of the walls already identified was the real outer wall of the city (it suggested an area too small in comparison to the classical descriptions). Layard reports that his excavations were conducted during a period of considerable local unrest, one consequence of which was that he was unable to excavate at Birs Nimrud.

At Tell Babil, Babylon's northernmost mound, Layard excavated buildings constructed in later periods from recycled Nebuchadnezzar bricks (still visible on the surface of the mound today), and burials dating to the Seleucid, Parthian and Sasanian periods. He also found some original Neo-Babylonian masonry, presumably a part of what Koldewey would later identify as Nebuchadnezzar's Summer Palace. Layard also noted local traditions on Tell Babil, which more than Babylon's other ruins stands as a high isolated mound in the landscape. He recalls Benjamin of Tudela's medieval informants, who (according to Layard's reading) gave this as the location of the Fiery Furnace of Daniel,[67] and notes that in his own day 'the ruin is not without its Mohammedan tradition. Within it are suspended by the heels, until the day of judgement, the two fallen angels, Harut and Marut, and the Arabs relate endless tales of the evil spirits which haunt the place.'[68]

At the Kasr, Layard saw the visible ruins of Nebuchadnezzar's monumental building programme. He found that:

Piers, buttresses, and pilasters may be traced; but the work of destruction has been too complete to allow us to determine whether they belong to the interior or exterior of a palace. I sought in vain for some clue to the general plan of the edifice.[69]

Layard also saw the continuing industry of extracting bricks:

> To this day there are men who have no other trade than that of
> gathering bricks from this vast heap and taking them for sale to
> the neighbouring towns and villages, and even to Baghdad.
> There is scarcely a house in Hillah which is not almost entirely
> built with them; and as the traveller passes through the narrow
> streets, he sees in the walls of every hovel a record of the glory
> and power of Nebuchadnezzar.[70]

The contrast between past grandeur and present decay was by now a
standard feature of European travel writing on the Middle East; that
the phenomenon should present itself to Layard in this light is
unsurprising. Nonetheless, like de Beauchamp, Layard realized that
the diggers might be an excellent source of information. However, he
did not have his predecessor's good fortune in informants: 'Those who
had been engaged from childhood in the brick trade, assured me that
no sculptures or inscribed slabs had been discovered in their time,
and that no remains of stone walls existed in any part of the
mound.'[71] The last part of the answer must reflect his own question:
were there parallels here to the Assyrian reliefs? The answer was no,
and his own soundings also yielded only brickwork, though he did
note the colourful fragments of glazed brick that could be found here,
and to which we will return in the next chapter. His finds were
minimal, although they did include a noteworthy ninth- to eighth-
century BC relief fragment.[72]

Further south, at Amran, Layard also discovered later material:
Aramaic incantation bowls, whose interest in terms of Jewish history
at Babylon he immediately recognized.[73] Once again, however, he
was unable to find the clear remains of ancient structures. Overall,
Babylon had been a disappointment, certainly when compared to the
wondrous Assyrian discoveries:

> Such then were the discoveries amongst the ruins of ancient
> Babylon. They were far less numerous and important than I
> could have anticipated, nor did they tend to prove that there

were remains beneath the heaps of earth and rubbish which would reward more extensive excavations. It was not even possible to trace the general plan of any one edifice; only, shapeless piles of masonry and isolated walls and piers, were brought to light – giving no clue whatever to the original form of the buildings to which they belonged.[74]

Hormuzd Rassam

Excavations were performed at Babil in 1864 by Arnold Kemball,[75] and between 1878 and 1882 at Babylon as well as nearby Birs Nimrud[76] and Sippar by Hormuzd Rassam, Layard's assistant, friend and successor as agent of the British Museum in Iraq (Figure 12).[77] Rassam supervised many excavations simultaneously during this period but was inadequately resourced to do so, with the result that recording is often minimal. After beginning excavations at the site he would leave overseers in charge of the work, but none had his training or was really qualified for the work. Moreover, for a variety of reasons Rassam himself was only present in the field for part of the time.[78] He was conscious of the inadequacy of these arrangements, but the trustees of the Museum did not share his view. He was, after all, tasked specifically to recover tablets for the Museum's collections, and for this reason was unable to persuade the trustees of the necessity of either an epigraphist in the field or of a camera for himself. It is unfair that the resulting loss of information has frequently been blamed on Rassam. The greater fault surely lies with the Museum's policy of treating the excavations simply as a mechanism for recovering tablets.[79]

One reason for Rassam's anxiety about the difficulty of recording data in the field was the fact that not all of the tablets excavated stood a good chance of survival. Unbaked tablets do not survive well once excavated, and much of what Rassam's workmen discovered must surely have crumbled. Anxious that so much information was thus being lost in the disintegration of cuneiform tablets at the sites themselves, Rassam – following experiments performed by one of his workmen – pioneered the practice of baking tablets in order to conserve them.[80] Recovering tablets was almost the only goal, and indeed a huge part of the British Museum's incredible cuneiform collection comes from Rassam's excavations.[81] Of Babylon itself, he wrote that 'Had it not been for my scruple not to waste public money on such an object, which is of no material benefit to the British Museum, I should certainly have gone about differently to discover some clue as to the positions of the important parts of the old city'.[82] Like his predecessors he had great trouble in identifying even the extent and boundaries of Babylon, though he was certain that Birs Nimrud was a separate city. At the latter he even produced a good plan of the Nabu Temple,[83] though again his focus was necessarily on recovering texts.

Rassam's best results in terms of the recovery of tablets came at Amran, the southernmost of Babylon's major mounds, near to the modern village of Djimijma.[84] Here, largely in the vicinity of what was later revealed to be Esagila, the greatest of all Babylon's temples, Rassam's workmen recovered large numbers of inscriptions, the most famous of which by far is the Cyrus Cylinder (see Chapter 2). This object, whose significance only became clear once it had been translated in London, was of particular value because of its biblical connection, a factor of no small importance in Rassam's own fascination with the ancient past. Like many of his English contemporaries (but unlike Layard)[85] Rassam was acutely alive to the biblical relevance of his work. He believed strongly in divine involvement in history, both in the ancient past and in the present:

There is another striking proof of the fulfilment of prophecy in the utter destruction and annihilation of the Assyrian and Babylonian monarchies for their rebellion and pride. God, through his omnipotent power, left no remnant of their sovereignty not a vestige of their grandeur [...]. But the Persians whom God raised to chastise the rebellious nations have held their own up to day, because it was divinely decreed that they should conquer and be victorious; and in return for the victories which God bestowed upon them, they ordered the rebuilding of His temple at Jerusalem, and thus Persia has remained an independent monarchy as it was then, and where God Jehovah is acknowledged as the only Lord and King with the revealed religion of the Jews and Christians at the base of their belief in Mohammed.[86]

Late nineteenth-century Britain is a world away from the seventeenth-century Amsterdam of Athanasius Kircher, but treatment of the confusion of tongues as a historical event survives in a few theories on linguistic development even now. Discussing Birs Nimrud, which he believes to be the Tower of Babel, Rassam comments:

> The most striking proof, in my mind, of the confusion of languages, and the dispersion of mankind after that event, is the widespread affinity existing in different parts of the world of Semitic derivation of words.
>
> The learned Colonel Vallancy says, 'that the descendants of Japhet peopled China as well as Tartary, we have no reason to doubt (though when they arrived in that country we cannot pretend to say), and that the language of the Chinese was pretty nearly related to the Hebrew and other tongues, which the learned consider as dialects of it.'[87]

Rassam goes on to cite supposed identifications of Hebrew and Gaelic names or roots in Native American and Pacific languages. Rassam himself was not a philologist and his views were not shared by Assyriologists such as Rawlinson, but the survival of this literal reading of Genesis is noteworthy nonetheless. It was precisely to the study of Semitic languages, however, that Layard and Rassam's work contributed most profoundly, and in which unimaginable leaps toward the real Babylon were being taken in their own time.

Cuneiform decipherment and the birth of Assyriology

The resurrection of ancient Mesopotamian language and literature after its complete extinction and an interval of 2,000 years is one of the greatest achievements of modern philology. As with Egyptian hieroglyphs, trilingual inscriptions were to play a crucial role in the decipherment. In this case, however, the trilingual inscriptions involved no known script or language. The crucial inscriptions are those of the Achaemenid Persian kings, who recorded their deeds in Babylonian, Elamite and Old Persian, the latter presumably the language of the Achaemenid kings themselves and for which a new, much simplified cuneiform script was invented. Some examples reached Europe via the drawings of Carsten Niebuhr, but the most famous among these trilingual records is the great rock-cut inscription at Bisitun in western Iran. The steep cliff face at Bisitun overshadowed a valley on one of the principal routes through the Zagros mountains; Alexander and his army are known to have passed this way and seen the inscription, while other Hellenistic, Parthian and Sasanian monuments at the site attest its long-term importance. The monument consists of a relief carving showing a king facing a line of smaller figures (Ibn Hauqal, writing in the tenth century AD, had interpreted the scene as a teacher admonishing his pupils).[88] Less clearly visible is a prostrate figure below the king's foot. Surrounding this central relief are monumental carved inscriptions of some length. The whole group is positioned high up the cliff face, making it difficult to reach or to make out clearly from the valley floor.

The inscriptions were written in the cuneiform (wedge-shaped) script of which tiny samples had been known in Europe since the time of Don Garcia de Silva y Figueroa and Pietro Della Valle in the seventeenth century. Little progress had been made with the fragments and drawings that had trickled westward since that time, but developments at the beginning of the nineteenth century suggested that change was on the way. In 1802 Georg Grotefend, a German philologist – most of whose work was on Italian and Latin – succeeded for the first time in identifying the names of Persian kings on inscriptions from Persepolis that had been copied at the site by Carsten Niebuhr.[89] This he did by the logical process of assuming that the word 'king' would appear frequently in monumental inscriptions, followed by the names of kings whose names were still known to the modern world via Herodotus and other ancient Greek writers. Proceeding on this basis he succeeded in identifying the names of Darius, Xerxes and Hystaspes. Grotefend also correctly deduced several characteristics of the inscriptions: that they must read from left to right (confirming the conclusions of Pietro Della Valle and Niebuhr), that the inscriptions were in fact of three different kinds (also suggested by Niebuhr) and that probably they were therefore a trilingual version of the same text, that two of the scripts were syllabic and that the third, simpler one in which he was able to identify kings' names was alphabetic, and consisted of 40 characters.[90] He believed that the language used was Middle Persian,[91] and was on the right path, since the actual language of the simpler inscription, today known as Old Persian, was indeed an Indo-Iranian one. Further progress was made by the Norwegian Christian Lassen and Frenchman Eugène Burnouf, the latter of whom was able in 1836 to identify in one of the texts copied by Niebuhr a list of the Satrapies of the Achaemenid Empire.[92] Again, the existing comparative sources on these were ancient Greek.

The second major development of the early nineteenth century was the work of Claudius Rich, whose researches in Mesopotamia included collecting tablets and inscribed bricks. The material acquired by Rich that would eventually reach the British Museum was modest compared to the later discoveries of Layard (whose observation that until his own discoveries 'a case scarcely three feet square inclosed all that remained, not only of the great city, Nineveh, but of Babylon itself!'[93] is only slightly exaggerated), but it greatly increased the quantity available for study in Europe and was accompanied by some extremely accurate copies of cuneiform inscriptions produced by Rich's private secretary, Carl Bellino. A little earlier, other individual inscriptions of particular value had reached London and Paris, most notably the East India House inscription, a large stone monumental inscription from Babylon that would eventually be found to record the restoration and rebuilding of the city's temples, palaces and defences by Nebuchadnezzar himself. At this stage the content remained wholly inaccessible; all this was to change, however, in the 1840s, and particularly with the close study of the inscriptions at Bisitun.

The celebrated hero of decipherment, remembered today for both his genius and his adventurous exploits in Persia, was Sir Henry Creswicke Rawlinson. Rawlinson was a gifted linguist, who while serving in the East India Company army not only rapidly acquired Persian (the language of Indian administration and government inherited by the British from the Mughals) but also studied several Indian languages. Once posted to Persia, Rawlinson began to study ancient inscriptions, and in 1836 he was fortuitously posted near to Bisitun, where he was to spend the next two years. During this time he made strenuous efforts to produce good copies of one inscription (the Old Persian), returning to the site in 1844 and 1847 to recopy this and to produce casts and copies of the other two (Elamite and Babylonian).[94] Although the Bisitun inscriptions were difficult to reach, Rawlinson realized their importance as tools for decipherment: lengthy trilingual texts would allow the kind of comparative work that might unlock the mysteries of cuneiform. It is not necessarily Rawlinson's fault that in imperial folklore these efforts were later imagined to consist of Rawlinson himself scaling the cliff and risking his life while being lowered on ropes to make the copies. The idea seemed to fit with his deserved reputation as a great sportsman and an exceptional rider. In fact Rawlinson did climb on ledges, but was assisted by local boys in his work, and as a feat of mountaineering his accomplishment has been exaggerated for the sake of a good story. What is more unjust, and results both from Rawlinson's own behaviour and from the somewhat partisan biography of him produced by his brother,[95] is that posthumously at least he ended up gaining the whole credit for achievements in decipherment that should at least have been shared with the Irish clergyman Edward Hincks. The latter was a far less glamorous figure and one of less worldly power, but the two worked in parallel, as rivals, and reached similar conclusions at a similar pace. Today Assyriologists generally agree that although Rawlinson deserves primacy in the case of Old Persian (where his knowledge of modern Persian proved a great advantage), Hincks pre-empted many of Rawlinson's conclusions in the decipherment of Babylonian, and that he ultimately deserves more of the credit.[96] There is of course quite enough credit to share:

three quite different languages written in different cuneiform scripts; two of these involving gigantic syllabaries and all three unknown – the achievement of decipherment was enormous. Nonetheless it was the Babylonian part of the trilingual inscriptions that would prove of the greatest importance in the grander scheme of things. Old Persian is confined to Achaemenid royal inscriptions, whereas Babylonian is a major branch of Akkadian, one of the two principal languages of Mesopotamian cuneiform (the other, Sumerian, was not convincingly deciphered until the twentieth century). Akkadian is a Semitic language related to Hebrew, Aramaic and Arabic, but the syllabic script in which it was written made its decipherment substantially more difficult than that of Old Persian. The reward, however, was correspondingly great: Hincks, Rawlinson and others were unlocking the vast corpus of texts surviving in the form of cuneiform tablets in Mesopotamia. The reward also constituted a helpful resource, since for the decipherment of Akkadian scholars had more examples of text available to them than was the case for either Old Persian or Elamite.

Progress on decipherment was made throughout the 1840s and 1850s, but the date generally accepted as a watershed is 1857. In this year William Henry Fox Talbot, another significant contributor to decipherment, moved to address growing public scepticism (induced not least by disagreements between, particularly, Rawlinson and Hincks themselves) by asking the Royal Asiatic Society to hold a test, or 'competition', to establish the progress that had been made. An Akkadian inscription[97] was sent to Talbot himself, Rawlinson, Hincks and Jules Oppert. The four scholars sent their individually produced, sealed translations to the Royal Asiatic Society in London, where they were found to be so similar as to admit of no doubt that decipherment had been achieved.

What of the content of the Bisitun inscriptions themselves? The monument would prove to be the record of an event once thought to be pure fancy on the part of Herodotus. The king represented on the relief is Darius I (550–486 BC). The man he is crushing underfoot is named Gaumata. According to Darius' own account Gaumata had claimed to be none other than Bardiya, brother of the reigning king Cambyses II (530–522 BC) and who, again according to Darius, the king had in fact already murdered. Gaumata provoked a rebellion against Cambyses in his absence and masquerading as Bardiya claimed the throne. Darius states that he served as lance-bearer for Cambyses until the king's death, at which point he and his allies attacked and defeated Gaumata. The inscription commemorates the event, and the smaller figures standing before Darius on the Bisitun relief are those of the satraps who unwisely supported Gaumata, now in chains. Darius, naturally, is proclaimed king. The account is very convenient from the point of view of Darius' accession – might he and his allies not have fought and murdered the real Bardiya to claim the throne? – but does accord remarkably well with what had seemed to be the far-fetched version given by Herodotus. In this account both Bardiya and Gaumata are named Smerdis; Herodotus distinguishes between the two by calling the latter as false king Pseudo-Smerdis. Again Cambyses, on campaign in Egypt, has his brother murdered, though this time it is the official he has left to rule in his absence, Patizeithes, who betrays him, allowing his brother to present himself as his namesake Smerdis, to whom he bears a close physical resemblance.[98] Again, Darius defeats the usurper and claims the throne. That the story appears in Herodotus does nothing to support Darius' claim to legitimacy, but does show that what Herodotus was recounting in this case was not fantasy or folklore, but the Achaemenid official version of events.

The contents of the Bisitun description, remarkable as they were, were only the first in what has proven to be a constant procession of discoveries in cuneiform texts that bear on, reveal more about or on occasion directly contradict the classical and biblical accounts that had for so long been the only sources available. The impact of this change has been enormous, and is perhaps best illustrated through its most famous manifestation: the discovery of the so-called Flood Tablet, a discovery that was also the culmination of the remarkable Assyriological career of George Smith.

As a young man Smith trained and worked as an engraver of banknotes. His developing fascination with the famous achievements of Layard and Rawlinson, however, led him to spend as much of his spare time as possible at the British Museum, studying the

Mesopotamian antiquities. In this way he came to the attention of Samuel Birch, the Keeper of the Department of Antiquities,[99] in 1861, and at some time in the next two years he was able to secure a junior post in the department. The self-taught Assyriologist (this in itself a remarkable achievement) quickly rose as his talents became clear, and by 1870 he was senior assistant to Birch himself. His triumph, however, came in 1872 when, to his own amazement, he translated a text whose resemblance to the Genesis account of the Flood was simply too close to ignore. The tablet[100] described a character named Uta-Napishtim, the survivor of a great deluge. Like the biblical Noah, Uta-Napishtim had received divine warning of the coming catastrophe and had built a boat to carry himself and his family, as well as animals and craftsmen. Smith's discovery was a Victorian sensation, attracting huge interest, and his lecture given to the Society of Biblical Literature in December 1872 was even attended by the prime minister, William Gladstone. The *Daily Telegraph* went so far as to sponsor Smith to travel to Mesopotamia (for the first time in his career) the following year in order to search for more of the story of which the Flood Tablet was obviously only a part. He succeeded, and the Flood Tablet was found to be part of the legend known today as the *Epic of Gilgamesh*. In the epic Gilgamesh, the hero king of Uruk, travels literally to the ends of the Earth in his quest for immortality. There he meets Uta-Napishtim, the only human being ever to have been granted eternal life by the gods, who does his best to convince Gilgamesh of the futility of his desire. To this day *Gilgamesh* remains by far the most famous piece of Babylonian literature, and several translations for the general reader exist.[101]

George Smith went twice more to Mesopotamia, now funded to do so by the British Museum, in 1873–4 and 1875–6. The second trip was to end in tragedy: suffering from dysentery, Smith collapsed at the village of Ikisji while making a journey between Mosul and Aleppo. He was brought to Aleppo but did not recover; he died in the city on 19 August 1876. He was only 36, yet he had lived to see the most dramatic of the transformations in his discipline. At the time of his birth the few brick fragments and undeciphered tablets collected by travellers still constituted all that the world knew of ancient

Mesopotamia beyond the biblical and classical sources. By the end of his life the sculpted reliefs of Assyrian palaces could be seen at the Louvre and British Museum, cuneiform had been deciphered, and Smith himself had contributed to the discovery that scholars now possessed documents older even than the earliest parts of the Bible, and which bore directly on the latter's content. Over the next 25 years excavators such as Rassam would continue to add to the collections of clay tablets from Mesopotamia, creating a resource that even now continues to pour forth new discoveries.

The most important trend in the accounts of travellers, from the pilgrims and merchants of the Middle Ages to the excavators of the nineteenth century, is a gradual, qualified, but definite shift toward a particular empiricism in which the perspective of the present-day, on-the-spot observer is privileged. This empiricism so underpins present-day attitudes to research that its absence, or rather weakness in relation to competing epistemologies, is difficult to imagine. It is an Enlightenment perspective, equally present in the competing bases for human knowledge put forward by Descartes and Vico (discussed below). Its absence leaves a very different, and at root more complex, set of mechanisms for verifying and establishing knowledge, in which cross-referencing and synthesis are of the highest importance. Attempting to appreciate this pre-modern perspective is central to understanding the early visitors' accounts of Babylon, and the transition to a more familiar humanist empiricism is equally important in understanding our later sources in terms of what they add and change.

In the accounts of visitors to Babylon there are some continuities and consistencies that are as remarkable as any change. The ubiquity of references to wild beasts, meaning the fulfilment of Isaiah and Jeremiah, is one such case; a fascination with the construction methods described by Herodotus another. Reinforcement and stability make knowledge, whether in the form of unquestioned assumptions or of the expectations one brings to one's investigations. Travel accounts form a part of this process, but by no means the whole. To enlarge our picture we must now return to the broader sweep of sources on Babylon, and the impact of their form and content on the study, representation and consumption of the Mesopotamian past.

Eighteenth- and nineteenth-century histories, art and literature

New approaches to the past

What, philosophically, underpinned the changes that separated scholars in the mould of Claudius Rich from their medieval forebears? The question is about knowledge, what it means and how it is to be gathered. The criteria for truth when studying knowledge historically do not have to be narrow or stringent. Just the reverse: what the authors of our sources considered to constitute truth is of great relevance, and any analysis must be sufficiently flexible to accommodate them.

One can seek to differentiate between different bases for knowledge, and hence between fundamentally different types of knowledge. There are many ways in which this can be done, for example by differentiating between scientific, moral and religious knowledge,[102] but the project of making such distinctions is an old one. Something of the sort occurs in Plato's *Republic*, in which it is suggested that the rational and emotional aspects of thought:

> Are two and different from one another, naming that in the soul whereby it reckons and reasons the rational and that with which it loves, hungers, thirsts, and feels the flutter and titillation of other desires, the irrational and appetitive – companion of various repelations and pleasures.[103]

Such distinctions need to be treated as tools or lenses of the interpreter, in which respect they are of enormous use in highlighting and isolating different patterns of logic, association and belief, and not as full-blown models of human cognition, which they are plainly not. The emphasis should therefore lie not on finding a single perfect distinction – it is unlikely to exist – but on tools appropriate for understanding a given process. The distinctions I outline here, therefore, are only those I see as most relevant to the historiographic treatment of the relationships between sources on Babylon. Others are equally possible.

In the case of Babylon, the first, perhaps historically the most important, form of knowledge that is apparent is that based on the authority of the Bible as revelation, as infallible and as literal truth: theocratic knowledge. This means primarily uses of scripture, but the term will be used here more loosely, wherever texts are treated as infallible authorities. A second form of knowledge to be considered is that which is grounded in allegory, which uses the past in moral or anecdotal rather than historical ways, and which, though often recounting or representing biblical material, does not depend for its message on the literal truth of that material. This we might term allegorical or mythic knowledge. It is not necessarily appropriate to talk of myth as knowledge as such, yet the history of Babylon as idea has involved great permeation of the mythic into the known, and this interaction is such as to suggest very strongly that myth can function as knowledge within the history of ideas. Crucially, the mythic includes moral knowledge embodied in allegory. The argument for its value as knowledge in this sense is encapsulated in Aristotle's contention that poetry is superior to history because it deals with the universal and with meaning where history can deal only with the particular.[104] Giambattista Vico made such 'poetic wisdom' a precursor and substitute for historical knowledge: each, for Vico, encapsulated its own form of philosophy and of science more generally.[105] The notion of the historical (or rational–empirical) supplanting the poetic in such a broad compass is an intriguing one, but perhaps not as promising as that of their coexistence and interaction in thought. In terms of cultural history and representation, the question is not so much one of the model as of practical influence: how, in practice, is the mythic used as knowledge, and how does it relate to or interact with other forms of knowledge?

The next broad category, humanistic knowledge, covers several distinct bases for truth-claims, whose shared feature is a grounding of knowledge in the human, whether in cognition or sensory perception. The most influential starting points for this anchoring in the human are those of Descartes (I think, therefore I am) and Vico (we can know only what we have made).[106] In practical terms at least, some form of humanism has underpinned the vast bulk of work in the fields we would now call the humanities and social sciences since the eighteenth century. Finally there is positivistic knowledge, whose basis is a physical universe whose properties can be measured in absolute (objective) terms and, in a pure positivism, without reference to the human except as an object of study. In archaeology as in many other fields, most research today operates through a hybrid, whereby in practical terms knowledge is treated as positive and the sensory perception underpinning it as accurate, while in philosophical terms limitations based on subjectivity are broadly accepted. The hybrid position is at least in part a consequence of the rise of atheism and the removal of the divine as an anchoring point for the human, and by extension for humanistic knowledge. In the absence of God the humanist cannot be studying the world as revealed by providence, nor can reason or the senses be trusted as accurate through the will of a divine creator. It therefore becomes necessary to anchor knowledge elsewhere, whether in human experience or in physical absolutes.

Knowledge derived empirically from observation and experiment can be humanist or positivist in character, because both forms of knowledge allow for hypothesis testing of a kind that is impossible for mythic knowledge and antithetical to theocratic knowledge. This ability to test is the basis on which the authority of academic research is most commonly validated: authority stems principally from the conception that the researcher tests claims according to reason and rational thought.[107] The high value placed on these principles originates in the Enlightenment, most importantly with Francis Bacon in the case of empiricism and with Descartes in that of rationalism. Despite their history of use in combination, however, the positions of Bacon and Descartes are not particularly compatible: Bacon put a faith in sensory data[108] that Descartes shunned, the latter arguing that only the mind and the capacity to reason are secure, and therefore favouring an inductive progression from abstract geometry, mathematics and logic to knowledge of the particular, as opposed to experiment and physical measurement of properties.[109] His belief in rational thought as the ideal basis for knowledge was strong enough to constitute its own form of positivism, an inward-looking metaphysical counterpart to the late-modern theories that have tried to achieve the same through the physical world:

> The long chains of simple and easy reasoning by means of which geometers are accustomed to reach the conclusions of their most difficult demonstrations, had led me to imagine that all things, to the knowledge of which man is competent, are mutually connected in the same way, and that there is nothing so far removed from us as to be beyond our reach, or so hidden that we cannot discover it, provided only we abstain from accepting the false for the true, and always preserve in our thoughts the order necessary for the deduction of one truth from another.[110]

Although he agrees with Descartes in placing the world of the human mind closest to God, expressing the relationships of knowledge visually in his frontispiece to the *New Science*,[111] Vico's position in this respect is closer to that of Bacon. The new science in question was that of the philosophy of history – the study of what we have made, which for Vico defined the limits of possible human knowledge – and therefore the primary science from which philosophy is derived.[112] This was a grand footing indeed on which to place historical research. For our purposes it is more important to note that it was an empirical one, with a foundation that was explicitly humanist.

One impact of rational–empirical models over time was to raise the status of the situated observer considerably, a phenomenon of which Claudius Rich's ability to argue points of detail with Herodotus is only one manifestation. There is no need to imagine that such models pushed other forms of knowledge to the sidelines, however. During the eighteenth century some believers in the importance of a good myth were only getting warmed up.

Voltaire

Athanasius Kircher's researches into the development of language and the antiquity of the Tower of Babel had appeared at an interesting time. Kircher was writing not long after Isaac Lapeyrère's *Preadamitaei*,[113] or *Men Before Adam* and, perhaps more importantly, after Lapeyrère's arrest in Treuremberg.[114] The establishment of a new, long chronology for humanity's existence was imminent, but the dangers of heresy were still very real. The eighteenth century would see rapid changes in the scope and influence of geology, natural history and antiquarianism. The growth of the Enlightenment tradition in humanism and science is today celebrated as the period in which many modern fields of study came of age. Not everyone had quite the proper reverence at the time, however, and by the mid-eighteenth century the increasing concern with empiricism and commitment to historical accuracy relating to the ancient Near East had, for Voltaire, become nothing less than a tremendous bore. His play, *Sémiramis* (completed 1748),[115] and the novels *Zadig, ou la destinée*[116] and *La Princesse de Babylone*,[117] are purely, determinedly fantastic. Their storylines are original, or at least owe more to the *Arabian Nights* than to Greek or biblical sources on Babylon. Even among the latter, the sources were selected for inspiration rather than plausibility. *Zadig* draws (via Photius) on the already fantastic *Babyloniaca* of Iamblichos, as well as the Venetian Michele Tramezzino's sixteenth-century *The Three Princes of Serendip*, itself supposedly based on a Persian folk tale, and the whole laced with references to contemporary French politics. Voltaire's Zadig is a Babylonian philosopher, but his main impact may have been on the modern detective novel: his prowess in deduction is thought to have inspired Edgar Allan Poe's C. Auguste Dupin, and possibly Arthur Conan-Doyle's Sherlock Holmes.[118] *Sémiramis* makes more use of the Babylon described by classical authors, particularly Ctesias, but also of the Armenian tradition. The play begins with the murder of Ninus by Semiramis and her lover Ashur, and ends with the ghost of Ninus orchestrating his revenge, guiding his son Ninyas to murder Semiramis. The play was later adapted for Rossini's 1822 opera *Semiramide*. The story is original but several elements, including Ninyas' estrangement from and eventual murder of Semiramis, are found in the Moses Khorenati account of Semiramis (see Chapter 4).

At times it seems that Mesopotamia is merely the source of exotic names and the glamorous location of Babylon, of which Voltaire offers a beautiful though entirely fanciful description at the start of *La Princesse de Babylone*. At the end of this romantic adventure the author characteristically steps into his story to make a rather unorthodox appeal to the Muses against the professors of the Sorbonne, whose usefulness he can nonetheless appreciate:

> I recommend you to [*sic*] my Princess of Babylon: say every thing you can against it, that it might be read [. . . E]ndeavour to prevail upon the Sieur Riballier to have the Princess of Babylon condemned by the Sorbonne: you will, thereby, afford my bookseller much pleasure, to whom I have presented this little history for his New Year's gift.[119]

Against such charm might be weighed the fact that Voltaire's work endorses the European use of the Middle East, ancient and modern, as an infinitely malleable resource for exotica. His distaste for the first serious attempts to learn about the Mesopotamian past expresses, for all its wit, a contempt for the subject matter as well as its students. This contempt is one side of a great ambivalence in Voltaire, who is by turns a fastidious historian (of France) and a committed sceptic of historical practice:

> So, although he engages in extensive historical research in search of facts, the simultaneous awareness of the probable inaccuracy of sources neither deters Voltaire from writing history nor does it inhibit him in the slightest [. . .] indeed, his method of systematic doubt renders him permanently assertive. The admission of both the practical impossibility of omniscience and of the philosophical pyrrhonism of history

illustrates how cavalierly the historian Voltaire could dismiss the fears of contemporary historians about their own inadequacies in relation to the chosen historical subject matter.[120]

In drawing out these problems of veracity, Voltaire echoes the approach taken in Lucian of Samosata's *True Stories*,[121] written *c*.170–80 AD, in which the author challenges the notion of historical truth by happily labelling himself a liar before launching into a series of stories that, though fantastic and magical, clearly parallel events described by historians, and take comparable forms.[122] Such pessimism and scepticism is especially easy to understand in the case of ancient Near Eastern history at this early stage, prior to the mid-nineteenth-century revolution in knowledge that came with excavation and decipherment. In the eighteenth century it cannot have been at all clear that historians would ever be able to move beyond their complete dependence on the biblical and classical sources for knowledge of this distant world. It is perhaps an indication of the environment within which he worked that Voltaire also wrote an article on Babel for the *Dictionnaire philosophique*, in which he comically dismisses the biblically-derived 'confusion' etymology for the name Babel itself, pointing out that this makes no sense for the capital of a great empire, and instead suggests 'the city of God, the holy city'. It was a guess, but one which brought Voltaire rather closer to the ancient (though probably still not etymologically correct) understanding of *bâb-ilu*, 'Gate of the gods'.[123]

In style very distant from Voltaire, two of the great English romantics (though neither used the term themselves) produced famous and influential representations of Babylon: William Blake and George Gordon, Lord Byron.

William Blake

William Blake's theological vision was completely unique. Pouring forth a mixture of prophecy, fantasy and polemic in his art and poetry, Blake developed a schema concerned with the placement of types, and represented these types through individuals or groups. The model is dominated by Blake's distinction between what he called innocence and experience, each of which could dominate in six types of being or matter: the divine, human, animal, mineral, vegetable and chaotic.[124] In Blake's imagery, Babylon appears as a manifestation of the mineral and of experience, i.e. as a physical (mineral) place whose characteristics are defined by worldly experience (and thus sin). At this point, however, the similarities with other visions of the city end. Although Blake placed sin on the side of experience, and virtue on that of innocence, what he meant by these terms was particular to his own work and extremely radical. For him, experience meant not only the kinds of sin with which Babylon has generally been associated, but also with all those institutions through which humans mitigate and restrain their desires; that is, law and society. Against this, uninhibited sexuality falls on the side of innocence, because it lies outside the production of social norms and controls.[125]

Blake argued that all forms of moral, religious and legal restraint sapped human energy, holding humanity back from innocence and salvation.[126] The idea of innocence as a powerful, primal force of desire checked by the world of experience leads to the conclusion that experience is straining against a stronger and more primitive force that will ultimately overwhelm it. This is exactly Blake's point, for innocence was also on the side of the New Jerusalem. Until its triumph innocence will strain and encroach upon the unnatural state of experience, and hence the manifestations of innocence will be seen as negative by the society they threaten. Blake's distrust of the constraints of society gives a foretaste of what, a century later, would resurface in the *fin-de-siècle* fascination with forbidden sexuality. To see uninhibited sexuality as redemptive, however, seems at first somewhat at odds with Babylon's traditional place as the home both of sin in general and of carnal sin in particular.

Blake produced several images relating to Babylon, of which by far the most famous is the large colour print *Nebuchadnezzar* (Figure 13).[127] This shows the Nebuchadnezzar of Daniel 4: 31–3, during his seven years in the wilderness. He is mad, naked, and crawling on all fours like a beast, a pose drawn from Albrecht Dürer's depiction of St John Chrysostomos and producing a deliberate circularity since, at least in legend, the latter consciously based his own penance on the wilderness years of Nebuchadnezzar.[128] The probable partner to this image is the figure of Newton, in this case embodying an excess of reason against Nebuchadnezzar's madness. Blake originally used Nebuchadnezzar in plate 24 of *The Marriage of Heaven and Hell*,[129] the major differences being that in the earlier image Nebuchadnezzar wore a crown, in reference to the recent fall of the French monarchy, and that beneath it sits the caption 'One Law for the Lion & Ox is Oppression', a phrase repeated in the accompanying paragraph.[130] Blake shows Nebuchadnezzar living and suffering by the law of the beasts, i.e. ruled by the senses, and gives a devil (the roles of devils and angels are deliberately confused in the work) a speech in which he argues that Christ himself broke several of the Ten Commandments. This theme is reprised in *The Everlasting Gospel*,[131] whose argument is that no moral teaching of Jesus was original and that the real substance of the Gospels is, simply and exclusively, the forgiveness of sin. Blake argues for licence, particularly for the great, and scorns 'moral virtues'. For him they are part of experience, and false:

> The Heathen Deities wrote them all:
> These Moral Virtues great and small.
> What is the Accusation of Sin
> But Moral Virtue's deadly Gin?
> The Moral Virtues in their Pride,
> Did o'er the World triumphant ride
> In Wars & Sacrifice for Sin,
> And Souls to Hell ran trooping in.[132]

Blake's position with respect to Babylon, however, remains superficially traditional. It remains for him the city of sin, yet that sin is not luxury or amorality. As with Bruegel, Babylon is not only itself but also the city of Blake's own experience, and its sins are as much the artifice of order and restraint as the excesses of the Great Whore; for him the two go hand-in-hand. In 1809 Blake produced a nightmarish depiction of Revelation's Whore of Babylon.[133] She also appears in his sketches of *c.*1810 for what Dante Gabriel Rossetti

later named *A Vision of the Last Judgement*,[134] which, though
unfinished, makes Babylon's place in Blake's religious schema
explicit.[135] With its swirling masses of bodies rising toward Christ or
descending to hell, *A Vision of the Last Judgement* strongly echoes
Michelangelo's Sistine Chapel *Last Judgement*. The Great Whore, here
found in the bottom centre of the composition, is an important
element in Blake's crowded, chaotic work, but what she stands for is
the deviant, misguided power that experience has created. Her sexual
sins, we can therefore conclude, are of a character wholly alien to the
free sexuality of Blake's innocence, and like all other experience are
destroyed in the birth of the New Jerusalem, represented by the
coming of Christ at the top of the picture. Thus *A Vision of the Last
Judgement* makes explicit the metaphor of experience buckling under
the pressure of innocence. Blake's images were unique, but the use of
Babylon and apocalyptic to comment on contemporary society was a
common thread in nineteenth-century English culture. One might
point to the vast outpouring of religious pamphlets on the theme, or
to the dramatic, apocalyptic works of John Martin.[136]

Byron

Perhaps the most important literary sources for the early nineteenth
century are the immensely popular works of Byron. His *Hebrew
Melodies* are concerned with the Babylonian Captivity, and naturally
incorporate Old Testament references throughout. The best known of
these song-poems today is *The Destruction of Sennacherib*, or rather its
opening verse:

> The Assyrian came down like the wolf on the fold,
> And his cohorts all gleaming in purple and gold;
> And the sheen of their spears was like stars on the sea,
> When the blue wave rolls nightly on deep Galilee.[137]

The poem describes the miraculous destruction of the Assyrian army
on the eve of their seemingly inevitable sack of Jerusalem. The
sentiment of this and the other *Hebrew Melodies* is nationalist, and
concentrates on the message that a nation dedicated to and loved by

God can and must endure any enemy. This is a use of the Old Testament that is very much of its time: Blake's 'And Did Those Feet in Ancient Time' later to become the lyric of the popular English patriotic song 'Jerusalem', dates to the same period.[138] For Byron there was little to differentiate the oppression of the Assyrians and that of the Babylonians, in which respect he shared a perspective with many ancient authors. His 'By the Rivers of Babylon We Sat Down and Wept', closely based on Psalm 137, emphasizes resistance to those oppressors:

> While sadly we gazed on the river
> Which roll'd on in freedom below,
> They demanded the song: but, oh never
> That triumph the stranger shall know!
> May this right hand be wither'd forever,
> Ere it string our high harp for the foe![139]

This is to be expected, and is not a distortion of the psalm's message, but it is worth remembering that the Old Testament itself is not so consistent as later tradition would make it. Several biblical sources, most prominently the early part of Isaiah, counsel acceptance of God's punishment in the form of the Captivity and advise the Israelites to build new lives for themselves in Babylon. This inconsistency better reflects the complex historical experience of displacement, with resistance, adaptation and integration all parts of the story, but would hardly serve Byron's purpose. *The Vision of Belshazzar* reprises an 1814 occasional piece, *To Belshazzar*, and covers the Daniel account of the writing on the wall. The subject of the Israelites' exile was a particularly poignant one for the romantic pessimist Byron, in whose eyes it symbolized the sorrow and pain of human existence itself.[140]

Clearly, there is a tragic aspect to Byron's outlook. Though on other topics his wit shines, here the contrast with the quick and flippant Voltaire could hardly be greater. Both authors, however, were immensely popular in their own lifetimes, and are often cited as defining examples of the great cultural movements of their times. Byron's work clearly struck a chord with a wide readership, and its sentiment cannot therefore be dismissed as entirely misrepresentative. Romanticism brought a powerfully emotional element, by turns moving and cloying, into cultural life; one whose tone has fallen in and out of favour with modern scholars ever since, but whose impact in all fields of nineteenth-century cultural life was undeniably profound.

Byron's largest work on a Mesopotamian theme is the play *Sardanapalus*, completed in 1821 and first performed in 1834. The subject and its treatment have little in common with the *Hebrew Melodies*. Here Byron concentrates on the downfall of a flawed ruler, though his treatment is not entirely unsympathetic. The main source is not biblical but Greek: the account of Ctesias preserved in Diodorus Siculus. Byron's play was written 20 years prior to the rediscovery of Assyrian cities and the decipherment of cuneiform, and so Ctesias remained the best available source.[141] Several other major productions were based on Byron's *Sardanapalus*, including one, *Sardanapal, Historische Pantomime*,[142] which came to play an important role in the German reception of Babylon (see Chapter 6). Most notably, Byron's play provided the inspiration for Delacroix's *Death of Sardanapalus*, one of the most famous Orientalist paintings ever produced.

Verdi

Also focusing on the plight of the exiled Judaeans, Giuseppe Verdi's *Nabucco* (originally *Nabucodonosor*, i.e. Nebuchadnezzar) is, by far, the grandest and most famous musical representation of ancient Babylon. First performed in Milan in 1842, the opera's libretto (by Temistocle Solera) was based on an 1856 play and 1838 ballet of the same name.[143] As the title suggests, the sources from which the plot is derived are biblical rather than classical, though a large part is also modern invention.[144] The Babylonian Captivity is the opera's setting and core theme, and is complemented by elements including an original version of Nebuchadnezzar's madness and a story in which non-biblical character, Abigaille, attempts to seize the throne of Babylon. The opera is best known for its Chorus of the Hebrew Slaves. In *Nabucco* Verdi foregrounded the chorus to a previously unknown degree, a musical innovation which also carried, or perhaps more accurately developed, political significance. 'Va pensiero', the most famous chorus, became associated with Risorgimento-era popular ardour for a unified homeland and political freedom. At Verdi's funeral in 1901, the chorus of La Scala led the huge crowds in a rendition of 'Va pensiero'. Once again the historically specific events of the Captivity had taken on a modern, universalizing importance far removed from their original context.

Nabucco, the opera which first brought Verdi real fame, has remained among his most popular and frequently staged works ever since.[145] Following the Second World War, the opera was the first to be performed at the reopened La Scala in 1948. The sets were designed by Zampini, the costumes by the celebrated Caramba (Luigi Sapelli), after whom La Scala's costume facility is now named. A surviving photograph held by the Royal Opera House, London, shows that the sets to this production incorporated features now known from the early twentieth-century excavations at Babylon, including the glazed-brick bulls and dragons of the Ishtar Gate.

'Assyriana': reception and consumption in mid-nineteenth-century Europe

The European impact of the Assyrian discoveries of the 1840s was substantial, and certainly affected the representation of Babylon well before that city had itself been excavated. The majority of the materials Layard had uncovered went to the British Museum, but some did find other homes.[146] Two famous examples are the set of jewellery, itself now held in the British Museum, that was produced for Enid Guest's wedding to Layard in 1869 from real Assyrian cylinder seals (and worn by her for the Layards' dinner with Queen Victoria in 1873),[147] and the Nineveh Porch at Canford Manor, home of Layard's cousin, patron, from 1869 mother-in-law – and in her own right an important translator (most notably of the *Mabinogion*), collector and business-woman – Lady Charlotte Guest.[148] These two uses for the Assyrian discoveries testify eloquently to their meaning and worth socially. If the British Museum collections symbolized national greatness, those privately held did as much for their discoverer and his circle. John Malcolm Russell, who has studied the history of the Nineveh Porch and the papers of Charlotte Guest in detail, considers what the reliefs at Canford Manor meant to their owner:

> Lady Charlotte's experience of the Nineveh marbles both parallels and contrasts with that of the British public. She appreciated their biblical and aesthetic value, but they also offered her the unique opportunity to compete with the national museums of England and France.[149]

This, of course, says a great deal about the wealth and social standing of Lady Charlotte and her husband Sir John Guest, a prominent industrialist.[150] Russell is able to cite the owner's own comments on the use of the Nineveh Porch:

> Lady Charlotte envisaged it as 'a beautiful and interesting object' and 'as interesting a little spot of ground that Porch as any in England.' Such an interesting object must be shown off and Lady Charlotte clearly enjoyed doing so, as evidenced by her numerous diary references to visits to the Porch by guests in 1853 and 1854.[151]

Lady Layard's jewellery could be said to fulfil a similar role: a talking point focussed on Henry Layard's status and success. It was the crowning glory of a trend for 'Assyriana', some examples of which are also retained in the collections of the British Museum. There was certainly an element of fashion. The French artist Gustave Courbet, referring to his own beard, noted that he himself possessed an 'Assyrian profile',[152] and incorporated postures from Botta's Khorsabad reliefs into his own compositions on non-Mesopotamian subjects.

Seductions east and west

IOKANAAN Back! Daughter of Babylon! Come not near the chosen of the Lord. Thy mother hath filled the earth with the wine of her iniquities, and the cry of her sinning hath come up even to the ears of God.

SALOME   Speak again, Iokanaan. Thy voice is as music to
                mine ear.[153]

The identification of Babylon with sin and amoral luxury is
longstanding. The major influences here are Old Testament sources,
but their fortuitous compatibility with Greek representations of
Achaemenid Persia can also be fairly said to have contributed to
later attitudes to the Middle East as a whole. The moral meaning of
biblical texts could even take it outside this geographical context,
as in Spenser's conscious modelling of the *Faerie Queene*'s Duessa
after the Whore of Babylon described in Revelation, and of Lucifera
as the Daughter of Babylon, guilty of pride.[154] It comes as no
surprise, then, that Babylon should be a popular subject in
Orientalist art. The story of Salome, of course, has nothing to do
with Babylon, and yet Wilde's reference above is not only simple
and clear, but there is also a more than allegorical truth in it. Salome
and her real mother, Herodias, are indeed the kin of Revelation's
Great Whore: neither are meaningful as individual characterizations, but both work as specific embodiments of a female type.
Babylon and Salome are, throughout their literary careers, fatally
seductive and corrupting to men. What makes Wilde's *Salome* so
interesting is that it explicitly makes Salome's seductions the heart
of the play, and emphasizes them far more than the virtue of the
saint. Wilde even sexualizes the conclusion of the story, turning
John the Baptist's resistance to Salome into a macabre triumph for
her as she kisses his severed head: 'they say that love hath a bitter
taste, but what matter? I have kissed thy mouth, Iokanaan, I have
kissed thy mouth'.[155] This was Salome, but it could have been
Lilith, Ishtar or Semiramis. As Zainab Bahrani puts it in her study
Women of Babylon:

> Ancient goddesses have been the subject of both scholarly and
> popular fascination since the earliest days of archaeological
> discovery in Babylonia and Assyria. Exoticising fantasies of
> cultic prostitution and illicit sexual practices were woven
> around historically attested female deities in the scholarly

literature, and these descriptions eventually became part of a larger imaginative picture of Oriental antiquity.[156]

This is a type also represented in semi-mythologized Greco-Roman history: Livia, wife of Augustus, or Olympias, mother of Alexander. In the Homeric tradition their luxury is not as clear, or at least not as material, yet their function still exists. Here it is found not in Helen, who like all the *Iliad*'s mortal protagonists is a pawn of the gods, but in the Sirens or the nymph Calypso. When Babylon is anthropomorphized in art and literature, this is the category in which it is consistently placed. We can explore this idea further by looking at two Mesopotamian characters who come to us from ancient Greece: Sardanapalus and Semiramis.

The stories of Sardanapalus and Semiramis have much in common. They both involve sexual deviancy and violence, power and the abuse of power. They also specifically involve the blurring of gender and sexuality. There is a rich literature on the European representation of Eastern man and Eastern woman, but they are as a rule treated as separate types in representation, and separate conclusions are drawn about them. Frequently, however, they are not different types at all. Instead, they are both parts of a fantasy of seduction and transgression being played out in modern, male, upper-class European minds. On this subject Anne McClintock's *Imperial Leather* is a key work, bringing together gender, sexuality, class and race in describing imperial discourse. McClintock looks at Victorian culture, identifying cultural taboos and boundaries and then looking at their transgression.[157] She concentrates on the ways in which fantasies are played out and constrained, and this often hidden tension is very relevant to the representation of characters like Sardanapalus and Semiramis.

The transgressions of Sardanapalus and Semiramis are represented, in modernity as in antiquity, as basically negative, Sardanapalus' entirely so. Semiramis is brave and cunning in her military career, but she abuses her power and her very success undermines the male kings of Mesopotamia, since in classical Greek literature female intervention in war is either reserved for immortals or treated as abhorrent, as in the case of the Amazons. Insofar as these characters carry an explicit lesson in modern paintings and plays, that lesson is about the dangers of such transgression. Rather than screening out such sin, however, nineteenth-century painters in particular seem to have revelled in it. Presented with an image such as Delacroix's *Death of Sardanapalus*[158] it is hard to deny that the artist dwells on the sexual transgressions, and that the viewer is encouraged to do the same. The public material plays an unspoken sexual, almost pornographic, role codified in just such a way as to be ideologically acceptable within a relatively prudish modern culture. This role is not simply a matter of the nudity of female figures found in many 'fall of Babylon' images, but rather the fantasy of transgression and sin for which they are ciphers. The feminized bisexual tyrant Sardanapalus and the masculinized, sadistic Semiramis represent everything forbidden, yet they and their behaviour are accessible because they are legitimated as culturally worthwhile subject matter by high culture and history. Such characters and their stories form a taboo-breaking aspect of a high culture created by and for a rich, powerful, but socially quite constrained audience, and this is the context in which their cultural significance makes most sense.

One important transgression of the taboo is missed as long as we treat the representation of men and women as distinct categories. These representations are laden with gender blurring and the reversal of traditional sexual roles and categories (as is also the case with Ishtar, analysed by Bahrani).[159] Sardanapalus and Semiramis are part of the same, modern fantasy, and their representation ties in well with a more widely documented Victorian fascination with the androgyne.[160] In the representation of Babylon, fantasies of transgression occur again and again, so much so that there evolves a standard way of mediating them and making them acceptable in modern society: that mediation is the performance of a seduction, yet sin and responsibility for sin are transferred away from the viewer. When the Sardanapalus story is presented as both a historical education and a moral lesson, for example, it can hardly be the fault of the producers for being faithful to history and morality, or of the audience if they witness all the sins of the ancient East.

The arrival of excavated Mesopotamian material in Europe and the decipherment of cuneiform did not in themselves do anything to undermine this tendency in art. Indeed, they could easily be co-opted to complement it. Edwin Long's 1875 *Babylonian Marriage Market* is a representation of particular interest to archaeologists and Assyriologists, incorporating an enormous amount of detail sourced from the Assyrian collections of the British Museum (Figure 14). Meticulous use of the Assyrian reliefs is everywhere in evidence, giving the impression that it represents a major break with what has gone before, and that Long's painting is far more accurate and authentic a representation of Babylon than its predecessors. No doubt this is true at the level of decorative detail, Long using the closely-related arts of Assyria rather than, for example, the classical sources of the Flemish Tower of Babel images. In theme and narrative, however, Long's choice of subject puts his work firmly into the category of Orientalist sexual exotica. Long drew the painting's narrative not from ancient Mesopotamia but from Herodotus, and in particular his far-fetched story of an annual market where the dowries of less attractive women are covered by the bride prices paid by rich men for the beauties (see Chapter 3). There is truth in the statement that 'the new archaeological approach signified a desire to engage more directly with the past and to recreate it more authentically than ever before,'[161] but this desire was realized in practice as an authentification of the fantastic. Just as Said argued with regard to orientalist scholarship and art more generally, meticulous attention to detail in history painting could mask a lack of factual foundation for the overall subject and its subjective treatment in moral terms.[162]

A large part of the legitimacy this sourcing of detail brings stems from the belief that objects are able in some way to speak for themselves. Layard himself felt that there were occasions on which even Assyrian art, alien as it was to the Victorian public, might speak

Figure 1 Hammurabi of Babylon (1790–1752 BC) stands before the sun-god Shamash, from the Code of Hammurabi. Musée du Louvre.

Figure 2 Stela of Marduk-apla-iddina II (721–710 BC, 703–702 BC). Vorderasiatisches Museum, Staatliche Museen zu Berlin.

Figure 3 Reconstructed view of sixth-century BC Babylon from the north.
Produced by Herbert Anger based on Robert Koldewey's excavations, 1927.

The Ishtar Gate appears in the foreground, with the Processional Way
leading into the city and the ziggurat Etemenanki, unidentified until the
German excavations, appearing in the distance. Beside the Ishtar Gate can
be seen the north-western corner of Nebuchadnezzar II's Southern Palace,
including lush greenery in the area Koldewey believed to have been the site
of the Hanging Gardens.

Figure 4   The Tower of Babel in the *Bedford Hours*. Bedford Master (probably Haincelin of Hagenau) and Parisian studio, 1410–30 (this fol. 1430). British Library.

Figure 5   The destruction of Babylon in the *Apocalypse of Angers*, Nicolas Bataille and Robert Poinçon after designs by Hennequin de Bruges, 1377–82. Château d'Angers, Angers, France.

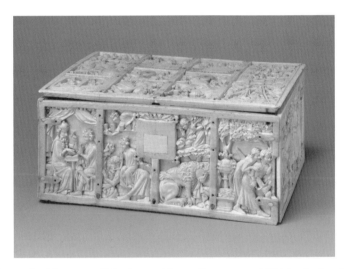

Figure 6   The story of the doomed lovers Pyramus and Thisbe depicted on a medieval ivory casket. Front panel, from left to right: Aristotle teaching Alexander; Phyllis riding Aristotle; the lion with Thisbe's cloak; death of Pyramus and Thisbe. French, early fourteenth century. The Metropolitan Museum of Art, gift of J. Pierpont Morgan, 1917; The Cloisters Collection, 1988.

Figure 7 Albrecht Dürer, *The Whore of Babylon, the Destruction of Babylon, and the Knight Called Faithful and True,* c.1496–7. The Metropolitan Museum of Art, Rogers Fund, 1918.

Figure 8 Pieter Bruegel the Elder, *Tower of Babel*, 1563. Kunsthistorisches Museum, Vienna.

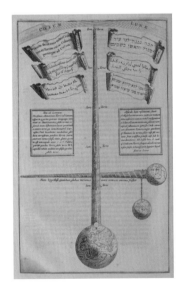

Figure 9 'Why the Tower Cannot Reach the Moon'. Conraet Decker after Lievin Cruyl in Athanasius Kircher's *Turris Babel*, 1679.

Figure 10 Rembrandt van Rijn, *Belshazzar's Feast*, *c*.1636–8. National Gallery, London.

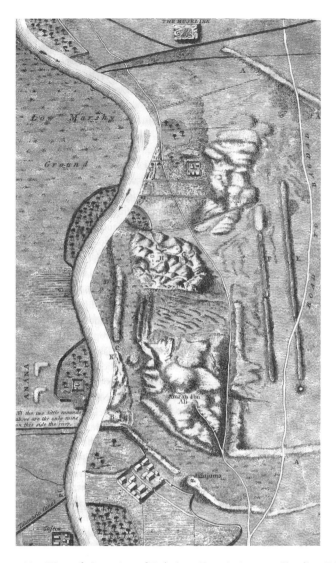

Figure 11 Plan of the ruins of Babylon. Frontispiece to Claudius Rich, *Memoir on the Ruins of Babylon*, 1815. The three major mounds are Tell Babil (north, here labelled 'Mujelibe'), the Kasr (centre, also known as the 'Mujelibe'), and Amran (south), with the shrine of Amran ibn 'Ali on top. To the south and west of Amran are the modern villages of Djimijma (here 'Jumjuma') and Anana, which still border the site today.

Figure 12   Arthur Ackland Hunt, Portrait of Hormuzd Rassam (1826–1910), 1869. The British Museum.

Figure 13   William Blake, *Nebuchadnezzar*, 1795/*c*.1805. Tate Britain.

Figure 14   Edwin Long, *The Babylonian Marriage Market*, 1875. Royal Holloway College, London.

Figure 15   Robert Koldewey at the Babylon expedition house, photographed by Gertrude Bell, March–April 1914. Gertrude Bell Archive, Newcastle University.

Figure 16   Early stages in the excavation of the Ishtar Gate, 1902.

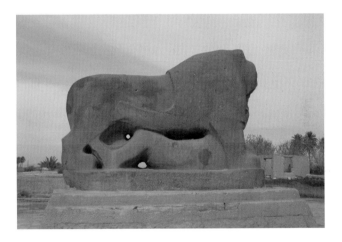

Figure 17   The Lion of Babylon. Possibly seen by Joseph de Beauchamp at the end of the eighteenth century, and certainly by Claudius Rich at the beginning of the nineteenth, the enigmatic statue remained a mystery. (The statue's identification is difficult because it is unfinished, but it is unlikely to be a Babylonian product.) By Koldewey's time the lion had acquired a local folklore of its own.

Figure 18 Walter Andrae, set design for *Sardanapal*, 1907. Staatsbibliothek zu Berlin.

Figure 19 Preparations for Ishtar Gate reconstructions: sorting glazed-brick fragments in Berlin, 1927.

Figure 20 The completed Ishtar Gate reconstructions at the Vorderasiatisches Museum today.

Figure 21 Glazed-brick lion relief from the Processional Way. The Metropolitan Museum of Art, Fletcher Fund, 1931.

Figure 22   The colossal Babylon set in D. W. Griffith's *Intolerance*, 1916.

Figure 23   Gertrude Bell at Babylon, 1909. Gertrude Bell Archive, Newcastle University.

Figure 24 Excavated ruins of the Northern Palace (left) and 1980s reconstructions at the Southern Palace (right) at Babylon.

Figure 25 Modern brickwork at the Southern Palace reconstructions, with Arabic inscription of Saddam Hussein.

Figure 26 Ceiling mural depicting Iraqi history, from Saddam Hussein's palace at Babylon.

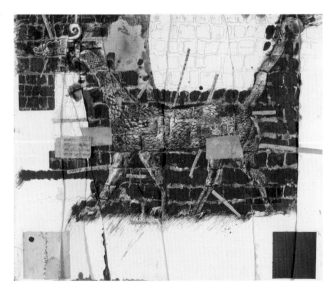

Figure 27 Hanaa Malallah, *The God Marduk*, 2008.

in such clear terms. Describing the great gateway sculptures that were to become the best-known examples of Assyrian art, he wrote:

> They could find no better type of intellect and knowledge than the head of the man; of strength, than the body of the lion; of ubiquity, than the wings of the bird. These winged, human-headed lions were not idle creations, the offspring of mere fancy; their meaning was written upon them.[163]

In a similar vein, it has been suggested that there was something of a happy coincidence between the form of these particular statues and the aesthetics of the modern culture into which they were received, that 'these enormous Assyrian bulls had something very much in common with the ponderous, conservative philosophy of the Mid-Victorian period'.[164] Some proof of the limitations of this belief can be found in the mixed reception the sculptures received as art. Layard championed Assyrian art as important and worthy of study, but his view was by no means shared by the British Museum's trustees or other art experts of the time, who judged the Mesopotamian reliefs and statues by comparison with a Greco-Roman standard for aesthetic perfection and – inevitably, since they failed to take the Assyrian material on its own terms – found them wanting.

The veracity *The Babylonian Marriage Market* achieves in detail misleads for two reasons. First, once the authority of the artist who has studied the Assyrian sources is confirmed in the viewer's mind, the legitimating detail serves partly to confuse: that some aspects of the painting are more firmly grounded than others is easily forgotten. In this case that legitimation extends not only to the Herodotus story of the marriage market, but also to the Victorian equation of skin colour with beauty. The girls appearing first at auction (the more beautiful in Herodotus' story) are white, with skin colour darkening as the queue to the auction block progresses from left to right across the canvas. Second, the level of detail, and of a kind of photo-realism in the depiction of people and objects, serves to disguise the extent to which the image is not and could not be drawn as a single study from life. This seems obvious given the ancient subject of the work, but the illusion here is not that Long was somehow present at an actual marriage market at the time of Herodotus, but that in his sources he had access to a coherent whole from which to copy. In eliding the composite nature of the work, its creator also conceals the selection and manipulation of a diverse set of texts and material culture to a particular end.

Conclusion: The experience and the idea

Close attention to the detail of one epistemology and set of sources in the production of a representation by no means precludes the effective dominance of another. Ideas or whole systems of knowledge can be overturned in theory and yet continue to exert an influence in practice. Stephanie Moser's study *Ancestral Images* traces the development of an iconography for human origins, revealing a surprising continuity in the face of major paradigm shifts, including the rise of evolutionary theory itself.[165] The relative stability in the iconography of 'primitive' humans over centuries is shown not only to survive but even to undermine new understandings of hominid evolution, and to contribute significantly to quite recent popular and scholarly images of Neanderthals and earlier hominids. In this case technical details receive close scientific attention, while important but less tangible factors (such as the facial expressions, posture, social groupings and gaze of figures) are treated far less critically, with the result that dramatic change in scientific theory has masked incredible continuity in representation. The history of Babylon's representation has taken a different course, but the intertwining of biblical, classical and later sources has produced a comparable degree of inconsistency and complexity in the relationship between current ideas on the ancient city in theory and its representation in practice. A simplistic model of intellectual change, in which new ideas and understandings neatly displace their predecessors, will tend to impose order and consistency on the sources where there is little to be found, and to obscure some of the less reasoned but more pervasive cross-pollination that has influenced everything from representation in art to the questions asked by excavators. Ideas too have their afterlives, and these can easily take on visual forms.

The dynamics of change and continuity are key to understanding the historical dimension of representation. One myth to be dispelled, particularly in the case of classical sources, is the notion of change exemplified by medieval decay and modern recovery, the belief that knowledge of the ancient past was once ungarbled and unambiguous, was gradually forgotten, and was eventually recovered and re-established by modern scholarship. This is a model of scholarly recovery based on particular ideals, especially a certain modern scientific positivism, not a historical pattern readily observed in practice. To demonstrate this point, we can return to our key early Greek accounts of Babylon. The combined writings of Herodotus, Ctesias and Berossus do not add up to a coherent and consistent account of Babylon or of Babylonia and Assyria. There is very little consistency in terms of historical events, king-lists, details of the great engineering works or the roles of individual rulers. There is often direct contradiction, and usually very little scope for an ancient reader to verify a given claim. Further, it seems probable that the lost elements of Berossus, especially if based on Babylonian primary sources, would throw up even more contradictions than those of which we are already aware. Later writers and artists have been forced to reconcile and homogenize the three very different accounts, or to favour one to the exclusion of the others. In its earliest stages, the literary reception of Babylon was already plural and inconsistent. Even allowing for the better-informed account of Berossus, there never was a correct single account of Babylon to lose, nor would there be if we went back further, to the Babylonian sources themselves or even to a set of hypothetical 'perfect' sources, in which residents of Babylon described the city in depth and detail. Such sources are impossibilities, of course, and all description is by its nature situated, partial, partisan and reductive. It can never be complete or absolute. The brief window in the early- to mid-twentieth century when positivism in archaeology briefly made the idea of a single accurate scholarly picture of the ancient past seem an achievable or at least an appropriate goal is not the consequence of progressive generations of scholars narrowing down the range of the possible. If anything it is an exception, a fleeting moment inconsistent with a history in which subjectivity and uncertainty have been accepted as the inevitable operating mode of historians. Although difficult to apply sensibly and constructively to the fragmentary remains of the ancient past, the pluralism and multi-vocality seen in contemporary critical theory and anthropology better suit the data and their problems, even if they lack the allure of completion and closure.

Any historical perspective shows knowledge and understanding to exist in states of perpetual flux, and their study, through representation as much as through philosophy, requires a concentration on the ebb and flow of epistemologies and values. There is a great deal of existing work on the patterns of gradual and dramatic, accretive and paradigmatic change in knowledge within the humanities, social sciences and natural sciences. A model of minor incremental change punctuated by dramatic revolution was the basic thesis of Thomas Kuhn's hugely influential *The Structure of Scientific Revolutions*.[166] There is a strong case for this understanding of the history of science: Bachelard argued that it does not apply equally to the humanities, which develop more incrementally,[167] yet while this objection may hold true to some extent there is no need to polarize or draw strong distinctions between the sciences and the humanities. Rather, both incremental and revolutionary processes operate in both contexts. In the history of science, of the humanities or of any scholarship, abrupt revolutionary change may be of great importance without implying total discontinuity or wholesale destruction. Since we are dealing here with the history of archaeology, we in any case find ourselves at the border between the two worlds.

The visits of travellers to Babylon frequently involved the conscious use of biblical and classical sources in more-or-less confined situations, whereby specific aspects of a visitor's experience were related in their accounts to specific aspects of the two textual traditions. Time, repetition and selective borrowing all contributed to a process by which observations and traditions became entangled, but this entanglement was frequently balanced by scholarly visitors such as Niebuhr and Rich, whose tendency to return to and compare their older sources did much to refresh and clarify the historiographic basis of the tradition. Representations in art and fiction developed in a different way, and their interrelation over time is as much a matter of narrative and theme as of historical detail. It is possible to identify the most popular and influential narratives and their biblical or classical roots, yet by the nineteenth century the overwhelming impression is of a single canon rather than two separate and conflicting biblical and classical traditions. The connection is sin: the moral and sexual deviancy of Sardanapalus and Semiramis tie in quite comfortably with the despotism of Nebuchadnezzar, or the hubris of Nimrod.

When ancient Assyrian material culture began arriving in Europe in the mid-nineteenth century, its iconography was applied to themes from both the biblical and classical traditions, lending the credibility of history and the support of physical evidence. The impact of decipherment played a similar unifying and legitimating role. The discovery of the palace sculptures of Ashurbanipal at Nineveh gave European scholars a credible historical Sardanapalus, while another Ninevite palace really was that of the biblical Sennacherib, complete with vivid depictions of his campaigns in the Levant. An understanding of the chronological and familial relationship between the two kings gave new weight to the biblical and classical accounts in equal measure.[168] There may be a reflection of this in the travellers' accounts, where observations on the fulfilment of biblical prophecy were increasingly supplemented by discussion of Herodotus' description of the walls of Babylon and temple of Bel.[169] This shift, however, could more convincingly be explained as the product of Herodotus' greater suitability to the types of topographical and architectural question and investigation that became important for visitors in the eighteenth and nineteenth centuries.

The sexualized and sinful aspects of Babylon in modern European culture would ultimately become the elements that lend the greatest potency and relevance to Babylon's representation in the present. Sin is as near to a universal theme as could be imagined, and in terms of Babylon's enduring relevance as a cultural symbol this is enormously important. We seek the difference of the past, yet it is recognition that fascinates. Leonard Woolley, excavator of Ur, observed that 'the surprise which a visitor to a museum expresses at the age of a given object is in exact proportion to his recognition of the object's essential modernity – it is the surprise of one who sees his horizon suddenly opening out'.[170] This precise and elegant explanation of archaeology's appeal brings us to the very heart of the relationship between the academic study of the past and its treatment in other cultural forms. The recognition of the object's essential modernity, in this case, is a sleight of hand: it stems from the fact that the object, be it painting, play, poem or opera, actually *is* modern, and thus able to bridge the gap and manufacture the desired mix of strangeness and familiarity. To satisfy this appeal, increasing empiricism is the last thing needed from travellers' accounts (as Voltaire recognized), yet this was occurring at just the same time as orientalist fantasies flourished. It is only as this conflict develops that the worlds of antiquarian, historical and archaeological study and the artistic representation of the past truly diverge. It was not, for example, a problem faced by Athanasius Kircher, even if his inclusion of Pietro Della Valle's pictures of Tell Babil alongside other, more fantastic, images is a part of its genesis. The firm separation of empirical, archaeological approaches as a distinct category, both in performance and in publication, is a recent development in our relationship with the human past. The consolidation and consequences of this change will be seen more clearly as we move into the twentieth century, and the German archaeological excavations at Babylon.

CHAPTER 6

THE GERMAN EXPERIENCE: EXCAVATION AND RECEPTION

The excavation of Babylon and its immediate reception in Germany mark a substantial change in the relationship between ancient Babylon and the present. Robert Koldewey's excavations revealed the monumental architecture at the heart of the ancient city itself, while in Berlin the Assyriologist Friedrich Delitzsch rose to great prominence as the academic authority on Babylon and as its chief publicist. This chapter examines the roles of individuals and institutions in the imperial German archaeological experience of Babylon, and the relationship between that experience and older forms of knowledge and representation.

Robert Koldewey

It would be misleading to draw too many parallels between the role of Koldewey in Babylonia and Germany and that of Layard in Assyria and England 50 years earlier (Figure 15). Crucially, Layard himself took charge of the promotion of his excavations to the British public,[1] as well as producing the more lavish *Monuments of Nineveh* volumes.[2] He was better known, if not more respected academically, than his peers in the subject, and through his willingness to communicate with the public became the defining figure in both the excavation and English reception of Assyria. Koldewey, by contrast, took little interest in fame in Berlin, and in any case worked in a different academic system within which, whatever his achievements in Mesopotamia, such fame might not have been a possibility. His background was in art and architecture, which he had taught, and he had excavation experience in Italy, Sicily and the Aegean as well as Syria and Iraq prior to his work at Babylon.[3] He was not of particularly high academic standing, and in this respect might even have been considered under-qualified for the task eventually allotted to him. He can be seen as the originator of that project, however, if not a great player in engineering the conditions under which it would receive support. Prior to the excavations he had made two previous visits to Babylon and had collected examples of the glazed bricks found on the surface. The second of these trips, in 1897–8, was made with the Berlin University orientalist Eduard Sachau.[4] The bricks proved important in Koldewey's efforts to gain support for the excavations, but the processes leading towards a large German archaeological project in Mesopotamia were really happening independently of him.

At this time, the priorities of the young Germany were mixed, but a general doctrine of the need to strengthen the republic through expansion, *Weltmachtpolitik* and a stake as a major imperial power were broadly agreed upon.[5] Whether the priorities were economic strength or cultural identity as a power to match England and France, the strength of a united Germany needed to find material expression and to be manifested in the world of culture. The political centre in imperial Germany engaged with only a limited part of the German cultural sphere, since unlike in England and France literary and artistic productivity were less concentrated in the political capital: Berlin was not the equivalent of London or Paris. Academic research and science, however, were perhaps exceptions.[6] Even before unification Prussia had, through a combination of royal patronage and individual initiative, developed as a leading centre of scholarship. The Humboldt University was founded in 1810; its humanist aims and mixture of teaching and research came to influence the form of modern universities across the world, while Humboldt himself ensured an expansion of the traditional curriculum. Prussian royalty had long supported scolarship – Sophie-Charlotte of Hanover (Electress of Brandenburg from 1688 and first Queen of Prussia 1701–5) was even a protégé of Leibniz. So whilst Berlin was not Germany's cultural centre to the same degree as the French and English capitals, it was nonetheless the established centre of modern scientific research.

That oriental studies and Near Eastern archaeology fell within this latter category is informative in itself. It might be possible to make comparisons with French imperial *savants*, but not with a scholarly culture rooted in *belles lettres*. Nor can an easy analogy be drawn with the English exploration of the Mesopotamian past, in which colonial administrators and gentleman adventurers had played such important roles. In the German case, the key actors were professionals working for and from institutions. The social makeup of this group was largely middle class, liberal and Protestant. Importantly, it was a demographic with a strong vested interest in contributing to German national and imperial culture, as their class prospered in industry and rose in social standing. Bismarck's careful maintenance of aristocratic, and particularly Prussian *Junker*, power[7] was eroded by rapid industrialization and the economic rise of the middle classes, and a bourgeoisie that sought a major role in national culture emerged. Seen by its instigators, most crucially Bernhard von Bülow (Chancellor 1900–9), as a tool for establishing domestic stability through national unity of purpose, *Weltpolitik* aimed to service these desires. (Not without a degree of cynicism: von Bülow fully understood the domestic value of imperialist pomp.[8])

The Deutsche Orient-Gesellschaft was founded with the aim of archaeological acquisition, for Germany, from major excavation projects in the Middle East and particularly within the weakening Ottoman Empire, which in broader political terms seemed at the time an area on which the latecomer on the imperial scene could focus and attempt to gain a foothold. Following great successes at Pergamon and Olympia, German excavations at classical sites in Asia Minor had already multiplied during the 1890s, with much of the new funding coming ultimately from the state.[9] The founding at the Deutsche Orient-Gesellschaft seems in some ways a natural extension of this existing German stake in the archaeology of the western part of the Ottoman Empire. Perhaps more interesting than the territorial expansion the society represented, however, was expansion of another kind: into the non-classical Near Eastern past, whose study had previously been restricted in Germany almost entirely to philology and biblical studies. Even here, although Germany had become a centre for textual criticism of the Old Testament, the same could not be said of Assyriological research: until the late nineteenth century German cuneiform researchers – including the young Friedrich Delitzsch – had to do much of their work abroad, predominantly in London among the rapidly expanding cuneiform collections of the British Museum.[10] Now ancient Mesopotamia and even Near Eastern archaeology were to share some of the limelight that throughout the nineteenth century in Germany had been reserved almost exclusively for the Graeco-Roman past.

It should be stressed that the society was founded with acquisitions for the nation as an explicit goal. It was modelled on the Kaiser-Friedrich-Museum Society (a group formed by collectors aiming to acquire fine art for the state), and was envisaged as performing a broadly equivalent function.[11] The main contributors, listed in each issue of the *Mitteilungen der Deutschen Orient Gesellschaft*, were Kaiser Wilhelm II himself and major business figures, and these were the interests that carried the most weight within the society. The picture is complicated by that part of the membership based more on scholarly interest than any substantial ability to invest: scholars, churchmen and other enthusiasts were part of the society, alongside the great industrialists. Nonetheless, the latter were enormously important, and it is notable that many had business concerns in Constantinople, and specifically in the great project of a 'Baghdad-Bahn'.[12]

The Baghdad-Bahn was at the economic heart of Germany's Mesopotamian interests.[13] Competing with Britain for control and a leading role in the creation of a strategically important new land route between Europe and the Persian Gulf, the railway as envisaged by Germany would eventually run all the way to Constantinople. In classic imperial fashion, this strategic commercial and military goal quickly acquired the trappings of an altruistic civilizing mission, and just as the new railway would contribute to the economic and technological development of the backward Ottoman Empire, so too German activity in the cultural sphere was conceptualized as beneficial to both parties, bringing progress, friendship and even a 'spiritual bond'.[14] The economic and cultural projects were therefore closely linked, both in theory and in the less altruistic fact that both endeavours were strongly in the national interests of the unified and expansionist new Germany.

Although the membership of the society was diverse, it is perhaps not so mysterious that its early drive and purpose were apparently unified. The interests of scholars, industrialists and the Kaiser could all be served by a large, prestigious German excavation project in the Near East, just at the time Robert Koldewey was looking for support for a project at Babylon. Koldewey's glazed bricks certainly helped. As he put it:

> The peculiar beauty of these fragments and their importance for the history of art was duly recognised by His Excellency R. Schöne, who was then Director-General of the Royal Museums, and this strengthened our decision to excavate the capital of the world empire of Babylonia.[15]

This is a polite way of saying that they suggested something visually spectacular would emerge from an excavation, and that visually impressive museum pieces were what the Deutsche Orient-Gesellschaft sought. This position may be less mercenary than it first appears to the present-day reader. Many scholars held that a fairly direct relationship existed between quality of aesthetic production and the historical significance or state of cultural development of a society.[16] The belief can be traced directly to Winckelmann, as can the position of classical Greek art as the benchmark for perfection in the aesthetic sphere. There was therefore an intellectual as well as an imperial imperative to access the finest artistic products of an ancient civilization. Of course, the name of Babylon was undoubtedly a great lure, and surely the only project that could match the discovery of Nineveh for prestige and public interest. On the other hand, it presented a risk in two respects. First, although the general location of ancient Babylon was clear, it was not at all apparent prior to Koldewey's excavations what was and was not Babylon itself. Claudius Rich had already failed to find the massive city wall described by Herodotus, for example,[17] and neither Layard nor Botta had managed to replicate their successes in Assyria here. Second, no excavation in southern Mesopotamia had yet proved satisfactory in terms of exposing architecture. The decision to support Koldewey only made sense if one assumed he would be successful. Perhaps his sponsors did, but in reality the young Deutsche Orient-Gesellschaft was taking an expensive gamble. Fortunately the gamble paid off, and Koldewey's work was a success from the very beginning.

Koldewey at Babylon

Robert Koldewey's work at Babylon from 1899 to 1917 forms the basis of our archaeological understanding of the site today, and his importance in the development of excavation methods in Mesopotamia is enormous.[18] The work was conducted on a huge scale. Excavations were concentrated in a scatter along the east bank of the river, in the very centre of the city's walled enclosure, and focused mainly on the large palaces, temples and fortifications of the inner city (Figure 16). Equally important, the publication of the work was exemplary, far ahead of its time, and included excellent technical drawing and recording.[19] Significantly, it also showed something of the detached, impersonal style of writing of the natural sciences.[20]

Koldewey had used the glazed bricks found at the site to help make the case for excavation, and unsurprisingly he concentrated first on their source. He aimed, in any case, to focus on the city's centre, where it was presumed that the most important palaces and temples were to be found. Babylon shares with most other early Mesopotamian excavations a concentration on large buildings and centres to the exclusion of ordinary residential areas. The latter have only received greater attention more recently, as research priorities have shifted away from elite political history and towards broader social and economic questions, and as new scientific techniques have made it possible to address these questions more effectively. The scale of earlier excavations relative to their successors, however, means that archaeologists today inherit a pronounced elite bias in the research materials that are available to work with. In addition, the particular interests of Koldewey and his colleagues were in architectural history, meaning the history of monumental architecture. All this said, some private houses were excavated at Babylon, and perhaps their inclusion at all in the Deutsche Orient-Gesellschaft project is more remarkable than their exclusion from early Mesopotamian excavations in general.

The ability to excavate Babylon's houses at all was owed, like the project's success in general, to the technical achievement of the Babylon excavations in carefully tracing and revealing mud-brick architecture. The development of these techniques benefitted Koldewey as well as posterity, since unlike their counterparts in Assyria even the grandest buildings in Babylonia were constructed of mud-brick. Modern buildings were made in the same way, and local workmen probably made a significant contribution to the achievement of successfully tracing and excavating mud-brick walls.[21] This is hard to confirm since these workers, never prominent and rarely named even in the personal, travelogue style of Layard, are even more elusive in Koldewey's writing, although they do appear in Walter Andrae's paintings[22] and some site photographs. There are other occasions when the interpretation of Koldewey himself was informed by his experience of living at Babylon, for example on practical matters such as building layout, where he noted that:

> [I]n all the great courts the largest buildings lay to the south, so in each of these houses the principal chamber lay on the south side of the court; and this must have been the pleasantest part of the whole house, as it lay in shadow almost all day. Owing to the peculiar climate of Babylon it is obvious that in laying out a

house, only the summer and the heat would be taken into
consideration [...]. We have observed a maximum of $49\frac{1}{2}$
grades Celsius in the shade, and 66 in the sun, and the heat lasts
for many hours of the day [...]. Rain is very scanty. I believe if
all the hours in the whole year in which there were more than a
few drops of rain were reckoned up, they would barely amount
to 7 or 8 days.[23]

This attention to the weather is also to be found in Koldewey's
frequent reports in the *Mitteilungen der Deutschen Orient-Gesellschaft zu
Berlin*, which often end with a short note on climate and
environmental conditions. In a similar vein, he debunks the common
myth that Babylonia is an obvious and particularly easy place for
astronomy to develop based on his own experience:

> Owing to excessive dryness, the air is almost opaque at a
> distance, and the horizon up to a height of 10 or 20 grades is a
> dusky circle of dust, through which the sun and moon often
> assume torn and distorted forms, if their setting can be seen at
> all [...]. The greatly-renowned clearness of the Babylonian sky
> is largely a fiction of European travellers, who are rarely
> accustomed to observe the night sky of Europe without the
> intervention of city lights.[24]

Koldewey's main interest, owing to his own academic and
professional background, was in the ancient city's architecture, and
one respect in which Babylon certainly did live up to its reputation
was palatial opulence, at least in terms of sheer scale. The palaces (of
which there are three: the 'Southern', 'Northern' and 'Summer'
palaces) contain hundreds of rooms and gigantic courtyards and
throne-rooms. The largest, the Southern Palace, measured almost
300 metres on its longest side and contained over 200 rooms set
around its five major courtyards. As impressive as their dimensions
are, however, the Babylonian ruins are of a type that makes their
original state difficult to imagine at all, although photographs from
the German excavations provided a glimpse of the city in a form more

comprehensible to the non-archaeologist, as their exposure of the architecture covered large areas and often revealed high standing walls or foundations. The recording of these standing remains was excellent; even greater care was taken later at Ashur, where Andrae performed what are generally considered the first stratigraphic soundings in Mesopotamian archaeology.[25] Although borrowed from geology, in some ways stratigraphic excavation was a natural development from excavation with an eye to architecture. Koldewey was interested in identifying the construction phases of buildings at Babylon, resulting in section drawings of walls that were in effect stratigraphic.[26]

The process of excavation was inevitably a demystifying one in some ways: good for archaeological and historical knowledge, not necessarily for the romantic. The reduction of a legend to the dimensions of a physical place was more than figurative. With Koldewey's confirmation of what Rich had first observed almost a century earlier, Babylon literally shrank:

> In fact, it was natural that several of the early travellers should have regarded the whole complex of ruins, which they saw still standing along their road to Baghdad, as parts of the ancient city; and it is not surprising that some of the earlier excavators should have fallen under a similar illusion so far as the area between Bâbil and El-Birs {Birs Nimrud} is concerned. The famous description of Herodotus, and the accounts other classical writers have left us of the city's size, tended to foster this conviction; and, although the centre of Babylon was identified correctly enough, the size of the city's area was greatly exaggerated. Babylon had cast her spell upon mankind, and it has taken sixteen years of patient and continuous excavation to undermine this stubborn belief.[27]

L. W. King's phrase here captures an aspect of Koldewey's work that is of particular relevance in terms of representation: a scholarly thoroughness and detachment brought to bear on this most romanticized of ancient cities. 'But', as King goes on to note, 'in the process of shrinkage, and as accurate knowledge has gradually given place to conjecture, the old spell has reappeared unchanged.'[28] He refers here to the archaeological questions excavations had left unanswered, but also to the survival of Babylon's mystique and of the biblical and classical narratives associated with it. Even in the early twentieth century, with a full-scale excavation, decipherment of cuneiform scripts and languages, the translation of Akkadian texts in particular at an advanced stage and a climate in which a literal adherence to biblical accounts was no longer the only available option when discussing them academically, research still did little to directly contradict the history of Daniel, the prophecies of Isaiah and Jeremiah, or even the physical descriptions of parts of the city found in Herodotus, Ctesias, Xenophon, Strabo, Philo the Paradoxographer of Byzantium[29] or Pliny the Elder. Koldewey could offer strong candidates for both the Tower of Babel and the Hanging Gardens. The first was the ziggurat Etemenanki, a cuneiform description of which had already been found by George Smith[30] but whose physical remains were only now identified: the tower had been destroyed in antiquity and so much of its rubble re-used elsewhere that little trace remained, hence the tendency of earlier visitors to identify 'Aqar Quf, Birs Nimrud or Tell Babil as the Tower of Babel.[31] For the second, Koldewey proposed the 'vaulted building' in the north-eastern corner of the Southern Palace, of which he wrote:

> That the identification when studied in detail bristles with difficulties, will surprise no one who has more than once had to bring ancient statements of facts into accordance with discoveries of the present day. We can always rejoice when they agree in the main points.[32]

The agreement to which Koldewey refers is the unusual presence of stone vaulted arches, tallying particularly with the account of Diodorus but also with those of Berossus, Strabo and Quintus Curtius Rufus.[33] There was also a candidate for Ctesias' picture of Semiramis in the 'Persian Building', where Koldewey interpreted the only two human figures seen in relief at Babylon (as part of a hunting scene) as Ninus and Semiramis.[34] And although Herodotus' description of the walls of Babylon makes them too long, his account of their thickness at least was supported by the Deutsche Orient-Gesellschaft's findings, while his description of bricks interspersed with layers of reed matting had already been confirmed by European travellers (see Chapter 4). As for the biblical descriptions, it remains true that their content is not often of a type on which archaeological investigation would have a great bearing, since they contain virtually no physical description of the city. It is difficult and uncommon for an archaeological investigation to confirm or refute a personal narrative such as the career of Daniel, who is listed as a historical individual alongside Nebuchadnezzar in the writings of early twentieth-century Mesopotamian archaeologists, including Koldewey. This level of compatibility is enough to prompt further speculation. Koldewey felt it obvious that the dragon associated with Marduk related to Bel and the Serpent:

> This 'dragon of Babylon' was the far-famed animal of Babylon, and fits in admirably with the well-known story in the Apocrypha of Bel and the Dragon. One may easily surmise that the priests of Esagila kept some reptile, possibly an arval, which is found in this neighbourhood, and exhibited it in the semi-darkness of a temple chamber as a living sirrush. In this case there would be small cause for wonder that the creature did not survive the concoction of hair and bitumen administered to it by Daniel.[35]

The name Koldewey gives as *sirrush* is now translated as *mushhushshu*, an onomatopoeic name recalling a serpent's hiss, whose literal meaning is 'furious snake'. The dragon is associated with Marduk and his son Nabu, the god of writing and wisdom and another major figure in the Babylonian pantheon. The other animals represented in the glazed bricks of the Ishtar Gate and Processional Way are bulls and lions, equally rich in their divine associations.

Koldewey might also have been tempted to associate the latter with Daniel and the lions' den, but shows himself a more cautious interpreter. As regards the lions in relief, he simply notes that 'The lion, the animal of Ishtar, was so favourite a subject at all times in Babylonian art that its rich and lavish employment at the main gate of Babylon, the Ishtar Gate, is by no means abnormal'.[36] Even faced with the decidedly abnormal basalt 'Lion of Babylon' (Figure 17), which had already been suggested as a monument to the event raised after Daniel became governor of Babylon,[37] Koldewey still resists endorsing the interpretation:

> Some see in it Daniel in the lions' den, and others Babylonia above defeated Egypt. But a concrete past is throughout this period never represented otherwise than in reliefs, and, on the other hand, it is foreign to Babylonian art to take as a basis the representation of an abstract idea.[38]

These are not the only interpretations Koldewey has to dismiss. He also records a local tradition attached to the lion:

> [The left hand of the man being trampled by the lion] has been chopped away by superstitious hands, and he is marked all over by the stones and flint balls that have been, and are still, flung at him; for he is regarded as the much-feared 'Djin.' On one side the Arabs have dug out a deep hole in his flanks, which is now filled with cement. The reason of this is as follows. A European once came here, and inquired about the lion, which he had probably read of in the books of earlier travellers. The Arabs showed it to him, and after looking at it attentively, he chose from among the small holes in the basalt the right one, into which he thrust a key and turned it, whereupon his hand was immediately filled with gold pieces. Having accomplished his practical joke, the traveller went his way, unable as he was to speak Arabic. The worthy Arabs, however, in order to render the treasure available, hammered this hole in the lion, which must have caused them immense labour, for the stone is extremely hard.[39]

The story is meant to highlight the simplicity of those who recounted it, but now appears as a rather telling commentary on contemporary local perceptions of European travellers and archaeologists. The story makes a wonderful allegory, and it is a shame that those telling it could not see the Assyrian-themed silver casket with which Austen Henry Layard had been presented with the Freedom of the City of London in 1854.[40] The Europeans certainly did come with knowledge that could be used to convert Iraq's standing and buried monuments into capital, whether that capital was cultural, social, political, material or a combination of the four. The work of the Deutsche Orient-Gesellschaft was intended very much as a continuation of this process, and Koldewey's differences from his predecessors are not so great that his work cannot be subjected to many of the same criticisms. Archaeological work in general is intimately bound up with possession, whether through the physical acquisition of objects or the accumulation (and in this case export) of knowledge. Maps and plans are important in this form of possession, but there is also a more personal side to the process, less imperial in motivation but arguably more so in fact. However noble its aims, academic research frequently generates feelings of propriety, ownership and jealousy. It is a sense of ownership for which it is possible to compete, but for which a provincial Ottoman town could hardly have competed with a well-funded research project from imperial Germany. Koldewey's work inevitably affected the status of local knowledge, both as a source for European visitors and, one must assume, locally as well. Moreover, his practical power and control of the site could be naturalized by his expertise and ownership of knowledge. There is nothing unusual or even particularly avoidable about these processes in such an excavation, but their relationship to more formal and more planned narratives of imperial possession should be noted.

The excavations at Babylon set a number of methodological precedents. The standards of excavation and recording were ahead of their time in Mesopotamia and beyond: the excavators worked 'with a patience and methodical ingenuity which set an entirely new standard for the conduct of archaeological excavations in all parts of the world'.[41] This point deserves attention, because it cannot easily be seen as a necessary consequence of the cultural milieu in which the Deutsche Orient-Gesellschaft was formed and the expedition conceived. What German archaeologists did at Babylon and Ashur makes little sense from the point of view of what was expected of them in Berlin. They had been engaged, bluntly put, to dig for treasure. Monumental art and inscribed tablets were the concerns of their patrons, who sought national glory, and of the academic establishment in Berlin, whose expertise lay in the study of cuneiform texts and for whom archaeology was still primarily thought of as a means of accessing this material. By contrast, Koldewey is remembered for developing excavation techniques that furthered neither of these causes, and even hindered the large-scale rapid acquisition of tablets and art. In much the same way it becomes easy to forget, looking at Koldewey's long stay at Babylon, his apparently good relationship with the local population and his diffidence regarding public life in Germany, that he had been sent to Mesopotamia for the glory of empire. His biographers, including Andrae, describe an eccentric, strong-willed personality, fiercely dedicated to his research – and apparently for himself far more than for an organization or state. One is left with the impression that Koldewey was happy to keep a continent between himself and Berlin, removed from the power-play and atavism of the system his work fed. The full consequences of his political disengagement are more complicated than this, however, and will be examined later in this chapter.

Koldewey's work, as he saw it, was only half-done at Babylon. He had worked almost continuously at the site, mostly on an enormous scale, and had exposed far more of it than any present-day excavation could, but much more remained unexplored. He had already made the site his life's work, and would gladly have devoted the rest of it to that work's continuation. The preface in which he stressed the importance of the work's completion was written at Babylon and is dated 16 May 1912, by which point war in Europe threatened. In April 1914 Gertrude Bell, who had visited the site previously and been deeply impressed by its excavators, made 'a brief visit to Babylon to pay homage to the work of her friend Professor Koldewey

of Berlin before war brought such peaceable pleasantries to an end'.[42]
War, of course, also brought an end to the excavations, though
incredibly Koldewey did continue working at a much reduced level
until the approach of the British Mesopotamia Expeditionary Force
in 1917. Deutsche Orient-Gesellschaft fieldwork – indeed European
fieldwork generally – was never to resume on the same scale.[43]

Friedrich Delitzsch

For all his achievements, Koldewey was not the figure with whom
Babylon came to be associated for the German public. This honour fell
instead to Friedrich Delitzsch, director of the newly founded
Vorderasiatische Abteilung (Near Eastern Section) of the Berlin
museums. The son of the Lutheran theologian Franz Delitzsch, he had
risen to prominence within the academic discipline of Assyriology. His
work remains an important part of the subject's foundations, and he
can be seen to be part of a movement that did as much for the study of
ancient Near Eastern texts as the excavations at Babylon did for
archaeological method. German philologists of Delitzch's generation
produced the dictionaries, grammars and sign-lists that underpin the
subject today, and Delitzsch's personal contribution to the study of
both Akkadian and Sumerian was enormous.[44] His is also of the
generation from which the first great German teachers of Assyriology
in America were drawn.[45] Additionally, Delitzsch had from an early
date recognized and engaged with the potential for his subject to
inform biblical studies,[46] and had produced a widely acclaimed and
explicitly nationalist call for support of the newly founded Deutsche
Orient-Gesellschaft in *Ex Oriente Lux! Ein Wort zur Förderung der
Deutschen Orient-Gesellschaft.*[47]

Although already a respected scholar and professor, Delitzsch was
a new arrival in Berlin in 1899, being appointed simultaneously to
his museum post in the Vorderasiatische Abteilung and to a
professorship at Berlin University. Again there is a parallel with
Koldewey, in the sense that Delitzsch also benefited from a rise in the
prominence of ancient Near Eastern studies driven by forces that had
little to do with his own work. Unlike Koldewey, however, Delitzsch

became very much involved with these forces. He was uniquely able to do so: his position was a powerful and prestigious one, making him the obvious authority in both university and museum. With his involvement in the Deutsche Orient-Gesellschaft his influence spanned the full breadth of Near Eastern studies in Germany, from academic philology to the allocation of excavation funding. Given the great personal interest taken by Kaiser Wilhelm II in the ancient Near East, Delitzsch's position was seen as one of particular influence.

Delitzsch's authority afforded him a privileged position in presenting ancient Mesopotamia to the public, a task to which he took with zeal. Bohrer argues that in performing this role he relied heavily on the historical precedents of France and England. His chosen vehicle for announcing Koldewey's early success was the *Illustrierte Zeitung*,[48] a journal designed to follow the format of the *Illustrated London News*. Layard had risen to fame in the pages of the latter, and the remarkable commercial success of *Nineveh and its Remains* owed a considerable debt to the sustained and positive coverage the Assyrian excavations received in the *Illustrated London News*. It has been suggested that the approach was now out of date,[49] although perhaps the problem was not the medium as such: in Britain the *Illustrated London News* itself continued to function as a popular and effective vehicle for communicating archaeological research to the public well into the twentieth century, publicizing the work of Leonard Woolley and Max Mallowan in Iraq and playing its own part in the reception of the discovery of Tutankhamun's tomb in Egypt.[50] It is true, however, that new, lighter publications had emerged and that Delitzsch fared badly in the changed media environment. Poor judgement of the press was only one factor contributing to his loss of face and media victimization, however. The main element was what came to be known as the 'Babel–Bibel' affair, and the espousal of views that led to considerable religious controversy.

Babel–Bibel

From 1902 Delitzsch was to give a series of three high-profile lectures on the theme of *Babel und Bibel*,[51] aimed at demonstrating the relevance of the Deutsche Orient-Gesellschaft's work to Germany. They were not designed to be particularly original in content, but to communicate scholarly research to a wider audience. Perhaps strangely, given Koldewey's recent successes, Delitzsch did not focus on the excavations at Babylon, but on his own strengths in philology and on discoveries that had been made prior to the Babylon excavations: the many Assyriological discoveries, well known to scholars though not to the wider German public, with a bearing on the Old Testament.

The first lecture[52] was delivered on 13 January 1902 to a prestigious audience at the Singakademie, Berlin, and was repeated three weeks later at the imperial palace – the emperor himself attended both performances. In his lecture Delitzsch outlined several ideas already current within the academic community, notably that the Bible was not the world's oldest literature and that parts of the ancient Mesopotamian corpus bore close similarities to parts of the Old Testament. He went on to attribute a number of supposedly Hebrew innovations, including extant religious narratives and ritual practices, to Babylonia. He was not the first to express these ideas, but he did bring them to a broader (and much more difficult) audience:

> The school of Wellhausen dominated the German theology at the time, and its emphasis on a strictly literary/critical approach to an analysis of the Old Testament left little space for the new, predominantly historical evidence. The prevailing view of both the theological professors and the general public was that the monotheistic religion of the Jews was to be seen and understood as a truly unique phenomenon, growing directly out of the nomadic, primitive world of the tribes.[53]

Delitzsch's view on these matters was part of a broader intellectual movement, complementing the 'pan-Babylonian' ideas of, particularly, Hugo Winckler, who won a substantial following at the beginning of the twentieth century for his arguments that Babylonian culture lay at the root of all later religion and mythology. The first *Babel und Bibel* lecture was controversial, but did gain Delitzsch and Near Eastern studies a great deal of publicity. It certainly succeeded in its aim of showing the relevance of the field to modern German cultural life: Mesopotamian texts were now at the centre of a national theological argument, given its intensity by the contemporary assumption that there was one overarching truth, to be found at any cost. This was not a question on which the parties concerned could agree to differ.[54]

The next lecture was delayed in order to allow the situation to calm down somewhat. 'Richard Schöne, Delitzsch's superior at the Berlin museums, providentially sent Delitzsch away from Berlin for most of the rest of the year'[55] and the second lecture was not given until early 1903.[56] Once again he spoke at the Singakademie, and once again with the Kaiser in attendance. Delitzsch now took his assertions of the previous year significantly further. Supported by the Mesopotamian precedents for much Old Testament material, he explicitly denied that the Old Testament was divinely inspired revelation. The preface added to the published version of the lecture is fascinating, and shows the meeting of several facets of Delitzsch's character: the son of the great theologian, the polemicist, the earnest scientific thinker and, most importantly of all, the man who saw his Assyriological work as intimately bound up with the future spiritual and moral wellbeing of a nation. It is worth quoting at some length. Having first given a particularly fiery quotation from the Book of Isaiah,[57] Delitzsch begins:

> Surely, both in diction, style, and spirit a genuine Bedouin battle-song and ode of triumph? No! This passage, with a hundred others from prophetical literature that are full of unquenchable hatred directed against surrounding peoples – against Edom and Moab, Assyria and Babylon, Tyre and Egypt – that for the most part, too, are masterpieces of Hebrew rhetoric, must represent the ethical prophets and prophecy of Israel, even at their most advanced stage! The outcome of certain definite events, these outbursts of political jealousy and

of a passionate hatred, which judged from the human standpoint, may, perhaps, be quite natural and comprehensible enough – such outbursts on the part of generations long since passed away must still do duty for us children of the twentieth century after Christ, for the Christian peoples of the West, as a Book of Religion, for morality, and for edification! Instead of immersing ourselves in 'thankful wonder' at the providential guidance shown by God in the case of our own people, from the earliest times of primitive Germany until to-day, we persist – either from ignorance, indifference, or infatuation – in ascribing to those old-Israelitish oracles a 'revealed' character which cannot be maintained, either in the light of science, or in that of religion or ethics. The more deeply I immerse myself in the spirit of the prophetic literature of the Old Testament, the greater becomes my mistrust of Yahwè, who butchers the peoples with the sword of his insatiable anger; who has but one favourite child, while he consigns all other nations to darkness, shame and ruin; who uttered those words to Abraham (Gen. xii. 3): 'I will bless those who bless thee, and those who curse thee will I curse' – I take refuge in Him who, in life and death, taught 'Bless those who curse you'; and, full of confidence and joy, and of earnest striving after moral perfection, put my trust in the God to Whom Jesus has taught us to pray – the God Who is a loving and righteous Father over all men on earth.[58]

This was a position Delitzsch would stick to and later firmly entrench with his last work, the openly anti-Semitic 1920–1 *Die grosse Täuschung* ('The Great Deception', referring to the status of the Old Testament as revelation).[59] Unsurprisingly the second lecture led to hostility from several quarters, and Delitzsch's views were the more reviled for apparently influencing the Kaiser. The emperor quickly distanced himself from the affair and from Delitzsch, writing an open letter advising that the latter should not dabble in theological matters to the president of the Deutsche Orient-Gesellschaft, Admiral Hollman.[60]

The third and final *Babel und Bibel* lecture came in October 1904.[61] In some ways the lecture was a penance (delivered this time not in front of the Kaiser in Berlin but to the literary societies of Barmen and Cologne), yet still it contains much that is incendiary. It was here that the anti-Semitism implicit in the first two lectures began to crystallize into something more overt. Drawing on the recent development of scholarship on the (non-Semitic) Sumerian language, Delitzsch argued that the culture, society and religion of ancient Mesopotamia were all Sumerian creations, adopted by the Semitic peoples who later settled in Babylonia and Assyria.[62] It was this non-Semitic origin, he contended, that explained many of the virtues of Babylonian society, as exemplified in the Code of Hammurabi, newly discovered by Jacques de Morgan at Susa and popularly celebrated, then as now, as the earliest expression of the very concept of the rule of law.[63] He also argued that this was why the morality of ancient Mesopotamian societies was in fact *superior* to that of Israel as expressed in the Old Testament. Confusingly, Delitzsch denied that his views were anti-Semitic;[64] nonetheless, his explanation for the virtues of Babylonian culture and for the defects he perceived in the Old Testament was clearly and explicitly based on race.

Sardanapal, Historische Pantomime

In the wake of Babel–Bibel, a more traditional emphasis in the representation of the Mesopotamian past seemed essential to the Deutsche Orient-Gesellschaft. The result was an opera, *Sardanapal, Historische Pantomime,*[65] recently studied in detail by Frederick Bohrer.[66] This hybrid production, incorporating a range of influences from biblical narratives to nineteenth-century romanticism to the recent excavations of Koldewey at Babylon and Walter Andrae at Ashur, is a particularly interesting example of the interaction of archaeological and non-archaeological understandings of the past.

Celebrating ten years of the Deutsche Orient-Gesellschaft,[67] *Sardanapal* was supposed to present a vision of Mesopotamia that was as accurate as modern scholarship allowed. Even the opera's title, however, suggests something more complex. An up-to-date title would have been *Assurbanipal* (Ashurbanipal), referring to the Assyrian king whom scholars at the time unproblematically identified with the legendary Sardanapalus.[68] Neither the name nor the story of Sardanapalus have any root in modern Assyriology; rather they first appear in the *Persica* of Ctesias, reproduced in the *Bibliotheke Historica* of Diodorus.[69] Ctesias' description, epitomizing the decay of a powerful pagan empire, provided fuel for the romantic imagination. Sardanapalus had become a particularly popular theme in the nineteenth century, the most famous representations being Byron's 1821 play *Sardanapalus* and Delacroix's 1827–8 painting *The Death of Sardanapalus*. In using both the theme and the name the Berlin production recalls this trend, and attempts to recapture its success, removed from the controversies of Babel–Bibel.

There is little reason to imagine that Ctesias was considered a more reliable source in 1908 than today. In his late nineteenth-century translation, Gilmore points out that 'though the ancients generally adopted Ktesias' chronological scheme, they had a low opinion of his veracity'.[70] Once the decision to follow the Sardanapalus story has been made, the Mesopotamia of archaeology and Assyriology becomes at best a source of visual detail for an understanding of the Mesopotamian past that is already established. Even the focus on Babylon is subservient to this aim. Although Ctesias' description itself had complex origins,[71] Sardanapalus is a king of Nineveh, not of Babylon or even of Ashur, the other jewel in the society's Mesopotamian crown. The sets of *Sardanapal*, however, aim to create a Nineveh that is also Babylon and Ashur, incorporating detail from the sites and aiming to resonate with German archaeological achievements rather than those of the French and English at Khorsabad, Nimrud and Nineveh. If an Assyrian city is intended to be associated with the production it is Ashur, excavated by Walter Andrae. Andrae's sketches, commissioned for the opera while he was still in Iraq, were one of the major visual sources for *Sardanapal* – their grand final form astonished Andrae himself (Figure 18).[72]

The audience of *Sardanapal* was not presented with an event that happened to take place in Mesopotamia, but with an epitome of

Mesopotamia itself. Sardanapalus was *the* Assyrian king. In one respect this shows great authenticity, being entirely faithful to the narrative aims of the Greek original in which he is clearly described as a type, representative of the culmination of vices common to all Assyrian rulers from Ninyas onward. The problem is that for all the attention lavished on detail to legitimate the opera as historically accurate (in some cases taken to extremes: the philologist Delitzsch required accuracy in the cuneiform inscriptions used in the play's sets), that detail is employed not in presenting a new vision of the past but in legitimating a very old one, specifically a Sardanapalus not substantially different to the king described by Ctesias 24 centuries before. *Sardanapal's* relationship to the empirical research that informed its sets is superficial. It is as though a cartographer has carefully laid out the gridlines, scales and keys for a map, then drawn an imaginary landmass and claimed it as authentic on the basis of these convincing trappings. Perhaps what should be of most concern is that, at least on the evidence of *Sardanapal*, the strategy works very well. In the absence of more information the fantastic map seems quite acceptable – its internal coherence and surrounding scholarly apparatus argues for its accuracy. This was the case with the academically sanctioned representation of Mesopotamia, and *Sardanapal, Historische Pantomime* received positive reviews as an accurate representation of the ancient past.[73] Its negative press was garnered simply for being dull.[74]

The Berlin reconstructions, 1927–30

Expertise in architecture is a long-standing strength of German archaeology, and the attention paid to architecture is certainly a striking feature of the Deutsche Orient-Gesellschaft's work in Mesopotamia. Robert Koldewey and Ludwig Borchardt had both worked with the architect Wilhelm Dörpfeld,[75] and Walter Andrae also had architectural training. Through Andrae's drawings and reconstructions in particular, an expertise and passionate interest is readily apparent. It is fitting, then, that his work should culminate in one of the most remarkable architectural reconstructions ever accomplished: the Ishtar Gate and Processional Way of Babylon in Berlin, opened in October 1930.[76] Monumental though it is, the enormous scale of the end product (the reconstructed gate is over 14 m high, the section of the Processional Way reconstructed 30 m in length on both sides) is itself dwarfed by that of the work which lay behind it. Andrae's team used original bricks to reconstruct the lions, dragons, bulls and other decoration. The bricks' colouration had survived excellently, but they were nonetheless fragmentary and in need of desalination treatment once excavated. The almost industrial-scale desalination and the daunting work of matching fragments with their original neighbours (in fact, into their original patterns – the repetition of animal forms, originally produced from the same moulds, helped reproduce them accurately, but often prevented the identification of a particular paw with one of many identical lions, for example) (Figure 19), was accompanied by the production of a special kiln to make the modern bricks replacing areas of plain colour as authentic in appearance as possible while still differentiating clearly between ancient and modern elements.[77] The first sign of Andrae's interest in the reliefs' construction is a short publication in the *Mitteilungen der Deutschen Orient-Gesellschaft* on the glazed bricks, written in December 1901 and published in May 1902.[78] Here he presents two isometric exploded diagrams showing the system of signs on the top and bottom surfaces of the bricks used to ensure that they were correctly fitted together. Later this would become a practical and logistical concern for Andrae himself.

Prior to the First World War Andrae had worked in Iraq. Having worked as Koldewey's first assistant at Babylon and been given experience of direction there as well as at Birs Nimrud and Fara in 1901 and 1902, he directed excavations at Qalat Sherqat, ancient Ashur, between 1903 and 1914. A proportion of the excavated material from this site was shipped back to Europe – albeit only as far as Lisbon, where it was confiscated when Portugal entered the war against Germany – while the rest was sent to Istanbul according to an agreement made with the Ottoman antiquities authorities when excavation permits were issued.[79] Most of the excavated material from Babylon stayed in Iraq for the duration of the war, thus falling under British control with the arrival of the British Mesopotamia Expeditionary Force in 1917.

A 1915 portrait by J. Walter-Kurau shows Andrae standing in front of one of the lions from the Processional Way. On closer inspection Andrae's own epigram can be seen in the lower-right corner, above Walter-Kurau's signature, revealing that Andrae was posing in front of his own painting. The initial impression is certainly that he is standing in front of the relief itself, however, and but for the date one would assume that the Berlin reconstructions already existed. In fact at this stage there were only a few individual panels, reconstructed using cases of fragments shipped to Germany in 1903. It took a further eight years after the war for Germany to recover the rest of the excavated material from Iraq and Portugal. Success in both cases came in 1926–7, when the Portugese government accepted an exchange for other material from the Berlin Museums, while Gertrude Bell approached the Vorderasiatisches Abteilung offering to return the material from Babylon in 1926.[80] Bell would have supervised the division of finds between Germany and Iraq, but died before Andrae, as Germany's representative, reached Babylon. Andrae's series of drafts for the reconstructions are dated 1927. Andrae became director of the Vorderasiatische Abteilung in 1928,[81] and presided over the two-year process of desalinating and reconstructing the Babylonian reliefs.

The finished reconstructions are a triumph. Not only visually powerful, they also allow the museum visitor, through reference to smaller architectural models, to gain a sense of the place and scale of the Ishtar Gate and Processional Way in their original contexts (Figures 20 and 21). Before 1930, however, there was no public display of Mesopotamian artefacts in Berlin at all, and between 1930 and 1934 the Vorderasiatische Abteilung consisted of only three rooms, the other 13 opening in 1934.[82] This is an important contrast with England and France in the mid-nineteenth century, not only because of the greater time-lag itself, but also because in these countries the peak of public interest had coincided with the arrival and display of Mesopotamian antiquities in European museums, as opposed to their actual period of excavation. Andrae's reconstruction was classically imperial in its demonstration of Germany's ability to understand and possess an ancient empire, but politically speaking it came too late. Transporting, enclosing and explaining the grandest monuments of another culture, the Ishtar Gate and Processional Way reconstructions signified imperial possession and in this sense were not unique at all. The Vorderasiatische Abteilung's finished reconstructions and superb collections from Mesopotamia would have been highly appropriate to Germany's nascent imperial culture; however, they were overtaken by world events. By the time of their construction and opening, Germany had been weakened and impoverished by the First World War and the impossible reparations required by the Treaty of Versailles. The stately permanence and paternalistic confidence of the universal museums so befitting a nineteenth-century European empire seems anachronistic in this context. This could be said of the entirety of Berlin's Museumsinsel, whose plans had been laid prior to the First World War in a burgeoning, supremely confident imperial state. Today the context is very different, and the original goal of matching London and Paris has been achieved, not only because of the grandeur and world class collections of today's Museumsinsel, but also since the millions of tourists that museums such as the Pergamon, Louvre and British Museum now serve today are unlikely to give much thought to the different histories of the three; they are equally naturalized as parts of their cities' imperial heritage. To the casual observer, present-day Unter den Linden and Museumsinsel are as convincing as the centre of a great nineteenth-century European empire to the casual observer as their English and French counterparts – more so for their careful preservation and restoration following reunification. In reality, however, their roles in such a context were extremely short-lived, and never matched Germany's territorial aspirations. The whole as seen today is a true modern cultural capital, but also the reconstructed centre of an empire that never quite was.

The German experience and its consequences

Germany's interest in Mesopotamia had been conceived as a primarily imperial one, and the work of the Deutsche Orient-Gesellschaft can be seen as the cultural aspect of a much broader imperial ambition. At the end of the nineteenth century the area seemed to hold great commercial promise as part of an overland route between Europe and India, and the possibility of sending German colonists to Iraq was seriously considered.[83] The link between imperial and archaeological ambition was so clear as to allow Budge to write that 'as for excavations in Assyria and Babylonia, many shrewd observers have remarked that Germany only began to excavate seriously in those countries when she began to dream of creating the German Oriental Empire'.[84] (The assertion is largely correct, if rather brazen coming from a British Museum Keeper at a time when Britain still held an empire of its own.) It is worthwhile considering the writing of Koldewey, Delitzsch and others as a form of imperial literature, created within the context of a young state's expansionist ambition, if not necessarily acting consciously to legitimate it.

Delitzsch was well aware of the political implications of his work, and far from perceiving a constraint or conflict of interests in this saw instead a legitimate reason and motivation. Though a scholar, he fell easily and confidently into the strong rhetoric and ambition of the statesman. In *Die deutsche Expedition nach Babylon*[85] he set out clearly his ambition of linking Germany with Babylon just as England was now linked with Nineveh. Although they turned into a great religious controversy, the Babel–Bibel lectures were intended to celebrate Germany's success in doing just this. They had caused great controversy in practice, but Delitzsch's goal in giving the lectures had been profoundly conservative and populist: to stake a claim for Assyriology in Germany's newfound sense of national destiny, and for himself in its public promotion.

Robert Koldewey, by contrast, writes of the site and the excavations themselves almost exclusively. *The Excavations at Babylon* does not contain any argument for the relevance of Babylon to an expansionist, ambitious Germany. Its style and format make such an inclusion almost unthinkable. Even the bulk of Koldewey's preface is devoted to the chronology of the excavations and acknowledgements: of the Berlin Museums, the Deutsche Orient-Gesellschaft, the Kaiser, Delitzsch (as a translator) and his most important staff in the field, first among whom is listed Walter Andrae. Koldewey's silence on politics is at least as interesting as Delitzsch's forthright imperialism. There are several questions to consider, one of which is particularly intriguing at a biographical level: did Koldewey agree with the purpose of his and his colleagues' work as expressed by Delitzsch? Others are more interesting from the point of view of historiography. Did Koldewey seek to appear more objective and/or scientific through adopting a consciously self-effacing style in his writing? This seems very likely: his dry but precise style is very much that of the contemporary natural sciences. Personal reflections are few, and the focus is on a thorough description of the site, with abundant plans and technical illustrations. The only exceptions are a few scattered anecdotes, relating usually to local traditions on the ancient ruins such as the story of the foreign visitor and the Lion of Babylon. Even these, however, are rare. The result was that Koldewey's work, despite its great academic significance, had comparatively little impact on the popular representation of the Mesopotamian past in Wilhelmine Germany.

The separation in the roles of Koldewey and Delitzsch is significant in terms of subsequent archaeological practice and writing. In eschewing the political aspect of his situation to concentrate on the site, Koldewey did what gradually became the norm in archaeology. In effect, he ceded control to the Berlin establishment, and that Delitzsch was his academic senior only matters in this regard insofar as it placed him at the right intersection to speak for that establishment and for the discipline of ancient Near Eastern studies simultaneously. It was Koldewey's work that became a model for good archaeological practice and publication, and it was a model that tried very hard to place itself outside the political world. This can be a quite admirable trait in terms of Koldewey's putting research questions above satisfying the imperial ambitions of Deutsche Orient-Gesellschaft backers in Berlin, but perhaps also came at a price. Koldewey never wrote about the broader contemporary implications of his work, and lost his right to a voice in the national debate. This in turn gives us the superficial impression that he had no part in these processes, specifically the bolstering of German claims to power in southern Mesopotamia. In addition, the excavator himself and the contemporary world within which he operated are effectively written out of *The Excavations at Babylon*. This self-effacing style, stressing close description and objectivity, would ultimately replace the less detailed but more open style of men like Delitzsch and of earlier English and French writers on the ancient Near East, though claims of greater objectivity accompanying the trend have met with increasing scepticism.[86] The detail and clarity in recording is greatly to be admired, but the format and approach tend towards the loss of information on the social context of excavations.

Within the events above, and particularly Babel–Bibel, there emerged the beginning of another religious controversy within German Near Eastern studies. Although a famous proponent of a pan-Babylonian argument Delitzsch was by no means alone, nor was he the most extreme. In later years his denunciation of the Old Testament was set in the most forthright terms with *Die grosse Täuschung*, the work in which he would argue not only that Christianity did not need the Hebrew Scriptures but that Christ himself was not a Jew.[87] His work supported the idea, current among some anti-Semitic pastors of the time, that Germany needed a new, German Christianity, founded in the New Testament and in celebrations of Germanic heroism such as Wilhelm Schwaner's *Germanen-Bibel*.[88] In particular, his work tied in well with the views of the nationalist anti-Semitic activist and pastor Friedrich Andersen, who argued that Christ was not Jewish, that the Christian God had little in common with Yahweh of the Old Testament, and that in Germany Jews sought to undermine Christian racial and religious identity.[89] Delitzsch himself died in 1922, but his academic assault on the Old Testament, in combination with the use of his conviction that Mesopotamian culture itself was essentially non-Semitic as part of the explanation for the great political and cultural achievements of Assyria and Babylonia, appears in retrospect as an early step in the process which by the 1930s saw a growing section of the German scholarly community producing work that served to legitimate the rising anti-Semitism visible in society at large.

The vanishing moment

By the time of *Die grosse Täuschung* the Babylon excavated by Koldewey was already beginning to disappear. The achievements of the excavation were not matched by conservation. Once exposed, the delicate sun-dried mud-brick architecture began to deteriorate:

> [I]n Budge's sense, the 'buildings were laid bare'; and yet to those who visit the site today the result is somewhat disappointing. Here are no tidy and comprehensible ruins, such as one sees in Greece or Egypt; for it is in the nature of mud-brick walls that their remains, once exposed, are difficult to preserve. As a result, save for the dominating outline of the more massive structures, and some recent reconstructions, the site presents for the modern visitor a scene of devastation almost as complete as when first discovered by European travellers.[90]

Seton Lloyd's description emphasizes the feeling that destruction and disappearance are somehow fitting here, that in narrative terms they give symmetry to the story and frame it. The event gives the Babylon of the present continuity with that visited by the early European travellers, and this is not the only way in which the description reconnects with older sources. As he wrote, Lloyd was aware that the 'scene of devastation' was a part of Babylon, and that it should be included: after all, physical disappearance is common to a great many sites, but rarely is it highlighted in this way. Destruction is part of Babylon's identity, either explicitly represented or clearly implied in almost every pre-modern source on the city. The return to ruin is more than physical; the city's destruction is part of its moral meaning, aesthetic and narrative. Cottrell ends his popular description of the Babylon excavations in much the same way, adding with some bitterness that 'since the Germans left the Arab builders of Hillah have quarried away practically every brick of the Ziggurat of Etemenanki'.[91] The aesthetic of ruin is a genre of representation in itself, and one within which Babylon plays a dual role. On the one hand, it can fairly be numbered among the ancient cities that inspire with the distance of their dramatic histories; cities whose very ruin is an integral part of the awe they provoke.[92] On the other, this is not the only factor at work in the case of Babylon, whose appeal to travellers, artists and writers also came to be bound up with notions of exoticism and transgression as an outgrowth from the idea of the city's divine punishment.

As in other aspects of his work, Koldewey is a notable exception to the narrative rule. The very title of his German publication, *Das wieder erstehende Babylon* ('Babylon Rises Again') emphasizes his lack of interest in a melancholy discussion of its fall, something he would also surely have considered to be outside the remit of his work. His avoidance of the established narrative forms and rhetorical flourishes for Babylon in general is as much a part of his move away from the mythic and towards the empiricist and even positivistic as his methodical thoroughness itself.

Koldewey's book was a success in terms of its influence on archaeological writing, less so in terms of public communication. To quote Seton Lloyd once more:

> If any reservation is to be made in praising the Germans [at Babylon and Ashur], it is in connection with the public presentation of their results. Total preoccupation with scientific minutiae robbed their writings of all but academic appeal, and the educative potential of their work suffered accordingly.[93]

The style Lloyd criticizes here is clearly archaeological, as opposed to historical. Koldewey's 'scientific minutiae' and their dry presentation are the fruit of a process begun in the nineteenth century, when archaeology, or at least questions of evolution and origins, began to move away from the humanities and towards the natural sciences in approach and style.[94] The style has a purpose and makes a programmatic statement of its own: it emphasizes the author's respect for and aspiration to emulate the modern successes of the natural sciences, and implies that such emulation is possible within and appropriate to his subject. This is not to suggest that such a move was purely stylistic: archaeology's development did indeed rely on and bring it closer in content to the sciences, especially the natural science of geology and the human science of anthropology.[95] Particularly notable in the German context is the extent to which this trend served to differentiate the excavators of the Deutsche Orient-Gesellschaft from their classical counterparts in the Deutsches Archäologisches Institut. The former were usually younger, and were more likely to have backgrounds in technical disciplines such as architecture and engineering than in classics or philology.[96]

Of Koldewey's writing on Babylon, what is remembered, ironically enough, is that which relates to older, more poetic accounts, specifically the unearthing of the city wall described by Herodotus and Koldewey's suggestion of a location for the Hanging Gardens. This is one good illustration of the extent to which the concerns of classical historians continue to influence patterns of research into modernity. Indeed, the relevance of their interests to our own is demonstrated by the continuing contemporary debate on the location of the Hanging Gardens.[97] Of Delitzsch's arguments, it was the idea of a Christianity that owed nothing to Judaism that eventually proved popular and influential, as part of an ideology that had nothing to do with Babylon.[98]

The popular success in terms of representing Babylon in Germany is *Sardanapal, Historische Pantomime*. It was the least accurate and least progressive of the three approaches, but this was no barrier. Quite the reverse: conservatism and a readiness to subserviate archaeological detail to the story of Sardanapalus were the very guarantors of its positive public reception. *Sardanapal* met expectations by using an established narrative. It did this, however, while simultaneously claiming to be the most advanced and accurate reconstruction of ancient Mesopotamia possible. It would be ridiculous to argue with Delitzsch on the accuracy of the cuneiform inscriptions he specified – if Assyriologists today could criticize them they could do so only because their discipline has built on Delitzsch's work.[99] Nor does it particularly matter that large parts of the Assyria on stage were based on Babylonian models – that such a distinction could be made at all is largely thanks to the German excavations. What matters is that the wealth of detail, the selective but nonetheless painstaking accuracy, was nothing more than a framing device for an Orientalist fantasy, itself drawn from ancient Greece, and some heavy-handed twentieth-century moralizing on the fate of empires, neither of which owed anything to the excavations. The role of archaeology here was not to update the image of Mesopotamia at all, but to validate existing preconceptions.[100] This success, of course, is no success at all. It is hollow both as academic communication and as an artistic achievement.

The contribution of Koldewey and Andrae's work, by contrast, was profound. The systematic excavation of Babylon and the spectacular reconstructions in Berlin required both ability and great stubbornness. Their projects brought a truly new vision of ancient Babylon – the archaeological and architectural – into the academic and public consciousness as never before. On the other hand, they were the product of a grand European imperial project that was among the last of its kind. Even as Koldewey was excavating the world was changing rapidly, and the political context of archaeology with it.

CHAPTER 7

THE LIBRARY OF BABEL: BABYLON AND ITS REPRESENTATION AFTER THE EXCAVATIONS

The German excavations were greatly scaled down with the outbreak of the First World War, and in 1917 were forced to cease completely. By 1918, the world was already transformed, and a period of unprecedented upheaval, uncertainty, creation, destruction and change, Eric Hobsbawm's 'age of extremes',[1] was underway. The upheaval was felt in intellectual terms in forces that fundamentally affected the place of archaeology and history: a great rise in atheism and a diminishing role for the humanities, the latter reduced, according to some, to mere luxuries that the dangerous new world could do very well without, and the withering in the face of modern atrocities not only of the notion of progress that placed modern Europe at history's pinnacle, but also of the more benign hope of progress as a general belief in human ability to build toward positive goals in the long term.[2] Significantly from the point of view of Babylon's representation, the period also witnessed the fragmentation of Europe's shared elite cultural canon, due to the emergence of increasingly cosmopolitan, multi-ethnic, multi-lingual, multi-confessional societies, the demise of the Bible as a source of narratives familiar to and accepted by all and new approaches to education. Perhaps most importantly, the period is that of the rise and fall of grand theoretical models for understanding – and in politics even directing – human behaviour.

This chapter focuses on approaches to Babylon within and without archaeology after the First World War, and follows three basic threads: the development of German archaeological theory; Babylon's twentieth-century reception and representation outside archaeology; and the role of the Mesopotamian past in Iraq's history as an independent state.

German archaeological discourse to 1933

Nowhere was the tumult of twentieth-century European political, social and cultural change so acutely felt as within its young but powerful new focus: unified Germany. The economic performance of Germany in its first few decades of existence, including and backed by phenomenal industrial and military development, left Britain and France, for all their global reach, relatively weak in continental Europe itself. By the eve of the First World War, Germany could boast school and university systems that were the envy of the world and a huge industrial output, as well as unequalled military resources.[3] Even Britain's once unassailable naval dominance became a gap that Admiral Tirpitz aimed to close at speed.[4] The language of German politics had grown correspondingly ambitious: 'Weltpolitik meant for Germans in the 1890s the invention of a new world mission for Germany worthy of her industrial, technological, cultural and military strength.'[5] Small wonder, then, that the fight for the nation's identity and destiny was intense. Between the late nineteenth-century foundation of proto-imperial organizations such as the Deutsche Orient-Gesellschaft and the rise to power of the Nazi party, the discipline of archaeology in Germany was the focus of intense political and ideological battles whose implications continue to affect us in the present. It was also a period of great technical and scientific innovation in the subject, again centred on Germany.[6] This potent combination, as events were to show, was ripe for exploitation by political extremists.

Returning to Delitzsch and Babel–Bibel, we are already witness to perhaps the first major derailment of German imperialist archaeological discourse by religious and racial concerns. That it was a derailment is itself one of the most important points to note about the situation. Nineteenth- and early twentieth-century imperialist archaeologies in which racial hierarchies of various kinds were implicit, assumed or consciously developed as explanatory models and the specifically twentieth-century archaeologies that were explicitly driven by racial and ethnic theories have many parallels and connections, but the two are absolutely not continuous nor even particularly compatible. The Babel–Bibel affair provides a good case in point. The lectures were conceived as a staged, controlled public spectacle, and as such had a clear intended narrative. The narrative ought to have been straightforward: what was wanted of Delitzsch was simply to highlight to the nation and the world at large the great steps that studies of the ancient Near East had taken in Germany over a short period of time, and to emphasize that Germany was now the equal of Britain and France in the archaeology and ancient languages of the region. They were not planned as the spur to a national outcry or the condemnation of philological research as blasphemous. The clue that this is what Delitzsch's lectures would induce, however, was to be found very close to home, within the German academy itself. The recent rise of grand theory on race, language and human development, of which pan-Babylonianism was only one manifestation, appears in retrospect as a bellwether. As has been mentioned above, the foci of academic research on the past are often linked to the pressing concerns of the present, and the public reaction to the first two *Babel und Bibel* lectures more than matched academic interest in the issues they discussed. Later, those who, like Delitzsch, drew explicitly anti-Semitic conclusions from their study of ancient texts were part of a broader cultural movement that had as much to do with old stereotypes and new insecurities as with philological considerations.

In other areas of history, archaeology and ethnography, theories of race were coming to the fore. The name most strongly associated with this new emphasis is that of Gustav Kossinna, whose model of culture history both served the racial political vision of Nazism and exerted a more positive influence on academic archaeology, leading scholars such as Gordon Childe to develop approaches that did much to systematize and encourage comparative approaches in the study of human prehistory.[7] Kossinna was hardly alone in promulgating confusion between linguistic, racial and ethnic identities in his work, but his conclusions drew on multiple strands of nationalist desire. Not only could his theories legitimate a sense of German superiority, they could also incorporate ancient Greece.[8] This inclusion was enormously important because in Germany – perhaps more even than in Britain, where imperial experiences had promoted a yet greater interest in the Roman Empire[9] – ancient Greece had a decidedly special place in history. The great art historian Johann Winckelmann had first constructed the typology that formally put Greek art at the pinnacle of human aesthetic achievement in the eighteenth century. Enlightenment thought was both ideologically open to and strongly affected by his view of the greatest aesthetic achievement being reached through the greatest personal freedom[10] (though Winckelmann himself did not follow the model consistently, frequently showing great admiration for works produced under autocratic regimes).[11] Many of the most important writers influenced by Winckelmann were German speakers and wrote in German, further heightening his impact on the high culture of the Germanic kingdoms including, crucially from the point of view of later history, Prussia. The historian of archaeology Alain Schnapp highlights Winckelmann's particular resonance in the original German:

> Mid-eighteenth century Germany, which worshipped daily at the shrine of Greek art, was to find in Winckelmann an inspired singer of the praises of antique art, who expressed in a new kind of German prose the matchless quality of Greek art [. . .]. Winckelmann transcended archaeology in the relevance of his analyses, but above all in the quality of his style and the ambition of his aesthetic.[12]

Winckelmann's *Geschichte der Kunst des Alterthums*[13] became canonical, its status only entrenched by the increasing volume of northern European travellers to Greece and the shipment of greater quantities of antiquities north from Greece and Italy during the nineteenth century. The overwhelming dominance of the classics in Prussian intellectual life was only beginning to shift at the turn of the twentieth century,[14] a process helped, ironically, by the great achievements of German scholars in classical philology and archaeology in the nineteenth. Excavations revealed quantities of pre-classical material, Mycenean, Geometric and Archaic, that did not fit easily into Winckelmann's scheme and provoked new approaches.[15] The exploration of prehistory created new problems of classification, as well as a need for explanation of historical processes in the absence of written records. Kossinna's solution was to combine the art historical approach associated with Winckelmann with a form of social Darwinism, building up an ethno-linguistic model that placed Germanic Aryans at its peak. This might at first seem incompatible with an idolization of ancient Greek art and architecture; the answer for Kossinna (and thereafter for culture and historical archaeology in general) was migration. His model could explain great cultural achievements in other parts of the world through the migration of *Kulturvolker*, a term coined by Gustav Klemm to designate culturally creative peoples as opposed to passive *Naturvolker*.[16] For Kossinna *Kulturvolker* meant essentially Germanic peoples, and so for him the Greeks and Romans became groups of Germanic colonists whose genius had been gradually corrupted by inferior local blood. This explanation emphasized the idea of Germany's special position and destiny in *Kulturgeschichte* while avoiding a total renunciation of ancient Greek culture and its merits. The model was a racial adaptation of Winckelmann's doctrine of the downfall of art through superfluity. The artist, in Winckelmann's opinion:

[A]t last gradually raised art among the Greeks to the highest beauty. After all the parts constituting grandeur and beauty

were united, the artist, in seeking to embellish them, fell into
the error of profuseness; art consequently lost its grandeur; and
the loss was finally followed by its utter downfall.[17]

In due course, new waves of Germanic peoples overwhelmed Rome.
Here, Kossinna looked further back, to Tacitus. (As one commentator
notes, 'The most salient fact about the Gothic migrations is that they
forcefully underscore how old theories never die'.[18]) The journal set
up by Kossinna to disseminate the findings of the Deutscher
Gesellschaft für Vorgeschichte, of which he was the first president,
was named *Mannus* after a founding god of the Germanic peoples
named in the *Germania*.[19] Tacitus himself regarded the Germanic
peoples 'as aboriginal, and not mixed at all with other races through
immigration or intercourse', albeit for rather different reasons than
Kossinna. For him, '[Q]uite apart from the danger of a rough and
unknown sea, who would abandon Asia or Africa or Italy for
Germania, with its unlovely landscape and harsh climate, dreary to
inhabit or behold, if it were not one's native land?'.[20] For Kossinna,
the important aspect was purity of German blood. Nietzsche's
aristocratic supermen, already innately superior and devoid of any
responsibility to the rest of humanity, and already driven by the
megalomaniac *raison d'être* of the Will to Power, could now take on
a racial character.[21]

There is little common ground between the ideas of Delitzsch
and Kossinna. *Ex oriente lux* could not sit easily with a model that
made Germany the font of all cultural innovation. For his part
Kossinna dismissed Near Eastern, Egyptian, and even classical
studies as unpatriotic in the conclusion to his *Die deutsche
Vorgeschichte: eine hervorragend nationale Wissenschaft* ('German
prehistory: A supremely national science').[22] Nonetheless,
Delitzsch's controversy is one that, as much as Kossinna's work, is
relevant to the later use of archaeology in legitimating anti-Semitic
persecution.[23] Moreover, they shared a position in the changes then
sweeping through the German academy. Suzanne Marchand
characterizes Kossinna and the arch pan-Babylonianist Hugo
Winckler as examples of a contemporary type:

[A]spirants to cultural prestige [... who] would look to the universities for cultural legitimation [...] most leading para-academic existences [...]. Importantly, these academic outcasts generally spoke to rather large popular audiences composed of educated laypeople and local elites, evinced sympathy for the natural sciences, and, usually working in areas less attractive to the classicising professorate (such as indology, German prehistory and Near Eastern studies), drew popular attention to the insularity and obsolescence of neohumanist academe.[24]

Although he can hardly be seen as a rank outsider or 'para-academic', some of the characteristics identified by Marchand extend even to the august Delitzsch. Certainly his speeches to a broad public brought a new relevance and urgency to the work of his discipline. As in the case of Kossinna, however, his controversial interventions foreshadowed the Nazi use of his subject. For Delitzsch and others it was not the Bible as a whole that was undermined, but specifically the Old Testament. For Delitzsch, the existence of Mesopotamian comparators negated the status of the Old Testament as revealed knowledge, but had no bearing on and could not undermine the New Testament. In the 1930s this fringe position was to move to the very centre of German religious politics. Although he did not live to see this dark conclusion, Delitzsch would have been well aware that his work was politically meaningful. Political anti-Semitism, never entirely absent in European history, had been a significant factor in German politics since the late 1870s, associated with extreme nationalism and at least tolerated by Bismarck for the purposes of 'negative integration', whereby the perception of some internal enemies helped to unify and stabilize relations between other groups.[25] Anti-Semitic movements were fuelled by the uncertainties and removal of traditional structures associated with industrialization and urbanization, for which Jews made convenient scapegoats.[26] They also became linked with nationalism, another factor relevant to the work of Delitzsch. The link was a strong one: according to Pulzer, 'Nationalism had, by the beginning of the twentieth century, become the main driving force behind anti-Semitism'.[27]

Babylon outside archaeology

The twentieth century saw the emergence of an exciting new tool for representing the past. The early history of cinema contains many examples of biblical and Near Eastern subject matter, and a number of very early Italian and French films feature Babylon and other Near Eastern subjects, including brief but often highly original adaptations of the stories of Belshazzar, Semiramis and Sardanapalus.[28] Babylon continued to appear as films became longer and more complex. Cecil B. DeMille's 1919 *Male and Female*, an adaptation of J. M. Barrie's *The Admirable Crichton*, contains a remarkable Babylonian dream sequence, prompted by the W. E. Henley poem 'To W. A.':

> Or ever the knightly years were gone
> With the old world to the grave,
> I was a king in Babylon
> And you were a Christian slave.

In the dream sequence Crichton, the butler who has risen above his former mistress in the social order after the two and their party have been shipwrecked and cut off from civilization, becomes the king of Babylon, wearing a loosely Assyrian-derived costume and an exaggerated cruel sneer. On either side of his throne stand winged bulls, at least in profile. In frontal view they resemble Norse heroes, though what look like swords they hold are actually snakes. Other parts of the scenery include bricks after those of Babylon and Susa, while the king's throne carries Assyrian rosettes and a lotus decoration. For reasons that are unclear, the king of Babylon's servants are African, but true to Daniel he is in possession of a fully functional lions' den, in which are kept the 'sacred lions of Ishtar'. The sequence is fun and extravagant, but it is relevant that in a story focusing on class and power Babylon is the venue chosen for an essay on extremes of despotic cruelty, luxury and absolute power. For similar reasons, though in a more lurid context, Gore Vidal's novel *Myron* (1974) chooses 'Siren of Babylon' as the appropriate fictional film into which to transport its protagonist for a provocatively explicit story centred on sexual transgression.

Babylon's most noteworthy appearance of all comes in D. W. Griffith's epic motion picture *Intolerance: Love's Struggle Through the Ages* (1916). Griffith's Babylon returned to Edwin Long and to Herodotus for inspiration, yet in some respects *Intolerance* is also an emphatic indicator of change in Babylon's meaning in representation, and a departure from the nineteenth-century sources that provided its visual inspiration.[29]

What is apparent to any viewer of *Intolerance* is the scale of Griffith's ambition (Figure 22). The film was exceptional in a number of ways and was very consciously a work of innovations and superlatives, explicitly intended to break new ground and expand the horizons of the young motion-picture industry. The film was technically and thematically ambitious in equal measure, and expensive beyond all probability for such an original venture. *Intolerance* was the first multi-reel motion picture, and its three hours of footage dwarfed anything previously seen. Its high production values were equally novel, particularly in the American film industry, which at this time was less lavish in most respects than those of Italy and France. Griffith, who had already produced hundreds of more conventional silent pictures,[30] had enjoyed great success with *The Birth of a Nation* (1915), and intended to surpass his achievements here in *Intolerance*. *The Birth of a Nation* was a deeply racist work, including positive portrayal of the Ku Klux Klan.[31] Even at the time some attempts were made to ban the film, and limited censorship was imposed by the National Board of Review, although this censorship seems to have been only of white racism and racist violence, that is, to produce a yet more positive portrayal of whites' behaviour.[32] Nonetheless, *The Birth of a Nation* was received as the biggest commercial and artistic success of American cinema, in which Griffith demonstrated a new mastery of cinematography, leading commentators to claim erroneously that he had actually invented techniques such as the close-up and fade-out.[33] *Intolerance*, a relatively difficult academic piece produced on an enormous scale, did not enjoy the same commercial success, and financially ruined Griffith, though his bankruptcy at least came about through employing the original cast of thousands and creating the most lavish and spectacular art. The scale, aesthetic merit and intellectual ambition of *Intolerance* mark it out as an important moment in the history of cinema. Kenneth Anger's *Hollywood Babylon*, whose title celebrates the seedier side of Hollywood excess and takes Babylon into yet another locale, opens with an evocation of how Griffith's sets, now ruins in their own right: came to loom over Hollywood:

> A make-believe mirage of Mesopotamia dropped down on the sleepy huddle of mission-style bungalows amid the orange groves that made up 1915 Hollywood, portent of things to come [...]. And there it stood for years, stranded like some gargantuan dream beside Sunset Boulevard. Long after Griffith's great leap into the unknown, his Sun Play of the Ages, *Intolerance*, had failed; long after Belshazzar's court had sprouted weeds and its walls had begun to peel and warp in abandoned movie-set disarray; after the Los Angeles Fire Department had condemned it as a fire hazard, still it stood: Griffith's Babylon, something of a reproach and something of a challenge to the burgeoning movie town – something to surpass, something to live down.[34]

The film's theme is an eternal conflict between love and intolerance, as expressed through four historical studies: ancient Babylon, Judea at the time of Christ, the persecution of the Huguenots in sixteenth-century Paris and the industrial development of early 1900s America. Of these, the first and last receive most attention. The film is best remembered for the Babylonian section[35] and particularly its sets, probably still the largest and in real terms most expensive in the history of cinema. The Babylonian storyline was inspired by Edwin Long's *Babylonian Marriage Market* of 1875.[36] Once again a Greek source, Herodotus, is used in preference to newly-available Mesopotamian themes, and this at a time when the American academy was rapidly achieving parity with European institutions in the study of ancient Mesopotamia.[37] Not to say that these studies were discarded. Rather, as with Long's painting, they were collected fastidiously and then employed selectively: the effort towards authenticity is focused exclusively on object detail. Unusually, a source survives showing vividly how this was accomplished: Griffith and his researchers put together a scrapbook (now held by the Museum of Modern Art in New York) whose combination of sources from archaeology and European art is reflected in the film itself. In costume a similar process married the most exotic and interesting of the ancient Near East with the requirements of contemporary celluloid glamour. As McCall notes, the result perhaps carried just a hint of gender bias:

> The men wore woollen robes with heavy embroidery and look completely authentic, as did the soldiers, priests, and kings, but the women had suffered the same fate as Long's maidens: they had been prettified to conform with modern tastes and wore flimsy robes that clung or were shaped to the body with jewelled girdles. The women had to be recognisably 'Babylonian' to western eyes, that is exotic, mysterious, and beautiful, and prone to lounge on tiger skins.[38]

As with Long's painting, this highly selective attention to detail elicited scholarly approval: A. H. Sayce lauded Griffith's attention to detail enthusiastically in an unpublished letter, and his praise is repeated in the souvenir programme of *Intolerance*.[39] Where Griffith's work differs from Long's is that in *Intolerance* Herodotus only sets the initial conditions; the story is Griffith's and is absolutely modern. An uncouth mountain girl, representing one of the less attractive women from Long's painting, attempts to escape from the vicissitudes of the marriage market and decide her own fate. Her will in the story represents love, her oppression intolerance. Even if Herodotus was not wholly sincere in his praise of the marriage market as a system (see Chapter 3), nor is the independent and non-conforming mountain girl of *Intolerance* by any means the better alternative he meant to imply. For Long in 1875 the same character, pictured at the end of the line of maidens at the bottom right of the image, is little short of an ogre. Her unrefined posture and coarse expression, which in Griffith's work represent a vital and positive will to freedom, in Long's image are presented as monstrous and frightening, as evidenced by the horrified male figure pictured above this girl, his own youth and delicate fineness of feature intended to contrast with her coarse image. In *Intolerance* the wild mountain girl is played by Hollywood beauty Constance Talmadge and is the heroine of a romance. Meaning here has changed radically within, ostensibly, the same story.

The clearest example of this kind of shift in meaning, however, is the twentieth-century reception and representation of the Tower of Babel.[40] Griffith's use of an Orientalist history painting as his starting point is, if not anachronistic, certainly late. In contrast with the sexually charged exoticism of the *fin-de-siècle*, perhaps the most prominent feature of Babylon's treatment in twentieth-century culture has been the Tower of Babel's popularity as a motif in philosophical work on identity, knowledge and the complexity of the world at large. In the twentieth century a very old theme, the nature of the confusion of tongues, returns to the fore. Stripped of the certainty of divine will at its centre, however, the Babel of Genesis becomes a very different subject, whose relevance to the emergent and in some ways genuinely new patterns of living in the globalizing twentieth century possessed substance and depth as well as the emotive strength of a well-chosen cipher. A 1950 article analyses five near-contemporary works of fiction in which the theme of Babel occurs specifically in a context clearly linked to the anxieties of the present, the author noting that 'It is probably more than mere coincidence that five works, published between 1934 and 1948, describe the Devil's dealings with our world by tracing deterioration in language and speech'.[41] In cinema a comparable use of the Tower of Babel can be seen in Fritz Lang's *Metropolis* (1927), in which the 'New Tower of Babel' is the symbol of a futuristic dystopia in which workers and technocrats have lost contact with one another and can no longer communicate. A flashback to the ancient Babylon shows armies of slaves being whipped on as they drag the blocks to build the tower for their priestly masters. Both towers, ancient and futuristic, owe something to the imaginings of Bruegel and his successors. By the time the film was produced it would have been quite possible to include a more ziggurat-like reconstruction, but to draw on the tower as known through the centuries in European culture has its own validity and seems wholly appropriate here: the Babel with which works like *Metropolis* are concerned is very much that of art and theology.

The modern transformation in the meaning and resonance of the Tower of Babel story is never clearer than in the stories of Jorge Luis Borges, whose work epitomizes some distinctively twentieth-century uses of Babylon. One of the great modern short story writers, in his playful interest in the absurd Borges is reminiscent of Lewis Carroll, and the two writers also share a tendency to employ mathematical games in their work. Infinity is a recurring theme in Borges' writing, as is the labyrinth (not, as in common usage, a maze, but in the stricter sense of a single, folding path leading to a central place). Borges saw the labyrinth as symbolic of – perhaps actively constituting – a form of thought or meditation.[42] His two stories with supposedly Babylonian settings are both contained within a series called *The Garden of Forking Paths*, and both concern infinity and the labyrinth. Against first impressions, both also concern Babylon in more than name.

The Library of Babel[43] is named for the confusion of tongues. It consists of the description of a library consisting of hexagonal chambers, in which every possible combination of 25 printed characters over 410 pages is given. The text's narrator maintains that the library is infinite in time and endlessly cyclical in space, on account of his awareness of a finite number of combinations but inability to conceive of a finite universe. Borges uses this structure to play with the subjects of authorship, language and knowledge. In particular, he draws out the self-referential nature of all written knowledge in the library, since it contains:

> Everything: the minutely detailed history of the future, the archangels' autobiographies, the faithful catalogue of the Library, thousands and thousands of false catalogues, the demonstration

of the fallacy of those catalogues, the demonstration of the fallacy of the true catalogue, the Gnostic gospel of Basilides, the commentary on that gospel, the commentary on the commentary on that gospel, the true story of your death, the translation of every book in all languages, the interpolations of every book in all books.[44]

The problem of drawing meaning from such a library, of transferring knowledge out of this self-referential system, is analogous to Derrida's web of infinite signification: the assertion that signifiers such as words correspond not to signifieds, i.e. things and concepts in the world, but to more signifiers, that these in turn do the same, and that it is therefore impossible to give a perfect description of an object or for a sign to be discrete. Instead any one sign must refer ultimately to the whole of language.[45] Derrida's (for some) systematic undermining of the human capacity for making meaning sparked strong reactions, and it is a similar problem that Borges presents to the reader. Although the very first sentence of the story begins 'The universe (which others call the library)...', it becomes apparent only gradually that the point being made extends beyond the problems of infinite signification within texts. In *The Library of Babel* the question of infinity and significance is ultimately made physical and tactile. The impotence of the librarians, trapped within their self-referential library, becomes the reader's own. The sense is that of being entirely lost, searching hopelessly for meaning that one knows, from a structural point of view, cannot be reached.

The problems raised by *The Library of Babel* are wholly modern, yet the endeavours of the librarians reflect an older approach to knowledge and language; the belief in something divine underlying the chaos. The reconstruction of the original Adamite language was, in earlier discourse, a subject of much speculation and scholarly inquiry, of which Kircher's comparative linguistic studies in works such as *Turris Babel* are outstanding examples. More interestingly, the study of the origins and development of languages remained the preserve of philologists closely allied to archaeology, and not least the archaeology of Iraq. The land of

Babel, coincidentally, became the best place to study some of the earliest written language and to witness linguistic change over time. The gulf between a philological work and a philosophical meditation on the properties of written language is vast, yet both are ways of addressing the same subject matter. The question of how one might begin to integrate the two raises many interesting possibilities. The point here, however, is that the biblical confusion of tongues did not cease to be a relevant and intriguing subject in terms of the human condition, but that archaeology, once formed into its twentieth-century shape and removed from a literal understanding of the Genesis account, was no longer equipped for such meditations, more natural heirs to this role being found in students of language much further from archaeology such as Borges, or more recently Umberto Eco.[46] It thus becomes apparent that the location of some parts of Babylon's identity and mythology outside archaeology does not mean that those aspects cease to function in important ways, even within academia, once archaeology's purposes and position are relatively established. Returning to Babylon's parallels in representation with Venice (noted above in Chapter 3), one is reminded here of Italo Calvino's *Invisible Cities* (1974), and a more philosophical engagement with the relationship between personal experience and the identity of the city as a concept.

In *The Lottery in Babylon*,[47] Borges may have been inspired in part by classical material, either in the marriage market of Herodotus or the story of Semiramis tricking Ninus from his throne in Plutarch (see Chapter 3). The story is original, however, and its concerns modern. In it a state lottery extends beyond money to consume all aspects of life, as the lottery's architects attempt to turn it into a just and complete redistributive system. The result is dystopian, and Borges uses it to explore the modern condition of existence in a world whose systems and scale of operations are inhuman (the company running the lottery seems omnipotent to Borges' narrator) and, from the perspective of the individual within them, mystifying, yet which at the level of the state have a curious logic of their own. This problem of perspective is also a characteristic of *The Library of Babel* and of the labyrinth, whose aesthetic is 'based on the fact that, fully perceived and appreciated, the maze transcends apparent disorder to reveal a grand design'.[48] Biblical Babel, built too high and with ambitions too great for humanity's own good, is a perfect setting for such an exploration.

The Babel and Babylon imagined by Borges have many visual equivalents, including some images based explicitly on his work. There are many twentieth-century representations of the Tower of Babel, and their emphasis is most often on a world that has grown too large and complex for human habitation. Often they reflect the inhuman scale of twentieth-century skyscrapers, as is the case in Fritz Lang's *Metropolis*. This is part of another modern trope: Babylon as urban dystopia. The confusion of Babel, the luxury and degeneracy described in the ancient Greek sources and the prophecies of destruction in the Old Testament and Revelation all feed into this image. Nowhere is this dystopian strand more powerfully evoked, however, than in the rhetoric of exile and return.

Babylon and exile: Zionism and Rastafari

The nineteenth and twentieth centuries saw unprecedented levels of deportation, exile, enslavement, displacement and alienation of all kinds. For some groups the struggles of the ancient Israelites in the Babylon of Nebuchadnezzar provided compelling parallels with their own situations, and the desire for a return to Zion became a very modern rallying point for the dispossessed. Most obviously there is modern Zionism itself. Demands for the creation of the modern state of Israel were always couched in an acute historical awareness of a long history of persecution and oppression, starting with the trials of the Old Testament, both in Exodus and in the Captivity, and it is in this broadest sense that the term Zionism is used here.

The use of Babylon and Zion in Zionism involves both historical and allegorical references to both cities. Even the return to Jerusalem itself has been, for some, much more than a literal territorial goal:

The important distinction [in evaluating the past results and contemporary relevance of Zionism] in this regard is between Herzl's school of 'political Zionism' and Ahad Ha'am's school of 'spiritual Zionism.' [. . .] According to Ahad Ha'am, Zionism's primary aim was to overcome the threat to the survival of the Jews as a nation due to historical processes such as emancipation and secularisation, which drove many Jews to assimilate. Ahad Ha'am sought to cope with the threat by establishing a 'spiritual centre' in the Land of Israel, one destined to foster a Jewish national culture that would unify the Jewish people and preserve their historical continuity.[49]

Babylon survives as a rhetorical device in Zionism, although the most influential developments in the binary pairing of the cities have been those of Christian sources, specifically Revelation and St Augustine. The actual modern displacement of the Iraqi (Babylonian) Jews reverses the biblical situation: over the course of the twentieth century, virtually the entire Jewish population of Iraq was forced out of the country. Rakowitz lists factors including 'Arab nationalism, Germanophilia, British colonialism'[50] – all of which led to anti-Semitism in Iraq during the 1930s, and the *farhud* riots of 1941[51] – but most importantly the creation of the state of Israel. After 1948 the situation for Jews in Iraq rapidly became untenable, and in 1950–1 all but a few thousand of Iraq's over 100,000 Jews emigrated, principally by means of airlifts to Israel. Iraq's Jewish population could trace its origins in the country back 2,500 years to the Babylonian deportations, and their loss both of home and of a stake in Iraq's national identity can hardly be seen as liberation.

Another politicized use of Babylon is made in Rastafarian rhetoric. Zionist and Rastafarian uses of Babylon share a great deal because the symbolism of Babylon is relevant to those aspects of the two that are most alike in political and religious terms. First, both are explicitly political movements with explicitly religious foundations. Second, both are very seriously concerned with place, exile and homeland. Finally, both are affected by the fear of loss of identity through 'assimilation' into white and Gentile power structures and societies, respectively.[52] Rastafarian usage of Babylon is also interesting in its differences from that of Zionism, however, and particularly its explicit relocation of both Babylon (to America and other sites of black oppression) and Zion (to Africa, and specifically Ethiopia under Hailie Selassie). The use of parallels with the Babylonian Captivity in this case serves to underline the emotive power of biblical metaphors. After all, the metaphor of the Babylonian Captivity is less horrific and far smaller in scale than the effects of the Atlantic slave trade it has come to symbolize, yet that symbolism has remained of paramount importance.

Emperor Haile Selassie's construction of a messianic self-image in Ethiopia was taken up with great enthusiasm in Jamaica, where an existing politicized Afrocentrism influenced by the founder of the Universal Negro Improvement Association, Marcus Garvey,[53] who appeared to have prophesized the reign of Haile Selassie,[54] could fuse with strong Christian traditions. At its inception, Rastafari had a pre-existing political base and a core theology familiar to all Christians. This strong, shared and well-known core theology could be argued to be the great advantage of allegory over (or perhaps as a facilitator for) the explicit use of more recent history in rhetoric. Parallels with the Babylonian Captivity also helped legitimate the idea of Haile Selassie as a new Messiah: the closer the correspondence of recent history with scripture, the more confidently and convincingly these links could be drawn on to affirm his status. The allegory gave religious narrative weight to the forced movement of so many Africans to the Americas, turning oppression into a step on a pre-ordained and righteous path to glory, giving meaning to past suffering and promising future redemption and restoration. The establishment of a divine plan in history is an important aspect of Christian theology's influence on historical scholarship generally,[55] and the role played by Babylon as the Americas here is exactly the same as that of Babylon as Rome in Revelation, transferring biblical narratives and thus the history of God's chosen people beyond 'Bible Lands' and into contemporary politics. Indeed, Haile Selassie's own use of biblical epithets shows the same concern for emphasizing significance in this greater, religious history: his titles drew on Isaiah

('Conquering Lion of Judah') and Revelation ('King of Kings', 'Lord of Lords').[56] Some reference to Rome also survives within the Rastafarian usage of Babylon, with reference to its status as the centre of the Roman Catholic Church, seen as colluding with states and with colonialism.[57] Beyond even this, the movements and relocations of Babylon in Rastafarianism are growing yet more complex. The socio-political appeal of Rastafari has proven broader than its original Jamaican context, and indeed has found support beyond African diaspora communities, both in other groups marginalized by colonialism (Maori in New Zealand) and increasingly in Africa itself.[58]

Heritage and identity in modern Iraq

Iraq is a young state, often considered 'artificial', in the sense of having been set up by European powers with insufficient regard for older cultural affinities and boundaries that the new borders of the post-1918 Middle East ignored. It is not true, however, that the three former Ottoman provinces of Basra, Baghdad and Mosul were thrown together arbitrarily. In many ways the creation of the modern state of Iraq cemented what had been an informal grouping of the provinces under Ottoman rule, and an even longer history of close relations.[59] The designation of the whole area as Iraq is certainly over 1,000 years old, and is found in the geographies of Ibn Hauqal, al-Muqadassi and Yakut al-Hamawi.[60] Moreover, the influence of Baghdad could be felt throughout this area, and had never been confined only to the province that bore its name. One example of this ambiguous relationship would be the way in which European travellers used the city as a hub for all three provinces, Joseph de Beauchamp and Claudius Rich both living there for substantial periods.

There is a tradition of capital cities with pan-Mesopotamian territory and power in central Iraq stretching back to ancient Babylon itself, and interrupted only by the Mongol sack of Baghdad in 1258 and the subsequent Turkoman Il-Khanate period, 1258–1534, during which strong centralized power was absent and Baghdad's role as capital supplanted by Tabriz in north-western Iran.[61] Rather than creating something wholly new, therefore, the establishment of the British Mandate following the First World War was perhaps most significant in changing international relationships and reinforcing an existing but weaker pattern of centralization, reorienting the country from its place in the Ottoman Empire and its connections with Turkey and Syria, towards a reinforced centrality for Baghdad.[62]

A significant special case was Kuwait, which was already under British control to a great extent prior to 1914 and which, though part of Ottoman Basra, had always retained substantial autonomy.[63] Its future as a separate state was effectively guaranteed by a July 1914 Anglo–Ottoman agreement, specifying Kuwait's borders and legitimating Britain's special authority in the (still Ottoman) region. The separation of Kuwait, then, while certainly a product of British economic interest (as a terminus of the proposed British version of the Baghdad railway originally conceived by Germany), did not constitute a sudden or unexpected appropriation of an area controlled by Baghdad prior to the establishment of nation-states and borders. The extent to which the formation of modern Iraq was subject to fleeting European economic concerns, while significant, should not therefore be emphasized to the exclusion of a pre-existing Iraq with comparable borders and an economic and administrative hub in Baghdad. Indeed, while the assertion of Iraq's borders as arbitrary is usually intended as a criticism of British imperialism, it is potentially much more damaging for Iraq itself, serving to dent the modern state's legitimacy and talk down the potential for peaceful coexistence.[64] It was also one of the arguments frequently used in the legitimation of Saddam Hussein through the perceived need for a 'strong' central government. The argument remains relevant, and its implications serious and immediate, in the post-Saddam era, where political freedom, independence, interdependence and representation are central concerns for all involved and, despite Iraq's experience of Saddam Hussein, calls for a dictatorial 'strong man' figure can still be heard. For the same reason, the claim of artificiality has served to excuse tyranny in the past[65] and economic exploitation by foreign powers in the present.[66] The claim to artificiality is both historically unconvincing and politically dangerous. Continuity at this level, however, by no means implies stability or unity. Rather, with such diverse stakeholders, Iraq's national identity has been and continues to be a site of intense conflict. It should come as no surprise that the past has been of great importance here, or that huge efforts have been made to shape its representation in support of present-day political goals.

An appropriate starting point for this topic is the Ottoman 'reconquest' of Iraq in 1831. In reality this was more of a centralization and reassertion of Ottoman power than a reconquest of lost territory. The governors of both Baghdad and Basra were mamluk, while in Mosul the al-Jalili family were semi-autonomous. When Da'ud Pasha, the governor of Baghdad, refused to comply with the so-called *Nizam-i Cedid* (New Order) and give up his office, an army led by 'Ali Rida Pasha, governor of Aleppo, captured Da'ud Pasha and put the three provinces under direct rule from Istanbul.[67] As a result, the provinces were more heavily affected by the Ottoman drive for reform based on European systems of government and, crucially, education. The failure of these reforms to prevent the continuation of old hierarchies, alongside the introduction of European-style education that had an impact on political thought and activity, would lead ultimately to the Young Turks, and to the rapid transformation of the terms of political participation throughout the Ottoman Empire.

The Young Turk revolution of 1908, which forced the Sultan to reintroduce the Ottoman constitution and saw the emergence into the open of the Committee of Union and Progress (CUP), allowed many of the hitherto suppressed currents of political opinion within the three Mesopotamian provinces to find public expression, as they did elsewhere in the empire. The proliferation of clubs, groups and societies after 1908, as well as the explosion of journals and newspapers (an estimated sixty titles were published at various times in the three provinces in the years following the revolution of 1908), is testimony to the political engagement of growing numbers in Mosul, Baghdad and Basra.[68]

It was thus a highly unstable Ottoman Empire that entered the First World War, and one widely expected to be succeeded by a very different political landscape regionally. In the short term the Iraqi provinces came under the rule of another empire. In 1914 the British army occupied Basra, followed by Baghdad in 1917 and Mosul in 1918. Iraq was officially ruled by British Mandate from 1920, an arrangement which in turn immediately gave fuel to a nationalist movement aiming at independence. The British solution was the installation of the Hashemite Emir Faisal as King Faisal I in 1921.[69] This move involved both practical and symbolic concerns, of which the latter were particularly bound up with heritage. One advantage of Faisal was his Hashemite lineage, through which he could claim descent from the Prophet.[70] This made up somewhat for the fact that the new king would be a foreigner: he was a son of the Sharif of Mecca, and his new station (following a very brief reign as King of Greater Syria in 1920 before being driven out in the Franco–Syrian War of 1920–1) was effectively a reward from the British for his success as a leader in the Arab Revolt during the First World War.

The period of the British Mandate and the Hashemite monarchy also involved a reinforcement of Britain's archaeological interests in Iraq. This is the period of Leonard Woolley's famous discoveries at Ur.[71] Following their time together as both archaeologists and spies, resulting simultaneously in detailed geographical information for the British government and an acclaimed piece of archaeological survey work,[72] T. E. Lawrence went on to become more deeply involved in politics, advising in the Arab Revolt led by Sharif Husain of Mecca and his sons, most importantly Faisal, while Woolley continued with archaeology, and through his work at Ur became one of its most famed practitioners.

One of the most important British figures in Iraq's political history, Gertrude Bell, was also heavily involved with the country's heritage and archaeology (Figure 23). She was officially Oriental Secretary to Civil Commissioner Arnold Wilson in the original 1920 British Mandate administration, but her actual role was unique and wide-ranging. In politics she is remembered for the influence of her views on Iraqi self-government, of which she began as an opponent and ended as a strong advocate, although continuing to see a senior, even paternalistic role for Britain in managing the country's affairs.[73] She was instrumental in the installation of King Faisal,[74] and arguably in speeding the end of the British Mandate. In archaeology it was she who, as Director of Antiquities, presided over the foundation of the Iraq Museum in Baghdad (which opened in June 1926, only shortly before her death on 12 July of the same year) and the introduction of new laws restricting the export of Iraqi antiquities, making all excavated material the property of the state and guaranteeing Iraq a share in material excavated by foreign archaeologists.[75] Bell was also responsible for regulating the quality of excavation methods, and for requirements that teams excavating in Iraq had, for example, an epigraphist, an architect and a photographer.[76] All of these were standard in the Deutsche Orient-Gesellschaft excavations that had so impressed Bell before the outbreak of war in 1914, and it seems quite possible that what she had seen at Babylon and Ashur encouraged her in promoting these new requirements. Under the auspices of Gertrude Bell, British archaeology in Iraq flourished, and the legacy of her support for the field can still be felt: her memorial fund formed the core of funding for the British School of Archaeology in Iraq, founded in 1936.[77]

Bell was adventurous, and travelled extensively in Iraq without a motor car and with only her servants for a male escort.[78] She also spoke good Arabic, and in the First World War had been assigned by the British Secret Service to promote Arab uprisings against the Ottoman government. She visited the excavations at Babylon for the first time in April 1909,[79] and would later be responsible for the decision to send finds from pre-war German excavations to Berlin, first in the case of Samarra immediately after the war,[80] and later in the case of Babylon (see Chapter 6). In general, however, she is remembered for working to keep material from new excavations for Iraq, making sure that the young state got the best of divisions of finds and providing collections for the new Iraq Museum. She retained her position in the early years of the monarchy, and Amatzia Baram notes Faisal's unconcern at the continued European control of archaeology in Iraq:

[W]hile King Faisal I was very particular about the choice of
the man who would run his Ministry of Education (i.e., Sati'
al-Husri), as he wanted to ensure that a radical pan-Arabist
would be in charge of molding the minds of the Iraqi younger
generation, he was perfectly happy to have the Department of
Antiquities headed by a British colonial officer. Indeed, the first
non-European Director of Antiquities, none other than al-
Husri, was only appointed as late as October 1934 [...].
Secondly, apparently because they were all aware of the fact that
the digs were being conducted in hopes of discovering pre-Arab
and pre-Islamic civilizations, neither Faisal nor any of his
ministers [...] considered the need to enact a Law of
Antiquities until they were prodded to do so by Bell.[81]

There are some qualifications to be made here. Winstone describes
Faisal as 'anxious to protect the country's archaeological heritage',[82]
and his government's decision to appoint Gertrude Bell as (Hon.)
Director of Antiquities was an effective way to ensure such
protection. Bell maintained strong friendships with many of the
archaeologists while still proving a powerful advocate for the claims
of the Iraqi state. In his memoirs, the British archaeologist Max
Mallowan defends the somewhat cosy situation, recalling that:

> During my first two seasons at Ur, Gertrude herself acted as
> Director of Antiquities and would spend several days battling
> with Woolley over their share of the finds. The division was
> supposed to be on a fifty-fifty basis, but no tigress could have
> safeguarded Iraq's rights better.[83]

With regard to Baram's second point, the responsibility of
enacting a law of antiquities really lay with the British Mandate
authorities, since its establishment, as Baram acknowledges, was
specified as a requirement in the Mandate Charter itself. The fact
remains, however, that in archaeology British influence, and that of
Gertrude Bell in particular, continued prominently and formally
after the Mandate.

Gertrude Bell was succeeded by several further, generally short-lived, English Directors of Antiquities, most notably the British Museum's Sidney Smith (1928–31), and by the German Julius Jordan (1931–4).[84] Significant change came in 1934 with the appointment of the Arab nationalist intellectual and politician Sati' al-Husri to the post.[85] Al-Husri immediately introduced a far more stringent antiquities law, against which, predictably, the foreign and especially British archaeologists who lost most through the changes protested, sometimes vehemently.[86] In reality the changes ought to have been expected: there had already been Iraqi protests that the old law had been too soft and had allowed foreign archaeologists to export too much, nor were the new arrangements less favourable to foreign excavators than those adopted by many other states. Sati' al-Husri also made a significant departure from the pre-Islamic focus of foreign expeditions, founding the Islamic Museum at the fourteenth-century caravanserai Khan Murjan, Baghdad,[87] and encouraging excavations of Islamic sites including the medieval city of Wasit and the great mosque at Kufa.

Al-Husri's background was international. Born in Yemen in 1882, his family were Syrian and his education was that of the Ottoman elite, including a spell in Paris. Before becoming Minister for Education in Faisal's Iraq, he had also been part of the short-lived Faisal government in Syria. Against the structure of state boundaries imposed on the Middle East by the 1916 Sykes-Picot agreement – though entirely in accordance with the terms of victory as the Allies had led Faisal, T. E. Lawrence and others to believe during the war, and for which the Arab Revolt had been fought – al-Husri was a strong advocate of a vast, politically unified Arab state. Following German romantic nationalist ideas of nations as organic, naturally occurring entities,[88] he argued that the Arab world constituted a single nation on linguistic and cultural grounds, and that the political unification of this nation was a goal of the greatest importance for Arab leaders. The view had direct implications for his work on education and as Director of Antiquities. In both cases it made sense to shift the emphasis away from the pre-Islamic heritage (which was both uniquely Iraqi and traditionally of greater interest to

Western than Arab historians) and towards the Islamic past, where a
sense of shared heritage and Arab identity could most effectively be
fostered. Such virtues, however, were very much a matter of political
persuasion. For those whose nationalism was Iraqi rather than pan-
Arab the approach held equal political disadvantages. A large part of
Iraq's population was not Arab but Kurdish, and while the rest of the
Arab world was overwhelmingly Sunni, in Iraq the existence of a
Shiite majority made unification based on Islamic history very
difficult. The holy cities of Karbala and Najaf and the martyrdoms of
'Ali and Hussein lie at the root of Sunni–Shi'a religious differences.
The ancient past of Sumer, Babylonia and Assyria, just as its
specificity to Iraq was a disadvantage from the point of view of Arab
nationalism, held great potential for Iraqi nationalists, particularly
since those groups in Iraq who claimed a more direct connection to
this past than others (Assyrian Christians, for example) were
minorities rather than any of the major ethnic or religious groups.
The idea of a pre-Islamic national past in which all, Arab and Kurd,
Sunni and Shi'a, could feel an equal stake was to become an important
cultural tool for Iraqi politicians.

To say that 'all' could have a stake in the new Iraqi national
heritage, however, is to ignore the fate of one important part of the
country's population. Another, tragic, development of the early
twentieth century was the effective termination of two and a half
millennia of Judaism in Iraq. What had begun with the Babylonian
Captivity had become a major Jewish minority in Iraq, with its own
culture and traditions but also a strong stake in Iraqi national life. To
be an Arab Jewish Iraqi nationalist was not, in the early twentieth
century, an uncommon position. Increasing anti-Semitic feeling in the
middle of the century reached boiling point with the establishment
of the state of Israel in 1948. Conditions for Iraqi Jews became
impossible, and from 1950 many thousands of Jewish families had no
option but to take advantage of a new law allowing them to leave
Iraq, giving up their nationality as they did so. They went to Israel,
from where many moved on to Britain and the United States. In 1947
the Jewish population of Iraq was 117,000; by 1952 practically all
had left the country.[89] Continuing persecution made life impossible

for the few who stayed, eventually forcing more families to leave and reducing Iraq's Jewish population almost to nil.[90]

Heritage and archaeology in Ba'thist Iraq

The role of heritage in Ba'thist Iraq has been explored by Amatzia Baram, who has studied the selective preservation and establishment of cultural festivals as well as uses of ancient material and iconography.[91] More recently, Zainab Bahrani has discussed both Saddam Hussein's association of himself with the militant kings of Assyria and Babylonia mentioned in the Old Testament, and his representation in terms of these leaders' despotic reputations abroad.[92] Baram charts a gradual permeation of pre-Islamic Mesopotamian components into Iraqi national identity during the 1930s–50s, but a major boost in 1958 following the successful coup of 'Abd al-Karim Qasim, and an even greater one with the Ba'th party's consolidation of power from 1968.[93] The party was pan-Arabist in its ideals, but political circumstances, including the increasingly concrete reality of the existing states and their borders and a permanent schism between the Ba'th parties of Syria and Iraq, created a use for the specifically Iraqi ancient heritage in practice.

Saddam Hussein made extensive use of the ancient past, investing heavily in heritage and, particularly, in enormous reconstructions at Babylon, work on which began in 1978 but which became far more ambitious from the mid-1980s onward. Archaeological work was well supported by the state. The antiquities budget doubled in the first four years of Ba'th rule, increasing much further after 1979, while decades of prior investment paid off in the form of a growing pool of highly trained Iraqi archaeologists, many employed by the Department of Antiquities and complemented by an extensive network of site inspectors and site guards.[94] Iraqi and foreign excavations and research projects continued throughout the Iran–Iraq War, with a brief return of large-scale foreign research projects, many intended as long-term, between that war's end and the 1990–1 Gulf War,[95] after which foreign projects ceased and Iraqi projects were greatly reduced.

For the promotion of nationalism by the Iraqi government, the ancient past not only had the advantage of being shared but also served to differentiate secular Iraq from its revolutionary neighbour. Following the 1979 revolution, Iran's new government set about consciously removing the many symbols of pre-Islamic heritage associated with the Shah, and a major shift in emphasis towards Iran's Islamic heritage began. Iraq, whose Ba'th government was at least nominally socialist and explicitly secular, was already well positioned to emphasize its difference from the Iranian theocracy, but the aggressive rhetoric of the new government in Tehran and fear of the Islamic revolution spreading to Shi'ite southern Iraq gave special impetus to the promotion of Iraq's ancient past by the state. Saddam Hussein's identification with Assyrian and Babylonian kings focused on their strength and power through force, showing him playing the role of an ancient king.[96] These themes are also encapsulated in what is possibly Baghdad's most famous modern monument, the giant 'Victory Arches' completed in 1989. Also known as the Hands of Victory or Swords of Qadisiyya, the arches commemorate Iraq's victory over Iran in the Iran–Iraq War (itself highly questionable: the war ended in what was in reality an immensely costly stalemate).[97] The Battle of Qadisiyya to which the monument also refers is a great Arab victory over Sasanian Persian forces in the seventh century, the decisive engagement that led to the Islamic conquest of Persia and thus a useful parallel for Saddam Hussein to draw with the modern conflict, also playing to the anti-Persian racism that had been a part of state historical rhetoric since the time of Sati' al-Husri.[98]

The site of Babylon was to be a major focus for activity. Beginning in 1978, the State Organization of Antiquities and Heritage embarked upon an ambitious programme of reconstructions.[99] Nebuchadnezzar's Southern Palace, the Ishtar Gate and Processional Way, the Ninmakh temple and the Greek theatre (as the name suggests, a Hellenistic-era rather than Neo-Babylonian building) were all restored (Figure 24), and work continued on the reconstructions despite the colossal drain on resources of the Iran–Iraq War. 1987 saw the first Babylon International Festival, with work on the reconstructions greatly sped up (to the detriment of quality) in order to be ready in time.[100] These large-scale events, intended to celebrate the glories of the past and the leadership of Saddam Hussein in the present, continued annually until 2002, save for the interruption of the 1990–1 Gulf War.[101] Unfortunately the reconstructions, carried out directly on top of the actual walls of the ancient buildings, were in many respects very far from ideal. Famously, Saddam Hussein echoed Nebuchadnezzar by having his name stamped on bricks in the reconstructions (Figure 25). They read, 'In the era of President Saddam Hussein of Iraq, the protector of Great Iraq and reproducer of its reawakening and the builder of its civilization' or 'In the era of Saddam Hussein, protector of Iraq, who rebuilt the royal palace'.[102] The modern yellow bricks themselves have also been criticized as an inappropriate building material for the reconstructions. Other works carried out at the site were not reconstructions of any kind: three artificial lakes and three extremely large artificial mounds were created at the site, upon one of which was built a palace for Saddam Hussein (Figure 26). This mound may also be the most damaging of the three archaeologically since its site, now on the eastern bank of the Euphrates, lies directly over the ancient course of the river and encroaches upon some of the most important remains of the city's Neo-Babylonian centre. The modern village of Qweirish also stood here; Koldewey's team had used a house here as their headquarters, and many workmen on excavations at Babylon then and since had come from the village. It was demolished and its population displaced when the mound was built.[103]

Other initiatives under Saddam Hussein were deliberately destructive. Perhaps the most dramatic example is the draining of southern Iraq's marshlands, areas that had long acted as refuges for political dissenters and opponents of the government. For thousands of years their environmental conditions had effectively rendered them remote and difficult of access, harder to monitor than the rest of the country. This changed in the 1990s, when Saddam Hussein began the systematic destruction of this environment. Following the Shi'ite uprisings in the wake of the Gulf War, which did not receive the foreign military support they had been led to expect,[104] and which the government punished with massacres:

Some of those who eluded capture and death escaped into the
marshes of southern Iraq, where they were given haven by the
marsh Arabs, a group of some 200,000 Shi'as whose culture
traces back to the ancient Sumerians. The retaliatory responses
of the government have included draining up to two-thirds of
the marshes and exterminating several Marsh Arab tribes. The
government has cut off the tributaries that feed the marshes,
blocked the entrance of food and medicine, and shelled the reed
huts in which the people live. In September 1993 a government
campaign forced tens of thousands of Marsh Arabs to flee to
Iran. The United Nations High Commissioner for Refugees
reported that some 7,000 Iraqi refugees entered Iran in one
year, June 1993 to June 1994, and SAIRI [the Supreme
Assembly for the Islamic Revolution in Iraq] reported that
another 6,000 severely malnourished Shi'as entered Iran in late
1994.[105]

Variants on the phrase 'whose culture traces back to the ancient
Sumerians' occur in almost all popular references to the persecution of
the marsh Arabs. Heritage was an important part of rhetoric against
the marsh drainage, even when the humanitarian crisis was on the
scale described by Wiley. As the journalist Robert Fisk put it, 'The
man who rebuilt Babylon in his own image was destroying Sumeria'
(*sic*).[106] The accusation of cultural barbarism was thus linked
rhetorically to far more serious crimes.

We must also consider the impact of Saddam Hussein's rule on the
intangible heritage, a term which can be misleading, and whose
tangible qualities are easily appreciated in the Iraqi case. It denotes
those aspects of cultural heritage that are harder to legislate for on the
basis that there is not necessarily a material or clearly definable object
to protect.[107] Most commonly this means the cultural practices,
memories and identities of living people, and so the suggestion that
legislation to protect this form of heritage does not or has not until
recently existed is inaccurate – protection of what we now call the
intangible heritage is implicit in the most fundamental human rights
legislation. The protection of cultural heritage in this form consists

principally in a person's right to live and in their freedom of expression. This is not to say that the problem of such protection is a simple one, or that a concern for cultural heritage does not raise important issues that concern for the other basic freedoms of water and food, shelter, physical safety, status in law, democratic rights and education would not in themselves include; only that the intangible heritage is already a part of this package, and that the most effective legislation in this field will always be that which protects human life and freedom of expression, since it is in these that this heritage primarily exists.

If not completely suppressed, cultural works carry their own survival mechanisms, and there is significant interdependence between memory, cultural identity and freedom in the present. Exposure to diverse cultural sources, and ideally to critical treatment of those sources, engenders the ability to consider a world outside one's own present-day reality, to be aware of the possibility – the certainty – of change and difference in the world, and to experience the humanity of someone else, particularly someone whose outlook differs substantially from one's own. All of these capacities are anathema to political dictatorship, to the denial of human rights, and to the oppression of others based on a perceived inherent inferiority. For this reason most aspects of heritage termed 'intangible' could more accurately be described as aspects of cultural rights or cultural freedom. This view carries with it the implication that policy relating to them ought to be treated in these terms, which perhaps helps to explain the feeling that they are not adequately treated in cultural heritage legislation: the latter was originally intended to preserve objects whose very stasis was perceived to be their most important characteristic. Rights and freedoms, by contrast, are performed actively and in need of constant renewal. Without the capacity for cultural expression, the ability to resist propaganda or the will of the state is greatly reduced.

How, then, to speak of the damage to cultural rights and freedoms that Iraq has undergone, both very recently and under Saddam Hussein, whose ability to prevent freedom of speech and expression underpinned his rule for over two decades? Kanan Makiya's *Republic of*

Fear: The Politics of Modern Iraq describes the mechanisms through which Saddam Hussein's control became so complete.[108] Despite the subject matter, the author's approach in describing the rise and consolidation of the Mukhabarat, the Iraqi president's secret police, of torture as routine, and of the establishment of an all-pervading culture of fear and distrust is sober and academic. Only rarely does Makiya allow himself to lament the impact of these changes in general terms:

> Authority used to be the butt of popular jokes, anecdotes, and satirical poems, cultural safety valves that provided relief from the traditional oppressiveness of the state. But all that is gone now. No one dares ridicule authority any longer in Iraq because everyone is afraid. The tone of political culture has become Kafkaesque: saturated with a sense of the impersonality of sinister and impenetrable forces, operating on helpless individuals, who nonetheless intuit that they are being buffeted about by a bizarre, almost transcendental kind of rationality.[109]

Such a climate of fear and repression destroys cultural life, especially where, as with the marshlands of southern Iraq, economic and environmental change have been absolutely inseparable from change in cultural practices.[110] Human rights should in any case take precedence for their own sake, but we should also make the point that no amount of state-funded excavation or research can outweigh serious political and cultural oppression in its long-term impact on the study of a country's past. Equally, in the years following 2003 a climate of fear generated by lawlessness reinforced ethnic and religious divisions to such an extent that Baghdad's once mixed neighbourhoods are now firmly segregated and likely to remain so for the foreseeable future, again impoverishing Iraq socially and culturally.

Babylon in the present

In 2003 a US-led coalition invaded and occupied Iraq, deposing and ultimately arresting Saddam Hussein and many other senior Ba'th party figures. Saddam Hussein himself was executed in December 2006; others, including his sons Uday and Qasay, were killed rather than captured.

In the immediate aftermath of the Iraqi government's collapse and the occupation of the country by coalition forces, several days of looting saw most government buildings stripped. This was entirely predictable, and indeed predicted not only by experts concerned with the safety of cultural sites,[111] but also by the coalition, who had drawn up a list of buildings to protect in the city. On this list the Iraq Museum was ranked third.[112] This list, however, apparently did not reach the commanders responsible for planning and executing the occupation of Baghdad itself. At a public forum held at the British Museum on 15 June 2004, Peter Galbraith, former US Ambassador to Croatia, stated that he believed the list, approved by Secretary of Defence Donald Rumsfeld, had disappeared 'just above the uniformed military'.[113] As a result the Iraq Museum was not protected. This explanation differs from that of Colonel Matthew Bogdanos, the US investigator into the Museum's looting, who asserts that for much of the time such protection was impossible and that delays in responding to appeals for protection resulted from inevitable battlefield confusion and an advance into Baghdad whose speed, Bogdanos argues, outstripped the expectations and ability to keep up of military planners.[114] Compounding this, the Museum itself was caught up in the fighting.[115] There is also disagreement in detail between Bogdanos' account and that of another key eyewitness, Dr Donny George of the Iraq Museum, in whose view it would have been possible for the US Army safely to secure the Museum and prevent the looting.[116] Whatever the case, failure to protect the Museum from looting came to symbolize for critics the ignorance of and indifference to history and culture represented by, particularly, the attitude of the American government. At the same time, many of Iraq's other museums and libraries, including the national library, were similarly victims of looting and its attendant damage, but it was the Iraq Museum itself that came to represent them all in global media coverage. Some information about Iraq's cultural and historical importance had been conveyed through the media during the build-up to war, and so public awareness was at least sufficient to provoke a global outcry when the looting actually occurred.[117]

Inevitably, the high level of attention initially focused on this crisis waned, and the subsequent looting of sites across Iraq received far less coverage. This looting, however, is of greater concern to archaeologists than even the damage done to cultural institutions such as the Iraq Museum, because the looting of sites represents an even greater loss of information. As is easily appreciated when faced with the aerial photographs of low tell sites in southern Iraq, now peppered with the marks of hundreds of small-scale illicit excavations;[118] the damage done means that it is not only the material that is actually removed from the site that loses its context, but a much larger category of disturbed material. The loss to humanity's knowledge of its own past this represents will be felt only gradually, as future researchers at critically important sites find their ability to analyse and interpret material permanently handicapped by the disruption. In sum, the looting of museums, libraries and archaeological sites in Iraq represents a catastrophic destruction and devastation of heritage.

The site of Babylon itself suffered no such looting, although the site's two museums and the offices were ransacked. The artefacts stolen and damaged from the museums were copies, but a far more significant loss was the burning of the library and archives in the site offices.[119] Sadly, however, Babylon suffered great harm of another kind. A coalition army camp built on the site in the aftermath of the occupation has itself damaged the site irreparably. Initially small, the camp expanded to cover 150 hectares in the centre of the ancient city; at its height 2,000 soldiers were based there.[120] Among the main problems that emerged once archaeologists were able to assess damage at the site were: the passage of heavy vehicles across much of central Babylon, including the ancient paving of the Processional Way; the use of material from the site in sandbags; the importing, when this practice had ceased, of material from other archaeological sites for use in sandbags, which becomes mixed with that of Babylon as these sandbags biodegrade; the spreading of chemically-treated gravel over large parts of the site; the use of part of the site as a helipad; the placement of toilet blocks on the site; and the surface disruption attending any occupation on the scale of a large military camp. Full reports are now available on the details of this damage.[121]

For the present, the only part of the site of Babylon itself most people are likely to see is that section of it that has been reconstructed in Berlin. Andrae's vision has remained a defining one in terms of archaeology's presentation of Babylon to the public. At one time this looked set to change: among their several purposes, the reconstructions at the site of Babylon were originally conceived as a potential international tourist attraction. At the time of writing, the prospect of such tourism, or even of a full return to normal life in Iraq, remains distant. The work of rehabilitating the site is only just beginning and the conservation demands immense. Preparations for a formal application for United Nations Education, Scientific and Cultural Organization (UNESCO) World Heritage status are under way (the site is at present on the tentative list), while planning for the future of research and tourism remain at the very earliest and most tentative stages. On the other hand, the site is a high priority for the Iraq State Board of Antiquities and Heritage, who have been working independently and with the World Monuments Fund on site management, documentation and conservation programmes.[122] It is hoped by all that the work now underway at Babylon will lead in time to its revival as a centre for research, education, cultural events and tourism. Whatever the uncertainties, it is clear that the site will continue to play a significant role in Iraq's national cultural life.

CHAPTER 8

CULTURE AND KNOWLEDGE

Discussions of Babylon traditionally lead to meditations upon its fall. There is one sense in which the city is indeed falling, along with every other component of the historical grand narrative within which that fall fits. Babylon had a definite place, albeit an unenviable one, in the biblical and classical sources carefully reconciled in the Middle Ages and developed through many permutations to underpin modern narratives of human progress. Today the tide of scholarly thought has begun to turn away from such unilinear narratives and towards understandings of history that, though dominated by interconnections as never before, nonetheless place great value on the particular and the local for their own sake, and resist regarding one particular grouping or locale as more significant in terms of the human condition than any other.

The various manifestations and offshoots of postcolonial studies, fields dealing constantly with the mechanics of the interconnected and the particular, represent a revival of that beauty seen by medievalists in the encyclopaedic nature of their scholarly work: the great but finite complexity of a world of particulars, all of which must be understood in relation to one another. This new particularism differs from the old in two crucial respects, however. First, though all is explicable within its terms, it allows dissonance and discord in all things because these are reflective of the multiplicity of perspectives and perceptions that make up human experience.[1] The purpose of the growing search for subaltern voices in colonial literature, for example, is not to erase and replace the colonial literature but to complement it, expand its scope and balance its inherent biases.[2] Second, it is a particularism without an obvious linear focus. Previously there have been two such foci: the divine will, as in medieval and Renaissance conceptions, and the fate of humanity (as in Enlightenment, romantic and modern models). Although the concept of humanity's fate as defined by the will of the gods is of great antiquity, that of the divine as structuring linear history is medieval, a product specifically of Jewish apocalypticism but adopted by both Christianity and Islam. It is a conception according to which the history of the world is not cyclical and will end, and whose entry into historiography is usually attributed by philosophers of history to St Augustine and *The City of God*.[3] This history 'sees humanity as in process toward a not yet attained but ultimate condition of mankind'[4] at the end of time. Importantly, this type of history made a project of the unification and harmonization of source material, working towards a single figuration, to use Erich Auerbach's term, of humanity and history.[5]

Such approaches, with their ultimately religious structures and understandings, were gradually supplanted by models of humanity's progress in which human agency increasingly made history until, in modern thought, progress became the goal and responsibility of humanity, something that it was possible to strive for and obtain. The idea of control over history is utterly alien to *The City of God*, but the linear structure is shared.[6] Where St Augustine's historical model was firmly grounded in providential history, however, modern linear perspectives have pursued philosophical models as potential keys to future utopias, driven by the very modern idea of humanity's own perfectability.[7] One product of such ambition is disillusionment, as witnessed in the modern flowering of dystopian fiction whose greatest exemplars, *Brave New World* and *Nineteen Eighty-Four*, were both written in the mid-twentieth century.[8] The dangers attached to thinking of human history as project and destiny have also been amply demonstrated in the real history of the twentieth century. Karl Popper dedicated his argument against historical prediction as an intellectual goal, *The Poverty of Historicism*, to the 'memory of countless men and women of all creeds or nations or races who fell victims to the fascist and communist belief in Inexorable Laws of Historical Destiny'.[9]

It makes sense that postcolonial thought should be so much less utopian in character, generally eschewing overarching structures and pointing toward more complex and pluralistic histories whose patterns need not be progressive or degenerative, and which lead neither to a utopia nor to the Last Judgement. One implication of this is a radically reduced significance for previously critical historical loci, such as Nebuchadnezzar's Babylon, classical Athens or imperial Rome, because their stories are no longer considered to structure the whole of human history in the way that they once were. This, at least, is the theory. Cultural canons have not historically changed quickly, however, and as icons in representation alone one would expect the constituent parts of the grand narrative to prove tenacious in practice.[10] In the case of Babylon there is already a long history of temporal and geographical displacement beginning with Revelation, and the continuation of this phenomenon seems certain. In one sense this makes the city important in a distinctly pre-modern, moral and quasi-religious way. If we return to the rough distinction between classical sources on Babylon as more descriptive and biblical sources as more moralizing, we will see its reestablishment here very clearly, remarkably intact after so many integrations and reconciliations of the two groups. For a Babylon whose meaning is abstract, ahistorical and largely moral biblical sources are far more relevant, and therefore are drawn upon more extensively. This is true on the one hand for twentieth-century images of the Tower of Babel, rarely located in a historical Iraq and no longer related to ziggurats but only to an allegorical or even atheistic and metaphorical reading of Genesis, and on the other for the many cities that have been called Babylon – Paris, London, New York, Los Angeles – where the prophets and particularly Revelation are the source. It is the classical sources that are directly affected by the Deutsche Orient-Gesellschaft excavations; their descriptions did become less authoritative, and have been supplanted by the writings of Koldewey, his colleagues and their successors in archaeology and Assyriology as the most authoritative sources on the geography of Babylon.

Knowledge and hybrids

The representation of Babylon offers practical examples of almost every conceivable transformation in epistemology and knowledge that a historical subject might undergo. Particularly interesting are the abiding presence and influence of a mythic component and the near-ubiquity of hybrid understandings that incorporate several different kinds of knowledge with quite different bases. Mythic elements are present where we might instinctively expect knowledge that was neatly and absolutely theocratic; in the case of Revelation the allegorical aspect of Babylon's use is mythic, as is the archetype of the worldly city in St Augustine. On the other hand, we find both allegorical and theocratic knowledge permeating humanist empiricism with regard to Babylon. When explorers, antiquaries and archaeologists sought the Tower of Babel, that search could be defined either as theocratic or, where Genesis is seen as a reliable (as opposed to infallible) reference to an actual building regardless of whether that building really was the site of divine punishment and the confusion of tongues, as humanist. The tension between different epistemological bases is particularly pronounced in Athansius Kircher's *Turris Babel*, a product of the author's attempt to reconcile biblical and classical sources with far more recent visitors' accounts. Voltaire's use of Babylon championed the use of the past as an effectively timeless, placeless setting for storytelling, i.e. as a site for myth and fantasy, but in a way that absolutely depended upon an empiricist approach against which to kick. Medieval travellers, whose visits to Babylon we are inclined to privilege on the grounds that they involve empirical observation, frequently turn out to be primarily theocratic, displaying a tendency for the observed world to be tested against that of the text rather than *vice versa*. The medieval encyclopaedic compilation and resolution of written sources is certainly theocratic in a broad sense, but also contains an Aristotelian forerunner to the Cartesian privileging of rational thought in the high value placed on logic, particularly important in medieval European education and in evaluating, resolving and sometimes rejecting incompatible claims. The conceivably equally encyclopaedic (though far less orderly) outcome of a postmodern and postcolonial scholarship that rejects grand narratives and is sceptical of claims to objectivity would be thoroughly humanist in the importance it places on the human subject and subjective knowledge, but also prone to the development of unchallengeable, unempirical claims on the basis of individual subjectivity and the equal validity of subjects' perceptions.

Despite taking place in a very different world, the German excavations and German reception of Babylon in the early twentieth century shared with Kircher's work a noticeable strain in the effort to resolve different kinds of knowledge into an absolute. The attempt at resolution proved antagonistic, hence the crisis of Babel–Bibel. The perceived value of excavations in terms of producing knowledge is obviously empirical, but the nationalist or imperialist desire to lay claim to the discovery of biblical sites where the production of extra knowledge about them was arguably irrelevant is a different matter. To the extent that this is about knowledge at all it is theocratic. *Sardanapal: Historische Pantomime* can be seen as an acknowledgement of and an attempt to redress the failure of academic research to satisfy the mythic component of people's understanding of Babylon. The development of a division that put this component outside the scope of archaeologists' work should not be taken for granted – the values attached to particular forms of knowledge are changeable and historically situated, and perhaps even now it is possible to discern some movement back towards a broader remit for archaeological interpretation, including serious academic consideration of communicating archaeology through fiction.[11] Similarly, the nature and implications of literary fiction's interventions in historical discourse have been analysed by Price,[12] and the interplay between literature and history has been the subject of a volume edited by Caldicott and Fuchs.[13] This is a new exploration of an old idea: in some ways it echoes the Aristotelian view of poetry's value over history.[14] Meanwhile, Michael Shanks' work as been particularly influential in introducing consideration of the human and creative elements in archaeological expression and practice.[15] One recent volume is dedicated to the possibilities of academic archaeological engagement with and expression in the creative arts,[16] a development better described as resurgent than new, while another considers archaeological writing for its own sake and as an integral part of the interpretative process.[17] The significance of Stephanie Moser's work on representation and iconography lies in her demonstration of these elements as acting on interpretation and constituting arguments about the past in their own right.[18] All of these recent works can be seen as part of a resurgence that is closely related to the broader acknowledgement of academic archaeological writing and practice as situated, contingent and subjective.[19]

Robert Koldewey occupies a significant point on this trajectory, as part of the turn towards detached and transparent description as the proper goal of a scholar describing an ancient site, and the introduction of conventions shared with the natural sciences in recording and writing. Within the specific context of Iraq, the departure Koldewey's publication represents from preceding English and French works on the Mesopotamian past is substantial, as discussed in Chapter 6. With Babylon, as with archaeology more generally, however, some resurgence in the role of narrative can be seen more recently. Marc Van De Mieroop has focused on the ideological messages of Babylon's monumental architecture and its self-representation in texts,[20] while Zainab Bahrani's *The Graven Image* analyses the roles of representation within Babylonian and Assyrian culture more broadly.[21] Their interest in capturing Babylonian modes of thought has much to do with a critical self-consciousness of subjectivity and perspective. On the other hand, more traditional approaches continue to play a central and essential role. Just as we are still dependent on the Deutsche Orient-Gesellschaft excavations and their publication for our understanding of the ancient city of Babylon, so too we still share for practical purposes an empirical, more-or-less positivistic outlook with the excavators of the early twentieth century, and much of the difference between their work and that of the present has to do with technical innovation and a broadening of interest in, for example, the study of residential areas, rather than a challenge to the basis of their approach. As a fundamental tool for gathering archaeological data we still value archaeological excavations for much the same reasons as Robert Koldewey.

There is value in all these forms and manifestations of knowledge, and certainly a great deal that is productive stems from their hybridity. One huge factor to consider is the serendipitous creation of knowledge in one category through the pursuit of ideas in another. Umberto Eco has written brilliantly on this topic, selecting examples such as scholarship building on the Ptolemaic universe and Columbus' discovery of the Americas,[22] but there are many other cases. The scale and diversity of such serendipity that can be demonstrated around the study of Babylon, for example, threatens to dwarf that progress which has been directed and intentional. Returning to origins, the Tower of Babel in Genesis inspired much scholarship. On the one hand searches for the original language, while acting on the basis of a narrative many Christians in the twentieth century would not treat as literal, produced much valuable and useful knowledge on the relationships between languages, and thus some of the foundations of present-day comparative linguistics. On the other, searches for the physical site of Babylon's Tower, not to mention its Hanging Gardens, walls, incalculable wealth and evidence of its decimation by God, led to the discovery and decipherment of Mesopotamian cuneiform script and the Akkadian and Sumerian languages; Iraq's is the most completely preserved of ancient literatures and, as it happens, the best-positioned for establishing that the Hebrew of the Old Testament formed part of a complex and geographically wide-ranging linguistic history, and was not the divine or Adamite language various Christian and Jewish scholars, including St Augustine, had at times argued.[23] As we have seen, the biblical fame of Babylon was an important factor in the Deutsche Orient-Gesellschaft's decision to finance excavations there, and thus in large part to generate an 'archaeological' identity for the city. The idea that this archaeological identity might compete with or harm the legitimacy of others was not part of the imperial agenda; rather the assumption was that it would confirm and complement what was already known and believed. Meanwhile, the study of languages, initially developed (like archaeology) in the belief that it might take humanity closer to a divine Truth, would lead eventually to a great destabilizing of textual authorities: to post-structuralists such as Derrida, Barthes and later Baudrillard; and of course coming full circle in Borges' *The Library of Babel*. All of these developments can be seen, in whole or in part, as serendipitous. Nonetheless they form a part of Babylon's intellectual history, which is one of unintended consequences as well as grand visions.

It can be difficult to connect this interplay of epistemological bases and understandings in fact, however, to a formulation of their value in principle. An instructive example is the case of William Blake and his (probable)[24] pairing and juxtaposition of Newton and Nebuchadnezzar. Blake's interest was of a moral and theological kind, taking the history of Daniel and from it producing a visual meditation on reason, unreason, punishment and redemption. It is inappropriate to weigh this kind of production of knowledge against the historical misrepresentation of Nebuchadnezzar (or even Nabonidus – see Chapter 3) as a crazed and piteous man/animal on some absolute scale of merit, because allegorical art and humanistic Assyriology produce meaning according to different criteria of value and truth. Not that this implies a splendid isolation of science from art; Blake's emotive image, though but a further mythologization of Daniel's Nebuchadnezzar, directly affects conceptions of the historical king, and not only for those who believe in the literal truth of his years living as a wild beast. It is neither easy nor very natural to disentangle the different sources on a historical character: our instinct is instead to pull together and reconcile what we 'know.' In many cases, but particularly those of the Deutsche Orient-Gesellschaft production of *Sardanapal* and Edwin Long's *Babylonian Marriage Market* painting, the intention is to blur such distinctions, and to naturalize or efface the application of a mythic framework to new empirical research. In such blurring, and in the uncritical reproduction of stereotypes without empirical foundation in books that do claim such authority, such hybrids can indeed pose serious problems. Nonetheless, it is a mistake to think of the purpose of studying representation in archaeology as the identification and refutation of empirical inaccuracy ('errors' would imply that these are always accidental and made in ignorance) and stereotyping. This is useful work, with the prospect of incrementally improving popular representations of the past in the sense of bringing them into closer harmony with the archaeological research they represent, but it does not begin to reflect the full relevance and importance of representation for students of the human past.

Differentiation between different forms of knowledge is surely useful in interpretative terms. How one acts on this understanding, however, depends in large part on what one considers archaeology *should* be. The current interest in the roles of oral history and narrative in archaeology, for example, show that this is an open debate. Attempts by archaeologists to engage with other approaches to the past are laudable and potentially very constructive. The archaeologist has every right, even a professional duty, to assert his or her views on truth and falsehood within such a dialogue, and no doubt generally adds new insights to others' knowledge of the past through doing so. It does not follow that the archaeologist should be automatically hostile to other uses of the past. Scholarly, humanistic archaeology and history have already won popular respect, a democratic sanction for academic expertise in which we should perhaps have more confidence.[25] The archaeologist's duty, based on a belief that theirs is indeed a particularly rigorous and epistemologically valid way in which to investigate the past, is to the differentiation of understandings and the dissemination of their expert knowledge, not to destruction or censorship.[26]

The central theme of this book has been the interaction of different ideas, understandings and forms of knowledge. We have seen many combinations of hybrids, rarely keeping to the boundaries of epistemological consistency in themselves or in their influence upon one another. In representation, we have seen the capacity for myth and legend to act on interpretations produced by empirical research and humanist criticism without subjection to their tests of truth. Understanding this entanglement is all-important if we aim to produce meaningful knowledge of the past.

POSTSCRIPT: THE BABYLON
EXHIBITIONS

In 2008–9 a unique collaboration between the Musée du Louvre and Réunion des Musées Nationaux de France, the Staatliche Museen zu Berlin and the British Museum resulted in a cycle of three major exhibitions on Babylon.[1] I was fortunate enough to be involved with the British Museum exhibition. Although the three versions differed greatly (this was not a travelling exhibition but a sharing of objects, expertise and resources), all three dealt both with the ancient city of Babylon itself and with its later representation in art and culture.

In the London exhibition we attempted to tell a story that moved back and forth between the ancient city and its later image, particularly the fragments that survive in contemporary popular culture such as the Hanging Gardens, the Tower of Babel, Babylon's reputation as the city of sin and the phrase 'the writing on the wall'. We wanted to show how the legends had developed and how they related to the ancient city itself. To do this we used a relatively small number of objects (a little over 100) and an exhibition structure based on a single, strong linear narrative. We conceived the exhibition as telling a particular story, focused on specific aspects of the city's identity and later reputation. In terms of ancient material we concentrated exclusively on the period of the Neo-Babylonian

Empire, *c.*612–539 BC, because it is this very short period that has most shaped Babylon's later representation.

The Paris exhibition took a different approach, consisting of two parts, the first a chronological survey of Babylon's history and archaeology, and the second a chronological survey of the city's reception and representation. The result is that the exhibition and its catalogue came as close as possible to providing a broad representative sample both of Babylon's ancient material culture and of the city's representation in art.[2] The material referred to in the present book is only a small sample of the vast wealth of representations of ancient Babylon in art and literature, and the Paris catalogue perhaps gives some sense of the quantity and variety of material that exists.

The exhibition in Berlin, the largest of the three, actually consisted of two physically separate exhibitions, entitled *Mythos* (myth) and *Wahrheit* (truth). Both were held in the Pergamonmuseum, Berlin, the latter in the Vorderasiatisches Museum itself, which was converted to house it. This meant that the archaeology of the city could be displayed alongside the great Ishtar Gate and Processional Way reconstructions. The separation of the two themes led to an exhibition structure that differed both from Paris and from London. The presentation in both cases was thematic, but the themes were quite different. Where the archaeological, *Wahrheit* side of the exhibition focused on subjects such as everyday life, work and religion, the *Mythos* component took themes such as Semiramis, the Tower of Babel and the confusion of tongues. This exhibition also contained more modern art than the other two, although the London exhibition did include a selection of modern works based on the Tower of Babel.

Exhibitions such as these reach a wider audience than that to which Mesopotamian archaeology is normally accustomed. All three were extremely popular, and together they attracted around one million visitors. This popularity partly reflects the enduring appeal of Babylon's name, but it is also perhaps the product of a strange disjunction between this familiarity and an inability to place the city historically. During preparations for the exhibition our initial surveys established what we already suspected, namely that although everyone questioned had heard of Babylon, very few knew that it was a city in ancient Iraq and indeed a majority of those surveyed were unsure whether Babylon was a real place.[3] This meant that we could offer visitors an unusual combination: a famous and familiar name but new and unfamiliar content. The situation is also interesting because I believe that the results of the visitor survey reflect Babylon's particular history in culture. The obvious, rather lazy conclusion one might first draw is that in general people are simply not that aware of ancient history, but this hardly explains the situation. After all, *everyone* had heard of Babylon. The phenomenon to be explained is the yawning gap between the city's fame and even the most basic specific knowledge about it. Why were people unsure where Babylon was located, or whether it was a real place?

There is a good reason in intellectual history for the disjunction. Specifically, the blame for Babylon's paradoxical combination of fame and obscurity should be laid squarely at the door of St John the Divine. It was Revelation, after all, that first took the powerful prophetic language of the Old Testament denunciations of Babylon and applied them in a much broader compass, transferring them specifically to first-century AD Rome and more generally to refer to aspects of all human societies. In doing so it created a powerful metaphor and a rhetorical tool that have been in constant use ever since. The moral meaning of Babylon's story (or at least the particular story of its fall) was thus uncoupled from specific geography and history. At the same time it was mythologized, taking on the proportions of the Apocalypse itself. This is the Babylon with which people today are most familiar: a construct created specifically to talk about sin and destruction. It is not an accident that the real city has become obscured by its myths: the use of Babylon in Revelation is universalizing, and is intended to encourage the application of the story to other, contemporary contexts. Examples of attempts to make the past 'live in the present' have been noted in earlier chapters, particularly in the cases of Bruegel and Rembrandt. Revelation, in these terms, is perhaps the ultimate example: it has caused the past to live in the present so successfully as to obscure the ancient history on which its language is based.

At the time the exhibitions were held it was still not possible to collaborate closely with the Iraq Museum, or to borrow objects from Baghdad. Five years after the invasion of 2003, Iraq remained unstable and unsafe, while the destruction of cultural heritage in the country remained a subject of prime importance. We used the final section of the British Museum exhibition to concentrate on the fate of Babylon in recent years, both under Saddam Hussein and as the site of a military camp post-2003. This was done in the form of a simple slideshow, which had a visibly sobering effect on visitors at the end of what had otherwise been (we hoped) an enjoyable journey through the exhibition. The exhibition gave us a chance to show something of the ancient Mesopotamian heritage itself, as well as its historical legacy, and thus to bring home the significance of the depredations suffered by the site of Babylon in recent decades.

Another way to make sense of this kind of loss is through art. Timed to coincide with the Babylon exhibition in London was a smaller exhibition, also held at the British Museum, entitled *Iraq's Past Speaks to the Present* and curated by Venetia Porter.[4] The exhibition consisted of works by contemporary Iraqi artists that connected to the country's ancient past, sometimes alongside relevant ancient objects from the British Museum's collection. The works were extremely varied, but several contained references to the recent destruction of heritage in Iraq and the suffering of the country in recent years more generally. This book has focused on Babylon's representation in European culture, but I would like to finish by mentioning the work of these Iraqi artists. They constitute a new turn in the history of Babylon's representation, and one whose iconography is largely drawn not from European traditions but from ancient Mesopotamian artefacts themselves. In theory this has been possible for around 150 years, but only now, and only because of artists approaching the subject in terms of contemporary identity and Iraqi cultural heritage, has the archaeology and visual culture of ancient Mesopotamia itself begun to feed back into art in forms more meaningful and substantial than as sources of material detail for Orientalist paintings. Hanaa Malallah's *The God Marduk*[5] (Figure 27) uses the image of a Babylonian *mushhushshu* as found by archaeologists in the glazed-brick reliefs of the Ishtar Gate, yet incorporates this image into a book with a system of overlapping, fragmentary pages, collage and burn marks, creating a piece that reflects on the fragility and loss of heritage in a way that archaeology is perhaps unable, and certainly in a manner more eloquent than could be achieved in an archaeological report. By rendering in fine calligraphy a passage from the first Arabic translation of the ancient *Epic of Gilgamesh*, Mustafa Ja'far unites ancient and modern culture in Iraq.[6] In the powerful *Cry of Mesopotamia*,[7] Suad al-Attar places present suffering in Iraq in the context of the country's long history. Works of this kind show the continuing importance of artistic engagements with the ancient past. The role they play in connecting past and present is one that co-exists very well with the scholarly disciplines of history and archaeology, and that the latter will never truly be able to supplant.

NOTES

Chapter 1   A city and its ghosts

1 See Matthews 2003a: 10 for the example of Telloh.
2 Koldewey 1914: v.
3 Klengel-Brandt 1995: 19.

Chapter 2   Ancient Babylon

1 The earliest possible reference to the city – a text whose author is the *Ensí* (governor) of a city called *Ba₇-ba₇* (BAR.KI.BAR), and which mentions the construction of a 'temple of Marduk' – dates to the first dynasty of Ur, *c.*2500 BC (Sollberger 1985). André-Salvini (*Babylone*: 28), explains the probable etymology of a link to the name of Babylon (Akkadian *Bâbilu* or *Bâbilim*). Occasional early references to the city's patron deity, Marduk, as the son of the sun god Shamash, suggest that Babylon was originally a satellite in the political orbit of the sun god's city, Sippar (Lambert 2011).
2 The temple of the supreme god Enlil at Nippur was a shared concern of Mesopotamian cities, hence its regular receipt of large offerings from them. The Ur III period texts list Babylon as making annual offerings of sheep, goats, cows, tamarisk wood and beer (the latter in particularly large quantity), as well as *corvée* labour for the harvest of temple lands (Renger 1979; Sollberger 1985).
3 With the expansion of many settlements in the fourth millennium BC, but especially the city of Uruk. It is increasingly clear, however, that large-scale settlements also began to appear in northern Mesopotamia at around the same time.

4 Charles 1988.

5 See, for example, chapters in Rothman 2001.

6 *Histories* 1.193. The date-palms remain a distinctive characteristic of the landscape and economy today.

7 The case made for cooperative irrigation projects as a spur for the rise of organized states (specifically despotic states) by Wittfogel (1957) was highly influential but became increasingly untenable as evidence emerged that irrigation systems employed in the earliest cities and states were much smaller projects (Adams 1966, 1970). Increasing evidence for very early urban development at Tell Brak in Syria, based on rain-fed agriculture, also weakens the case for irrigation as a primary cause for urbanization (Oates et al. 2007; Ur et al. 2011). For the developed system of the mid–late third and early second millennium see Adams 1981: 1–11; Charles 1988; Pemberton et al. 1988; Steinkeller 1988; Renger 1990; Pollock 1999: 28–34; Postgate 1994: 173–90.

8 See, for example, Herodotus' description of the legendary queen Nitocris changing the course of the Euphrates: 'by cutting channels higher upstream she made it wind about with so many twists and turns that now it actually actually passes a certain Assyrian village called Ardericca three separate times [...]. In addition to this she constructed embankments on both sides of the river of remarkable strength and height, and a long way above the city, close beside the river, dug a basin for a lake some forty-seven miles in circumference' (*Histories* 1.185).

9 Nebuchadnezzar I (1125–1104 BC). The sack of Susa occurred in 1110 BC.

10 Or so the prologue to the Code of Hammurabi implies.

11 About whom very little is known. Lambert (1974) suggests that their capital, E'uruku(g) or Uruku(g), may have been al-Hiba (Lagash).

12 Specialists generally refer to such texts as collections rather than codes, since the latter term tends to suggest a complete and systematic treatment, rather than a collection of particular examples (VerSteeg 2000: 13).

13 For example the laws of Lipit-Eshtar, a king of the first dynasty of Isin, produced *c.*1930 BC (Roth 1997: 23–35; *Babylone* no. 15), or those ascribed to Ur-Nammu (2112–2095 BC or his son Shulgi (2094–2047 BC) (Kramer 1954; Roth 1997: 13–22, 36–59; Canby 2001).

14 For a current view of the monument's importance see André-Salvini 2003.

15 Brinkman 1974: 396, no. 7.

16 Adams 1981; Richardson 2007: 17.

17 Clayden 1996.

18 See esp. Collins 2008; Aruz et al. 2008, 2013.

19 On Babylonian participation in the Amarna correspondence see Westbrook 2000.

20 Grayson 1975: 175–6.

21 Kravitz 2010: 125–6.

22 Grayson 1987: 245.

23 Shutruk-Nahhunte's son, Kudur-Nahhunte, was forever condemned in Babylonian literature for the act (Oates 1986: 97).

24 Foster 2005: 350–401. The date of composition is uncertain as the epic is known only through later texts, however both content (the centrality of Babylon and Marduk) and language suggest a date in the late second millennium BC (Lambert 1984). See now Lambert 2013: 439–44.

25 Oates 1986: 223. On Chaldean and Aramean tribes in Babylonia and their ongoing conflicts with Assyrian power, see Fales 2011.

26 Frame 1992: 38.

27 Ousting the short-lived king Marduk-zakir-shumi II, whom the rebellion had initially brought to power (Brinkman 1973: 91).

28 Parpola 1972.

29 Brinkman 1973: 93.

30 In this respect it was successful, at least temporarily. There was no further rebellion during Sennacherib's reign (Frame 1992: 53).

31 Luckenbill 1924: 83–4.

32 Brinkman 1983, 1984: 67–8. A notable exception is Nabonidus' frank description of the destruction and removal of Marduk's statue (Langdon 1912: 270–2).

33 Babylonian chronicles and the Ptolemaic Canon both refer to this period as 'kingless' (Brinkman 1984: 69).

34 There is a possibility that the statue was actually destroyed and a replacement fashioned in Nineveh under Esarhaddon before its 'return' from Ashur to Babylon under Ashurbanipal (Frame 1992: 56–7).

35 Grayson 1975: 131.

36 Brinkman 1984: 34.

37 Frame 1992: 67 for discussion of the date; Borger 1956: 14–26 for Esarhaddon's account of the destroyed city and its rebuilding.

38 Brinkman 1984: 73.

39 Brinkman 1984: 103–4.

40 Harper 1892–1914: no. 972.

41 Cogan and Tadmor 1981: 232–3.

42 Steiner and Nims 1985; André-Salvini in *Babylone*: 394.

43 See Chapter 3.

44 British Museum, BM 124945–6, from room M of the North Palace of Ashurbanipal at Nineveh. Barnett 1976: 46–7, pl. 35; Novotny and Watanabe 2008.

45 According to Berossus he was a brother of Shamash-shuma-ukin, and therefore also of Ashurbanipal (Schnabel 1968 (1923): 269–70). It is not impossible that Kandalanu is merely a throne name of Ashurbanipal, or a statue that represented Ashurbanipal at key Babylonian cultic events such as the New Year (Oates 1965: 158–9; Reade 1970: 1). Two earlier Assyrian kings who had held the Babylonian kingship, Tiglath-pileser III and Shalmaneser V, are known by the strange names of 'Pul(u)' (also in the Old Testament, 2 Kings 15.19; 1 Chronicles 5.26) and 'Ulayu', respectively, in the Babylonian chronicles and

king-lists (Kuhrt 1995a: 580); however these are rather different cases in terms of the sources in which they appear (Frame 1992: 303–4).

46 There is also a strong argument for dating Ashurbanipal's death earlier, in 631 BC (Na'aman 1991), which if correct would confirm that Ashurbanipal and Kandalanu were not one and the same (Zawadzki 1995).

47 Grayson 1975: 19, 99.

48 Burstein (1978: 26) suggests that Nabopolassar may be the same individual as 'Bupolassaros', a general of Assyrian forces according to Berossus.

49 Wiseman 1985: 7.

50 Brinkman 1984: 110. The source identifying Nabopolassar as a king of the Sealand (Hunger 1968: no. 107) is of much later (Seleucid) date, while biblical and classical sources seem to use 'Chaldean' simply as a synonym for 'Babylonian'.

51 Jeremiah 52.30.

52 For a general overview of the Assyrian practice and its development see Grayson 1995.

53 Yamauchi 2002: 365.

54 British Museum, BM 45690. Lambert 1965; Taylor in *Babylon: Myth and Reality*: 66–7.

55 See, for example, the East India House Inscription (British Museum, BM 129397) and inscription from the Ishtar Gate (Vorderasiatisches Museum, SMB, Berlin).

56 Amel-Marduk (biblical Evil-Merodach) is a throne name. It is thought that as prince Amel-Marduk was the Nabu-shuma-ukin known from a highly unusual prison lament (Finkel 1999).

57 Pritchard 1969: 309.

58 Dougherty 1929: 73.

59 Josephus, *Against Apion* 1.147–9.

60 The king's background is discussed by Dougherty (1929: 16–28). Nabonidus' famous claim to be the son of a nobody has also been translated (as in the quotation above) as 'the lonely one who has nobody' and as 'the only son who has nobody'.

61 *Histories* 1.74.

62 Pritchard 1969: 562.

63 Pritchard 1969: 311–12.

64 Pritchard 1969: 561.

65 Beaulieu 1993: 243.

66 Gadd 1958: 56–9; Wiseman 1991: 246.

67 DSS 4Q242.

68 Kinnier Wilson and Finkel 2007: 18–20.

69 Schaudig 2001: 563–78.

70 This is a debatable point, but the emphasis placed on the *akitu* festival by texts such as the *Verse Account* and Cyrus Cylinder suggests that it did have a special importance.

71 *Nabonidus Chronicle* (Pritchard 1969: 305–7).

72 Cited in Josephus, *Against Apion* 1.152–3, although see the alternative account of Xenophon (*Cyropedia* 7.5.30), describing Nabonidus' murder in the palace by two of Cyrus' nobles.

73 The others were Persepolis in Persia, Susa in Elam and Ecbatana in Media. Although themselves separated by hundreds of miles and lying in different provinces, the four capitals were nonetheless all positioned relatively near the centre of the vast empire.

74 Announcing the discovery to the Royal Society in November 1879, Henry Rawlinson mistakenly presented the Cylinder as excavated at Birs Nimrud. Rassam was able to correct him, having seen the report of the Royal Society meeting in the following day's *Times*. From Rassam's correspondence it is clear that the Cylinder was discovered during excavations at Babylon's Amran mound (Rassam refers to Jumjuma, apparently meaning the southern part of this mound, although the name is more properly that of the modern village, now Djimijma, lying a short distance to the south, from which many of the workmen came).

75 For the history of the Achaemenid period, including Babylon's role, see Briant 2006.

76 Support but not direct corroboration. Notwithstanding the existence of several bogus translations online, the text of the document does not mention Jerusalem or the Judaeans. The passage in question speaks of returning gods and their personnel to their temples, and although the return of the Judaeans to Jerusalem and the rebuilding of the Temple there is surely the result of the same policy, the examples actually mentioned in the text of the Cyrus Cylinder are all Mesopotamian. At the same time, however, the text of the Cyrus Cylinder shows striking parallels with parts of the Second Isaiah account. For a tabular comparison of the relevant sections see Smith 1963: 416. Smith argues that a divergence between the two accounts on events following the fall of Babylon is the result of the Second Isaiah text having been produced prior to the capture of the city, based on Persian propaganda that also formed the basis of the (post-conquest) Cyrus Cylinder. It is true that the violence of the conquest prophesied in Second Isaiah diverges substantially from the Cyrus Cylinder, describing a sack that the latter is at pains to deny:

> I will go before you
> and will level the mountains;
> I will break down gates of bronze
> and cut through bars of iron.
> I will give you the treasures of darkness,
> riches stored in secret places,
> so that you may know that I am the Lord,
> the God of Israel, who summons you by name.

(Isaiah 45.2–3)

77 For which reason a copy of the Cylinder is displayed in the United Nations building in New York. The cylinder also remains a highly potent political symbol in contemporary Iran. On the Cylinder in general see now Curtis 2013 and Finkel 2013.

78 The story of Xerxes' wrath in Greek sources (Arrian, *Anabasis* 3.16.4–5, 7.17.1–3) may be exaggerated, but Waerzeggers (2003/4) argues that there is strong evidence for a major disruption in the archives. For an opposing view, see Briant 2006: 544–5.

79 Though Kuhrt cautions some scepticism regarding the accounts of successive conquerors – Sargon, Cyrus, Alexander – being welcomed into Babylon by cheering crowds (Kuhrt 1990).

80 British Museum, BM 36761. Sachs and Hunger 1988: no. 330.

81 Briant 2005: 17. On the other hand we should be clear that Alexander did not adopt many of the formal trappings of the Achaemenid Great King, and seems to have seen his role differently (Fredricksmeyer 2000).

82 'On entering Babylon Alexander directed the Babylonians to rebuild the temples Xerxes destroyed, especially the temple of Baal, whom the Babylonians honour more than any other god [...]. At Babylon he met the Chaldaeans, and carried out all their recommendations on the Babylonian temples, and in particular sacrificed to Baal according to their instructions' (Arrian, *Anabasis* 3.16.4–5). Here 'Baal' is Marduk. The latter was commonly referred to simply as Bel, 'lord', leading Greek writers to believe this was the actual name of the god.

83 Plutarch, *Alexander* 54.3–55.1; Arrian, *Anabasis* 4.10.5–4.12.5; Curtius, *History of Alexander* 8.5.5–24.

84 Plutarch (*Alexander* 54.5–6) and Arrian (*Anabasis* 4.12.3–5) describe how Callisthenes avoids performing *proskynesis* before Alexander, while elsewhere (Arrian, *Ababasis* 4.10–11; Curtius, *History of Alexander* 8.5.13–21) he is described as arguing publicly that Alexander should receive neither divine honours nor *proskynesis*. For discussion of the affair see Bosworth 1988: 284–6, 1995: 77–90; Atkinson 1994: 201.

85 If indeed it was: Diodorus and Arrian locate the funeral at Babylon, Plutarch and Justin do not. McKechnie (1995) argues that the pyre at Babylon is pure invention, its ultimate origin lying in Ephipphus of Olynthus' *The Funeral of Alexander and Hephaestion*, of which only fragments survive, and conveyed via Ptolemy. The main basis for this scepticism, however, is a conflict beween Diodorus *Bibliotheke Historica* 17.115 and 18.4. The latter suggests that the pyre, or possibly a permanent momument, had not yet been built at the time of Alexander's death. (The theory has Ptolemy colluding in a fictional account of Hephaestion's death in order to support his own transport of Alexander's body to Alexandria.) The sources agree, however, on a lavish monument and funeral, and the former had surely been begun in some form. The details he gives for the pyre may well be false but if, as seems to be the case, Diodorus used Cleitarchus and Ptolemy as sources, the presumption should remain that Hephaestion's funeral really did take place at Babylon. Here I follow Lane-Fox

(2004), who places the pyre at Babylon but doubts both the physical descriptions and whether it was ever completed.

86 Diodorus Siculus, *Bibliotheke Historica* 17.115.1.

87 *Bibliotheke Historica* 17.115.2–4.

88 *Bibliotheke Historica* 17.114.1. The astronomical cost of the funeral is given by Diodorus as 12,000 talents, while Plutarch (*Alexander* 72.3) and Arrian (*Anabasis* 7.14.8) put the figure at 10,000 talents.

89 In Diodorus the death of Hephaestion and the royal honours he receives are used to presage the death of Alexander, although the other accounts (Plutarch, Arrian, Justin) do not make the same use of this device (McKechnie 1995: 420). In Arrian (*Anabasis* 7.24.1–3), Diodorus (*Bibliotheke Historica* 17.116.2–4) and Plutarch (*Alexander* 73.7–9) there is also what sounds very much like the Babylonian procedure of killing a 'substitute king' to divert an ill-omen – probably misunderstood by Alexander as a bad omen in itself (Boiy 2004: 113).

90 Suspicion fell almost immediately upon the family of Antipater, a suspicion actively fanned by Alexander's mother Olympias. Plutarch, Arrian, Quintus Curtius Rufus and Justin all record a story in which Cassander brought the poison to be administered by Iolaus at the house of Medius of Larissa (Bosworth 1971: 112–14). Against this, however, can be weighed the time that elapsed (itself disputed) between the banquet and Alexander's sickening, and the further days that passed before his death. It has been pointed out that a poison that could act so slowly and still guarantee death was almost certainly beyond the technical capacity of ancient poisoners (Lane-Fox 2004).

91 Strabo, *Geography* 16.1.

92 Though the extent to which existing cultures and traditions could be said thereby to have become *Hellenized* is a different question. Mesopotamian institutions and civic life show substantial continuity with earlier periods, and despite the presence of outward signs in names and artworks recent commentary on the subject has tended to support Sack's view that 'only a light veneer of hellenism coated institutions in the important city-states of Babylonia' (Sack 1990: 117).

93 On the division of empire, Seleucus at Babylon and the founding of Seleucia on the Tigris see Boiy 2004: 117–37.

94 Ibn Hauqal, *Surat al-Ardh* (Hilprecht 1903: 13).

95 Foster 2005: 436–86. See now Lambert 2013.

96 For example, Pritchard 1969: 267. The name Sargon means 'true king', as a result of which it is widely assumed that Sargon was a usurper.

97 Musée du Louvre Sb 4.

98 Grayson 1975: 149.

99 Aka the *Esagila Chronicle*. Grayson 1975: 43–5, 141–51; Glassner 2004: 263–9. Another version of the story exists in the *Chronicle of Early Kings* (Grayson 1975: 45–9, 152–6; Glassner 2004: 268–71).

100 Not that the situation is entirely clear. The text reads, '... Bel [...] he dug up the dust of its pit [...] In front of Agade he made another city and cal[led] it

Babylon' (Grayson 1975: 149). In this case 'Agade' (or Akkad) is probably Babylon (the city has many names, of which Akkad is one of the more common), but there is no denying that the situation is confusing. An alternative interpretation (although the two are not wholly incompatible) is that the text describes a symbol of Akkad's dominance over Babylon, and that this is the hubristic act which angers Marduk. Grayson (1975: 153–4) cites descriptions of Shalmaneser I, Sennacherib and Ashurbanipal in which the conqueror sets up a mound of dust from the conquered city next to his own city.

101 Grayson 1975: 149. The *Chronicle of Early Kings* also mentions famine:

> He dug up the dirt of the pit of Babylon and
> made a counterpart of Babylon next to Agade.
> Because of the wrong he had done the great lord Marduk became angry
> and wiped out his family by famine.
> They (his subjects) rebelled against him from east to west
> and he (Marduk) afflicted him with insomnia.
>
> (Grayson 1975: 153–4)

102 As shown in a compendium of ancient signs with contemporary equivalents and secret numbers, written in the Neo-Babylonian period or later (Pearce 1996; Finkel in *Babylon: Myth and Reality*: 83–7).

103 Little is known of Cyrus' own religious beliefs. It is often assumed that he worshipped Ahura Mazda and practised a form of Mazdaism similar to that of later Persian kings, but no direct evidence exists for this.

104 Kuhrt 1990.

Chapter 3   Tyrants and wonders: The biblical and classical sources

1 The latest documents of all, which are undated, may date to the third century.

2 Genesis 11.1–9.

3 Considine 2003: 3; Freedman et al. 1992: I, 561; Gérard 1989: 120–1.

4 Descendants of Shem (Genesis 11.10–25) and descendants of Terah (Genesis 11.26–32).

5 Freedman et al. 1992: I, 561–2 (where on the basis of the strongly anti-Babylonian slant an Israelite origin for the text is also preferred); O'Connell 2003: 129.

6 Lambert and Millard 1969; Dalley 1989: 1–38.

7 Guinan 2002: 24.

8 Josephus, *Jewish Antiquities* 1.109–19.

9 *Jewish Antiquities* 1.113, following the implication of Genesis 10.8–10 that it is Nimrod who first settles in the land of Sumer. Inconsistencies in the two texts show that Genesis 10 and 11 were originally separate units, although

clearly their juxtaposition in Genesis is deliberate and structured (O'Connell 2003: 128).

10 *Jewish Antiquities* 1.118.

11 For examples see George 2005–6.

12 On George Smith, see pp. 158–60, this volume.

13 Genesis 10.6; 10.9.

14 See Levin 2002 for two arguments on Nimrod: (1) that 'Cush' should be the Mesopotamian city name Kish, and that its misunderstanding as Cush explains Nimrod's attribution to the otherwise African lineage of Ham; and (2) that the Genesis passage on Nimrod ultimately relates to the mythologized biography of Sargon of Akkad.

15 Genesis 10.10–12.

16 On the debate, see Freedman et al. 1992: VI, 1012–19.

17 Psalms 137.1–9.

18 Larsen 1996: 278.

19 Jullien and Jullien 1995: 23.

20 2 Kings 25.1–21.

21 2 Chronicles 36.17–21.

22 Jeremiah 52.3–30.

23 Finkelstein and Silberman 2002: 48–71.

24 2 Kings 25.27–30.

25 Keck and Tucker 1992: 14.

26 See Chapter 2.

27 2 Chronicles 36.22–3/Ezra 1.1–3.

28 Ezra 1.3–4.

29 1 Esdras 2.3–7. NB – Esdras is the Greek form of Ezra used in the Apocrypha. Ezra is the supposed author of 1 and 2 Esdras, which continue the historical narrative from 2 Chronicles and end on the only apocalyptic sequence in the Apocrypha in 2 Esdras.

30 Stoyanov 2000: 49–50.

31 Isaiah 14.12–17.

32 The chronology of the oracles against the nations in First Isaiah is complex, since the text weaves a core of eighth- to seventh-century BC oracles against Assyria, Egypt, Damascus, Israel and Judah together with later, exilic material on Babylon, Persia, Moab and Tyre (Freedman 1992: III, 485–6; Hill 2003: 596). An exilic origin makes political sense and would imply Nebuchadnezzar or the Neo-Babylonian kings generally. However, see Sweeney (1996: 232) for the alternative view that Isaiah 14 is part of the much earlier body of core material, and that the 'king of Babylon' should be equated with the eighth-century BC Assyrian king Sargon II.

33 McGinn 1998: 7.

34 Collins 1998: 87–8. There are further reasons for believing that the combined text takes its final form in the 160s BC, since it is widely agreed that the text

refers to the period of Antiochus' persecution of traditionalist Jews following the Maccabean rebellion.

35 Both Cyrus himself and the Median king Astyages have been suggested as possibilities.

36 The early part of the Book of Daniel explains how 'some of the Israelites from the royal family and the nobility – young men without any physical defect, handsome, showing aptitude for every kind of learning, well informed, quick to understand, and qualified to serve in the king's palace' (Daniel 1.3–4) received training in the scribal arts and preparation for a life at the Babylonian court.

37 Collins 1998: 86–7. Whether this truly is the same Daniel as the prophet of the Exile is disputed, however, as the name occurs as *dan'el* in Ezekiel as opposed to *daniyyel* in Daniel (Lucas 2000: 68).

38 See pp. 24–5, this volume.

39 The *Verse Account of Nabonidus* records that '[As for his …] they tore out its image; [from all mon]uments his name was obliterated' (Pritchard 1969: 312–15). A surviving stela of Nabonidus, its inscription carefully removed, may show the policy in action (Finkel in *Babylon: Myth and Reality*: 165).

40 Daniel 3.25.

41 Daniel 3.29.

42 Daniel 4.

43 See p. 25, this volume.

44 See pp. 24–5, this volume.

45 Kinnier Wilson and Finkel 2007: 18–20.

46 Sack 1991: 103.

47 Daniel 5.30–1. See note 35 above on Darius the Mede.

48 Sachau 1879: 297.

49 Dougherty 1929: 11–13.

50 Daniel 5.23–8. *Mene, tekel* and *parsin* refer to the currency weights mina, shekel and half-shekel. *Peres*, the singular of *parsin*, also refers to Persia.

51 Daniel 11.40.

52 Daniel 11.2–4. The prophecy has been reinterpreted to suit political and religious agendas throughout history, most famously Moscow's claim to be the 'third Rome' and defender of Christianity following the Ottoman conquest of Constantinople in 1453.

53 Jeremiah 50.39–40.

54 Though brief references to the historical Babylon and the Exile do appear: Matthew 1.11, 12, 17; Acts 7.43. The reference at 1 Peter 5.13 is probably symbolic of Rome in the same manner as the Babylon of Revelation (Freedman 1992: I, 565).

55 Apparently completed during the reign of Domitian, AD 81–96.

56 Revelation 17.1–6.

57 Dronke 1986: 71.

58 Jeremiah 51.7.

59 *Histories* 1.

60 Diodorus Siculus, *Bibliotheke Historica* 2.

61 *Histories* 1.178–9.

62 Herodotus' 200 cubits is around 102 m (for a comparison of the dimensions given by classical authors see *Babylon: Myth and Reality*: 115). Marincola (2003: 633) suggests a Homeric reference to 'hundred-gated Thebes' (*Iliad* 10.383). The exact locations of some of Babylon's eight gates are not known, but their names and relative positions on the inner city wall are well established from textual sources (see George 1992).

63 Oates 1986: 148.

64 Mellor 1999: 7.

65 Aristotle, *Generation of Animals* 756b7. See Grant 1970: 52.

66 Sayce 1883.

67 Sayce 1883: xi–xii.

68 Tanner 1992: 4.

69 Particularly relevant here is MacGinnis 1986, a point-by-point reassessment of Herodotus' account which concludes that a large proportion of his description holds up very well against what is known archaeologically and from the cuneiform sources.

70 Reade 2000: 198.

71 Dalley 1994, 2002, 2003b.

72 Hyginus, *Fabulae* 233.

73 Pliny, *Natural History* 19.19.49.

74 Budge 1920: 297.

75 Reade 2000.

76 Reade 2000: 198.

77 Van De Mieroop 2004.

78 Dalley 2003a. There seem at least to have been significant family connections between the Neo-Assyrian and Neo-Babylonian courts, while to a non-Mesopotamian it is probable that the empire – still ruled from Iraq, and covering similar territory – seemed to change very little.

79 Dalley 2003b: 179; 2008.

80 No one doubts that both cities had royal gardens. In the case of Babylon, however, the surviving evidence is limited a single text (BM 46226), describing plants in the garden of Marduk-apla-iddina II (Brinkman 1964; Wiseman 1983: 142–3; Finkel in *Babylon: Myth and Reality*: 110).

81 Dalley 2003b.

82 Kuhrt and Sherwin-White 1987: 69–78.

83 Although the Achaemenid-period form of the ritual is unknown. This is significant since the later (Hellenistic) period ritual of the same name differs greatly from its Neo-Babylonian forbear. For the *akitu* festival in general see Bidmead 2002.

84 'At that time [Sayce's, writing in 1883] the Assyrian reading of the name written ^{d}NIN.LÍL had not been established. Now we have found out that it was

read Mulissu in Assyrian [. . .] Herodotus' Mylitta can be accepted as a genuine piece of information' (Dalley 2003b: 172–4).

85 Arieti 1995: 181–7.

86 Redfield 2002: 24–5.

87 *Histories* 1.196.

88 Arieti 1995: 183–4.

89 Judging that 'The agonistic – and antithetical – character of the story marks it as quintessentially Greek' (McNeal 1988: 63).

90 McNeal 1988: 71.

91 On points of comparison between Babylonian and Hippocratic medical traditions see Geller 2004.

92 See note 84 on Aphrodite/Mulissu/Mylitta.

93 *Histories* 1.199.

94 *Histories* 1.178.

95 Diodorus, *Bibliotheke Historica* 2, covering Ctesias, *Persica* 1–5/6; Photius, *Bibliotheke* codex 72, covering the last 17 books of the *Persica*. See now Llewellyn-Jones and Robson 2010 for an edition and commentary including all the surviving fragments.

96 Megasthenes' *Indica*, Diodorus, *Bibliotheke Historica* 2.35–42; Agatharchides, Diodorus, *Bibliotheke Historica* 3.18–43 (Gilmore 1888: v).

97 Murphy 1989: ix.

98 Budge 1920: 297.

99 Stevenson 1997: 2.

100 Roux 2001: 147.

101 Llewellyn-Jones and Robson: 2–3.

102 *Bibliotheke Historica* 2.2.1.

103 *Bibliotheke Historica* 2.2.3.

104 It has been suggested that the Greek legend may have its origin in the career of the Middle Assyrian king Tukulti-Ninurta I (1243–1207 BC) and the foundation of his eponymous capital, Kar Tukulti-Ninurta (Oates 1986: 96).

105 *Bibliotheke Historica* 2.3.2–4.

106 *Bibliotheke Historica* 2.8.6–7.

107 Dalley 2003b: 183.

108 *Bibliotheke Historica* 2.8.4.

109 Koldewey 1914: 129–31.

110 These links were deep and pervasive, but perhaps the most striking uses of Babylonian and Assyrian models in Achaemenid royal architecture are the glazed-brick reliefs of the palace of Darius I at Susa and the winged bulls of Persepolis respectively.

111 *Histories* 1.185.

112 *Geography* 16.1.2.

113 Grayson 1991: 138–9. The possibility that elements of Naqia/Zakutu can be found in legends of Semiramis has been discussed by Lewy (1952) and by Nougayrol and Parrot (1956). An alternative suggestion is that Nitocris'

legend originates in the person of Adda-Guppi, the formidable mother of Nabonidus (Grayson 1982: 244). Röllig (1969) considers both possibilities.

114 Athenagoras, *Plea for the Christians* 30.

115 The story is mentioned by a daughter of Minyas:

> Her joyful sisters bid her to begin,
> but which of the many stories that she knows
> should she relate? Long she pondered, doubtful:
> your story, Babylonian Derceto?
> A woman who, as Syria supposes,
> was changed into a scaly thing that swims
> now in a little pool? Or how her daughter,
> transformed into a dove of purest white,
> spent her last years perched on lofty towers?
>
> (*Metamorphoses* 4.71–9)

116 Grayson 1982: 243–4.

117 Sammuramat also had a stela dedicated to her in the so-called *Stelenreihen* at Ashur. That she should be accorded such an honour is not actually unique: other stelae do bear inscriptions of women (Schram 1972: 519). Nonetheless it is sufficiently exceptional for the stela to remain a significant piece of circumstantial evidence for her importance. She is also included in a stela of Adad-nirari III, where her name follows that of her son the king (Grayson 1982: 275).

118 Weinfeld 1991.

119 *Bibliotheke Historica* 2.20.2.

120 *Bibliotheke Historica* 2.21, 23.

121 *Bibliotheke Historica* 2.22.1.

122 *Bibliotheke Historica* 2.21.1–2.

123 Aeschylus, *Persians*.

124 See p. 172, this volume.

125 *Bibliotheke Historica* 2.23.1–2.

126 *Bibliotheke Historica* 2.26.4.

127 *Bibliotheke Historica* 2.27.1–2.

128 *Bibliotheke Historica* 2.27.2.

129 Kuhrt 1995b: 57.

130 Kuhrt 1995b: 57.

131 André-Salvini in *Babylone*: 394.

132 Shamash-shuma-ukin's name also survives, as 'Saosdouchinos' in the Ptolemaic Canon, and 'Samoges' in Berossus (Oelsner 2012).

133 Van De Mieroop 2004: 4.

134 Dalley 2003b.

135 Dalley 2003b: 181.

136 Josephus, *Against Apion* 1.129–31. An account of Berossus' creation story does survive in sufficient detail to confirm that it is the Babylonian creation story familiar from *Enuma Elish*, with Marduk's battle with Tiamat; his creation of

the world from her body; and his creation of the stars and planets and of humanity. *FGrHist* 685F 1a–b.

137 See Verbrugghe and Wickersham 1996: 8.

138 Kuhrt 1995b: 63.

139 Athenaeus of Nacrautis, *Deipnosophistae* 639c; Stephens and Winkler 1995a: 26. Parpola (1993: xxx–xxxi, n. 16, 17) argues that this 'Sakaia' is probably not the substitute king ritual, for which the term is also used in Greek sources, but may refer to part of the Babylonian New Year festival in one of its later forms. De Breucker (2011: 642–3) also suggests an origin in a real, but unidentified, Babylonian ritual.

140 Plutarch, *Erotikos* 753d–e.

141 *Bibliotheke historica* 2.20.3–5. The Athenaeus referred to here is otherwise unknown.

142 Arnaud-Lindet 1990–91: vii; Brumble 1998: 302.

143 Orosius, *History Against the Pagans* 1.4.6–8.

144 Orosius gives Babylon 1164 years from its re-foundation by Semiramis (following the Genesis destruction of Babel) to its fall to Median forces and Rome 1164 years from its foundation to its sack by Alaric (Laistner 1940: 252).

145 Sack 1991: 35.

146 *Against Apion* 1.146–53; Eusebius, *Praeparatorio Evangelica* 9.

147 Alexander Polyhistor, *On the Jews*, cited in Eusebius, *Praeparatorio Evangelica* 9.

148 *Against Apion* 1.146–9.

149 The ancient practice of counting in full regnal years is generally also used by modern historians. Therefore, e.g., Nebuchadnezzar II came to the throne in 605 BC, but his first full regnal year was 604; thus his dates are given elsewhere in this book as 604–562. Berossus takes this into account, and so his dates better match the true reigns based on date of accession.

150 *Against Apion* 1.150–3.

151 Though see Dalley's argument that Nebuchadnezzar and Sennacherib were confused in later histories (Dalley 2003b: 179).

152 '... in the third book of his *History of Chaldaea*, where he censures the Greek historians for their deluded belief that Babylon was founded by the Assyrian Semiramis and their erroneous statement that its marvellous buildings were her creation. On these matters the Chaldaean account must surely be accepted' (Josephus, *Against Apion* 1.142–3). This summary also suggests that Berossus identified Semiramis as Assyrian, making it effectively the only recorded Babylonian comment on the queen and her identity.

153 Van der Spek 2008.

154 Josephus, *Against Apion* 1.141; see Josephus, *Jewish Antiquities* 10.11.

155 Discussed in Reade 2000.

156 Eusebius, *Chronicon* 46; *Armenian Chronicon*, pp. 44, 53.

157 There is a theory that Berossus' mention of the gardens itself is a later insertion by Alexander Polyhistor. I think it more likely that Berossus is tying up a loose end for non-Babylonian readers, showing where the Greek Hanging Gardens

story fits in the Babylonian history and correcting Persian (Ctesias) to Median for the identity of Nebuchadnezzar's queen. Accepting a later insertion, however, would only strengthen the argument that Berossus did not invent the story of Nebuchadnezzar's marriage to Amyitis for the sake of a neat fit with the Hanging Gardens story.

158 That Ctesias would confuse Media with Persia in his account demands an explanation: he knew Iran and the Achaemenid Empire at first hand. I agree with van der Spek (2008) that he does not confuse the two, but rather records a Persian variant of the story, with a Persian princess.

159 Gropp 1998: 23. The stories in question are those of Cyrus and Mandane, Semiramis and Zariadres and Cyrus the Younger and Syennesis' wife.

160 Although Cleitarchus might have had less direct access to the same story. Pliny the Elder claims that Cleitarchus went to Babylon with Alexander, but more likely he relied (as is known) on other sources (e.g. returning soldiers) who had. He may have 'corrected' Ctesias regardless of whether he had access to an alternative version, much as Ctesias can be shown to have done with Herodotus.

161 If this event is not real it is still notable that Berossus records the information from some existing source.

162 *Souda* Ξ.49.

163 Stephens and Winkler 1995a: 23.

164 Doro Levi judged that despite undergoing a substantial transformation, 'persons and elements of the old legend are still recognizable' (Levi 1944: 423), also pointing out several respects in which the novel is unusual: 'It rests upon a historical basis; love is not the result of a fortuitous meeting, but the fruit of long intercourse and of mutual inclination. Nor are fortuitous and aimless the adventures and wanderings of the hero, but dictated by high political and ethical reasons; the woman does not seem to follow her beloved in his travels, but to remain within the domestic walls waiting for his return' (Levi 1944: 424). This last is not absolutely clear, but assuming that it is correct it actually hinders the argument that the novel's departures from the norm can be attributed to the earlier legend: the Semiramis of Ctesias, after all, did follow Ninus to war. See also Kussl 1991: 84–95.

165 McCall 1998: 185.

166 Ninus as part of a genealogy: 'Agron, son of Ninus, grandson of Belus, great-grandson of Alcaeus' (*Histories* 1.7); Semiramis as a notable contributor to Babylon's defences (*Histories* 1.185).

167 Frustratingly, this problem recurs in pictorial representations: two surviving Roman mosaics appear to depict the story. That in Alexandretta names Ninus but is damaged and does not show the female figure. In the Antioch mosaic (now held by Princeton University) it is probable that either the painting held by a reclining male figure – almost certainly Ninus, on comparison with the Alexandretta mosaic (Levi 1944) – or the standing female figure represent Semiramis, but here no figures are labelled. Even ancient citations of the novel

cannot help us: an apparent reference in Lucian (*Pseudologista* 25) also mentions only Ninus!

168 'Derkeia' (*Ninus* fragment A.iv.14–15), from Derceto (Diodorus, *Bibliotheke Historica* 2.4.9).

169 One such account is recorded in Diodorus (Athenaeus, in *Bibliotheke Historica* 2.20.3); see also Plutarch, *Erotikos* 753d–e.

170 Stephens and Winkler 1995a: 23.

171 Photius, *Bibliotheke*, codex 94.

172 Stephens and Winkler 1995b: 179.

173 *Souda* I.26.

174 Photius, *Bibliotheke*, codex 94.

175 Ovid, *Metamorphoses* 4.87–227.

176 *Metamorphoses* 4.87–91.

177 A prominent landmark in the Babylon of classical imagination. Though he is as fictional as Pyramus and Thisbe, we nonetheless have a description of Ninus' tomb: 'Semiramis buried Ninos in the capital city, and over him she reared up an enormous mound, nine stades in height and, as Ctesias says, ten in width. Therefore since the city lay in a plain beside the Euphrates, this earthwork appeared from many stades away exactly as an acropolis; and they claim it exists until today, even though the Medes raised the city of Ninos when they overthrew the dominion of the Assyrians' (Diodorus Siculus, *Bibliotheke Historica* 2.7).

The height of the tomb is an impossible 1.6 km, but as Murphy (1989: 10) notes, the description otherwise answers very well to that of a large tell marking the ruins of any long-lived Mesopotamian city – perhaps even one of the huge mounds of Nineveh itself.

Chapter 4   The Earthly City: Medieval and Renaissance approaches

1 The same is not true of transmission in other fields such as medicine, astronomy and divination, where cuneiform sources were copied and translated into Greek and Aramaic for several centuries more.

2 Spiegel 1975: 316.

3 Spiegel 1975: 316.

4 See Freedman and Spiegel 1998 on the course of twentieth-century debates.

5 Villalba Ruiz de Toledo 2006: 31.

6 Hudson 1981: 2.

7 Hilprecht 1904: 13.

8 Also known as the *Sefer Masa'ot* or *Libro de Viages*. The supposition that Benjamin was a merchant is based on the expertise and interest in businesses and commercial matters shown in his account (Magdalena nom de Déu 2006: 22).

9 McCall 1998: 186.

10 As was already recognized by Adler (1907: 43). Lundquist (1995: 69) observes that Benjamin may have followed the same identification in the Talmud.

11 Benjamin of Tudela, *Itinerary* 102.

12 *Itinerary* 102.

13 Asher 1840–1: xi.

14 Asher 1840–1: xii. In this connection it is important to note that attempts in the seventeenth and eighteenth centuries to suggest Rabbi Benjamin never left Tudela (his account was seen as 'an attempt to aggrandize the real number and to represent under bland colours the state of the Jews in remote countries' [Asher 1840–1: xiii]) were part of a broader anti-Semitic position which Asher was quick to discredit and dissociate from his own claim.

15 Magdalena nom de Déu 2006: 24.

16 Signer 1983: 15.

17 See Irwin 2006 for a history of European academic Arabists.

18 Marco Polo, *Travels* 7. It should be noted, however, that it has been questioned whether the chapter divisions and rubrics used in most editions of the *Travels* and taken from text F (the Parisian Ms considered the most reliable and authentic of the surviving versions) are original, as the arrangement is absent in other versions (Latham 1958: 28).

19 *Travels* 7/Latham 1958: 51, 52.

20 Chiesa 2002: 6.

21 Chiesa 2002: 13–14.

22 Chiesa 2002: 10; Yule also thought the detour from Yazd unlikely.

23 Odoric, *Relatio* 4.

24 Telfer 1879: xxvii.

25 Telfer 1879: xviii-xix.

26 Telfer 1879: xix.

27 *Bondage and Travels of Johann Schiltberger* 34.

28 *Bondage and Travels* 15.

29 *Bondage and Travels* 34.

30 'Schatt' = *Shatt* (شط), 'coast'. The Arabic name of the Tigris, in Schiltberger's time as now, is *Dijla* (دجلة). The branch of the Euphrates passing through Babylon is known as the *Shatt al-Hillah*, whilst the confluence of the Tigris and Euphrates farther south is today called the *Shatt al-Arab*.

31 Bruun 1879: 167.

32 Bruun gives 'prison', although Arabic ربط (*rabat*), 'to bind,' and مربوط (*marbut*) 'bound', suggest bonds of Nimrod as an alternative translation.

33 *Itinerary* 102.

34 *Relation* 4.

35 *Bondage and Travels* 34.

36 Rauwolf 1583: 204.

37 Manwaring et al. 1825: 46.

38 Korte 2000: 23–4.

39 Mandeville, *Travels* 6.

40 *Travels* 6.

41 *Travels* 6. Baghdad in the fourteenth century was indeed ruled by the 'King of Persia', in the form of the il-Khanate, founded by Ghengis Khan's grandson Hulagu and initially subordinate to the Great Khans ruling the entire Mongol world. By Mandeville's time the system had broken down, with rival successor states (in Iraq and western Iran the powerful Jalayirids) competing within the il-Khanate.

42 Ooghe 2007: 234.

43 Rauwolf 1583: 203.

44 Rauwolf 1583: 204, my translation.

45 Hilprecht 1904: 14. It was Claudius Rich, at the beginning of the nineteenth century, who realized that in general what many of his predecessors had taken for ruined buildings were in fact disused canals.

46 Eldred 1903 (1592): 298.

47 The route seems first to have been described by the Portugese scholarly traveller Pedro Texeira (Ooghe 2007: 239). Four eighteenth-century accounts of the route Aleppo to Basra are reproduced in Carruthers 1929. Apparently the desert route greatly reduced the danger of bandits and the expense of charges levied by tribes through whose territory the river passed.

48 Budge 1925: 60.

49 Hilprecht 1904: 14.

50 Eldred 1903 (1592): 299. The comparison is picturesque, although for the proper effect it should be remembered that Eldred was writing well before the great fire of London in 1666, and hence before Christopher Wren had designed the present St Paul's cathedral, built 1675–1710. A model of the St Paul's Eldred had in mind – whose steeple was of greater height even than Wren's dome, though of a far smaller and less imposing mass – is displayed in the Museum of London.

51 Manwaring et al. 1825.

52 Cartwright 1633.

53 Tavernier 1676–7: 214.

54 Manwaring et al. 1825: 51–2.

55 Ooghe 2007: 236.

56 If any Islamic architectural model can be claimed to have influenced European depictions, it might be the square-towered minaret of the Ibn Tulun mosque in Cairo, which would have been seen by greater numbers of Europeans. Even this, however, seems to me unnecessary to explain the medieval images.

57 Blunt 1953; Invernizzi 2000, 2001.

58 Invernizzi 2000: 643–4. For the life and achievements of Don Garcia de Silva y Figueroa, whose work in Iran pre-empted that of Della Valle in several respects, see Córdoba 2006.

59 Budge 1925: 16.

60 Invernizzi 2000: 648.

61 Ooghe 2007: 240.

62 Invernizzi 2000: 646.

63 Kircher 1679.

64 Della Valle 1650–63. A further publication appeared in the nineteenth century (Della Valle 1843) and from this an abridged English translation has been produced (Bull 1989). For Italian edition and commentary see Invernizzi 2001.

65 For a drawing of this seal, see Tabouis 1931: 5.

66 Christoph Fernberger, *Reisetagebuch*: 58; Ooghe 2007: 237.

67 Lewis 1964: 11.

68 Lewis 1964: 10.

69 'That was the first thing that I ever learned from him: that even ideas can be tidied up to look like a salad rather than a stew. He hated mishmash. "The very seas would lose their shores," was a quotation from Ovid he was fond of, and he was much given to dividing ideas and keeping them apart' (Watson 1995: 230).

70 Bloomfield 1958: 75.

71 *Natural History* 7.2.

72 Korte 2000: 22.

73 Kendall 1978: 145.

74 Kendall 1978: 146–7.

75 Although it should be acknowledged that in the longer term the work would have been preserved without this translation, as Syriac and Armenian versions have also survived.

76 Rebenich 2002: 27.

77 Laistner 1940: 243.

78 Kelly 1975: 86.

79 Rebenich 2002: 52.

80 Bourke 1995: 295; Mommsen, T. E. 1995: 359.

81 Kaufman 1995: 75–6.

82 Daniel 7.7–8.

83 Pratt 1965: 31; Mommsen, T. E. 1995: 352–5.

84 Brown 2000 (1967): 248.

85 Lancel 2002: 396.

86 Augustine, *The City of God* 5.15.

87 *The City of God* 14.1.

88 *The City of God* 14.28.

89 Lancel 2002: 401.

90 Bittner 1999: 356.

91 A possible second reference, to the Tower of Babel, is Sura *An-Naḥl* (*The Bees*) 28–9, describing God's punishment in the form of a collapsing building (Janssen 1995: 138).

92 *Al-Baqarah* 102.

93 Vernay-Nouri in *Babylone*: 380.

94 Omission of Arabic sources is a recurring problem in the study of the reception of Near Eastern antiquity. Here I am deeply indebted to the excellent study of Janssen (1995), which collects and discusses the medieval Arabic sources on Babylon.

95 Sachau 1879: v–vi.

96 The frequent occurrence of the name Bel in diverse contexts reflects Greek confusion over what was actually a Babylonian term meaning 'lord,' applied to many gods but most often used as a synonym for Marduk.

97 Al-Biruni, *Al-Athar al-Bakiya* 87.

98 In al-Biruni's scheme called Thonos Konkoleros.

99 *Al-Athar al-Bakiya* 87; Sachau 1879: 100.

100 *Al-Athar al-Bakiya* 88. This attribution is never made in any of the European sources.

101 This is not Nebuchadnezzar I, but probably the early Neo-Babylonian king Nabonassar (747–734 BC).

102 The younger of the two (Bibliothéque nationale de France, department des Manuscrits, Arabe 1489, f.161v) is a close sixteenth-century copy of the older (University of Edinbugh Library, Ms 161, f.134b), which dates to AD 1307 (707 AH). Soucek 1975: 145–7; *Babylone*: 421; *Babylon: Myth and Reality*: 149.

103 Yaqut 1.447–9; Janssen 1995: 197.

104 Lewis 1982: 158.

105 Yaqut 4.798; al-Himyari 357. Janssen 1995: 166.

106 Janssen 1995: 197.

107 Yaqut 1.770; al-Himyari 73. Janssen 1995: 193.

108 Janssen 1995: 193, citing the *Arabian Nights*.

109 Al-Bakri 136.

110 Janssen 1995: 136.

111 Collins and Al-Tai 1994: 105.

112 Janssen 1995: 163–4.

113 Cohen 1967: xiii.

114 Chazan 1988: 42.

115 Cohen 1967: 168.

116 Ibn Daud, *Sefer ha-Kabbalah* 1.123–42.

117 *Sefer ha-Kaballah* 1.148–9.

118 *Sefer ha-Kaballah* 1.19–23.

119 Baron 1972: 342–3.

120 Vernay-Nouri in *Babylone*: 391. Ferdowsi reconciled earlier legends in which Zahhak was a monster with those that treated him as human. An incident in which he is tricked by the evil spirit Ahriman causes the human Zahhak of the *Shahnahmeh* to sprout snakes from his shoulders.

121 Hamza Isfahani, cited by F. Richard in *Babylone*: 392.

122 Al-Tha'alibi, cited by F. Richard in *Babylone*: 392.

123 Barnett 1982: 314.

124   A possible historical origin for Ara is the Urartian king Aramu (858–844 BC), whose kingdom was invaded and capital captured by the Assyrian king Shalmaneser III (859–824 BC).

125   The corpus of medieval manuscript images relating to Babylon is vast. For a variety of examples see *Babylone*: 399–414.

126   British Library Add. Ms 11695, ff.228v–229. Seymour in *Babylon: Myth and Reality*: 158–9; Williams 1994–2003: vol. 4, Ms 16, pp. 31–40, Figs 332a–b.

127   *Bible of Etienne Harding*, Bibliothèque Municipale, Dijon. The root of the Hebrews' representation of children is their description as 'young men' or 'youths' in the biblical account.

128   Augsburg School, *Shadrach, Meschach and Abednego*. Oil on panel, Barnes Foundation, Merion, PA.

129   For example, *Nebuchadnezzar questions Daniel and his companions*, Master of Marradi, Florence 1480–1500; *Daniel interprets Nebuchadnezzar's first dream*, Erasmus Quellinus, Flemish, mid–late seventeenth century.

130   For example, *Daniel before Nebuchadnezzar*, Salomon Koninck, Dutch, mid-seventeenth century; *Daniel interpreting Nebuchadnezzar's first dream*, Mattia Preti (Il Calabrese), Calabria, mid–late seventeenth century.

131   With the exception of that of Erasmus Quellinus, which resembles later romanticist images of Eastern courts, the settings of those examples listed above appear European.

132   *Nebuchadnezzar's dream*, Giovanni di Paulo, Tuscany *c.*1450. In Dante, *Commedia*. British Library Ms Yates Thompson 36.

133   *Nebuchadnezzar besieges Jerusalem*, Great Bible (Vulgate), England 1405–15. British Library Ms Royal 1E.1X.

134   British Library Ms Add. 18,850, f.17v. That a book of hours should contain an image of the Tower of Babel is unusual. It was one of four full-page miniatures depicting scenes from Genesis added later, when the book was given to the young King Henry VI.

135   Examples in *Babylone*: 410–11.

136   The tapestries were produced by Nicolas Bataille and Robert Poinçon after designs by Hennequin de Bruges, also known as Jean de Bondol. For the tapestries see Muel 1996; for the manuscript sources on which the images are based see Henderson 1985.

137   A further *c.*40 m of tapestry, constituting 30 of the original 100 scenes, has not survived.

138   Haskell 1993.

139   Often in the still not particularly accessible form of sculptures on column capitals, although an exception is a twelfth-century mosaic depicting the building of the Tower of Babel at Monreale Cathedral, Sicily.

140   On Chaucer's version see Spisak 1984.

141   The long hair of Venus may be a reference to the virtuous Semiramis, and thus a compliment to the unusually named Semiramide Appiani, for whose marriage

to Lorenzo di Pierfrancesco Medici the painting was produced. Michalski 2003; Seymour in *Babylon: Myth and Reality*: 119.

142   Mahon 1949; Seymour in *Babylon: Myth and Reality*: 118–22.

143   Judith 1.5.

144   Lewis 1964; see above, pp. 97–8.

145   Auerbach 1952: 6.

146   Dante, *Inferno* 12.104–5.

147   *Inferno* 4.129.

148   *Inferno* 28.

149   Dante, *Paradiso* 23.130–5.

150   *Purgatorio* 32.130–60.

151   *Inferno* 5.52–60.

152   Brumble 1998: 308.

153   Laistner 1940: 250.

154   Dante, *Paradiso* 10.118–20.

155   Dronke 1986: 95.

156   Dante follows the historical Virgil (*Aeneid* 12.899–900) in thinking people were physically larger before the Flood (Levine 1967: 457).

157   *Inferno* 31.76–81.

158   Janssen (1995: 157–72) finds a similar dissonance in Nimrod's representation in the medieval Arabic sources.

159   *Paradiso* 4.13–15.

160   Bartrum 1999: 165.

161   In fact borrowed from an earlier drawing by Dürer of a Venetian lady (Carey 1999: 138).

162   Revelation 17.4.

163   Revelation 18.21. One carries a millstone to be cast down into the sea, symbolizing that Babylon will no longer make bread. It is presumably the other angel who cries 'Babylon the great is fallen'.

164   Revelation 19.11.

165   Parshall 1999: 102.

166   Notable examples include series by Hans Burgkmair, Georg Lemberger and Jean Duvet.

167   Chastel 1984: 99; Allard in *Babylone*: 440.

168   The earlier of the two surviving oil on panel paintings, dated 1563, is held at the Kunsthistorisches Museum, Vienna, and the second, dated *c.*1568, at the Museum Boijmans van Beuningen, Rotterdam. A third painting, made in Rome and painted on ivory, recorded in the inventory and will of the Croatian miniaturist Giulio Clovio, is lost (Mansbach 1982: 43).

169   Van Mander 1604, reproduced in English translation in Grossman 1955: 7–9.

170   De Tolnay 1935.

171   For a recent general examination of Bruegel's circle and influences see Zagorin 2003.

172 According to Carel van Mander the drawings were burned 'because some were too critical or sarcastic' (quoted in Sybesma 1991: 467).

173 Sullivan (1991) demonstrates Bruegel's use of Latin and Greek proverbs, including specific instances of material drawn from Erasmus' *Adages*.

174 Sullivan 1991: 460.

175 *c.*1567, oil on panel, Kunsthistorisches Museum, Vienna.

176 *c.*1610, oil on canvas, Thomson Collection, Art Gallery of Ontario, Toronto.

177 Ferber's (1966) argument that a central figure in *The Massacre of the Innocents* represents Ferdinand Alvares, Duke of Alba, known for his harsh governorship of the Spanish Netherlands, is one of the more compelling reasons to interpret several of Bruegel's works as containing veiled attacks on Spain and the Catholic hierarchy, despite the fact that one of his significant patrons was Cardinal Antoine Perrenot de Granville, Philip II's regent in the Spanish Netherlands from 1567.

178 Mansbach 1982: 48, who also suggests (though without strong evidence) that another layer of meaning in the figure may be a reference to Alexander the Great and his attempted rebuilding of Babylon's ziggurat as described by Arrian (*Anabasis* 7.17) and Strabo (*Geography* 16.1).

179 It seems certain that the Rotterdam panel has been cut down on all sides (Lammertse 1994: 402–3), although one would have to imagine a quite dramatic reduction to remove a foreground figure group. If we do imagine such a major alteration, Lucas van Valckenborch's first two major works on the Tower of Babel, produced *c.*1568, may give some clue as to the original composition of Bruegel's Rotterdam painting, which they followed. If this is correct then later views of the Tower in a much broader landscape, *c.*1595, would have been Valckenborch's own innovation.

180 The very existence of so many arguments over meaning in Bruegel's paintings suggests that they were ambiguous even in their own time. Kavaler (1999) argues strongly that Bruegel deliberately produced works that were ambiguous, raising problems and questions for the viewer.

181 Seipel 2003. Again, we do not know what has been cut from the scene, but this would fit well with the idea that the absence of Nimrod from the scene represents political caution.

182 This image itself is no simple illustration of the Genesis account. The Tower is not explicitly destroyed in Genesis at all; this elaboration is found first in Josephus (see Chapter 3). The depiction of its destruction is not uncommon, but stranger is an inscription reading 'Genesis 14'. Genesis 14 does not refer to Babel or Babylon at all; the Tower of Babel is found in Genesis 11, and indeed it appears that this was what the original etched inscription read. The number 4 is an alteration. The amended inscription is almost certainly intended to make a link with Revelation 14, and thus to the dramatic destruction of Babylon as an allegory for Rome (Armstrong 1990: 105–14).

183 Ten Brink Goldsmith 1992: 208.

184 *Grimani Breviary*, Biblioteca nazionale Marziana, Venice, Ms Lat. I, 99 (2138); Kren and McKendrick 2003: no. 126; *Farnese Hours*, Pierpont Morgan Library, Ms M. 69.

185 The world landscape genre is investigated in depth by Gibson (1989).

186 Mansbach (1982) maintains that the Rotterdam Tower, rising above the clouds, is a firmly optimistic piece, describing the lighting of the Tower as bucolic. I prefer the standard interpretation of the light as ominous, combining with the darkening sky and gathering clouds to imply that the moment of reckoning is imminent, but the utopian interpretation is also possible and it is not unlike Bruegel to incorporate two contradictory lines of thought into a single, ambivalent composition. I would suggest, however, that a utopian meaning could not easily be primary in the picture, since the viewer can be expected to bring to the painting a definite understanding of the Tower of Babel as a lesson in the dangers of hubris and the punishment of pride.

187 Hankins 1945: 364. For example, Matthias Gerung's parallel images of the *Fall of Babylon* and *Fall of the Catholic Church* (Bartrum 1999).

188 These images are collected and discussed in Wegener 1995.

189 Lundquist 1995: 70.

190 Budge 1925: 63.

191 Kircher 1679.

192 Findlen 2004: 4.

193 Grafton 2004: 183.

194 Kircher 1679: vol. 1: 14.

195 *Bibliotheke Historica* 2.2.1.

196 Kircher 1679: vol. 1: 106.

197 Kircher 1679: vol. 1: frontispiece, 43. In another hunting scene with Ninus (Kircher 1679: vol. 1: 57), Semiramis is also shown in Roman robes and with a placid expression, although even here she is depicted as active and aggressive, in the act of shooting at a leopard.

198 As mentioned in Chapter 3, Kuhrt and Sherwin-White (1987) argue that this is a misinterpretation of the textual sources.

199 De Winkel 2006: 255–8.

200 The figure at right is drawn directly from Veronese's *Rape of Europa* of 1580 (Starcky 1990: 74). The most prominent of the figures in the left-hand group is a portrait of Rembrandt's wife Saskia.

201 Goetz 1938: 287–8.

202 For studies of Jewish connections and influence in Rembrandt's work see Zell 2002; Nadler 2003.

203 Sanhedrin 22a.

204 Evidence of Rembrandt's association with Menasseh is hotly disputed, and indeed the *Belshazzar's Feast* inscription itself has been the focus for much of this debate. Alternative Christian sources for the inscription have been proposed (Schwartz 2006, 2011); however, my colleague Irving Finkel and I can now offer what we believe is compelling evidence that Rembrandt

consulted a Jewish scribal source, in all probability Menasseh ben Israel (Finkel and Seymour in preparation).

205 The impression that the table itself is tipping, and a generally increased sense of the figures recoiling from the writing, owes to the fact that the painting has at some stage been cut down and its orientation slightly changed (Bomford et al. 2006: 113–14).

Chapter 5 Discoveries and fantasies: Enlightenment and modern approaches

1 Budge 1925: 61.
2 Also known as Ahmed ibn Lütfullah. Müneccimbaşı himself, however, was reliant on the same biblical and classical sources as European scholars.
3 Otter 1768: vol. 2: 209–11.
4 And indeed contemporaries, noting that the accounts of Edward Ives (1773) and G. A. Olivier (1789–90, 1801) did not make contributions of the same order (Hilprecht 1904: 20–1).
5 Hilprecht 1904: 18.
6 Niebuhr 1774–8.
7 Rich 1839: 301. See also Reade in *Babylon: Myth and Reality*: 27.
8 Beauchamp 1790–1800: 13.
9 McClintock 1995: 1–4.
10 Stanley 1998 (1886): 42.
11 Rich 1813, 1815, 1839.
12 Rich 1815: 5.
13 Budge 1920.
14 Rich 1815: 1–2.
15 Rich 1815: 15.
16 Rich 1815: 26.
17 Rennel 1800.
18 Ker Porter 1821–2; Buckingham 1827; Keppel 1827.
19 Rich 1815: 29.
20 Rich 1815: 17, referring to Xenophon, *Cyropaedia* 7. The *Cyropedia* is largely an imaginative exercise, and in reality very little is known of Cyrus' early life or education. Ancient Mesopotamian warfare did at times involve the diversion of water sources, but in this case the story conflicts directly with the Babylonian and Persian accounts, which suggest that Cyrus entered the city of Babylon freely following the defeat of the Babylonian army at Opis.
21 Gazin-Schwartz and Holtorf 1999.
22 Rich 1815: 29.
23 Reade 1999: 57.

24 Koldewey 1914: 160. The Arabic name transliterated as Mujelibè/ Mudshallibeh seems to be مجليبة (*mujaliba*), from جلب (*jalaba*), 'tumult, turmoil'.

25 Rich 1815: 26.

26 Discussed by Reade (2000: 196).

27 Rich 1815: 34.

28 Rich 1818.

29 Rich 1839.

30 Gadd 1936: 11.

31 Adelson 1995.

32 The massive Assyrian excavation projects of the mid-nineteenth century have been given excellent historical coverage, particularly in Mögens Trolle Larsen's *The Conquest of Assyria* and Nicole Chevalier's *La Recherche Archéologique Française au Moyen-Orient*, whose subject matter it will only be possible to sketch here. For a broad history of archaeology in the Ottoman Empire that gives full weight to Ottoman perspectives and action, see Bahrani, Çelik and Eldem 2011. Ottoman–French diplomacy is well covered by Chevalier 2002. For Mesopotamia, see also Bernhardsson 2005; Malley 2012.

33 Chevalier 2002: 21.

34 For the competing attitudes to non-classical sculpture and its relevance to the Museum's collections in the early nineteenth century see Jenkins 1992: 56–74; Moser 2006.

35 There were strong signs even before his departure from England that Layard's legal career would be brief. He had worked as a clerk at the solicitor's office of his uncle Benjamin Austen, but the work did not suit him and his departure in 1839 to seek employment as a barrister in Ceylon was also motivated by a desire to travel and explore. Beyond even this there is a disjunction between Layard's cosmopolitan childhood in France and Italy and the narrower professional world of his uncle. The journey itself was obviously a large part of Layard's purpose, and indeed he was commissioned by the Royal Geographical Society to research the terrain through which he travelled (Parry 2006).

36 Reade 1994: 121.

37 Layard 1849a: vol. 1: 13–14.

38 Holger Hoock (2007) rightly stresses that although private funding tended to underpin British excavations, they received a great deal of logistical support for free from the British army and navy, as well as the crucial help of the diplomatic service in obtaining permissions to excavate and to export antiquities. For two much larger studies of of the relationship between the state, military and cultural activity, especially collecting, in the British Empire see Jasanoff 2005; Hoock 2010.

39 Russell 1997: 120.

40 Layard 1849a; Botta 1849.

41 Layard 1849a: vol. 2: 173–4.

42 Jenkins 1992: 68.

43 Layard 1849a: vol. 2: 287–8.

44 Studied by Jenkins (1992).

45 Henry Rawlinson to Sir Stratford Canning, British Museum Original Correspondence 36, 30 August 1846; quoted at greater length in Jenkins 1992: 156.

46 Waterfield 1987: 13–14.

47 Reade 1987: 48.

48 Reade 1998: 915.

49 Bohrer 1989, 1992, 1998, 2003. On the reception of the Assyrian discoveries in England more broadly, see now Malley 2012.

50 Bohrer 1992: 85.

51 Layard 1852.

52 Layard 1849b.

53 Layard 1853a.

54 Phillips 2004: 109.

55 Comission des sciences et ars d'Égypte 1809–18.

56 Koldewey 1913, discussed in Chapter 6.

57 Layard was a remarkably talented draughtsman; his original drawings are held in the Department of the Middle East, British Museum.

58 See Richard Hingley's *Roman Officers and English Gentlemen*, which discusses both this point (Hingley 2000: 156) and the role of ancient Rome in British imperial identity more generally.

59 Hingley 2000.

60 Jenkins 1992; Moser 2006.

61 See Curtis 2010 for examples and a survey of Cooper's work with Layard.

62 The joins from reassembly can be seen clearly on the largest of the winged bulls at the British Museum, from Khorsabad. Each of the reassembled statues weighs approximately 16 tonnes.

63 Oppert 1863: vol. 1. The excavators were criticized at the time for failing to pay the necessary bribes or negotiate their passage with local tribal leaders (Matthews 2003: 9).

64 In the present we can cite the problems of looted clay tablets, which without conservation rapidly deteriorate, and the removal, again through looting in the aftermath of the 2003 Iraq war, of metal roofing installed to protect exposed parts of the Assyrian palace sites. The consequences of mud-brick architecture going without the maintenance it would in better times have received can also be seen at sites across the country.

65 Layard 1853b: 499–500. Layard was positive, however, about the usefulness of the more detailed survey due to be undertaken by Felix Jones for the East India Company. This was produced in 1855 but is lost; another was produced by Jones' successor, W. B. Selby (Selby 1859).

66 'There is no doubt that, by imagining a square large enough to include the smaller mounds scattered over the plains from Mohawill to below Hillah on one side of the river, and the Birs Nimroud at its south-western angle on the

other, the site of a city of the dimensions attributed to Babylon might be satisfactorily determined. But then it must be assumed, that neither the outer wall nor the ditch so minutely described by Herodotus ever existed' (Layard 1853b: 492).

67   See p. 83, this volume, for the relevant passage. To me the information does not seem clear enough to identify Tell Babil as the site intended, however, and it is certain that multiple locations at and near Babylon have been associated with the story. Reade (in *Babylon: Myth and Reality*: 23) thinks the mound of Ibrahim Khalil near Birs Nimrud a more likely candidate for Benjamin's Fiery Furnace.

68   Layard 1853b: 505. For Harut and Marut, see p. 104, this volume. NB that the site is not necessarily the same 'pit of Daniel' with which the burial of Harut and Marut was associated in the medieval Arabic sources.

69   Layard 1853b: 506.

70   Layard 1853b: 506.

71   Layard 1853b: 506.

72   Now British Museum N.2050. Layard 1853b: 508; *Babylone*: 140.

73   Layard 1853b: 509–26.

74   Layard 1853b: 527–8.

75   Kemball 1864; Reade 1999: 57–8; Mitchell 2008.

76   Rassam revives both the comparison to St Paul's Cathedral and the vitrification question, writing that 'it is against common sense that a huge tower like that of Birs Nimroud could be subjected to artificial heat after it was built. The tower must have been originally at least 200 feet high; and to build a furnace to envelope it would be just like trying to cover a solid mass equal in size to the whole dome of Saint Paul's Cathedral with one huge furnace, and subjecting it to artificial heat for the purpose of vitrifying it!' (Rassam 1884: 16)

77   On Rassam's career see Rassam 1897; Reade 1986a, 1986b, 1993, 1999, in *Babylon: Myth and Reality*: 74–80; Seymour 2013a.

78   'While Rassam's excavations in the Babylon area continued without interruption for some three and a half years, with work usually proceeding at two or three sites at once (notably Babylon, Borsippa, Sippar) and sometimes at other sites too, he was himself personally present in the region for little more than ten months out of all this time (9 February 1879, the day work began–24 March 1879, 23 May 1880–9 June 1880, 20 November 1880–3 May 1881, 22 April 1882–25 July 1882, the day work ended)' (Reade 1986a: 105–6).

79   Julian Reade (1986a, 1993) has done much to restore Rassam's reputation, which in his own lifetime suffered particularly from accusations made against him by E. A. Wallis Budge.

80   Reade 1986b: xxi.

81   See Reade 1986b, and in *Babylon*: 74–80.

82   Rassam 1897: 363.

83   Rassam 1897: pl. facing p. 224. See also Reade 1986a: 106–11 and pl. 13. Rassam's plans and sketches were not usually of this quality, however, and again

the trustees failed to supply him with professional assistance, in this case in the form of an artist or illustrator.

84 Rassam explains why this was the case, at least for the Kasr mound: 'I found it would only be a waste of money and labour to excavate at Imjaileeba, or kasir [Kasr], because from the deep ditches existing, and the nature of the rubbish which had been thrown up, I was convinced that there could be no ancient remains of any value left there, so I contented myself with having a trial at its centre for a week, and abandoned it for other localities not far distant which had not been so much turned up. These were the other ruins of the city called Omran [Amran] and Jimjima [Jumjuma], and in both these spots I was amply rewarded for my labours in Babylon' (Rassam 1881: 214–15).

85 Timothy Larsen (2013) discusses Layard's religious views, arguing that his interest in Assyria was primarily that of an art historian and connoisseur. Both Layard's own writings on Assyria and his later career lend support to this view.

86 Rassam 1894: 19–20.

87 Rassam 1894: 17. The reference is to Charles Vallancey (c.1726–1812), whose antiquarian interests in Ireland resulted in novel theories on the spread of languages. He argued for an Eastern (Semitic or Persian) origin for Irish language and civilization, but does not seem to have been taken seriously by scholars of his own day; the brilliant orientalist William Jones assisted him with Indian questions, but in a letter describes him as 'very stupid' (in Cannon 1970: vol. 2: 768, cited in Vance 2008). By the time of Rassam's Babylonian excavations a century later the use of Vallancey as an authority would have seemed highly anachronistic.

88 Le Strange 1905: 187.

89 Grotefend 1824.

90 The script actually consists of 36 phonemes (syllabic and alphabetic characters) and eight logograms, as opposed to the hundreds of signs used in other cuneiform scripts.

91 He writes 'Zend', meaning either the Pazend and Pahlavi commentaries on the *Avesta* known by the same name, or Avestan, the language of the *Avesta* themselves.

92 Weißbach 1938; Borger 1980–3.

93 Layard 1849a: vol. 1: xxv.

94 For chronology and a detailed study of Rawlinson's contribution see Daniels 2009.

95 Rawlinson 1898.

96 See Daniels 1994 and Larsen 1997 for comparisons between the work of the two scholars.

97 A prism carrying an inscription of Tiglath-pileser I (1114–1076 BC), British Museum, BM 91033.

98 *Histories* 3.61–5.

99 The division of British Museum antiquities departments over time is explained in Wilson 2002 (see especially p. 379, where the dates of the divisions are

presented diagrammatically). Under the present structure, all material from ancient Mesopotamia is the responsibility of the Department of the Middle East.

100 British Museum K 3375, excavated at Nineveh.

101 The best is that of George (2003a), who has also produced the authoritative scholarly edition (George 2003b).

102 Audi 1998: 250.

103 Plato, *Republic* 439d.1–4, cited in Giustiniani 1985: 167. This seems to me to be a binary division, a reading which agrees with those of Penner (1992: 129) and Williams (1973: 169, 1997: 58), however Giustiniani reads it as tripartite, consisting of 'the rational soul, the emotional soul, the appetitive soul' (Giustiniani 1985: 167).

104 Aristotle, *Poetics* 1451a. See Finley 1975: 11; Bartky 2002.

105 Whittaker 1926: 204; Levin 1966: 23.

106 Avis 1986: 137.

107 Shanks 1992: 16.

108 Bacon 1996 (1605): 32.

109 Thomas 2004: 16–18.

110 Descartes 1996 (1637): 47.

111 Vico 1999 (1744): 1.

112 Herrera 2001: 77–8.

113 Lapeyrère 1656.

114 Schnapp 1996: 222.

115 Voltaire 1814 (1748).

116 Voltaire 1749.

117 Voltaire 1768.

118 Ginzberg 1989: 116.

119 Voltaire 1768: 184; anonymous translation from Voltaire 1969 (1768): 127.

120 Pierse 2003: 79.

121 Lucian, *True Stories*.

122 Bowerstock 1994: 6.

123 Allard in *Babylone*: 447. On the city's earliest attestations and the probable etymology of the name, see André-Salvini in *Babylone*: 28; Lambert 2011.

124 Frye 1951.

125 Hagstrum 1964: 78.

126 Blunt 1943: 192.

127 1795/*c*.1805. Three versions of the image exist, the best-known of which is held by Tate Britain, London. See Butlin 1990 for bibliography.

128 Wind 1938.

129 Blake 1979 (1790).

130 The large prints of *Nebuchadnezzar* and *Newton*, the *Marriage of Heaven and Hell* plate, Dürer's image of St John Chrysostomos and a woodcut produced by Weiditz that also influenced Blake are reproduced together in *Babylon: Myth and Reality*: 166–9.

131 Blake 1979 (1818).

132 *The Everlasting Gospel* 2.5–12.

133 Butlin 1981: no. 523; Carey 1999: no. 5.34.

134 The three pen and watercolour sketches, dated 1806, 1808 and 1809, are part of the Stirling Maxwell Collection, Pollock House, Glasgow Museums.

135 Goldsmith 1993: 142. For Babylon in Victorian apocalyptic see Seymour in 2013a.

136 Seymour 2013a.

137 *The Destruction of Sennacherib* 1.1–4.

138 Originally from the preface to *Milton*, and set to music by Sir Hubert Parry in 1916.

139 'By the Rivers of Babylon We Sat Down and Wept' 2.1–6.

140 Gleckner 1967: 207–8.

141 Although in *Don Juan* Byron himself was to mention those few finds that had made their way back to England from Mesopotamia, noting that 'Claudius Rich, Esquire, some bricks has got, and written lately two memoirs upon't' (*Don Juan* 5.62).

142 Delitzsch and Taglionis 1908.

143 Auguste Amiet-Bourgeois and Francis Cornu, *Nabuchodonosor*, 1836; Antonio Cortesi, *Nabuccodonosor*, 1838.

144 For a summary see Seymour 2013b.

145 On settings for Babylon in the theatre and opera, and particularly *Nabucco*, see Allard in *Babylone*: 476–81; Nadali 2011.

146 Reliefs from Ashurnasirpal's Northwest Palace at Nimrud are in fact quite widely dispersed, with single pieces or small groups held in many locations worldwide. See Cohen and Kangas 2010, Paley 1976 and Russell 1997. For a full study of the reliefs' arrangement see Paley 1981–1992.

147 The jewellery is now held by the British Museum (BM 105111–105128, 115656), to whom it was bequeathed by Lady Layard. Barnett 1978; Rudoe 1987; Collon 1995.

148 Russell 1997: 9. The discovery by John Malcolm Russell of half a relief panel that had earlier been mistaken for a cast of itself in the Nineveh Porch – now the tuck-shop of Canford School – led to a very rare legal sale. The panel fetched £7.7 million at auction, at the time making it the most expensive antiquity ever sold (Russell 1997: 192).

149 Russell 1997: 121.

150 Wealth and social standing do not necessarily rise in parallel, however, and the marriage might have cost the aristocratic Lady Charlotte something in terms of status. Despite his wealth, the connection with John Guest still amounted to marrying into trade (John 2004).

151 Russell 1997: 121–2.

152 Lundquist 1995: 177.

153 Wilde 1998 (1894): ll. 283–7.

154 Hankins 1945: 366.

155 Wilde 1998 (1894), ll. 1066–8.

156 Bahrani 2001b: 141.
157 McClintock 1995.
158 1827, Musée du Louvre.
159 Bahrani 2001b: 146.
160 Busst 1967.
161 Cowling 2004: 15.
162 Said 1978, 1993; Nochlin 1989.
163 Layard 1852: 52.
164 Thompson and Hutchinson 1929.
165 Moser 1998.
166 Kuhn 1970.
167 Young 1990: 49.
168 Since Sennacherib, known from the Old Testament, was the grandfather of Ashurbanipal, equated at the time with the Sardanapalus known only from classical sources.
169 The most important example being the debate between Rich and Rennel in the early nineteenth century (see above, pp. 135–7).
170 Woolley 1937 (1930): 15.

Chapter 6 The German experience: Excavation and reception

1 Layard 1849a, 1852, 1853b.
2 Layard 1849b, 1853a.
3 On Koldewey's life, work and personality more broadly see Andrae 1952 and now Wartke 2008.
4 Sachau 1900; Rogers 1900: 247.
5 Hauser 2001: 214.
6 Mommsen, W. J. 1995: 120.
7 Williamson 1998 (1986): 53.
8 Mommsen, W. J. 1995: 151.
9 Marchand 1996: 193.
10 Marzahn in *Babylon: Wahrheit*: 67.
11 Bohrer 2003: 280.
12 Bohrer 2003: 280.
13 On the railway and Germany's broader imperial ambitions see McMeekin 2010.
14 Marchand 1996: 191.
15 Koldewey 1914: vi. Page references in this chapter are to this English edition; pagination differs slightly in the German original (Koldewey 1913).
16 Haskell 1993: 217–35; see also Wengrow 1999: 599, noting the significance of ceramics from the massive *Délégation Française en Perse* excavations at Susa, contemporary with Koldewey's work at Babylon.

17   Rich 1818. Herodotus gives the walls an impossibly large circuit of 480 stades (89 km), and other classical authorities give figures not much lower: Diodorus, Quintus Curtius Rufus and Strabo offer figures ranging from 360 to 368 stades. Modern estimates of the city's extent and boundaries varied so greatly that even in the mid-nineteenth century Jules Oppert was able to put forward a proposal that matched the enormous circuits described by classical authors (Oppert 1863). This plan described a perfect square so large as to contain not only all the major mounds of Babylon but also Birs Nimrud, actually the separate ancient city of Borsippa (Reade in *Babylon: Myth and Reality*: 113).

18   Strommenger and Stucky 1977: 10.

19   As well as Koldewey 1913, 1914, discussed in this chapter, see especially Koldewey 1911, 1918, 1931–2; Wetzel 1930; Wetzel and Weißbach 1938.

20   The major changes occurring in German scholarship at this time, the 'dethroning of the classical', the rise of technical subjects and non-classical backgrounds in organizations such as the Deutsche Orient-Gesellschaft, and the impact of the natural sciences have been brilliantly analysed by Marchand (1996, 2009).

21   Pollock 1999: 17.

22   Andrae and Boehmer 1989.

23   Koldewey 1914: 73–4.

24   Koldewey 1914: 195–6. He does, however, hold to the idea that 'so lofty a temple would be welcomed by the Babylonian astronomers as a platform for their observations' (1914: 195). It is probable that use of this sacred structure was extremely restricted, confined to particular religious functions and personnel. The vantage point might indeed have been useful for astronomers, but was probably not accessible.

25   Andrae 1922. Micale and Nadali (2008) trace the development of a stratigraphic approach in excavation and recording in Koldewey's work. On methodological innovations see also van Ess 2008.

26   Micale and Nadali 2008, who also note that 'These section drawings are, however, architectural sections aiming more at the identification of a building than at a sequence of archaeological deposits' (2008: 411).

27   King 1919: 15.

28   King 1919: 15.

29   See Dalley 2003.

30   Budge 1920: 300–3.

31   On the ziggurat's archaeology and treatment in cuneiform texts see Schmid 1995; George 2005–6. For a modern aerial photograph of the ruin see *Babylon: Myth and Reality*: 21.

32   Koldewey 1914: 95–6.

33   Diodorus, *Bibliotheke Historica* 2.10.1–6; Josephus, *Against Apion* I.141, *Jewish Antiquities* 10.11; Strabo, *Geography* 16.1.5; Curtius, *History of Alexander* 5.1.5.

34   Koldewey 1914: 130.

35   Koldewey 1914: 46.

36 Koldewey 1914: 46.
37 Keppel 1827: 123; see Myers 1875: 211.
38 Koldewey 1914: 160–2.
39 Koldewey 1914: 160.
40 *Illustrated London News* 1854. The casket is now held by the British Museum, BM 1976,0903.1. Rudoe 1994a: no. 127, 1994b: 260–3, pl. 1.
41 Lloyd 1980: 174. The 'new standard' took some time to become the norm. The German excavations do not resemble those of any other nation working in the Middle East prior to the First World War, nor were they quickly matched in the interwar period (Micale and Nadali 2008: 409).
42 Winstone 2004 (1978): 215.
43 Nagel 1976: 69.
44 Delitzsch 1889b, 1912, 1914a, 1914b.
45 Kucklick 1996.
46 Delitzsch 1881.
47 Delitzsch 1898.
48 Delitzsch 1899.
49 Bohrer 2003: 287.
50 For a selection of *Illustrated London News* coverage of archaeology see Bacon 1976.
51 Delitzsch 1902, 1903a, 1905, and collected in English translation 1903b, 1906. On the lectures see Johanning 1988; Larsen 1989, 1995; Lehmann 1994, 1999; Arnold and Weisberg 2002; Bohrer 2003: 286–96.
52 Delitzsch 1902.
53 Larsen 1989: 189.
54 Larsen 1989: 200.
55 Bohrer 2003: 290.
56 Delitzsch 1903.
57 The passage is Isaiah 63.1–6.
58 Delitzsch 1903b: 148–50; German original Delitzsch 1903a: iv–v.
59 Delitzsch 1920, 1921. He advocated that the Old Testament should be replaced in a new German Christianity by Wilhelm Schwaner's *Germanen Bibel* (Schwaner 1905), in which are collected the thoughts on divine matters of German heroes of the past (Delitzsch 1921: 97, cited in Arnold and Weisberg 2002: 446).
60 It should be noted that in later life the exiled Kaiser continued to follow Delitzsch's views, including his claim in *Die grosse Täuschung* that Jesus was not a Jew (Arnold and Weisberg 2002: 449).
61 Delitzsch 1905.
62 Delitzsch 1905: 32–7.
63 See Chapter 2.
64 Delitzsch 1904: 57–66.
65 Delitzsch and Taglionis 1908.

66 Bohrer 2003.

67 Renger 1999a: 1.

68 On Sardanapalus' origins, see p. 66, this volume.

69 *Bibliotheke Historica* 2.23.

70 Gilmore 1888: 3; see also pp. 59–60, this volume. If anything, Ctesias' reputation is only improving today, with a better understanding of his oral sources and their value as a window onto the culture of the Achaemenid court (Llewellyn-Jones and Robson 2010).

71 See Chapter 3.

72 Andrae 1961: 181; Bohrer 2003: 300.

73 Bohrer 2003: 303.

74 Bilsel 2012: 176.

75 Nagel 1976: 57.

76 Nagel 1976: 69. See also Andrae's own account, where he makes clear his feeling that the opening and display of the collections was long overdue (Andrae 1930). On the early history of the Vorderasiatische Abteilung see Crüsemann 2000a.

77 On the question of 'authenticity' in this and the other major architectural reconstructions at the Pergamonmuseum see Bilsel 2012.

78 Andrae 1902.

79 Klengel-Brandt 1995: 18.

80 Andrae 1927a, 1927b. For the negotiations surrounding the ownership and disposal of antiquities excavated in Iraq before 1914 that followed the First World War see Bernhardsson 2004: 72–92. As well as Babylon, large quantities of material had been excavated by German teams prior to the war at Ashur and Samarra. For a more detailed account of the case of Babylon see Crüsemann 2000a: 184–9; Salje 2008.

81 Which officially became the Vorderasiatische Museum not with the 1927–8 move into the Pergamonmuseum but later, in 1953 (Crüsemann 2000b: 3).

82 Nagel 1976: 69.

83 Hauser 2001: 215.

84 Budge 1925: 293.

85 Delitzsch 1899.

86 Wylie 1982, 1989.

87 Delitzsch 1921: 59–66.

88 Schwaner 1905.

89 Niewyk 1980: 49.

90 Lloyd 1980: 175–6.

91 Cottrell 1959: 47.

92 Macaulay 1953: 40.

93 Lloyd 1980: 178. Lloyd, it should be noted, is a thoroughly biased commentator in this respect, belonging as he does to a tradition of engaging popular writing in English studies of ancient Mesopotamia that runs through

Mallowan, Woolley, Budge, Layard and even beyond, to travellers such as Robert Ker Porter.

94 Morgan 2004: 89.
95 Schnapp 2000: 166–7.
96 Marchand 1996: 213.
97 Dalley 1994, 2003b; Foster 2004; Reade 2000.
98 Larsen 1995: 105.
99 Delitzsch's *Assyrische Grammatik/Assyrian Grammar*, published simultaneously in German and English (Delitzsch 1889a, 1889b), formed a cornerstone of Assyriology for the next century.
100 Bohrer 2003: 299.

Chapter 7   The Library of Babel: Babylon and its representation after the excavations

1 Hobsbawm 1994.
2 Herrera 2001: 11–12.
3 Roberts 1989: 223.
4 Hobsbawm 1987: 319.
5 Joll 1990: 91.
6 Arnold and Hassmann 1995: 71.
7 In his discussion of Kossinna, Ulrich Veit quotes Childe's positive assessment, noting that his view stands 'in sharp contrast to post-war comments on Kossinna which – in the light of the ideological takeover of archaeology during the Third Reich – reduced his contribution to an example of the abuse of prehistory for political reasons' (Veit 2002: 42).
8 Anthony 1995: 91.
9 Hingley 2000.
10 Podro 1982: 8.
11 Haskell 1993: 219–20.
12 Schnapp 1996: 258.
13 Winckelmann 1934 (1764).
14 Hauser 2001: 217.
15 Whitley 2000: 37.
16 Klemm 1843–52, cited in Trigger 1989: 165.
17 Winckelmann 2001 (1880): 134.
18 Burns 1982: 1.
19 *Germania* 2.3.
20 *Germania* 2.1–2.
21 It should be noted in passing that this development actually went against Nietzsche's own racial theories, in which racial mixtures were held to produce better human types and the notion of racial 'purity' was dismissed as a chimera (Lloyd-Jones 1982: 166).

22 Kossinna 1912.

23 Like Delitzsch, Kossinna did not live to see the eventual use to which his racial theories were put. He died in 1931.

24 Marchand 1994: 111.

25 Volkov 1978: 313–19.

26 Steinman 1998: 143.

27 Pulzer 1988: 221.

28 Studied by Regina Heilmann (2004).

29 Seymour in press c.

30 '[S]ome 485 one- and two-reelers made for the American Mutoscope and Biograph Company at the rate of two and three per week' (Merritt 1981: 17).

31 Kirby 1978: 121; Gallagher 1982: 69.

32 Rogin 1985: 174.

33 Matthews 2001.

34 Anger 1975: 6.

35 This section of the film was even re-released separately (with a revised ending) as *The Fall of Babylon* in 1919.

36 Discussed in Chapter 5. Other nineteenth-century artworks used prominently by Griffith for the Babylon sets are John Martin's *Belshazzar's Feast* and George Rochegrosse's *Fall of Babylon*. The latter, now in a private collection, had once hung in a New York restaurant, where it was presumably seen by Griffith (McCall 1998: 208).

37 Kucklick 1996.

38 McCall 1998: 210.

39 Both lecture and programme are held in the Griffith Archive, Museum of Modern Art, New York, and cited in Hanson 1972: 498.

40 Seymour in *Babylon: Myth and Reality*: 203–12.

41 Bonwit 1950. The five works are Joseph Roth, *The Antichrist*; Denis de Rougemont, *The Devil's Share*; C. S. Lewis, *That Hideous Strength*; Edward Wilson, *Memoirs of Hecate County*; and Thomas Mann, *Doctor Faustus*.

42 A perspective shared with Dante, whose journey in the *Divine Comedy* is a good example of a true labyrinth (Doob 1990: 66).

43 Borges 2000 (1964): 78–86.

44 Borges 2000 (1964): 81–2.

45 Derrida 1981.

46 Eco 1995.

47 Borges 2000 (1964): 55–61.

48 Doob 1990: 66.

49 Don-Yehiya 1998: 267.

50 Rakowitz 1997: 177.

51 Rejwan 1985: 217–24.

52 On perceived threats of assimilation in Zionism, Taylor 1972: 50; in Rastafari, Simpson 1985: 287.

53 Chevannes 1995: 10.

54 Watson 1974: 330.

55 See notes on apocalypticism, Chapter 3, and St Augustine, Chapter 4.

56 Chevannes 1995: 10.

57 Simpson 1985: 289.

58 Savishinsky 1994: 19–20.

59 Fattah 2003; Al-Tikriti 2009.

60 Bahrani 1998: 165; Bernhardsson 2005: 97.

61 Abdullah 2003: 43.

62 Abdullah 2003: 123.

63 Matthews 1993: 136–7.

64 Fattah 2003: 50.

65 Fattah 2003: 49.

66 For example, Black 2004; Chatterjee 2004; Klein 2004.

67 Tripp 2002: 14.

68 Tripp 2002: 22.

69 For a history of the British Mandate and the installation of Faisal see Sluglett 2007.

70 Abdullah 2003: 130. Saddam Hussein was later to claim Hashemite descent for this reason, although the implications of this did not include a thawing of relations with the Hashemite monarchy in Jordan, and the Iraqi president's political and military elite was always drawn from his actual tribe of Abu-Nasser (Hassan 1999: 96–8).

71 Woolley 1950 (1929); Woolley and Moorey 1982.

72 Woolley and Lawrence 2003 (1914–15).

73 Tripp 2002: 39.

74 Winstone 2004: 368.

75 Matthews 1997: 59.

76 O'Keefe and Prott 1984: 46.

77 In December 2007 the school changed its name and officially extended its academic remit to cover a broader spectrum of the humanities and social sciences, becoming the British Institute for the Study of Iraq (BISI). The organization's full name continues to include the phrase 'Gertrude Bell Memorial'.

78 Schiffer 2001: 309.

79 Andrae and Boehmer 1989: 34, 122.

80 Against the wishes of High Commissioner Sir Percy Cox and the advice of T. E. Lawrence, both of whom advocated that they go instead to the British Museum (Winstone 2004: 375; Bernhardsson 2005: 76–84).

81 Baram 1994: 282.

82 Winstone 2004: 374.

83 Mallowan 1977: 41.

84 The latter suffered from a conflict of interests, as he was also head of the German expedition at Warka (Bernhardsson 2005: 162).

85　He was to remain Director until 1941, when his support for the coup d'état of that year forced him to leave Iraq.

86　Bernhardsson 2005: 186–97.

87　Abdi 2008: 15.

88　Makiya 1998: 152.

89　Tripp 2000: 123–6.

90　Makiya 1998: 45–53.

91　Baram 1991, 1994.

92　Bahrani 1998, 2003. See also Seymour 2004 and Curtis in *Babylon: Myth and Reality*: 213–20.

93　Baram 1994: 300–3.

94　Rothfield 2009: 13–14.

95　Matthews 2003b: 19.

96　Some examples are shown in Baram 1991.

97　Al-Khalil (Makiya) 1991.

98　Makiya 1998: 13–15, 153–5.

99　Klengel-Brandt 1982: 178–81; Parapetti 2008; see also articles in *Sumer* 35 (1979). For a general survey of excavation and reconstruction projects at Babylon see Seymour in press a.

100　Baram 1991: 46; Abdi 2008: 19.

101　Curtis in *Babylon: Myth and Reality*: 215.

102　Curtis in *Babylon: Myth and Reality*: 213.

103　On the villages surrounding the site and the local impact of these works, see Seymour in press b.

104　Colin Powell had successfully lobbied for US observation of the will of the United Nations in this case, and the coalition did not have a mandate for regime change (Bush and Scowcroft 2003 (1998)).

105　Wiley 2003: 159.

106　Fisk 2001.

107　For example, Handler 2003: 356–7.

108　Makiya 1998, first published 1989 under the pseudonym Samir al-Khalil.

109　Makiya 1998: 45.

110　Hillel 1994: 101–2.

111　See esp. Stone 2005; Gibson 2008.

112　Bogdanos 2008: 110. The only buildings above the Museum on the list were the central bank and oil ministry.

113　*The Guardian*/British Museum public forum, held at the British Museum 15 June 2004 and chaired by Jon Snow, was entitled *Babylon to Baghdad: Can the Past Help Build a Future for Iraq?*. The participants were Neil MacGregor, Kanan Makiya and Ghaith Abdul Ahad.

114　Bogdanos 2005: 506–7.

115　For first-hand accounts of the events see George 2008; Bogdanos 2008.

116　George 2008.

117　Pollock 2003, 2005; Seymour 2004.

118 For an overview see Farchakh-Bajjaly 2008; Al-Husainy and Matthews 2008: 93–6; Stone 2008.
119 Moussa 2008: 144.
120 Curtis in *Babylon: Myth and Reality*: 216.
121 Curtis 2005, 2009; Ministry of Culture of the Republic of Poland: Bureau of Defence Matters 2004; UNESCO 2009; Russell 2010. See also Curtis in *Babylon: Myth and Reality*: 213–20; Moussa 2008; Parapetti 2008.
122 Peruzzetto, Allen and Haney 2011; World Monuments Fund/SBAH in press.

Chapter 8   Culture and knowledge

1   Loomba 1998: 13.
2   Gosden 2001; Spivak 1996.
3   Herrera 2001: 22.
4   Bourke 1995: 299.
5   Auerbach 1952: 6
6   Ricoeur 1965: 81.
7   Thomas 2004: 3.
8   Huxley 1955 (1932); Orwell 2000 (1949).
9   Popper 1957: v.
10 Moser 1998.
11 Nelson 2003.
12 Price 1999.
13 Caldicott and Fuchs 2003.
14 See p. 162, this volume.
15 Shanks 1992.
16 Jameson et al. 2003.
17 Joyce 2002.
18 Moser 1992, 1998, 2001, 2006; Smiles and Moser 2005.
19 See Wylie 1992.
20 Van De Mieroop 2003.
21 Bahrani 2003.
22 Eco 1998.
23 Eco 1998: 27.
24 Butlin 1990: 93.
25 Whatever beliefs individual members of the public may hold about individual points (where a misleading popular article or documentary, for example, may have had a powerful impact) most would agree that rigorous professional training and study is the best way to produce experts and that observation and critical analysis are the appropriate tools to produce what they would consider legitimate knowledge about the past.
26 A great fallacy in the relativism debate is the fear of opening the door to pseudo-science. In fact the debate is far more relevant to religious views than to pseudo-

scientific approaches which, as the name suggests, generally seek to masquerade as scientific. People who use pyramid-building aliens and discoveries of Atlantis to sell books are, as a rule, desperate to appear empirical. They can and should be criticized in conventional rational-empirical terms.

Postscript: The Babylon exhibitions

1 The exhibitions themselves were as follows: *Babylone*, Musée du Louvre, 14 March–2 June 2008; *Babylon: Mythos und Wahrheit*, Pergamonmuseum, 26 June–5 October 2008; *Babylon, Myth and Reality*, British Museum, 13 November 2008–15 March 2009.

2 *Babylone*.

3 I am grateful to the British Museum's Department of Learning and Audiences, and in particular to Rebecca Richards, for this information and for organizing the visitor research.

4 *Iraq's Past Speaks to the Present*, John Addis Islamic Gallery, British Museum, 10 November 2008–15 March 2009 (Porter 2008).

5 2008, mixed media on paper (Porter 2008).

6 Untitled calligraphy in muhaqqaq script. 2008, coloured inks on paper (Porter 2008).

7 2004, ink and watercolour on paper (Porter 2008).

BIBLIOGRAPHY

Editions

Aeschylus, *Persians*.
Sommerstein, A. H. 2009. *Aeschylus*. Loeb Classical Library. 3 vols. London: William Heinemann.

Anon, *Ninus Romance*.
Stephens, S. A. and J. J. Winckler 1995. *Ancient Greek Novels: The Fragments*. Princeton: Princeton University Press.

Arrian, *Anabasis of Alexander*.
Brunt, P. A. and E. I. Robson 1976–83. *Arrian, Anabasis of Alexander*. Loeb Classical Library. 2 vols. London: William Heinemann.

Athenaeus of Nacrautis, *Deipnosophistae*.
Gulick, C. B. 1927–41. *Athenaeus, The Deipnosophists*. Loeb Classical Library. 7 vols. London: William Heinemann.

Athenagoras, *Plea for the Christians*.
Pratten, B. P. 1867. *Athenagoras' Plea for the Christians*. In A. Roberts and J. Donaldson (eds), *Anti-Nicene Christian Library*. Edinburgh: T. and T. Clark. Vol. 3, pp. 375–421.

Augustine, *City of God*.
McCracken, G. E., W. M. Green, D. S. Wiesen, P. Levine, E. M. Sanford and W. C. Greene 1957–72. *Saint Augustine, The City of God Against the Pagans*. Loeb Classical Library. 7 vols. London: William Heinemann.

The Babylonian Talmud.
Goldwurm, H., Y. S. Schorr and C. Malinowitz 1980–2008. *Talmud Bavli. The Schottenstein Version of the Babylonian Talmud*. 73 vols. New York: Mesorah Publications/Artscroll.

Benjamin of Tudela, *Itinerary*
Signer, M. A. (ed.) 1983. *The Itinerary of Rabbi Benjamin of Tudela*. Malibu: Joseph Simon/Pangloss Press.

The Bible.
All translations of biblical passages are quoted from the New International Version (NIV).

al-Biruni, *Al-Athar al-Bakiya*.
Sachau, C. E. 1879. *The Chronology of Ancient Nations. An English Version of the Arabic Text of the Athâr ul-Bâkiya of Albîrûnî, or Vestiges of the Past Collected and Reduced to Writing by the Author in AH 390–1, AD 1000*. London: W. H. Allen.

Blake, William, *The Everlasting Gospel, The Marriage of Heaven and Hell* and *Milton*.
Johnson, M. L. and J. E. Grant (eds) 1979. *Blake's Designs and Poetry*. New York and London: Norton.

Byron, George Gordon, *To Belshazzar, Hebrew Melodies, Sardanapalus* and *Don Juan*
McGann, J. J. (ed.) 1980–93. *Lord Byron: The Complete Poetical Works*. 7 vols. Oxford: Clarendon Press.

Ctesias, *Persica*.
Llewellyn-Jones, L. and J. Robson (eds) 2010. *Ctesias' History of Persia: Tales of the Orient*. London and New York: Routledge.
(See also Diodorus Siculus).

Dante, *The Divine Comedy*.
Dale, P. 1996. *The Divine Comedy*. London: Anvil.

Diodorus Siculus, *Bibliotheke Historica*.
(1) Oldfather, C. H., C. L. Sherman, C. B. Welles, R. M. Geer and F. R. Walton 1933–67. *Diodorus Siculus, Library of History*. Loeb Classical Library. 12 vols. London: William Heinemann.

(2) Murphy, E. 1989. *The Antiquities of Asia: A Translation with Notes of Book II of the Library of History of Diodorus Siculus*. New Brunswick: Transaction Publishers.

Eusebius, *Praeparatorio Evangelica*.
Gifford, E. H. 1903. *Eusebius of Caesarea, Praeparatio Evangelica (Preparation for the Gospel)*. 2 vols. Oxford: Clarendon Press.

Eusebius, *Chronicon*.
Helm, R. 1956. *Eusebius, Werke* (2nd edn). Die Griechischen Christlichen Schriftsteller der Ersten Jahrhunderte 47. Berlin: Akademie Verlag. Vol. 7.

Ferdowsi, Abdolqasem, *Shahnahmeh*.
Davis, D. 2007. *Shahnahmeh: The Persian Book of Kings*. London: Penguin.

Fernberger, Christoph, *Reisetagebuch*.
Burger, R. and R. Wallisch 1999. *Fernberger, Georg Christoph: Reisetagebuch (1588–1593) Sinai, Babylon, Indien, Heiliges Land, Osteuropa. Lateinisch-Deutsch*. Beiträge zur Neueren Geschichte Österreichs 12. Frankfurt am Main: Peter Lang.

FGrHist.
Jacoby, F. 1923–99. *Fragmente der griechischen Historiker*. Berlin/Leiden: Brill.

Herodotus, *Histories*.
De Selincourt, A. (trans.) and J. Marincola (ed.) 2003. *Herodotus, The Histories*. London: Penguin.

Hyginus, *Fabulae*.
Waiblinger, F. P. 1996. *Hyginus, Fabulae/Sagen der Antike*. Munich: Deutsche Taschenbuch Verlag.

Iamblichos, *Babyloniaca*.
Stephens, S. A. and J. J. Winckler 1995. *Ancient Greek Novels: The Fragments*. Princeton: Princeton University Press.

Ibn Daud, *Sefer ha-Kaballah*.
Cohen, G. D. 1967. *A Critical Edition with a Translation and Notes of the Book of Tradition (Sefer ha-Qaballah) by Abraham Ibn Daud*. Philadelphia: Jewish Publication Society of America.

Ibn Hauqal, *Surat al-Ardh*.
Kramers, J.-H. and G. Wiet (eds) 1965. *Ibn Hawqal, Le Livre de la Configuration de la Terre*. Paris: Commission Internationale pour la Traduction des Chefs-d'Œuvre.

Josephus, *Jewish Antiquities* and *Against Apion*.
Thackeray, H. St. J., R. Marcus, A. Wikgren and L. H. Feldman 1926–81. *Josephus*. Loeb Classical Library. 14 vols. London: William Heinemann.

Lucien of Samosata, *True Stories* and *Pseudologista*.
Harmon, A. M., K. Kilburn and M. D. MacLeod 1913–67. *Lucian*. Loeb Classical Library. 8 vols. London: William Heinemann.

Mandeville, Sir John, *Travels*.
Moseley, C. W. R. D. 1983. *The Travels of Sir John Mandeville*. London: Penguin.

Marco Polo, *Travels*.
(1) Masefield, J. 1908. *Marco Polo's Travels*. London: J. M. Dent and Sons.
(2) Latham, R. 1958. *The Travels of Marco Polo*. London: Penguin.

Odoric of Pordenone, *Relatio*.
Chiesa, P. (ed.) and H. Yule (trans.) 2002. *The Travels of Friar Odoric*. Grand Rapids. Michigan: William B. Eerdmans.

Orosius, *Historiae Adversus Paganos*.
Arnauld-Lindet, M. P. 1990–1. *Orose: Histoires (Contre les Païens)*. Paris: Les Belles Lettres.

Ovid, *Metamorphoses*.
Martin, C. 2004. *Ovid, Metamorphoses*. New York and London: Norton.

Photius, *Bibliotheke*.
Henry, R. 1959–71. *Photius, Bibliothèque. Texte établi et traduit*. 6 vols. Paris: Société d'Édition "Les belles lettres".

Pliny the Elder, *Natural History*.
Rackham, H., W. H. S. Jones, A. C. Andrews and D. E. Eichholz 1938–62. *Pliny, Natural History*. Loeb Classical Library. 10 vols. London: William Heinemann.

Plutarch, *Life of Alexander* and *Erotikos*
Perrin, B., F. C. Babbitt, H. N. Fowler, W. C. Helmbold, H. Cherniss, P. H. De Lacy, B. Einarson, E. L. Minar Jr, F. H. Sandbach, L. Pearson, P. A. Clement, H. B. Hoffleit and E. N. O'Neil 1914–2004. *Plutarch*. Loeb Classical Library. 28 vols. London: William Heinemann.

Quintus Curtius Rufus, *History of Alexander*.
Rolfe, J. E. 1946. *Quintus Curtius, History of Alexander*. Loeb Classical Library. 2 vols. London: William Heinemann.

The Quran.
N. J. Dawood (ed.) 1990. *The Koran, with Parallel Arabic Text* (5th edn). London: Penguin.

Schiltberger, Johann, *Bondage and Travels*.
Telfer, J. B. 1879. *The Bondage and Travels of Johann Schiltberger, a Native of Bavaria, in Europe, Asia and Africa, 1396–1427*. London: Printed for the Hakluyt Society.

Souda.
Adler, A. (ed.) 1928–38. *Souda/Suias*. 5 vols. Leipzig: B. G. Teubner.

Strabo, *Geography*.
Jones, H. L. 1961. *The Geography of Strabo*. Loeb Classical Library. 8 vols. London: William Heinemann.

Tacitus, *Germania*.
Hutton, M., W. Peterson, C. H. Moore and J. Jackson 1914–37. *Tacitus*. Loeb Classical Library. 5 vols. London: William Heinemann.

Virgil, *Aeneid*.
Fairclough, H. R. 1916–18. *Virgil*. Loeb Classical Library. 2 vols. London: William Heinemann.

Xenophon, *Cyropaedia*.
Miller, W. 1914. *Xenophon, Cyropaedia*. Loeb Classical Library. 2 vols. London: William Heinemann.

References

Note: The catalogues of the three Babylon exhibitions held (2008–9) in Paris, Berlin and London are made up of many chapters and shorter entries and are frequently cited. References to these are therefore presented in the form 'Author in...' rather than as individual bibliographic entries. The catalogues themselves are as follows:

Babylone.
André Salvini, B. (ed.) 2008. *Babylone*. Paris: Hazan/Musée du Louvre Editions.

Babylon: Myth and Reality.
Finkel, I. L. and M. J. Seymour (eds) 2008. *Babylon: Myth and Reality*. London: British Museum Press. (Also published 2009 as *Babylon*. New York: Oxford University Press.)

Babylon: Mythos.
Wullen, M., Schauerte, G. and Strzoda, H. (eds) 2008. *Babylon: Mythos.* Berlin: Hirmer/Staatliche Museen zu Berlin.

Babylon: Wahrheit.
J. Marzahn, G. Schauerte, B. Müller-Neuhof and K. Sternitzke (eds) 2008. *Babylon: Wahrheit.* Berlin: Hirmer/Staatliche Museen zu Berlin.

Abdi, K. 2008. 'From Pan-Arabism to Saddam Hussein's cult of personality: Ancient Mesopotamia and Iraqi national ideology.' *Journal of Social Archaeology* 8 (1): 3–36.

Abdullah, T. A. J. 2003. *A Short History of Iraq from 636 to the Present.* London: Pearson Education.

Adams, R. McC. 1966. *The Evolution of Urban Society.* Chicago: Aldine.

———. 1970. 'The study of Ancient Mesopotamian settlement patterns and the problem of urban origins.' *Sumer* 25: 111–123.

———. 1981. *Heartland of Cities.* Chicago: University of Chicago Press.

Adelson, R. 1995. *London and the Invention of the Middle East: Money, Power, and War, 1902–1922.* New Haven: Yale University Press.

Adler, M. N. (ed.) 1907. *The Itinerary of Benjamin of Tudela: Critical Text, Translation and Commentary.* New York: Philipp Feldheim, Inc.

Andrae, W. 1902. 'Die glasierten Ziegel von der Südburg des Kasr.' *Mitteilungen der Deutschen Orient-Gesellschaft zu Berlin* 13: 1–12.

———. 1922. *Die archaischen Ischtar-Tempel in Assur.* Wissenschaftliche Veröffentlichungen der Deutschen Orient-Gesellschaft 39. Leipzig: J. C. Hinrichs.

———. 1927a. 'Der Rückerwerb der Assur Funde aus Portugal.' *Mitteilungen der Deutschen Orient-Gesellschaft zu Berlin* 65: 1–6.

———. 1927b. 'Reise nach Babylon zur Teilung der Babylon Funde.' *Mitteilungen der Deutschen Orient-Gesellschaft zu Berlin* 65: 7–27.

———. 1930. 'Das Vorderasiatisches Museum.' *Berliner Museen* 51: 108–113.

———. 1952. *Babylon. Die versunkene Weltstadt und ihr Ausgräber Robert Koldewey.* Berlin: de Gruyter & Co.

———. 1961. *Lebenserinnerungen eines Ausgräbers.* Berlin: Walter de Gruyter.

Andrae, E. W. and R. M. Boehmer 1989. *Bilder eines Ausgräbers/Sketches by an Excavator: Walter Andrae im Orient 1898–1919.* Berlin: Gebr. Mann Verlag.

André-Salvini, B. 2003. *Le Code de Hammurabi.* Paris: Éditions de la Réunion des Musées Nationaux.

Anger, K. 1975. *Hollywood Babylon.* New York: Dell Publishing.

Anthony, D. W. 1995. 'Nazi and eco-feminist prehistories: ideology and empiricism in Indo-European archaeology.' In P. L. Kohl and C. Fawcett (eds), *Nationalism, Politics and the Practice of Archaeology.* Cambridge: Cambridge University Press. pp. 82–96.

Arieti, J. 1995. *Discourses on the First Book of Herodotus.* Lanham, Maryland: Littlefield Adams Books.

Arnaud-Lindet, M. P. (ed.) 1990–1. *Orose: Histoires (Contre les Païens).* Paris: Les Belles Lettres.

Arnold, B. and H. Hassmann, 1995. 'Archaeology in Nazi Germany: The legacy of the Faustian bargain.' In P. L. Kohl and C. Fawcett (eds), *Nationalism, Politics and the Practice of Archaeology*. Cambridge: Cambridge University Press. pp. 70–81.

Arnold, W. T. and D. B. Weisberg 2002. 'A Centennial Review of Friedrich Delitzsch's "Babel und Bibel" Lectures.' *Journal of Biblical Literature* 121 (3): 441–57.

Aruz, J., K. Benzel and J. Evans (eds) 2008. *Beyond Babylon: Art, Trade, and Diplomacy in the Second Millennium B.C.* New York: The Metropolitan Museum of Art / Distributed by Yale University Press.

Aruz, J., Y. Rakic and S. Graff (eds) 2013. *Cultures in Contact: From Mesopotamia to the Mediterranean in the Second Millennium B.C.* New York: The Metropolitan Museum of Art / Distributed by Yale University Press.

Asher, A. (ed.) 1840–1. *The Itinerary of Rabbi Banjamin of Tudela*. 2 vols. New York: Hakesheth Publishing Co.

Atkinson, J. E. 1994. *A Commentary on Q. Curtius Rufus' Historiae Alexandri Magni, Books 5–7.2*. Amsterdam: Hakkert.

Audi, R. 1998. *Epistemology: A Contemporary Introduction to the Theory of Knowledge*. London and New York: Routledge.

Auerbach, E. 1952. 'Typological Symbolism in Medieval Literature.' *Yale French Studies* 9: 3–10.

Avis, P. 1986. *Foundations of Modern Historical Thought: From Macchiavelli to Vico*. London: Croom Helm.

Bacon, E. (ed.) 1976. *The Great Archaeologists and Their Discoveries as Originally Reported in the Pages of the Illustrated London News from 1842 to the Present Day*. London: Book Club Associates.

Bacon, F. 1996 (1605). 'The Advancement of Learning.' In J. Appleby, E. Covington, D. Hoyt, M. Latham, and A. Sneider (eds), *Knowledge and Postmodernism in Historical Perspective*. London and New York: Routledge. pp. 31–40.

Bahrani, Z. 1998. 'Conjuring Mesopotamia: imaginative geography and a world past.' In Meskell, L. (ed.), *Archaeology Under Fire: Nationalism, Politics and Heritage in the Eastern Mediterranean and Middle East*. London and New York: Routledge. pp. 159–174.

———. 2001. *Women of Babylon: Gender and Representation in Mesopotamia*. London and New York: Routledge.

———. 2003. *The Graven Image: Representation in Babylonia and Assyria*. Philadelphia: University of Pennsylvania Press.

Bahrani, Z., Z. Çelik and E. Eldem (eds) 2011. *Scramble for the Past: A Story of Archaeology in the Ottoman Empire*. Istanbul: SALT/Garanti Kültür A. Ş.

Baram, A. 1991. *Culture, History and Ideology in the Formation of Ba'thist Iraq, 1969–89*. New York: St. Martin's Press.

———. 1994. 'A case of imported identity: the modernizing secular ruling elites of Iraq and the concept of Mesopotamian-inspired territorial nationalism, 1922–1992.' *Poetics Today* 15 (2): 279–319.

Barnett, R. D. 1976. *Sculptures from the North Palace of Ashurbanipal at Nineveh (668–627 BC)*. London: British Museum Publications.

———. 1978. 'Lady Layard's jewelry.' In P. R. S. Moorey and P. J. Parr (eds), *Archaeology in the Levant: Essays for Kathleen Kenyon*. Warminster: Aris and Phillips. pp. 172–9.

————. 1982. 'Urartu.' In J. Boardman, I. E. S. Edwards, N. G. L. Hammond and E. Sollberger (eds), *The Cambridge Ancient History* (2nd edn). Cambridge: Cambridge University Press. Vol. 3, pt. 1, pp. 314–71.

Baron, S. W. 1972. *Ancient and Medieval Jewish History.* New Brunswick, NJ: Rutgers University Press.

Bartky, E. 2002. 'Aristotle and the Politics of Herodotus's *History.' The Review of Politics* 64 (3): 445–468.

Bartrum, G. 1999. Catalogue entries on 'Matthias Gerung (c. 1500–70), *The Destruction of Babylon* and *The Destruction of the Catholic Church.'* In F. Carey (ed.), *The Apocalypse and the Shape of Things to Come.* London: British Museum Press. pp. 164, 165.

Beauchamp, J. 1790–1800. *Mémoire sur la Carte de la Mésopotamie.* Unpublished manuscript, British Library Add. MS. 15,331.2.

Beaulieu, P.-A. 1993. 'An episode in the fall of Babylon to the Persians.' *Journal of Near Eastern Studies* 52 (4): 241–261.

Bernhardsson, M. T. 2005. *Reclaiming a Plundered Past: Archaeology and Nation Building in Modern Iraq.* Austin: University of Texas Press.

Bidmead, J. 2002. *The Akītu Festival: Religious Continuity and Royal Legitimation in Mesopotamia.* Piscataway, NJ: Gorgias Press.

Bilsel, C. 2012. *Antiquity on Display: Regimes of the Authentic in Berlin's Pergamon Museum.* Oxford: Oxford University Press.

Bittner, R. 1999. 'Augustine's philosophy of history.' In G. B. Matthews (ed.), *The Augustinian Tradition.* Berkeley: University of California Press. pp. 345–60.

Black, E. 2004. *Banking on Baghdad: Inside Iraq's 7,000-Year History of War, Profit, and Conflict.* Hoboken, NJ: John Wiley and Sons.

Blake, W. 1979 (1790). 'The marriage of heaven and hell.' In M. L. Johnson and J. E. Grant (eds), *Blake's Poetry and Designs.* London: Norton. pp. 88–102.

————. 1979 (1804). 'Milton.' In M. L. Johnson and J. E. Grant (eds), *Blake's Poetry and Designs.* London: Norton. pp. 237–306.

Bloomfield, M. W. 1958. 'Symbolism in medieval literature.' *Modern Philology* 56 (2): 73–81.

Blunt, A. 1943. 'Blake's pictorial imagination.' *Journal of the Warburg and Courtauld Institutes* 6: 190–212.

Blunt, W. J. W. 1953. *Pietro's Pilgrimage: A Journey to India and Back at the Beginning of the Seventeenth Century.* London: James Barrie.

Bogdanos, M. 2005. 'The casualties of war: the truth about the Iraq Museum.' *American Journal of Archaeology* 109: 477–526.

————. 2008. 'Thieves of Baghdad.' In P. J. Stone and J. Farchakh-Bajjaly (eds), *The Destruction of Cultural Heritage in Iraq.* Woodbridge: Boydell Press. pp. 109–34.

Bohrer, F. N. 1989. 'Assyria as art: a perspective on the early reception of ancient Near Eastern artefacts.' *Culture and History* 4: 7–33.

————. 1992. 'The printed Orient: the production of A. H. Layard's earliest works.' *Culture and History* 11: 85–105.

————. 1998. 'Inventing Assyria: exoticism and reception in nineteenth-century England and France.' *Art Bulletin* (June): 336–56.

————. 2003. *Orientalism and Visual Culture: Imagining Mesopotamia in Nineteenth-Century Europe.* Cambridge: Cambridge University Press.

Boiy, T. 2004. *Late Achaemenid and Hellenistic Babylon*. Orientalia Lovaniensia Analecta 136. Leuven, Paris and Dudley, MA: Peeters and Department Oosterse Studies, Leuven.

Bomford, D., J. Kirby, A. Roy, A. Rüger and R. White 2006. *Art in the Making: Rembrandt*. London: National Gallery.

Bonwit, M. 1950. 'Babel in modern fiction.' *Comparative Literature* 2 (3): 236–47.

Borger, R. 1956. *Die Inschriften Asarhaddons, Königs von Assyrien*. Archiv für Orientforschung, Beiheft 9. Graz.

———. 1980–3. 'Lassen, Christian.' In D. O. Edzard (ed.), *Reallexikon der Assyriologie und Vorderasiatischen Archäologie*. Band 6. Berlin and New York: Walter de Gruyter. p. 507.

Borges, J. L. 2000 (1964). *Labyrinths*. London: Penguin.

Bosworth, A. B. 1971. 'The death of Alexander the Great.' *The Classical Quarterly* (new series) 21 (1): 112–36.

———. 1988. *Conquest and Empire: The Reign of Alexander the Great*. Cambridge: Cambridge University Press.

———. 1995. *A Historical Commentary on Arrian's History of Alexander*. Oxford: Oxford University Press. Vol. 2.

Botta, P.-É. 1849–50. *Monuments de Ninive. Découvert et décrit par M. P.-E. Botta. Mesuré et dessiné par M. E. Flandin. Ouvrage publié par ordre du Gouvernement sous les auspices de M. le Ministre de l'Intérieur et sous la Direction d'une Commission de l'Institut*. 5 vols. Paris: Imprimerie Nationale.

Bourke, V. J. 1995. '*The City of God* and history.' In D. F. Donnelly (ed.), *The City of God: A Collection of Critical Essays*. New York: Peter Lang. pp. 291–304.

Bowerstock, G. W. 1994. *Fiction as History: Nero to Julian*. Berkeley: University of California Press.

Breucker, G. de 2011. 'Berossus Between Tradition and Innovation.' In K. Radner and E. Robson (eds), *The Oxford Handbook of Cuneiform Culture*. Oxford: Oxford University Press.

Briant, P. 2005. 'History of the Persian Empire 550–330 BC.' In J. E. Curtis and N. Tallis (eds), *Forgotten Empire: The World of Ancient Persia*. London: British Museum Press. pp. 12–17.

———. 2006. *From Cyrus to Alexander: History of the Persian Empire*. Winona Lake: Eisenbrauns.

Brinkman, J. A. 1964. 'Merodach-Baladan.' In R. D. Biggs and J. A. Brinkman (eds), *Studies Presented to A. Leo Oppenheim, June 7, 1964*. Chicago: Oriental Institute of the University of Chicago.

———. 1973. 'Sennacherib's Babylonian Problem: An Interpretation.' *Journal of Cuneiform Studies* 25 (2): 89–95.

———. 1974. 'The monarchy in the time of the Kassite dynasty.' In P. Garelli (ed.), *Le Palais et la Royauté*. Proceedings of the XIXème Rencontre Assyriologique Internationale, 1971. Paris: Paul Geuthner. pp. 395–408.

———. 1983. 'Through a glass darkly: Esarhaddon's retrospects on the downfall of Babylon.' *Journal of the American Oriental Society* 103: 35–42.

———. 1984. *Prelude to Empire: Babylonian Society and Politics, 747–626 BC*. Occasional Publications of the Babylonian Fund 7. Philadelphia: Babylonian Fund, Pennsylvania University Museum.

Brown, P. 2000. *Augustine of Hippo: A Biography* (3rd edn). London: Faber and Faber.

Brumble, H. D. 1998. *Classical Myths and Legends in the Middle Ages and Renaissance: A Dictionary of Allegorical Meanings.* London: Fitzroy Dearborn.

Bruun, P. 1879. 'Notes on the bondage and travels of Johann Schiltberger.' In J. B. Telfer (ed.), *The Bondage and Travels of Johann Schiltberger, a Native of Bavaria, in Europe, Asia and Africa, 1396–1427.* London: Printed for the Hakluyt Society.

Buckingham, J. S. 1827. *Travels in Mesopotamia. with Researches on the Ruins of Nineveh, Babylon, and Other Ancient Cities.* London: Henry Colburn.

Budge, E. A. W. 1920. *By Nile and Tigris: A Narrative of Journeys in Egypt and Mesopotamia on Behalf of the British Museum between the Years 1886 and 1913.* London: John Murray.

———. 1925. *The Rise and Progress of Assyriology.* London: Martin Hopkinson and Co.

Bull, G. (ed.) 1989. *The Pilgrim: The Journeys of Pietro Della Valle.* London: The Folio Society.

Burns, T. S. 1982. 'Theories and facts: the early Gothic migrations.' *History in Africa* 9: 1–20.

Burstein, S. M. 1978. *The 'Babyloniaca' of Berossus.* Malibu: Undena.

Bush, G. H. W. and B. Scowcroft 2003 (1998). 'Why we didn't go to Baghdad.' In M. L. Sifry and C. Cerf (eds), *The Iraq War Reader: History, Documents, Opinions.* New York: Simon and Schuster. pp. 101–2.

Busst, A. J. L. 1967. 'The image of the androgyne in the nineteenth century.' In I. Fletcher (ed.), *Romantic Mythologies.* London: Routledge and Kegan Paul. pp. 1–95.

Butlin, M. 1981. *The Paintings and Drawings of William Blake.* 2 vols. London and New Haven: Yale University Press.

———. 1990. *William Blake, 1757–1827.* London: Tate Gallery Publications.

Caldicott, E. and A. Fuchs (eds) 2003. *Cultural Memory: Essays on European Literature and History.* Oxford: Peter Lang.

Calvino, I. 1974. *Invisible Cities.* New York: Harcourt Brace Janovich.

Canby, J. V. 2001. *The Ur-Nammu Stela.* Philadelphia: University of Pennsylvania Museum of Archaeology and Anthropology.

Cannon, G. (ed.) 1970. *The Letters of Sir William Jones.* 2 vols. Oxford: Clarendon Press.

Carey, F. (ed.) 1999. *The Apocalypse and the Shape of Things to Come.* London: British Museum Press.

Carruthers, D. (ed.) 1929. *The Desert Route to India: Being the Journals of Four Travellers by the Great Desert Caravan Route between Aleppo and Basra 1745–1751.* London: Hakluyt Society.

Cartwright, J. 1633. 'Excerpta ex itinerario Ioannis Cartwright.' In J. de Laet (ed.), *Persia: seu regni Persici status, variaque itinera in atque per Persiam.* Antwerp: Elzeviriana, Lugduni Batavorum.

Charles, M. P. 1988. 'Irrigation in lowland Mesopotamia.' *Bulletin of Sumerian Agriculture* 4: 1–39.

Chastel, A. 1984. *Le Sac de Rome 1527. Du premier maniérisme à la Contre-Réforme.* Paris: Gallimard.

Chatterjee, P. 2004. *Iraq, Inc.: A Profitable Occupation.* New York: Seven Stories Press.

Chazan, R. 1988. 'Representation of events in the Middle Ages.' *History and Theory* 27 (4): 40–55.

Chevalier, N. 2002. *La recherche archéologique française au Moyen-Orient 1842–1947.* Paris: Éditions Recherche sur les Civilisations.

Chevannes, B. 1995. 'Introducing the native religions of Jamaica.' In B. Chevannes, (ed.), *Rastafari and Other African-Caribbean Worldviews.* Basingstoke: Macmillan. pp. 1–19.

Chiesa, P. (ed.) 2002. *The Travels of Friar Odoric.* Grand Rapids, Michigan: William B. Eerdmans.

Clarke, D. 1973. 'Archaeology: the loss of innocence.' *Antiquity* 47 (185): 6–18.

Clayden, T. 1996. 'Kurigalzu I and the Restoration of Babylonia.' *Iraq* 58: 109–21.

Cogan, M. and H. Tadmor 1981. 'Ashurbanipal's conquest of Babylon: the first official report: Prism K.' *Orientalia* 50: 229–40.

Cohen, A. and S. E. Kangas (eds) 2010. *Assyrian Reliefs from the Palace of Ashurnasirpal II: A Cultural Biography.* Hanover, New Hampshire: Hood Museum of Art, Dartmouth College; Hanover and London: University Press of New England.

Cohen, G. D. (ed.) 1967. *A Critical Edition with a Translation and Notes of the Book of Tradition (Sefer ha-Qaballah) by Abraham Ibn Daud.* Philadelphia: Jewish Publication Society of America.

Collins, B. A. and M. H. al-Tai (eds) 1994. Al-Muqaddasi, *The Best Divisions for Knowledge of the Regions. A Translation of Ahsan al-Taqasim fi Ma'rifat al-Aqalim.* Reading: Centre for Muslim Contribution to Civilization / Garnet.

Collins, J. J. 1998. *The Apocalyptic Imagination: An Introduction to Jewish Apocalyptic Literature* (2nd edn). Grand Rapids, Michigan and Cambridge: William B. Eerdmans.

Collon, D. 1995. Catalogue entry on 'Lady Layard's Jewellery.' In J. E. Curtis and J. E. Reade (eds), *Art and Empire: Treasures from Assyria in the British Museum.* London: British Museum Press. p. 220.

Comission des sciences et ars d'Égypte 1809–18. *Description de l'Égypte ou recueil des observations et des recherches qui ont été faites en Égypte pendant l'Expédition de l'Armée française, publiée par les ordres de Napoleon Bonaparte.* 23 vols. Paris: Imprimerie Impériale.

Conrad, J. 1990 (1897). 'An outpost of progress.' In C. Watts (ed.), *Joseph Conrad: Heart of Darkness and Other Tales.* Oxford: Oxford University Press. pp. 1–34.

Considine, J. S. 2003. 'Babylon, City of.' In B. L. Marthaler, G. F. L. N.ve, J. Y. Tan, R. E. McCarron and D. J. Obermeyer (eds), *New Catholic Encyclopedia* (2nd edn). 15 vols. Detroit: Gale. Vol. 2, pp. 3–4.

Córdoba, J. Ma. 2006. 'Don Garcia de Silva y Figueroa, and the rediscovery of Iran.' In J. Ma. Córdoba and C. Perez Díe (eds), *The Spanish Near Eastern Adventure (1166–2006): Travellers, Museums and Scholars in the Rediscovering of the Ancient Near East.* Madrid: Ministerio de Cultura de España. pp. 51–6.

Cottrell, L. 1959. *Lost Cities* (2nd edn). London: Pan.

Cowling, M. 2004. 'Archaeology and aestheticism: The Babylonian Marriage Market and high Victorian taste.' In *The Price of Beauty: Edwin Long's Babylonian Marriage Market (1875).* London: Libraries and Arts Service of the Royal Borough of Kensington and Chelsea. pp. 15–23.

Crüsemann, N. 2000a. *Vom Zweistromland zum Kupfergraben: Vorgeschichte und Entstehungsjahre (1899–1918) der Vorderasiatischen Abteilung der Berliner Museen vor fach- und kulturpolitischen Hintergründen.* Jahrbuch der Berliner Museen Beiheft 42. Berlin: Gebr. Mann Verlag.

———. 2000b. 'Die Berliner Sammlung vorderasiatischer Altertümer bis 1885.' In N. Crüsemann, U. Von Eickstedt, E. Klengel-Brandt, L. Martin, J. Marzahn and R.-B. Wartke (eds), *Vorderasiatisches Museum Berlin: Geschichte und Geschichten zum hundertjährigen Bestehen.* Berlin: Staatliche Museen zu Berlin, Preußischer Kulturbesitz. pp. 3–4.

Curtis, J. E. 2005. *Report on Meeting at Babylon 11th–13th December 2004.* London: British Museum.

———. 2009. *Inspection of Babylon on Behalf of UNESCO 25th to 29th February 2009.* [http://www.britishmuseum.org/pdf/Babylon%20UNESCO%20Report_.pdf/]

———. 2010. 'A Victorian artist in Assyria.' *Iraq* 72: 175–82.

———. 2013. *The Cyrus Cylinder and Ancient Persia: A New Beginning for the Middle East.* London: British Museum Press.

———. and J. E. Reade (eds) 1995. *Art and Empire: Treasures from Assyria in the British Museum.* London: British Museum Press.

D'Ablancourt, P. (ed.) 1977. *Histoire véritable de Lucien.* Nancy: Université de Nancy, Société Française de Littérature Générale et Comparée.

Dalley, S. M. 1989. *Myths from Mesopotamia: Creation, the Flood, Gilgamesh and Others.* Oxford: Oxford University Press.

———. 1994. 'Nineveh, Babylon and the Hanging Gardens: cuneiform and classical sources reconciled.' *Iraq* 56: 45–58.

———. 2002. 'More about the Hanging Gardens.' In L. al-Ghailani Werr, J. E. Curtis, H. Martin, A. McMahon, J. Oates and J. E. Reade (eds), *Of Pots and Plans: Papers on the Archaeology and History of Mesopotamia and Syria as Presented to David Oates on his 75th Birthday.* London: Nabu Publications. pp. 67–73.

———. 2003a. 'The transition from Neo-Assyrians to Neo-Babylonians: break or continuity?' In I. Eph'al, A. Ben-Tor and P. Machinist (eds), *Eretz-Israel: Archaeological, Historical and Geographical Studies. Volume 27: Hayim and Miriam Tadmor Volume.* Jerusalem: The Israel Exploration Society. pp. 25–8.

———. 2003b. 'Why did Herodotus not Mention the Hanging Gardens of Babylon?' In P. Derow and R. Parker (eds), *Herodotus and his World: Essays from a Conference in Memory of George Forrest.* Oxford: Oxford University Press. pp. 171–89.

———. 2008. 'Babylon as a name for other cities including Nineveh.' In R. D. Biggs, J. Myers and M. T. Roth (eds), *Proceedings of the 51st Rencontre Assyriologique Internationale, Held at the Oriental Institute of the University of Chicago, July 18–22, 2005.* Studies in Ancient Oriental Civilization 62. Chicago: The Oriental Institute of the University of Chicago. pp. 25–34.

Daniels, P. T. 1994. 'Edward Hincks's decipherment of Mesopotamian cuneiform.' In K. J. Cathcart (ed.), *The Edward Hincks Bicentenary Lectures.* Dublin: Department of Near Eastern Languages, University College Dublin. pp. 30–57.

———. 2009. 'Rawlinson, Henry ii: Contributions to Assyriology and Iranian studies.' *Encyclopedia Iranica* [online] <http://www.iranicaonline.org/articles/rawlinson-ii>.

Delitzsch, F. 1881. *Wo lag das Paradies?* Leipzig: J. C. Hinrichs.

———. 1889a. *Assyrian Grammar: With Paradigms, Exercises Glossary and Bibliography.* London: Williams and Norgate.

————. 1889b. *Assyrische Grammatik: mit Paradigmen über Übungsstücken, Glossar, und Literatur*. Berlin: Reuther's Verlagsbuchhandlung.

————. 1898. *Ex Oriente Lux! Ein Wort sur Förderung der Deutschen Orient-Gesellschaft*. Leipzig: J. C. Hinrichs.

————. 1899. 'Die Deutsche Expedition nach Babylon.' *Illustrierte Zeitung* 113: 541–43.

————. 1902. *Babel und Bibel: Ein Vortrag*. Leipzig: J. C. Hinrichs.

————. 1903a. *Zweiter Vortrag über Babel und Bibel*. Stuttgart: Deutsche Verlags-Anstalt.

————. 1903b. *Babel and Bible: Two Lectures Delivered Before the Members of the Deutsche Orient-Gesellschaft in the Presence of the German Emperor by Friedrich Delitzsch*. London: Williams and Norgate.

————. 1904. *Babel und Bibel. Ein Rückblick und Ausblick*. Stuttgart: Deutsche Verlags-Anstaldt.

————. 1905. *Babel und Bibel. Dritter (Schluss-) Vortrag*. Stuttgart: Deutsche Verlags-Anstaldt.

————. 1906. *Babel and Bible: Three Lectures on the Significance of Assyriological Research for Religion, Embodying the Most Important Criticisms and the Author's Replies*. Chicago: The Open Court Publishing Co.

————. 1912. *Assyrische Lesestücke mit den Elementen der Grammatik und vollständigem Glossar: Einführung in die assyrische und semitische – babylonische Keilschriftliteratur für akademischen Gebrauch und Selbstunterricht*. Leipzig: J. C. Hinrichs.

————. 1914a. *Sumerisch-akkadisch-hettitische Vokabularfragmente*. Berlin: Akademie der Wissenschaften.

————. 1914b. *Sumerisches Glossar*. Leipzig: J. C. Hinrichs.

————. 1920. *Die Grosse Täuschung* (I). Stuttgart: Deutsche Verlags-Anstalt.

————. 1921. *Die Grosse Täuschung* (II). Württemberg: Karl Rohm.

————. and P. Taglionis 1908. *Sardanapal, Grosse Historische Pantomime in 3 Akten*. Berlin.

Della Valle, P. 1650–63. *Viaggi di Pietro della Valle il Pellegrino Con minuto ragguaglio di tutte le cose notabili osseruate in essi, Descritti da lui medesimo in 54. Lettere familiari, Da diuersi luoghi della intrapresa peregrinatione, Mandate in Napoli all'erudito, e fra' più cari, di molti anni suo Amico Mario Schipano, Divisi in tre parti, cioè La Turchia, la Persia, e L'India, Le quali hauran per Aggiunta, Se Dio gli darà vita, la quarta Parte, Che conterrà le figure di molte cose memorabili, Sparse per tutta l'Opera, e a loro esplicatione*. Rome: V. Mascardi and B. Deversin.

————. 1843. *Viaggi di Pietro Della Valle il pellegrino descritti da lui medesimo in lettere familiari all'erudito suo amico Mario Schipano divisi in tre parti cioè: la Turchia, la Persia e l'India colla vita e ritratto dell'autore*. 2 vols. Brighton: G. Gancia.

Derrida, J. 1981. *Positions*. Chicago: University of Chicago Press.

Descartes, R. 1996 (1637). 'Discourse on method.' In J. Appleby, E. Covington, D. Hoyt, M. Latham and A. Sneider (eds), *Knowledge and Postmodernism in Historical Perspective*. London and New York: Routledge. pp. 42–9.

Don-Yehiya, E. 1998. 'Zionism in retrospective.' *Modern Judaism* 18 (3): 267–76.

Doob, P. R. 1990. *The Idea of the Labyrinth from Classical Antiquity Through the Late Middle Ages*. Ithaca: Cornell University Press.

Dougherty, R. P. 1929. *Nabonidus and Belshazzar: A Study of the Closing Events of the Neo-Babylonian Empire*. New Haven: Yale University Press.

Dronke, P. 1986. *Dante and Medieval Latin Traditions*. Cambridge: Cambridge University Press.

Eco, U. 1995. *Search for a Perfect Language*. Oxford: Blackwell.

———. 1998. *Serendipities: Language and Lunacy*. New York: Columbia University Press.

Eldred, J. 1903 (1592). 'John Eldred's narrative.' In R. Beazley (ed.), *Voyages and Travels, Mainly During the 16th and 17th Centuries*. 2 vols. London: Archibald Constable and Co. Ltd. pp. 295–303.

Fales, F. M. 2011. 'Moving around Babylon: on the Aramean and Chaldean presence in Southern Mesopotamia.' In E. Cancik-Kirschbaum, M. van Ess and J. Marzahn (eds), *Babylon. Wissenkultur in Orient und Okzident*. Topoi Berlin Studies of the Ancient World 1. Berlin: Walter De Gruyter. pp. 91–111.

Farchakh Bajjaly, J. 2008. 'Will Mesopotamia survive the war? The continuous destruction of Iraq's cultural heritage.' In P. G. Stone and J. Farchakh Bajjaly (eds), *The Destruction of Cultural Heritage in Iraq*. Woodbridge: Boydell Press. pp. 135–41.

Fattah, H. 2003. 'The Question of the "Artificiality" of Iraq as a Nation-State.' In S. C. Inati (ed.), *Iraq: Its History, People, and Politics*. New York: Humanity Books. pp. 49–60.

Ferber, S. 1966. 'Peter Bruegel and the Duke of Alba.' *Renaissance News* 19 (3): 205–19.

Findlen, P. 2004. 'Introduction: the last man who knew everything. Or did he? Athanasius Kircher, S. J. (1602–80).' In P. Findlen (ed.), *Athanasius Kircher: The Last Man Who Knew Everything*. London and New York: Routledge. pp. 1–48.

Finkel, I. L. 1999. 'The lament of Nabû-šuma-ukin.' In J. Renger (ed.), *Babylon: Focus Mesopotamischer Geschichte, Wiege früher Gelehrsamkeit, Mythos in der Moderne*. 2. Internationales Colloquium der Deutschen Orient-Gesellschaft 24–26. März 1998 in Berlin Saarbrücken: Saarbrücker Druckerei und Verlag. pp. 323–42.

——— (ed.) 2013. *The Cyrus Cylinder: The King of Persia's Proclamation from Ancient Babylon*. London: I.B.Tauris.

———. and M. J. Seymour in prep. 'A note on Rembrandt's *Mene Mene Tekel Upharsin*.' Publication TBC.

Finkelstein, I. and N. A. Silberman 2002. *The Bible Unearthed*. London and New York: Simon and Schuster.

Finley, M. I. 1975. *The Use and Abuse of History*. New York: The Viking Press.

Fisk, R. 2001. 'Their lagoons and reedbeds gone, the marsh Arabs have no refuge.' *The Independent* (19 May): News 3.

Foster, K. P. 2004. 'The Hanging Gardens of Nineveh.' *Iraq* 66: 207–20.

Foster, B. R. (ed.) 2005. *Before the Muses: An Anthology of Akkadian Literature*. Bethesda, MD: CDL Press.

Frame, G. 1992. *Babylonia 689–627 BC: A Political History*. Leiden: Nederlands Historisch-Archaeologisch Instituut te Istanbul.

Fredricksmeyer, E. 2000. 'Alexander the Great and the kingship of Asia.' In A. B. Bosworth and E. J. Baynham (eds), *Alexander the Great in Fact and Fiction*. Oxford: Oxford University Press. pp. 136–66.

Freedman, D. N., G. A. Herion, D. F. Graf, J. D. Pleins and A. B. Beck (eds) 1992. *The Anchor Bible Dictionary*. 6 vols. New York: Doubleday.

Freedman, P. and G. M. Spiegel 1998. 'Medievalisms old and new: the rediscovery of alterity in North American Medieval studies.' *The American Historical Review* 103 (3): 677–704.

Frye, N. 1951. 'Blake's use of the archetype.' In A. S. Downer (ed.), *English Institute Essays.* New York: Columbia University Press. pp. 170–96.

Gadd, C. J. 1936. *The Stones of Assyria: The Surviving Remains of Assyrian Sculpture, their Recovery and their Original Positions.* London: Chatto and Windus.

———. 1958. 'The Harran Inscriptions of Nabonidus.' *Anatolian Studies* 8: 35–92.

Gallagher, B. 1982. 'Racist ideology and black abnormality in *The Birth of a Nation.' Phylon* 43 (1): 68–76.

Gazin-Schwartz, A. and C. Holtorf (eds) 1999. *Archaeology and Folklore.* London and New York: Routledge.

Geller, M. J. 2004. 'West meets East: early Greek and Babylonian diagnosis.' In H. F. J. Horstmanshoff and M. Stol (eds), *Magic and Rationality in Ancient Near Eastern and Graeco-Roman Medicine.* Leiden: Brill. pp. 11–61.

George, A. R. 1992. *Babylonian Topographical Texts.* Orientalia Lovaniensia Analecta 40. Leuven: Peeters.

———. 2003a. *The Epic of Gilgamesh: the Babylonian Epic Poem and Other Texts in Akkadian and Sumerian.* London: Penguin.

———. 2003b. *The Babylonian Gilgamesh Epic: Introduction, Critical Edition and Cuneiform Texts.* Oxford: Oxford University Press.

———. 2005–6. 'The Tower of Babel: archaeology, history and cuneiform texts.' *Archiv für Orientforschung* 51: 75–95.

George, D. Y. 2008. 'The looting of the Iraq Museum.' In P. G. Stone and J. Farchakh Bajjaly (eds), *The Destruction of Cultural Heritage in Iraq.* Woodbridge: Boydell Press. pp. 97–107.

Gérard, A.-M. 1989. *Dictionnaire de la Bible.* Paris: R. Laffont.

Gibson, W. S. 1989. *Mirror of the Earth: The World Landscape in Sixteenth-Century Flemish Painting.* Princeton: Princeton University Press.

Gilmore, J. 1887. 'The origins of the Semiramis legend.' *The English Historical Review* 2 (8): 729–34.

———. (ed.) 1888. *The Fragments of the Persika of Ktesias.* London: Macmillan and Co.

Ginzburg, C. 1989. *Clues, Myths and the Historical Method.* Baltimore: Johns Hopkins University Press.

Glassner, J. J. 2004. *Mesopotamian Chronicles.* Writings from the Ancient World 19. Atlanta: Society of Biblical Literature.

Goetz, H. 1938. 'Persians and Persian costume in the Dutch painting of the seventeenth century.' *The Art Bulletin* 20 (3): 280–90.

Goldsmith, S. 1993. *Unbuilding Jerusalem: Apocalypse and Romantic Representation.* Ithaca: Cornell University Press.

Gosden, C. 2001. 'Postcolonial archaeology: issues of culture, identity, and knowledge.' In I. Hodder (ed.), *Archaeological Theory Today.* Cambridge: Polity Press. pp. 241–61.

Grafton, A. 2004. 'Kircher's chronology.' In P. Findlen (ed.), *Athanasius Kircher: The Last Man Who Knew Everything.* London and New York: Routledge. pp. 171–87.

Grant, M. 1970. *The Ancient Historians.* London: Weidenfeld and Nicolson.

Grayson, A. K. 1975. *Assyrian and Babylonian Chronicles.* Texts from Cuneiform Sources 5. Locust Valley, NY.

————. 1982. 'Assyria: Ashur-dan II to Ashur-nirari V (934–745 BC).' In J. Boardman, I. E. S. Edwards, N. G. L. Hammond and E. Sollberger (eds), *The Cambridge Ancient History* (2nd edn). Cambridge: Cambridge University Press. Vol. 3, pt. 1, pp. 238–81.

————. 1987. *Assyrian Rulers of the Third and Second Millennium BC (to 1115 BC).* Royal Inscriptions of Mesopotamia, Assyrian Periods (RIMA) I. Toronto: University of Toronto Press.

————. 1991. 'Assyria: Sennacherib and Esarhaddon.' In J. Boardman, I. E. S. Edwards, N. G. L. Hammond, E. Sollberger and C. B. F. Walker (eds), *The Cambridge Ancient History* (2nd edn). Cambridge: Cambridge University Press. Vol. 3, pt. 2, pp. 103–41.

————. 1995. 'Assyrian rule of conquered territory in ancient Western Asia.' In J. M. Sasson (ed.), *Civilisations of the Ancient Near East.* 4 vols. New York: Charles Scribner's Sons. pp. 959–68.

Gropp, G. 1998. 'The development of a Near Eastern culture during the Persian Empire.' In G. Trompf, M. Honari and H. Abramian (eds), *Mehregan in Sydney. Proceedings of the Seminar in Persian Studies during the Mehregan Persian Cultural Festival, Sydney, Australia, 28 October–6 November 1994.* Sydney Studies in Religion 1. Sydney: School of Studies in Religion, University of Sydney, with the Persian Cultural Foundation of Australia. pp. 17–24.

Grossman, F. 1955. *Bruegel, the Paintings: Complete Edition.* London: Phaidon Press.

Grotefend, G. 1824. 'Über die Erklärung der Keilschriften, und besonders der Inschriften von Persepolis.' In A. H. L. Heeren, *Ideen über die Politik, den Verkehr und den Handel der vornehmsten Völker der alten Welt.* 2 vols. Göttingen: Vandenhoek und Ruprecht. Vol. 1, pp. 325–400.

Guinan, A. 2002. 'A severed head laughed: stories of divinatory interpretation.' In L. Ciraolo and J. Seidel (eds), *Magic and Divination in the Ancient World.* Ancient Magic and Divination 2. Groningen: Styx. pp. 7–40.

Hagstrum, J. H. 1964. *William Blake: Poet and Painter.* Chicago: University of Chicago Press.

Handler, R. 2003. 'Cultural property and culture theory.' *Journal of Social Archaeology* 3 (3): 353–65.

Hankins, J. E. 1945. 'Spenser and the Revelation of St. John.' *PMLA* 60 (2): 364–81.

Hanson, B. 1972. 'D. W. Griffith: some sources.' *Art Bulletin* 54 (4): 493–515.

Harper, R. F. 1892–1916. *Assyrian and Babylonian Letters Belonging to the Kouyunjik Collections of the British Museum.* 14 vols. Chicago: University of Chicago Press.

Haskell, F. 1993. *History and its Images: Art and the Interpretation of the Past.* London: Yale University Press.

Hassan, H. A. 1999. *The Iraqi Invasion of Kuwait: Religion, Identity and Otherness in the Analysis of War and Conflict.* London: Pluto Press.

Hauser, S. R. 2001. 'Not out of Babylon? The development of ancient Near Eastern studies in Germany and its current significance.' In T. Abusch, P.-A. Beaulieu, J. Huehnergard, P. Machinist and P. Steinkeller (eds), *Proceedings of the XLVe Rencontre Assyriologique Internationale, Part I: Harvard University: Historiography in the Cuneiform World.* Bethesda, Maryland: CDL Press. pp. 211–38.

Heilmann, R. 2004. *Paradigma Babylon: Rezeption und Visualisierung des Alten Orients im Spielfilm*. Doctoral dissertation, Mainz.

Henderson, G. 1985. 'The manuscript model of the Angers "apocalypse" tapestries.' *The Burlington Magazine* 127: 208–19.

Herrera, R. A. 2001. *Reasons for Our Rhymes: An Inquiry into the Philosophy of History*. Grand Rapids: William B. Eerdmans.

Hill, W. 2003. 'Isaiah, Book of.' In B. L. Marthaler, G. F. LaNave, J. Y. Tan, R. E. McCarron and D. J. Obermeyer (eds), *New Catholic Encyclopedia* (2nd edn). 15 vols. Detroit: Gale. Vol. 7, pp. 594–99.

Hillel, D. 1994. *Rivers of Eden: The Struggle for Water and the Quest for Peace in the Middle East*. Oxford: Oxford University Press.

Hilprecht, H. V. 1904. *The Excavations in Assyria and Babylonia*. Philadelphia: Department of Archaeology of the University of Pennsylvania.

Hingley, R. 2000. *Roman Officers and English Gentlemen: The Imperial Origins of Roman Archaeology*. London and New York: Routledge.

Hobsbawm, E. J. 1987. *The Age of Empire, 1875–1914*. London: Weidenfeld and Nicolson.

———. 1994. *Age of Extremes: The Short Twentieth Century, 1914–91*. London: Michael Joseph.

Hoock, H. 2007. 'The British state and the Anglo–French wars over antiquities, 1798–1858.' *The Historical Journal* 50 (1): 49–72.

———. 2010. *Empires of the Imagination: Politics, War and the Arts in the British World, 1750–1850*. London: Profile.

Hudson, K. 1981. *A Social History of Archaeology: The British Experience*. London: MacMillan.

Hunger, H. 1968. *Babylonische und assyrische Kolophone*. Alter Orient und Altes Testament 2. Kevelaer and Neukirchen-Vluyn: Butzon und Bercker and Neukirchener Verlag.

al-Husainy, A. and R. J. Matthews 2008. 'Archaeological heritage of Iraq in historical perspective.' *Public Archaeology* 7 (2): 91–100.

Huxley, A. 1955 (1932). *Brave New World*. London: Penguin.

Invernizzi, A. 2000. 'Discovering Babylon with Pietro Della Valle.' In P. Matthiae, A. Enea, L. Peyronel and F. Pinnock (eds), *Proceedings of the First International Congress on the Archaeology of the Ancient Near East*. Rome: Universita degli Studi di Roma. pp. 643–49.

———. (ed.) 2001. *Pietro della Valle, In viaggio per l'Oriente: le mummie, Babilonia, Persepoli*. Alessandria: Edizioni dell' Orso.

Irwin, R. 2006. *For Lust of Knowing*. London: Allen Lane.

Ives, E. 1773. *A Voyage from England to India, in the Year 1754, and an Historical Narrative of the Operations of the Squadron and Army in India, Under the Command of Vice-Admiral Watson and Colonel Clive, in the Years 1755, 1756, 1757. Also a Journey from Persia to England by an Unusual Route. With an Appendix, Containing an Account of the Diseases Prevalent in Admiral Watson's Squadron, etc.* London.

Jameson, J. H. Jr., J. E. Ehrenhard and C. A. Finn (eds) 2003. *Ancient Muses: Archaeology and the Arts*. Tuscaloosa: University of Alabama Press.

Janssen, C. 1995. 'Bābil, the City of Witchcraft and Wine. The Name and Fame of Babylon in Medieval Arabic Geographical Texts.' *Mesopotamian History and Environment* Series 2, Memoirs 2. Ghent: University of Ghent.

Jasanoff, M. 2005. *Edge of Empire: Lives, Culture, and Conquest in the East, 1750–1850*. New York: Alfred A. Knopf.

Jenkins, I. 1992. *Archaeologists and Aesthetes in the Sculpture Galleries of the British Museum, 1800–1939*. London: British Museum Press.

Johanning, K. 1988. *Der Babel-Bibel-Streit. Eine forschungsgeschichtlicher Studie*. Frankfurt am Main: Lang.

John, A. V. 2004. 'Schreiber, Lady Charlotte Elizabeth.' *Oxford Dictionary of National Biography* (online edition). Oxford: Oxford University Press. [http://www.oxforddnb.com/view/article/24,832, accessed 21 Jan 2010]

Joll, J. 1990. *Europe Since 1870: An International History* (4th edn). London: Penguin.

Joyce, R. A. 2002. *The Languages of Archaeology: Dialogue, Narrative and Writing*. Oxford: Blackwell.

Jullien, C. and F. Jullien 1995. *La Bible en Exil*. Civilisations du Proche-Orient Serie III, Religions et Culture 1. Neuchâtel and Paris: Recherches et Publications.

Kaufman, P. I. 1995. 'Redeeming politics: Augustine's cities of God.' In D. F. Donnelly (ed.), *The City of God: A Collection of Critical Essays*. New York: Peter Lang. pp. 75–92.

Kavaler, E. M. 1999. *Pieter Bruegel: Parables of Order and Enterprise*. Cambridge Studies in Netherlandish Culture. Cambridge: Cambridge University Press.

Keck, L. E. and G. M. Tucker 1992. 'Literary forms of the Bible.' In M. J. Suggs, K. D. Sakenfeld and J. R. Mueller (eds), *The Oxford Study Bible: Revised English Bible with the Apocrypha*. Oxford: Oxford University Press. pp. 12–31.

Kelly, J. N. D. 1975. *Jerome: His Life, Writings, and Controversies*. London: Duckworth.

Kemball, A. 1864. *Report from Babylon*. Unpublished. British Museum Original Papers, vol. 79, no. 4448.

Kendall, C. B. 1978. 'Bede's *Historia Ecclesiastica*: the rhetoric of faith.' In J. J. Murphy (ed.), *Medieval Eloquence: Studies in the Theory and Practice of Medieval Rhetoric*. Berkeley: University of California Press. pp. 145–72.

Keppel, G. 1827. *Personal Narrative of a Journey from India to England*. London: Henry Colburn.

Ker Porter, R. 1821–2. *Travels in Georgia, Persia, Armenia, Ancient Babylonia, &c. &c. During the Years 1817, 1818, 1819, and 1820*. 2 vols. London: Longman, Hurst, Rees, Orme and Brown.

al-Khalil, S. (Kanan Makiya) 1991. *The Monument: Art, Vulgarity and Responsibility in Iraq*. London: André Deutsch.

King, L. W. 1919. *A History of Babylon from the Foundation of the Monarchy to the Persian Conquest*. London: Chatto and Windus.

Kinnier Wilson, J. V. and I. L. Finkel 2007. 'On *būšānu* and *dī'u*, or why Nabonidus went to Teima.' *Le Journal des Médecines* 9: 17–22.

Kirby, J. T. 1978. 'D. W. Griffith's Racial Portraiture.' *Phylon* 39 (2): 118–27.

Kircher, A. 1679. *Turris Babel, Sive Archontologia Qua Primo Priscorum post diluvium hominum vita, mores rerumque gestarum magnitudo, Secundo Turris fabrica civitatumque exstructio, confusio linguarum, et inde gentium transmigrationis, cum principalium inde enatorum idiomatum historia, multiplici eruditione describuntur et explicantur*. 3 vols. Amsterdam: Janssonis-Wassbergiana.

Klein, N. 2004. 'Baghdad year zero: pillaging Iraq in pursuit of a Neocon utopia.' *Harper's Magazine* (September): 43–53.

Klemm, G. F. 1843–52. *Allgemeine Cultur-Geschichte der Menschheit*. 10 vols. Leipzig: Teubner.

Klengel-Brandt, E. 1982. *Der Turm von Babylon. Legende und Geschichte eines Bauwerkes*. Leipzig: Koehler and Amelang.

Klengel-Brandt, E. 1995. 'The history of the excavations at Ashur and of the Vorderasiatisches Museum.' In P. O. Harper, E. Klengel-Brandt, J. Aruz and K. Benzel (eds), *Assyrian Origins: Discoveries at Ashur on the Tigris: Antiquities in the Vorderasiatisches Museum, Berlin*. New York: Metropolitan Museum of Art. pp. 17–20.

Koldewey, R. 1911. *Die Tempel von Babylon und Borsippa*. Wissenschaftliche Veröffentlichung der deutschen Orient-Gesellschaft 15. Leipzig: J. C. Hinrichs.

———. 1913. *Das wieder erstehende Babylon*. Leipzig: J. C. Hinrichs.

———. 1914. *The Excavations at Babylon*. London: MacMillan and Co., Limited.

———. 1918. *Das Ischtar-Tor in Babylon*. Wissenschaftliche Veröffentlichung der deutschen Orient-Gesellschaft 32. Leipzig: J. C. Hinrichs.

———. 1931–2. *Die Königsburgen von Babylon*, ed. F. Wetzel. 2 vols. Wissenschaftliche Veröffentlichung der deutschen Orient-Gesellschaft 54, 59. Leipzig: J. C. Hinrichs.

Korte, B. 2000. *English Travel Writing from Pilgrimages to Postcolonial Explorations*. London: Macmillan.

Kossinna, G. 1912. *Die deutsche Vorgeschichte: eine hervorragend nationale Wissenschaft*. Würzburg: Kabitzsch.

Kramer, S. N. 1954. 'Ur-Nammu law code.' *Orientalia* 23: 40–51.

Kravitz, K. F. 2010. 'Tukulti-Ninurta I conquers Babylon: two versions.' In J. Stackert, B. N. Porter, and D. P. Wright (eds), *Gazing on the Deep: Ancient Near Eastern and Other Studies in Honor of Tzvi Abusch*. Bethesda, MD: CDL Press. pp. 121–9.

Kren, T. and S. McKendrick (eds) 2003. *Illuminating the Renaissance: The Triumph of Flemish Manuscript Painting in Europe*. Los Angeles and London: J. Paul Getty Museum and Royal Academy of Arts.

Kucklick, B. 1996. *Puritans in Babylon: The Ancient Near East and American Intellectual Life 1880–1930*. Princeton: Princeton University Press.

Kuhn, T. S. 1970. *The Structure of Scientific Revolutions* (2nd edn). Chicago: University of Chicago Press.

Kuhrt, A. 1990. 'Alexander and Babylon.' In H. Sancisi-Weerdenburg and J. W. Drijvers (eds), *Achaemenid History V: The Roots of the European Tradition*. Proceedings of the 1987 Groningen Achaemenid History Workshop. Leiden: Nederlands Instituut voor het Nabije Oosten. pp. 121–30.

———. 1995a. *The Ancient Near East, c. 3000–330 bc*. 2 vols. London and New York: Routledge.

———. 1995b. 'Ancient Mesopotamia in Classical Greek and Hellenistic thought.' In J. M. Sasson (ed.), *Civilisations of the Ancient Near East*. 4 vols. New York: Charles Scribner's Sons. pp. 55–65.

———. and S. Sherwin-White 1987. 'Xerxes' destruction of Babylonian Temples.' *Achaemenid History* 2: 69–78.

Kussl, R. 1991. *Papyrusfragmente griechischer Romane. Ausgewählte Untersuchungen*. Tübingen: Gunter Narr.

Laistner, M. L. W. 1940. 'Some reflections on Latin historical writing in the fifth century.' *Classical Philology* 35 (3): 241–58.

Lambert, W. G. 1965. 'Nebuchadnezzar King of Justice.' *Iraq* 27 (1): 1–11.
———. 1974. 'The home of the first Sealand dynasty.' *Journal of Cuneiform Studies* 26 (4): 208–10.
———. 1984. 'Studies in Marduk.' *Bulletin of the School of Oriental and African Studies* 47: 1–9.
———. 2011. 'Babylon: origins.' In E. Cancik-Kirschbaum, M. van Ess and J. Marzahn (eds), *Babylon. Wissenkultur in Orient und Okzident.* Topoi Berlin Studies of the Ancient World 1. Berlin: Walter De Gruyter. pp. 71–6.
———. 2013. *Babylonian Creation Myths.* Mesopotamian Civilizations 16. Winona Lake: Eisenbrauns.
———. and A. R. Millard 1969. *Atra-Ḫasīs: The Babylonian Story of the Flood.* Oxford: Clarendon Press.
Lammertse, F. 1994. 'Pieter Bruegel the Elder, *The Tower of Babel*.' In *Van Eyck to Bruegel, 1400–1550: Dutch and Flemish Painting in the Collection of the Museum Boymans-van Beuningen.* Rotterdam: Museum Boymans-van Beuningen. pp. 400–3.
Lancel, S. 2002. *Saint Augustine.* London: SCM Press.
Lane-Fox, R. J. 2004. *Alexander the Great.* London: Penguin.
Langdon, S. 1912. *Die neubabylonischen Königsinschriften.* VAB 4. Leipzig: J. C. Hinrichs.
Lapeyrère, I. 1656. *Preadamitaei, sive exercitatio super versibus duodecimo, decimotertio et decimoquarto, capitiis quinti epistolae D. Pauli ad Romanos.* Amsterdam: Elsevier.
Larsen, M. T. 1989. 'Orientalism and the ancient Near East.' In M. Harbsmeier and M. T. Larsen (eds), *The Humanities Between Art and Science: Intellectual Developments 1880–1914.* Copenhagen: Akademisk Forlag. pp. 181–202.
———. 1995. 'The "Babel/Bible" controversy and its aftermath.' In J. M. Sasson (ed.), *Civilisations of the Ancient Near East.* 4 vols. New York: Charles Scribner's Sons. pp. 95–106.
———. 1996. *The Conquest of Assyria: Excavations in an Antique Land, 1840–1860.* London and New York: Routledge.
Larsen, T. 2013. 'Nineveh.' In D. Gange and M. Ledger-Lomas (eds), *Cities of God: Archaeology and the Bible in Nineteenth-Century Britain.* Cambridge: Cambridge University Press. pp. 111–35.
Latham, R. 1958. *The Travels of Marco Polo.* London: Penguin.
Layard, A. H. 1849a. *Nineveh and its Remains: With an Account of a Visit to the Chaldæan Christians of the Kurdistan, and the Yezidis, or Devil-Worshippers; and an Inquiry into the Manners and Arts of the Ancient Assyrians.* 2 vols. London: John Murray.
———. 1849b. *The Monuments of Nineveh.* London: John Murray.
———. 1852. *A Popular Account of the Discoveries at Nineveh.* London: John Murray.
———. 1853a. *A Second Series of the Monuments of Nineveh.* London: John Murray.
———. 1853b. *Discoveries in the Ruins of Nineveh and Babylon; with Travels in Armenia, Kurdistan and the Desert: Being the Result of a Second Expedition Undertaken for the Trustees of the British Museum.* London: John Murray.
Lehmann, R. G. 1994. *Friedrich Delitzsch und der Babel-Bibel-Streit.* Orbis Biblicus et Orientalis 133. Göttingen: Vandenhoeck und Ruprecht.
———. 1999. 'Der Babel-Bibel-Streit. Ein kulturpolitisches Wetterleuchten.' In J. Renger (ed.), *Babylon: Focus mesopotamischer Geschichte, Wiege früher Gelehrsamkeit, Mythos in der Moderne. 2. Internationales Coloquium der Deutschen Orient-Gesellschaft*

24–26 März 1998 in Berlin. Saarbrücken: Saarbrücker Druckerei und Verlag. pp. 502–21.

Le Strange, G. 1905. *The Lands of the Eastern Caliphate: Mesopotamia, Persia, and Central Asia from the Moslem Conquest to the Time of Timur.* Cambridge: Cambridge University Press.

Levi, D. 1944. 'The novel of Ninus and Semiramis.' *Proceedings of the American Philosophical Society* 87 (5): 420–8.

Levin, Y. 2002. 'Nimrod the Mighty, King of Kish, King of Sumer and Akkad.' *Vetus Testamentum* 52 (3): 350–66.

Levine, P. 1967. *Notes to Saint Augustine: The City of God Against the Pagans, Books XII–XV.* London: William Heinemann.

Lewis, B. 1982. *The Muslim Discovery of Europe.* London: Weidenfeld and Nicholson.

Lewis, C. S. 1964. *The Discarded Image: An Introduction to Medieval and Renaissance Literature.* Cambridge: Cambridge University Press.

Lewy, H. 1952. 'Nitokris-Naqî'a.' *Journal of Near Eastern Studies* 11 (4): 264–86.

Llewellyn-Jones, L. and J. Robson (eds) 2010. *Ctesias' History of Persia: Tales of the Orient.* London and New York: Routledge.

Lloyd, S. 1980. *Foundations in the Dust: The Story of Mesopotamian Exploration* (2nd edn). London: Thames and Hudson.

Lloyd-Jones, H. 1982. *Blood for the Ghosts: Classical Influences in the Nineteenth and Twentieth Centuries.* London: Duckworth.

Loomba, A. 1998. *Colonialism/Postcolonialism.* London and New York: Routledge.

Lowenthal, D. 1985. *The Past is a Foreign Country.* Cambridge: Cambridge University Press.

Lucas, E. C. 2000. 'Daniel: resolving the enigma.' *Vetus Testamentum* 50 (1): 66–80.

Luckenbill, D. D. 1924. *The Annals of Sennacherib.* Oriental Institute Publications 2. Chicago: University of Chicago Press.

Lundquist, J. M. 1995. 'Babylon in European thought.' In J. M. Sasson (ed.), *Civilisations of the Ancient Near East.* 4 vols. New York: Charles Scribner's Sons. pp. 67–80.

Macaulay, R. 1953. *Pleasure of Ruins.* London: Weidenfeld and Nicolson.

MacGinnis, J. 1986. 'Herodotus' description of Babylon.' *Bulletin of the Institute of Classical Studies* 33 (1): 67–86.

Magdalena nom de Déu, J. R. 2006. 'Benjamin de Tudela and his *Libro de Viajes* (12th Century).' In J. Ma. Córdoba and C. Perez-Díe (eds), *The Spanish Near Eastern Adventure (1166–2006): Travellers, Museums and Scholars in the History of the Rediscovering of the Ancient Near East.* Madrid: Ministerio de Cultura de España. pp. 22–6.

Mahon, D. 1949. 'Guercino's paintings of Semiramis.' *The Art Bulletin* 31 (3): 217–23.

Makiya, K. 1998. *Republic of Fear: The Politics of Modern Iraq* (2nd edn). Berkeley: University of California Press.

Malley, S. 2012. *From Archaeology to Spectacle in Victorian Britain: The Case of Assyria, 1845–1854.* Farnham: Ashgate.

Mallowan, M. E. L. 1977. *Mallowan's Memoirs.* London: Collins.

Mander, C. van 1604. *Het Schilder-Boek.* Haarlem.

Mansbach, S. A. 1982. 'Pieter Bruegel's Towers of Babel.' *Zeitschrift für Kunstgeschichte* 45 (1): 43–56.

Manwaring, G., A. Sherley et al. 1825. *The Three Brothers; or, the Travels and Adventures of Sir Anthony, Sir Robert and Sir Thomas Sherley, in Persia, Russia, Turkey, Spain etc. With Portraits*. London: Hurst, Robinson and Co.

Marchand, S. L. 1994. 'The rhetoric of artifacts and the decline of classical humanism: the case of Josef Strzygowski.' *History and Theory* 33 (4): 106–30.

———. 1996. *Down from Olympus: Archaeology and Philhellenism in Germany, 1750–1970*. Princeton: Princeton University Press.

———. 2009. *German Orientalism in the Age of Empire: Religion, Race and Scholarship*. Cambridge: Cambridge University Press.

Marincola J. (ed.) 2003. *Herodotus: The Histories*. London: Penguin.

Matthews, K. 1993. *The Gulf Conflict and International Relations*. London and New York: Routledge.

Matthews, R. J. 1997. 'History of the field: archaeology in Mesopotamia.' In E. M. Meyers (ed.), *The Oxford Encyclopaedia of Archaeology in the Near East*. 4 vols. Oxford: Oxford University Press. Vol. 3, pp. 56–60.

———. 2003a. *The Archaeology of Mesopotamia: Theories and Approaches*. London and New York: Routledge.

———. 2003b. 'Year zero for the archaeology of Iraq.' *Papers from the Institute of Archaeology* 14: 1–23.

Matthews, T. D. 2001. 'Friday review: "Move those 10,000 horses a trifle to the right."' *The Guardian* (January 5): Friday p. 8.

McCall, H. 1998. 'Rediscovery and Aftermath.' In S. Dalley (ed.), *The Legacy of Mesopotamia*. Oxford: Oxford University Press. pp. 183–213.

McClintock, A. 1995. *Imperial Leather: Race, Gender and Sexuality in the Colonial Context*. London and New York: Routledge.

McGann, J. J. (ed.) 1980–93. *Lord Byron: The Complete Poetical Works*. 7 vols. Oxford: Clarendon Press.

McGinn, B. 1998. *Visions of the End: Apocalyptic Traditions in the Middle Ages* (2nd edn). New York: Columbia University Press.

McKechnie, P. 1995. 'Diodorus Siculus and Hephaestion's Pyre.' *Classical Quarterly* 45: 418–32.

McMeekin, S. 2010. *The Berlin-Baghdad Express: The Ottoman Empire and Germany's Bid for World Power*. Cambridge, MA: Harvard University Press.

McNeal, R. A. 1988. 'The Brides of Babylon: Herodotus 1.196.' *Historia: Zeitschrift für Alte Geschichte* 37 (1): 54–71.

Mellor, R. 1981. 'Rescued from a perilous nest: D. W. Griffith's escape from theatre into film.' *Cinema Journal* 21 (1): 2–30.

———. 1999. *The Roman Historians*. London and New York: Routledge.

Micale, M. G. and D. Nadali 2008. '"Layer by layer…" of digging and drawing: the genealogy of an idea.' In R. D. Biggs, J. Myers and M. T. Roth (eds), *Proceedings of the 51st Rencontre Assyriologique Internationale, Held at the Oriental Institute of the University of Chicago, July 18–22, 2005*. Studies in Ancient Oriental Civilization 62. Chicago: The Oriental Institute of the University of Chicago. pp. 405–14.

Michalski, S. 2003. 'Venus as Semiramis: a new interpretation of the central figure of Botticelli's "Primavera".' *Artibus et Historiae* 24 (48): 213-22.

Mitchell, T. C. 2008. 'Two British East India Company Residents in Baghdad in the Nineteenth Century.' *Zeitschrift für Orient-Archäologie* 1: 376–95.

Mommsen, T. E. 1995. 'St. Augustine and the Christian idea of progress: the background to *The City of God*.' In D. F. Donnelly (ed.), *The City of God: A Collection of Critical Essays*. New York: Peter Lang. p. 353.

Mommsen, W. J. 1995. *Imperial Germany 1867–1918: Politics, Culture, and Society in an Authoritarian State*. London: Arnold.

Morgan, J. 2004. 'Myth, expectations and the divide between disciplines in the study of classical Greece.' In E. W. Sauer (ed.), *Archaeology and Ancient History: Breaking Down the Boundaries*. London and New York: Routledge. pp. 85–95.

Moser, S. 1992. 'The visual language of archaeology: a case study of the Neanderthals.' *Antiquity* 66: 831–44.

———. 1998. *Ancestral Images*. Stroud: Sutton.

———. 2001. 'Archaeological representation: the visual conventions for constructing knowledge about the past.' In I. Hodder (ed.), *Archaeological Theory Today*. Cambridge: Polity Press. pp. 262–83.

———. 2006. *Wondrous Curiosities: Ancient Egypt at the British Museum*. Chicago: Chicago University Press.

Moussa, M. U. 2008. 'The damages sustained to the ancient city of Babylon as a consequence of the military presence of coalition forces in 2003.' In P. G. Stone and J. Farchakh Bajjaly (eds), *The Destruction of Cultural Heritage in Iraq*. Woodbridge: Boydell Press. pp. 143–50.

Muel, F. 1996. *Tenture de l'Apocalypse d'Angers, l'Envers et l'Endroit*. Nantes: Inventaire général.

Murphy, E. 1989. *The Antiquities of Asia: A Translation with Notes of Book II of the Library of History of Diodorus Siculus*. New Brunswick: Transaction Publishers.

Myers, P. V. N. 1875. *Remains of Lost Empires: Sketches of the Ruins of Palmyra, Nineveh, Babylon, and Persepolis, with some Notes on India and the Cashmerian Himalayas*. London: Sampson Low, Marston, Low, and Searle.

Na'aman, N. 1991. 'Chonology and history in the late Assyrian empire.' *Zeitschrift für Assyriologie* 81: 243–67.

Nadali, D. 2011. 'L'archeologia di Nabucco: l'Oriente antico in scena.' *Studi Verdiani* 22: 73–87.

Nadler, S. 2003. *Rembrandt's Jews*. Chicago and London: University of Chicago Press.

Nagel, W. 1976. 'Die Deutsche Orient-Gesellschaft: Rückblick.' *Mitteilungen der Deutschen Orient-Gesellschaft zu Berlin* 108: 53–71.

Nelson, S. M. 2003. 'RKLOG: archaeologists as fiction writers.' In J. H. Jameson Jr., J. E. Ehrenhard and C. A. Finn (eds), *Ancient Muses: Archaeology and the Arts*. Tuscaloosa: University of Alabama Press. pp. 162–8.

Niebuhr, C. 1774–78. *Reisebeschreibung nach Arabien und andern umliegenden Ländern*. 2 vols. Copenhagen: Nicholas Möller.

Niewyk, D. L. 1980. *The Jews in Weimar Germany*. Manchester: Manchester University Press.

Nochlin, L. 1989. *The Politics of Vision: Essays on Nineteenth-Century Art and Society*. London: Harper & Row.

Nougayrol, J. and A. Parrot 1956. 'Asarhaddon et Naqi'a sur un bronze du Louvre.' *Syria* 33: 147–60.

Novotny, J. and C. E. Watanabe 2008. 'After the Fall of Babylon: a new look at the presentation scene on Assurbanipal relief BM ME 124945-6.' *Iraq* 70: 105–25.

Oates, J. 1965. 'Assyrian Chronology, 631–612 BC.' *Iraq* 27 (2): 135–59.

————. 1986. *Babylon*. London: Thames and Hudson.

————, A. McMahon, P. Karsgaard, S. al-Quntar and J. Ur 2007. 'Early Mesopotamian Urbanism: A New View from the North.' *Antiquity* 81: 585–600.

O'Connell, K. G. 2003. 'Tower of Babel.' In B. L. Marthaler, G. F. LaNave, J. Y. Tan, R. E. McCarron and D. J. Obermeyer (eds), *New Catholic Encyclopedia* (2nd edn). 15 vols. Detroit: Gale. Vol. 14, pp. 128–30.

Oelsner, J. 2012. 'Saosduchinus.' In *Brill's New Pauly*. Brill Online.

O'Keefe, P. J. and L. V. Prott 1984. *Law and the Cultural Heritage I: Discovery and Excavation*. Abingdon: Professional Books Limited.

Olivier, G. A. 1789–90. *Voyage dans l'Empire Othoman, L'Égypte et la Perse, Fait par ordre du Gouvernement, pendant les six premières années de la République*. Paris: Imprimeur-Libraire.

————. 1801. *Travels in the Ottoman Empire, Egypt and Persia, Undertaken by Order of the Government of France, During the First Six Years of the Republic, by G. A. Olivier*. London: Printed for T. N. Longman and O. Rees, Paternoster Row, and T. Cadell Jun. and W. Davies, the Strand.

Ooghe, B. 2007. 'The rediscovery of Babylonia: European travellers and the development of knowledge on lower Mesopotamia, sixteenth to early nineteenth centuary.' *Journal of the Royal Asiatic Society*, Series 3, 17 (3): 231–52.

Oppert, J. 1863. *Expédition Scientifique en Mésopotamie I: Relation du Voyage et Résultats de l'Expédition*. Paris: Imprimerie Impériale.

Orwell, G. 2000 (1949) *Nineteen Eighty-Four*. London: Penguin.

Otter, J. 1768. *Voyage en Turque et en Perse. Avec une Relation des Expéditions de Tahmas Kouli-Khan*. Paris: Chez les Frères Guerin.

Paley, S. 1976. *King of the World: Ashur-nasir-pal II of Assyria, 883–859 BC*. New York: Brooklyn Museum.

————. 1981–92. *Die Rekonstruktion der Reliefdarstellungen und ihrer Anordnung im Nordwestpalast von Kalḫu (Nimrūd)*. 3 vols. Mainz am Rhein: Philipp von Zabern.

Parapetti, R. 2008. 'Babylon 1978–2008, a chronicle of events in the ancient site.' *Mesopotamia* 43: 123–66, pls. II–VII.

Parpola, S. 1972. 'A Letter from Šamaš-šumu-ukīn to Esarhaddon.' *Iraq* 34: 21–34.

————. 1993. *Letters from Assyrian Scholars to the Kings Esarhaddon and Assurbanipal, Part II: Commentary and Appendices*. Alter Orient und Altes Testament 5/2. Neukirchen-Vluyn: Butzon and Bercker.

Parry, J. 2006. 'Layard, Sir Austen Henry, 1817–1894.' *Oxford Dictionary of National Biography* (online edition). Oxford: Oxford University Press. {http://www.oxforddnb.com/view/article/16,218, accessed 21 Jan 2010}

Parshall, P. 1999. 'The vision of apocalypse in the sixteenth and seventeenth centuries.' In F. Carey (ed.), *Apocalypse and the Shape of Things to Come*. London: British Museum Press. pp. 99–124.

Pearce, L. E. 1996. 'The number syllabary texts.' *Journal of the American Oriental Society* 116 (3): 453–74.

Pemberton, W., J. N. Postgate and R. F. Smyth 1988. 'Canals and bunds, ancient and modern.' *Bulletin of Sumerian Agriculture* 4: 207–21.

Penner, T. 1992. 'Socrates and the early dialogues.' In R. Kraut (ed.), *The Cambridge Companion to Plato*. Cambridge: Cambridge University Press. pp. 121–69.

Phillips, J. E. 2004. *The Past and the Public: Archaeology and the Periodical Press in Nineteenth Century Britain*. Unpublished Doctoral Thesis, University of Southampton.

Pierse, S. 2003. 'A sceptic witness: Voltaire's vision of historiography.' In E. Caldicott and A. Fuchs (eds), *Cultural Memory: Essays on European Literature and History.* Oxford: Peter Lang. pp. 69–84.

Podro, M. 1982. *The Critical Historians of Art.* New Haven: Yale University Press.

Pollock, S. 1999. *Ancient Mesopotamia: The Eden that Never Was.* Cambridge: Cambridge University Press.

———. 2003. 'The looting of the Iraq Museum: thoughts on archaeology in a time of crisis.' *Public Archaeology* 3 (2): 117–24.

———. 2005. 'Archaeology goes to war at the newsstand.' In S. Pollock and R. Bernbeck (eds), *Archaeologies of the Middle East: Critical Perspectives.* Oxford: Blackwell. pp. 78–96.

Popper, K. 1957. *The Poverty of Historicism.* London: Routledge and Kegan Paul.

Porter, V. 2008. *Iraq's Past Speaks to the Present* (exhibition guide). London: British Museum.

Postgate, J. N. 1994. *Early Mesopotamia: Society and Economy at the Dawn of History* (2nd edn). London and New York: Routledge.

Pratt, K. 1965. 'Rome as eternal.' *Journal of the History of Ideas* 26 (1): 25–44.

Price, D. W. 1999. *History Made, History Imagined: Contemporary Literature, Poiesis, and the Past.* Urbana: University of Illinois Press.

Pritchard, J. B. 1969. *Ancient Near Eastern Texts Relating to the Old Testament* (3rd edn). Princeton: Princeton University Press.

Pulzer, P. 1988 (1964). *The Rise of Political Anti-Semitism in Germany and Austria* (2nd edn). London: Peter Halban.

Rakowitz, R. N. 1997. 'Exodus from the Babylonian captivity: the Jews of modern Iraq.' *International Journal of Group Tensions* 27 (3): 177–91.

Rassam, H. 1881. 'Recent Assyrian and Babylonian research.' *Journal of the Transactions of the Victoria Institute* 14: 182–225.

———. 1894. *Babylonian Cities.* London: E. Stanford.

———. 1897. *Ashhur and the Land of Nimrod.* New York: Eaton and Mains.

Rauwolf, L. 1583. *Aigentliche beschreibung der Raiß / so er vor diser zeit gegen Aussgang inn die Morgenländer fürnemlich Syriam, Iudæam, Arabiam, Mesopotamiam, Babyloniam, Assyriam, Armeniam ιζ.* Lauingen: Georgen Willers.

Rawlinson, G. 1892. *A Memoir of Major-General Sir Henry Creswicke Rawlinson.* London: Longman, Greeen and Co.

Reade, J. E. 1970. 'The accession of Sinsharishkun.' *Journal of Cuneiform Studies* 23 (1): 1–9.

———. 1986a. 'Rassam's excavations at Borsippa and Kutha, 1879–82.' *Iraq* 48: 105–16, pls. XIII–XIX.

———. 1986b. 'Rassam's Babylonian collection: the excavations and archives.' Introduction to E. Leichty, *Catalogue of the Babylonian Tablets in the British Museum.* London: British Museum Publications. Vol. 6, pp. xii–xxxvi.

———. 1987. 'Reflections on Layard's archaeological career.' In F. M. Fales and B. J. Hickey (eds), *Austen Henry Layard tra l'Oriente e Venezia.* Rome: "L'Erma" di Bretschneider. pp. 47–53.

———. 1993. 'Hormuzd Rassam and his Discoveries.' *Iraq* 55: 39–62.

———. 1994. 'Les relations anglo-françaises en Assyrie.' In E. Fontan and N. Chevalier (eds), *De Khorsabad à Paris: La découverte des Assyriens.* Paris: Réunion des Musées Nationaux. pp. 116–35.

————. 1999. 'Early British Excavations at Babylon.' In J. Renger (ed.), *Babylon: Focus Mesopotamischer Geschichte, Wiege. Früher Gelehrsamkeit, Mythos in der Moderne*. Saarbrücken: Saarbrücker Druckerei und Verlag. pp. 47–65.

————. 2000. 'Alexander the Great and the Hanging Gardens of Babylon.' *Iraq* 62: 195–218.

Rebenich, S. 2002. *Jerome*. London and New York: Routledge.

Redfield, J. 2002. 'Herodotus the tourist.' In T. Harrison (ed.), *Greeks and Barbarians*. Edinburgh: Edinburgh University Press. pp. 24–49.

Rejwan, N. 1985. *The Jews of Iraq: 3000 Years of History and Culture*. London: Weidenfeld and Nicolson.

Renger, J. 1979. 'The city of Babylon during the Old Babylonian period.' *Sumer* 35 (1): 205–9.

————. 1990. 'Rivers, watercourses, old irrigation ditches and other matters concerning irrigation based on Old Babylonian sources (2000–1600 BC).' *Bulletin of Sumerian Agriculture* 5: 31–46.

————. 1999a. 'Babylon: Focus mesopotamischer Geschichte, Wiege früher Gelehrsamkeit, Mythos in der Moderne.' In J. Renger (ed.), *Babylon: Focus mesopotamischer Geschichte, Wiege früher Gelehrsamkeit, Mythos in der Moderne*. Saarbrücken: Saarbrücker Druckerei und Verlag. pp. 1–32.

Rennel, J. 1800. *The Geographical System of Herodotus Examined and Explained by a Comparison with Those of Other Ancient Authors, and with Modern Geography. In the Course of the Work are Introduced, Dissertations on the Itinerary State of the Greeks, the Expedition of Darius Hystaspes to Scythia, the Position of Ancient Babylon, and Other Subjects of History and Geography*. London: G. and W. Nicol.

Rich, C. J. 1813. 'Memoir on the ruins of Babylon.' *Mines de l'Orient / Fundgruben des Orients* 3: 129–62, 197–200.

————. 1815. *Memoir on the Ruins of Babylon*. London: Longman, Hurst, Rees, Orme and Brown and J. Murray.

————. 1818. *Second Memoir on Babylon: Containing an Inquiry into the Correspondence Between the Ancient Description of Babylon and the Remains Still Visible on the Site*. London: Longman, Hurst, Rees, Orme and Brown.

————. 1839. *Narrative of a Journey to the Site of Babylon. Edited by his Widow*. London: Duncan and Malcolm.

Richardson, S. 2007. 'The world of Babylonian countrysides.' In G. Leick (ed.), *The Babylonian World*. London and New York: Routledge. pp. 13–38.

Ricoeur, P. 1965. *History and Truth*. Evanston: Northwestern University Press.

Rives, J. B. (ed.) 1999. *Tacitus: Germania. Translated with Introduction and Commentary*. Oxford: Clarendon Press.

Roberts, J. M. 1989. *Europe, 1880–1945* (2nd edn). London: Longman.

Rogers, R. W. 1900. *A History of Babylonia and Assyria*. 2 vols. Freeport, NY: Books for Libraries Press.

Rogin, M. 1985. '"The sword became a flashing vision": D. W. Griffith's *The Birth of a Nation*.' *Representations* 9: 150–95.

Röllig, W. 1969. 'Nitokris von Babylon.' In R. Stiehl and M. E. Stier (eds), *Beitrage zur Alten Geschichte und deren Nachleben. Festschrift für Franz Altheim*. 2 vols. Berlin: Walter de Gruyter.

Roth, M. T. 1997. *Law Collections from Mesopotamia and Asia Minor*. Society of Biblical Literature Writings from the Ancient World Series 6 (2nd edn). Atlanta: Scholars Press.

Rothfield, L. 2009. *The Rape of Mesopotamia: Behind the Looting of the Iraq Museum*. Chicago and London: Chicago University Press.

Rothman, M. S. (ed.) 2001. *Uruk Mesopotamia and its Neighbours: Cross-Cultural Interactions in the Era of State Formation*. Santa Fe: School of American Research Press.

Roux, G. 1980. *Ancient Iraq* (2nd edn). London: Penguin.

———. 2001. 'Semiramis: The Builder of Babylon.' In J. Bottéro (ed.), *Everyday Life in Ancient Mesopotamia*. Edinburgh: Edinburgh University Press. pp. 141–61.

Rudoe, J. 1987. 'Lady Layard's jewellery and the "Assyrian style" in nineteenth century jewellery design.' In F. M. Fales and B. J. Hickey (eds), *Austen Henry Layard tra l'Oriente e Venezia*. Rome: "L'Erma" di Bretschneider. pp. 213–26.

———. 1994a. *Decorative Arts 1850–1950: A catalogue of the British Museum collection* (2nd edn). London: British Museum Press.

———. 1994b. 'Henry Layard et les arts décoratifs du style "Ninive" en Angleterre,' in E. Fontan and N. Chevalier (eds), *De Khorsabad à Paris, La découverte des Assyriens*. Paris 1994: Louvre, Département des Antiquités orientales; Réunion des Musées Nationaux. pp. 260–73.

Russell, J. M. 1997. *From Nineveh to New York: The Strange Story of the Assyrian Reliefs in the Metropolitan Museum and the Hidden Masterpiece at Canford School*. New Haven and London: Yale University Press.

Sachau, C. E. (ed.) 1879. *The Chronology of Ancient Nations: An English Version of the Arabic Text of the Athâr-ul-Bâkiya of Albîrûnî, or Vestiges of the Past Collected and Reduced to Writing by the Author in A. H. 390–1, A. D. 1000*. London: Oriental Translations Fund.

———. 1900. *Am Euphrat und Tigris. Reisenotizen aus dem winter 1897–1898*. Leipzig: J. C. Hinrichs.

Sachs, A. J. and H. Hunger 1988. *Astronomical Diaries and Related Texts from Babylonia Volume I: Diaries from 652 BC to 262 BC*. Vienna: Österreichische Akademie der Wissenschaften.

Sack, R. H. 1990. 'Review of A. Kuhrt and S. Sherwin-White (eds.), *Hellenism in the East: The Interaction of Greek and non-Greek Civilisations from Syria to Central Asia after Alexander.' Journal of the American Oriental Society* 110 (1): 117–8.

———. 1991. *Images of Nebuchadnezzar: The Emergence of a Legend*. London: Associated University Presses.

Said, E. W. 1978. *Orientalism*. London: Penguin.

———. 1993. *Culture and Imperialism*. London: Chatto and Windus.

Salje, B. 2008. 'Robert Koldewey und das Vorderasiatische Museum Berlin.' In Wartke, R.-B. (ed.), *Auf dem Weg nach Babylon. Robert Koldewey—Ein Archäologenleben*. Berlin and Mainz: Staatliche Museen zu Berlin—Stiftung Preußischer Kulturbesitz and Philipp von Zabern.

Savishinsky, N. J. 1994. 'Rastafari in the Promised Land: the spread of a Jamaican socioreligious movement among the youth of West Africa.' *African Studies Review* 37 (3): 19–50.

Sayce, A. H. 1883. *The Ancient Empires of the East: Herodotus I–III.* London: MacMillan and Co.

Schaudig, H. 2001. *Die Inschriften Nabonids von Babylon und Kyros' des Großen samt den in ihrem Umfeld entstandenen Tendenzschriften. Textausgabe und Grammatik.* Alter Orient und Altes Testament 256: Münster: Ugarit Verlag.

Schiffer, R. 2001. 'Agatha's Arabs: Agatha Christie in the tradition of British Oriental travellers.' In C. Trümpler (ed.), *Agatha Christie and Archaeology.* London: British Museum Press. pp. 303–33.

Schmid, H. 1995. *Der Tempelturm Etemenanki in Babylon.* Baghdader Forschungen 17. Mainz: Philipp von Zabern.

Schnabel, P. 1968 (1923). *Berossus und die babylonisch-hellenistische Literatur.* Leipzig: B. G. Teubner.

Schnapp, A. 1996. *The Discovery of the Past: The Origins of Archaeology.* London: British Museum Press.

———. 2000. 'L'archéologie classique face à l'histoire de l'archéologie.' In R. Étienne (ed.), *Les politiques de l'archéologie du milieu du XIXe siècle à l'orée du XXIe.* Athens: École Française d'Athènes. pp. 165–77.

Schramm, W. 1972. 'War Semiramis assyrische Regentin?' *Historia* 21: 513–21.

Schwaner, W. 1905. *Germanen-Bibel: aus heiligen Schriften germanischer Völker* (2nd edn). Schlachtensee: Volkerzieher Verlag.

Schwartz, G. 2006. *Rembrandt's Universe: his Art, his Life, his World.* London: Thames and Hudson.

———. 2011. *Meet Rembrandt: Life and Work of the Master Painter.* New Haven: Yale University Press.

Seipel, W. (ed.) 2003. *Der Turmbau zu Babel. Ursprung und Vielfalt von Sprache und Schrift, Eine Ausstellung des kunsthistorischen Museums Wien für die Europäische Kulturhauptstadt Graz 2003.* 4 vols. Graz: Skira.

Selby, W. B. 1859. *Memoir on the Ruins of Babylon.* Selections from the Memoirs of the Bombay Government, New Series 51. Bombay.

Seymour, M. J. 2004. 'Ancient Mesopotamia and modern Iraq in the British press, 1980–2003.' *Current Anthropology* 45 (3): 351–68.

———. 2013a. 'Babylon.' In D. Gange and M. Ledger Lomas (eds), *Cities of God: Archaeology and the Bible in Nineteenth-Century Britain.* Cambridge: Cambridge University Press. pp. 164–96.

———. 2013b. 'Power and seduction in Babylon: Verdi's *Nabucco.*' In S. Knippschild and M. Garcia (eds), *Seduction and Power: Antiquity in the Visual and Performing Arts.* London: Bloomsbury. pp. 9–20.

———. in press a. 'Appendix: history of excavation.' In World Monuments Fund and Iraq State Board of Antiquities and Heritage (eds), *Babylon Site Management Plan.* New York and Baghdad: World Monuments Fund and Iraq State Board of Antiquities and Heritage.

———. in press b. 'Appendix: social history.' In World Monuments Fund and Iraq State Board of Antiquities and Heritage (eds), *Babylon Site Management Plan.* New York and Baghdad: World Monuments Fund and Iraq State Board of Antiquities and Heritage.

———. in press c. 'The Babylon of D. W. Griffith's *Intolerance.*' In M. Garcia, P. Hanesworth and O. Lapeña (eds), *Imagining Ancient Cities on Film: From Babylon to Cinecittà.* London and New York: Routledge.

Shanks, M. 1992. *Experiencing the Past: On the Character of Archaeology.* London and New York: Routledge.

Signer, M. A. (ed.) 1983. *The Itinerary of Rabbi Benjamin of Tudela.* Malibu, CA: Joseph Simon/Pangloss Press.

Simpson, G. E. 1985. 'Religion and justice: some reflections on the Rasta movement.' *Phylon* 46 (4): 286–91.

Sluglett, P. 2007. *Britain in Iraq: Contriving King and Country, 1914–1932.* New York: Columbia University Press.

Smiles, S. and S. Moser (eds) 2005. *Envisioning the Past: Archaeology and the Image.* Oxford: Blackwell.

Smith, M. 1963. 'II Isaiah and the Persians.' *Journal of the American Oriental Society* 83 (4): 415–21.

Smith, W. R. 1897. 'Ctesias and the Semiramis legend.' *The English Historical Review* 2 (6): 303–17.

Sollberger, E. 1985. 'Babylon's Beginnings.' *Sumer* 41: 10–13.

Soucek, P. P. 1975. 'An illustrated manuscript of al-Bīrunī's *Chronology of Ancient Nations.*' In P. J. Chelkowski (ed.), *The Scholar and the Saint: Studies in Commemoration of Abu 'l-Raihan al- Bīrunī and Jalal al-Din al-Rūmī.* New York: New York University Press. pp. 103–68.

Spiegel, G. M. 1975. 'Political utility in medieval historiography: a sketch.' *History and Theory* 14 (3): 314–25.

Spisak, J. W. 1984. 'Chaucer's Pyramus and Thisbe.' *The Chaucer Review* 18 (3): 204–10.

Spivak, G. C. 1996 (1985). 'Subaltern studies deconstructing historiography.' In D. Landry and G. MacLean (eds), *The Spivak Reader.* London and New York: Routledge. pp. 203–36.

Stanley, H. M. 1998 (1886). 'The meeting with Livingstone.' In E. Boehmer (ed.), *Empire Writing: An Anthology of Colonial Literature 1870–1918.* Oxford: Oxford University Press. pp. 42–50.

Starcky, E. 1990. *Rembrandt.* London: Studio Editions.

Steiner, R. C. and C. F. Nims 1985. 'Ashurbanipal and Shamash-shum-ukin: a tale and two brothers from the Aramaic text in demotic script.' *Revue Biblique* 92 (1): 60–81.

Steinkeller, P. 1988. 'Notes on the irrigation system in third millennium southern Babylonia.' *Bulletin of Sumerian Agriculture* 4: 73–92.

Steinman, L. B. 1998. *Paths to Genocide: Antisemitism in Western History.* New York: St Martin's Press.

Stephens, S. A. and J. J. Winkler 1995a. 'Introduction to *Ninos.*' In S. A. Stephens and J. J. Winkler (eds), *Ancient Greek Novels: The Fragments.* Princeton, NJ: Princeton University Press. pp. 23–30.

———. and J. J. Winkler 1995b. 'Iamblichos: *Babyloniaka.*' In S. A. Stephens and J. J. Winkler (eds), *Ancient Greek Novels: The Fragments.* Princeton: Princeton University Press. pp. 179–245.

Stevenson, R. B. 1997. *Persica: Greek Writing about Persia in the Fourth Century BC.* Edinburgh: Scottish Academic Press.

Stone, E. C. 2008. 'Patterns of looting in Southern Iraq.' *Antiquity* 82: 125–38.

Stoyanov, Y. 2000. *The Other God: Dualist Religions from Antiquity to the Cathar Heresy.* New Haven: Yale University Press.

Strommenger, E. and R. Stucky 1977. 'L'exploration de l'ancienne Mésopotamie.' In R. Stucky (ed.), *Trésors du musée de Bagdad: 7000 ans d'histoire mésopotamienne. Exposition au Musée d'art et d'histoire à Genève, 10 décembre 1977–12 février 1978.* Mainz: Verlag Philipp von Zabern. pp. 8–15.

Sullivan, M. 1991. 'Bruegel's proverbs: art and audience in the Northern Renaissance.' *The Art Bulletin* 73 (3): 431–66.

Sweeney, M. A. 1996. *Isaiah 1–39, with an Introduction to Prophetic Literature.* The Forms of the Old Testament Literature 16. Grand Rapids: Eerdmans.

Sybesma, J. 1991. 'The reception of Bruegel's beekeepers: a mater of choice.' *The Art Bulletin* 73 (3): 467–78.

Tabouis, G. R. 1931. *Nebuchadnezzar.* New York: McGraw-Hill.

Tanner, A. 1992. *Venice Desired.* Oxford: Blackwell.

Tavernier, J.-B. 1676–7. *Les six voyages de Jean Baptiste Tavernier en Turquie, Ecuyer Baron d'Aubonne, en Perse, et aux Indes, pendant l'espace de quarante ans et par Toutes les Routes que l'on Peut Tenir: Accompagner d'Observations Particulieres sur la Qualité, la Religion, le Gouvernement, les Coûtumes et le Commerce de Chaque Païs, avec les Figures, le Poids, et la Valeur des Monnoyes qui y ont Cours.* Paris: G. Clousier.

Taylor, A. R. 1972. 'Zionism and Jewish history.' *Journal of Palestine Studies* 1 (2): 35–51.

Telfer, J. B. (trans.) 1879. *The Bondage and Travels of Johann Schiltberger, a Native of Bavaria, in Europe, Asia and Africa, 1396–1427.* London: Printed for the Hakluyt Society.

Ten Brink Goldsmith, J. 1992. 'Pieter Bruegel the Elder and the matter of Italy.' *Sixteenth Century Journal* 23 (2): 205–34.

Thomas, J. S. 2004. *Archaeology and Modernity.* London and New York: Routledge.

Thompson, R. C. and R. W. Hutchinson 1929. *A Century of Exploration at Nineveh.* London: Luzac and Co.

al-Tikriti, N. 2009. 'Was there an Iraq before there was an Iraq?' *International Journal of Contemporary Iraqi Studies* 3 (2): 133–142.

Tolnay, C. de 1935. *Pierre Bruegel l'Ancien.* 2 vols. Brussels: Nouvelle société d'éditions.

Trigger, B. G. 1989. *A History of Archaeological Thought.* Cambridge: Cambridge University Press.

Tripp, C. 2002. *A History of Iraq* (2nd edn). Cambridge: Cambridge University Press.

Ur, J., P. Karsgaard and J. Oates 2011. 'The spatial dimensions of early Mesopotamian urbanism: the Tell Brak suburban survey, 2003-2006.' *Iraq* 73: 1–19.

UNESCO International Coordination Committee for the Safeguarding of the Cultural Heritage of Iraq, Sub-Committee on Babylon 2009. *Final Report on Damage Assessment at Babylon.* Paris: UNESCO. {http://www.unesco.org/fileadmin/MULTIMEDIA/FIELD/Iraq/pdf/Report%20on%20Damages%20in%20Babylon.pdf, accessed July 2014.}

Vance, N. 2008. 'Vallancey, Charles (c. 1726–1812).' *Oxford Dictionary of National Biography* (online edition). Oxford: Oxford University Press. {http://www.oxforddnb.com/view/article/28,051, accessed 26 Jan 2010}

Van De Mieroop, M. 2003. 'Reading Babylon.' *American Journal of Archaeology* 107: 257–75.

————. 2004. 'A tale of two cities: Nineveh and Babylon.' *Iraq* 66: 1–6.

Van der Spek, R. J. 2008. 'Berossus as Babylonian chronicler and Greek historian.' In R. J. van der Spek (ed.), *Studies in Ancient Near Eastern World View and Society Presented to Marten Stol*. Bethesda, Maryland: CDL Press. pp. 277–318.

Van Ess, M. 2008. 'Koldewey—Pionier systematischer Ausgrabungen im Orient.' In Wartke, R.-B. (ed.), *Auf dem Weg nach Babylon. Robert Koldewey—Ein Archäologenleben*. Mainz: Philipp von Zabern. pp. 91–103.

Veit, U. 2002. 'Gustav Kossinna and his concept of national archaeology.' In H. Härke (ed.), *Archaeology, Identity and Society: The German Experience* (2nd edn). Frankfurt am Main: Peter Lang. pp. 41–66.

Verbrugghe, G. P. and J. M. Wickersham 1996. 'General introduction to *Berossos and Manetho*.' In G. P. Verbrugghe and J. M. Wickersham (eds), *Berossos and Manetho, Introduced and Translated*. Ann Arbor: Unversity of Michigan Press. pp. 1–11.

VerSteeg, R. 2000. *Early Mesopotamian Law*. Durham, NC: Carolina Academic Press.

Vico, G. 1999 (1744). *New Science: Principles of the New Science Concerning the Common Nature of Nations*. London: Penguin.

Vidal, G. 1974. *Myron*. New York: Random House.

Villalba Ruiz de Toledo, F. J. 2006. 'Medieval travellers and the reencounter with the Orient.' In J. Ma. Córdoba and C. Perez Díe (eds), *The Spanish Near Eastern Adventure (1166–2006): Travellers, Museums and Scholars in the History of the Rediscovering of the Ancient Near East*. Madrid: Ministerio de Cultura de España. pp. 31–6.

Volkov, S. 1978. *The Rise of Popular Antimodernism in Germany: The Urban Master Artisans, 1873–1896*. Princeton, NJ: Princeton University Press.

Voltaire (François Marie Arouet) 1814 (1748). *La Tragédie de Sémiramis*. Paris.

————. 1749. *Zadig, ou la Destinée. Histoire Orientale*. London: James Brindley.

————. 1768. *La Princesse de Babilone*. Geneva: Grasset.

————. 1969 (1768). *The Princess of Babylon*. London: Signet.

Waerzeggers, C. 'The Babylonian Revolt Against Xerxes and the "End of Archives".' *Archiv für Orientforschung* 50: 150–173.

Wartke, R.-B. (ed.) 2008. *Auf dem Weg nach Babylon. Robert Koldewey—Ein Archäologenleben*. Berlin and Mainz: Staatliche Museen zu Berlin—Stiftung Preußischer Kulturbesitz and Philipp von Zabern.

Waterfield, G. 1987. 'Reflections on A. H. Layard's Character and Early Life.' In F. M. Fales and B. J. Hickey (eds), *Austen Henry Layard tra l'Oriente e Venezia*. Rome: "L'Erma" di Bretschneider. pp. 7–23.

Watson, G. L. 1974. 'Patterns of black protest in Jamaica: the case of the Rastafarians.' *Journal of Black Studies* 4 (3): 329–43.

Watson, G. 1995. 'The art of disagreement: C. S. Lewis (1898–1963).' *The Hudson Review* 48 (2): 229–39.

Wegener, U. B. 1995. *Die Faszination des Maßlosen: der Turmbau zu Babel von Pieter Bruegel bis Athanasius Kircher*. Hildesheim: Olms.

Weinfeld, M. 1991. 'Semiramis: her name and origin.' In M. Cogan and I. Eph'al (eds), *Ah, Assyria: Studies in Assyrian History and Ancient Near Eastern Historiography Presented to Hayim Tadmor*. Scripta Hierosolymitana, Publications of the Hebrew University of Jerusalem 32. Jerusalem: Magnes Press. pp. 99–103.

Weißbach, F. H. 1938. 'Burnouf, Eugène.' In E. Ebeling and B. Meissner (eds), *Reallexikon der Assyriologie*. Band 2. Berlin and Leipzig: Walter de Gruyter. p. 82.

Wengrow, D. 1999. 'The intellectual adventure of Henry Frankfort: a missing chapter in the history of archaeoogical thought.' *American Journal of Archaeology* 103 (4): 597–613.

Westbrook, R. 2000. 'Babylonian diplomacy in the Amarna letters.' *Journal of the American Oriental Society* 120 (3): 377–82.

Wetzel, F. 1930. *Die Stadtmauren von Babylon*. Wissenschaftliche Veröffentlichung der deutschen Orient-Gesellschaft 48. Leipzig: J. C. Hinrichs. 30.

———. and F. H. Weißbach 1938. *Das Hauptheiligtum des Marduk in Babylon: Esagila und Etemenanki*. Wissenschaftliche Veröffentlichung der deutschen Orient-Gesellschaft 59. Leipzig: J. C. Hinrichs.

Whittaker, T. 1926. 'Vico's new science of humanity.' *Mind* 35 (138): 204–21.

Wilde, O. F. O'F. W. 1998 (1894). 'Salome.' In P. Raby (ed.), *Oscar Wilde: The Importance of Being Earnest and Other Plays*. Oxford: Oxford University Press. pp. 61–91.

Wiley, J. N. 2003. 'The Iraqi Shi'as: origin, ideology and current political goals.' In S. C. Inati (ed.), *Iraq: Its History, People, and Politics*. New York: Humanity Books. pp. 149–61.

Williams, B. 1973. *Problems of the Self: Philosophical Papers 1956–1972*. Cambridge: Cambridge University Press.

———. 1997. 'The analogy of city and soul in Plato's *Republic*.' In R. Kraut (ed.), *Plato's Republic: Critical Essays*. Lanham, Maryland: Rowman and Littlefield. pp. 49–59.

Williams, J. 1994–2003. *The Illustrated Beatus: A Corpus of Illustrations of the Commentary on the Apocalypse*. 5 vols. London: Harvey Miller.

Wilson, D. M. 2002. *The British Museum: A History*. London: British Museum Press.

Winckelmann, J. J. 1934 (1764). *Geschichte der Kunst des Alterthums*. London: Phaidon.

———. 2001 (1880). 'The history of ancient art, translated from the German by G. Henry Lodge.' In C. Bowman (ed.), *Essays on the Philosophy and History of Art: Johann Joachim Winckelmann* vol. 2–3. Bristol: Thoemmes Press.

Wind, E. 1938. 'The Saint as Monster.' *Journal of the Warburg Institute* 1 (2): 183.

Winkel, M. de 2006. *Fashion and Fancy: Dress and Meaning in Rembrandt's Paintings*. Amsterdam: Amsterdam University Press.

Winstone, H. V. F. 2004. *Gertrude Bell* (2nd edn). London: Barzan.

Wiseman, D. J. 1983. 'Mesopotamian Gardens.' *Anatolian Studies* 22: 141–47.

———. 1985. *Nebuchadrezzar and Babylon: The Schweich Lectures of the British Academy, 1983*. Oxford: Oxford University Press.

———. 1991. 'Babylonia 605–539 BC.' In J. Boardman, I. E. S. Edwards, N. G. L. Hammond, E. Sollberger and C. B. F. Walker (eds), *The Assyrian and Babylonian Empires and Other States of the Near East, from the Eighth to the Sixth Centuries BC*. Cambridge Ancient History (2nd edn). Cambridge: Cambridge University Press. Vol. 3, pt. 2, pp. 229–51.

Wittfogel, K. 1957. *Oriental Despotism: A Comparative Study of Total Power*. New Haven: Yale University Press.

Woolley, C. L. 1937. *Digging Up the Past* (2nd edn). Harmondsworth: Penguin.

———. 1950 (1929). *Ur of the Chaldees*. London: Penguin.

———. and T. E. Lawrence 2003 (1914–15). *The Wilderness of Zin*. London: Stacey International.

————. and P. R. S. Moorey 1982. *Ur of the Chaldees* (revised edition). Ithaca: Cornell University Press.

World Monuments Fund and Iraq State Board of Antiquities and Heritage (eds), *Babylon Site Management Plan*. New York and Baghdad: World Monuments Fund and Iraq State Board of Antiquities and Heritage.

Wylie, A. 1982. 'Epistemological issues raised by structuralist archaeology.' In I. Hodder (ed.), *Symbolic and Structural Archaeology*. Cambridge: Cambridge University Press. pp. 39–46.

————. 1989. 'Matters of fact and matters of interest.' In S. J. Shennan (ed.), *Archaeological Approaches to Cultural Identity*. London and New York: Routledge. pp. 94–109.

————. 1992. 'On "heavily decomposing red herrings": scientific method in archaeology and the ladening of evidence with theory.' In L. Embree (ed.), *Metaarchaeology*. London: Kluwer Academic Publishers. pp. 269–88.

Yamauchi, E. 2002. 'The Eastern Jewish Diaspora under the Babylonians.' In M. W. Chavalas and K. L. Younger (eds), *Mesopotamia and the Bible: Comparative Explorations*. London: Sheffield Academic Press. pp. 356–77.

Young, R. J. C. 1990. *White Mythologies: Writing History and the West*. London and New York: Routledge.

Zagorin, P. 2003. 'Looking for Pieter Bruegel.' *Journal of the History of Ideas* 64 (1): 73–96.

Zawadzki, S. 1995. 'A contribution to the chronology of the last days of the Assyrian empire.' *Zeitschrift für Assyriologie* 85: 67–73.

Zell, M. 2002. *Reframing Rembrandt: Jews and the Christian Image in Seventeenth-Century Amsterdam*. Berkeley and London: University of California Press.

INDEX